DEATH, OUR LAST ILLUSION

A SCIENTIFIC AND SPIRITUAL PROBING OF CONSCIOUSNESS THROUGH DEATH

SUSAN SHORE

DEATH, OUR LAST ILLUSION

A SCIENTIFIC AND SPIRITUAL PROBING OF CONSCIOUSNESS THROUGH DEATH

SUSAN SHORE

Common Ground

First published in Australia in 2011
by Common Ground Publishing Pty Ltd
at The Humanities
a series imprint of The University Press

The National Library of Australia Cataloguing-in-Publication data:

Death, our last illusion: a scientific and spiritual probing of consciousness through death
Susan Shore

Includes Index
Bibliography.
978 1 86335 627 5 (pbk.)
978 1 86335 628 2 (pdf)

1. Death.
2. Future Life.

128.5

Cover photograph: Australian Superb Blue Fairy Wren by artist-photographer Ute Klein.

Despite success with other bush creatures, Ute had failed to capture these elusive little angels in their natural setting. This one was taken by surprise in the gutter at Melbourne Zoo. It is symbolic of the soul captured, briefly, in the concrete world of matter.

Table of Contents

Chapter 1
Does our Attitude to Death Matter?

There is such a powerful taboo around death in our society, that even when a beloved parent or partner is dying, few of us have the courage (or is it the indiscretion) to ask 'How do you feel about this death which is now quite close?' It seems incredibly insensitive to raise the subject; much worse than referring to body odour or an un-zipped fly, but socially not dissimilar. It is an affrontingly personal question about the obvious, which in our society, should be tactfully ignored to take the mind of the dying person and everyone else, away from the unhappy prospect. And when death is less than certain, we dare not risk causing the patient to dwell fearfully on it, and perhaps hasten it.

What's the use of this book?

What about our own inevitable ending? 'I don't have time to worry about something that may not happen for decades yet!' was my response too. We ignore the subject until it is too late, and death is upon us. We have then left ourselves no time to prepare, or even to think clearly about the issues and form a more enlightened idea about the nature of death and its implications for living our lives right now. By the time we know that death is coming for us or for someone close to us, the time to prepare for it may have passed.

What is your attitude at this moment of your life, to death? When my sister was diagnosed with cancer, I chattered brightly about how we would finally go back to the Greek islands when she recovered, while I blocked out the possibility that she might die instead. This is what we do in the West-sit at the bedside in home or hospital, of a critically ill person, and propose loudly with stretched smiles, that she or he will get better soon. We joke that they'll soon be up and making dinner/ garden beds/ whoopee/ a nuisance of themselves. It's cheerful, it's funny, and it's false, even when the patient does actually recover. *'Get Well Soon!'* shout the bright cards on the bedside table-as if this were the only desirable or acceptable outcome. It's certainly the only one we're prepared to let anyone contemplate.

We do, as a society, seem to be groping towards a new awareness and sensitivity. Perhaps you have also been in the midst of offering this blind hope, and begun to suspect, as I did, that you weren't helping, and were possibly hindering, this beloved individual's journey towards acceptance of the coming death. Why was I behaving like this, I wondered? The answer is obvious: I was afraid. I had to confront my fear of death if I was going to be of any use to Anthea, or to my equally loved sister Meredith, whose chronic illness causes many close encounters with the Real Thing. If possible, I had to discover the truth about death.

Do I consider that I've succeeded? Yes; as a result I no longer see how there can be any doubt about the more-than-joy, bliss, in fact, and pervasive love, which await us beyond mere physical death. It has been an amazing journey, as I hope it will be for my readers, from holding to the theoretical possibility of some vague continuance, to encountering (and accepting) the very real and considerable evidence for survival of consciousness after bodily demise. More than that- I've arrived at the point, as does the book, where *the life after death makes sense*; where previously obscure and apparently conflicting schemes of the afterlife from separate traditions, come to agree, in quite surprising detail. And agree also, with the latest scientific evidence, from hospital and clinical studies.

I think of the beliefs of family and friends: *'When you're dead, you're dead'; 'I died for fifteen minutes; Kerry Packer's right-there's nothing there!'* (No, there isn't, for any of Kerry Packer's worldwide tribe! The reason becomes obvious later in the book.) *'I don't do God, though it's arrogant to be atheistic when we just don't know'; 'There can't be a God, there's too much suffering'; 'I believe in a Creator, but we don't survive death'; 'I've had a Near-death experience and know I will survive death'; 'This little life-short and brutish, and then – oblivion'; 'This one life preparing-and then back to God and Heaven!'; 'The one soul, but many lives to perfect it'; 'It's the Buddhist thing, no God, no soul; we disperse into the universe'; 'I believe there's something after, I just don't have a clue what'.*

While the sexes aren't quite at swords or saucepans drawn in their opposition, men gather more towards the materialist, atheist end and women towards a Superior Consciousness and continuity. Have the men studied more science? Or does this just reflect the difference between the fact-based (the men) and the feeling-based (the women) approach to life, the universe and everything? I have watched some of my friends react to the text with apparent discomfort and reluctance to disturb their universe: Regardless of where you fall in this continuum of belief, and whether one of my family, a cherished friend, or the Dear Reader to whom this book is addressed, I invite you to at least explore the possibility that death is no more than a transition. Will the arguments advanced here change your cosmos?

In this chapter, I ponder the following issues: **Death as the unacceptable** outcome; **The right to die** and a saner approach to death; **The challenge to 'Material Universe'** in our intuitive knowledge about death; **The deathbed vision**; Post-death visions and **bereavement 'hallucinations'**; Material Universe and the **Great Heresy** of Separateness; **Chance, Design and suffering**; Unusual states of consciousness-**delusional or empirically testable?**; Infantile to transpersonal- **the stages of cognition and consciousness development**; then Summaries for each chapter as a roadmap, followed by **How does it feel to die?** I report my sister's NDE under this last heading.

Death as the unacceptable outcome

The famous palliative care pioneer, Elisabeth Kubler-Ross, whose pioneering study *On Death and Dying* (1970) changed medical and hospital treatment of the dying, spent her life working to transform the culture of denial surrounding death and dying, and to institute compassionate care for the dying person as standard medical practice. (There have always been nurses and nuns, doctors and families, who have tenderly cared for the person, not just attended to physical disease.) Kubler-Ross witnessed dying patients neglected because they were doing what was unacceptable to modern medicine -- dying. She was dismayed by the *'sad, lonely and impersonal event'* that

3

dying had become in modern hospitals. The terminally ill lay in back rooms, and families were not allowed to be with them as they died; emergency patients were similarly isolated while medical staff and families ' *debated whether or not they should* [even] *be told what was wrong*' (1970, p.141).

Things are no longer so grim for the dying; Kubler-Ross' work, and that of those who followed, has changed attitudes so that at least we are likely to be told the truth about our condition. Yet a patient's death is still considered a medical team's failure; death is still a catastrophe, so everything possible must be done, and forced on the patient, to prevent it. As adult citizens in a pluralist democracy we are expected to take full responsibility for every aspect of our lives. Except our dying, as admired Australian journalist Pamela Bone discovered when she was diagnosed with cancer of the bone marrow. She wrote in *Bad Hair Days* that the alternative to long and painful treatment, which could not guarantee to even give her a little more time, was imminent death. As her specialist declared;

> *'You'd fairly quickly just sink into a coma and...that would be a very dumb option'. I don't believe I ever said whether I agreed to go ahead with the treatment. It was simply taken for granted, by the medical staff, by my family, by everyone, that I would. It was expected of me. It is expected of everyone that when they become ill they will have whatever treatment is necessary to save them. It is our moral duty to stay alive.*
>
> *Anyway, I went along with it because I am a conventional, law-abiding person. But how many times, in the weeks and months to come, did I wish I had taken that dumb option! How desirable would become the prospect of that kind coma* (Bone 2007, pp. 24-5).

Bone acknowledges, as honestly and courageously as she recognizes everything else about it, her true response to this confrontation with her death, calling one chapter *Not being brave*. This was not Pamela's only response: she was, later, grateful for the time she was given by the treatment. She had three precious extra years with her husband, daughters and grandchildren, and her work. And wrote this wonderful book. Does this change the central moral issues: the right to decide, and the responsibility? Not to have the decision made for us by a society too afraid to face the reality of death? Surely it is time we ceased being merely and passively 'conventional, law-abiding persons'. (Such brave words! What will I do when my turn comes?)

Conscious dying and a saner approach to death

A less frightened, more considered approach to death by the society could rid us of some of the suffering we experience during dying. This is a relief that is good medicine's intent, and which, interestingly, eighty percent of Australians consider their right[1]. Melbourne specialist Mr Rodney Syme confronts the issues, including the legal tangle that needs urgent attention, in his outspoken and courageous book *A Good Death (2008)*. Unbearable suffering, as defined by the patient, *should* be relieved by the medical profession, through sensible and safe hastening of inevitable death when needed and requested-voluntary euthanasia. And it should be legal to do so, Syme argues. *A Good Death* is the record of Syme's own journey as he confronted the issue through striving to meet the needs of his patients. He did this within the laws where possible, but pushed the legal boundaries for humane treatment when there was no option. The book is an attempt to stir up the debate that Syme sees as necessary to the needed legal reform. I must note that Kubler-Ross disagreed. At the end of a wonderful holiday back in Switzerland with her family, Elisabeth was stunned by a direction from her mother: *'If I ever become a vegetable, I want you to terminate my life.'*

'Stop with such nonsense', Elisabeth protested; *'Nothing like that is going to happen.'* She finally told her mother she was *'against suicide'* and would never assist anyone, especially her own mother, *'the loving person who gave birth to me and kept me alive'.* She would do as with all her patients, and help her mother to live until she died. She returned to

---

1. Two Right to Die practitioners deserve mention — American Jack Kevorkian, and Australian Philip Nitschke of Exit International, who has long campaigned to obtain this right for us despite increasing obstacles. In September 1996, the Northern Territory legislation which made doctor-assisted voluntary euthanasia legal there under strict controls, the world's first, was overridden from the Federal level. A Private Member's Bill was introduced by MP Kevin Andrews for the Right to Life lobby, who regard euthanasia as a crime. Rather than monitor the effects of the Rights of the Terminally Ill legislation and recommend changes, both sides of parliament appeared to capitulate to a minority opinion, forcing it on the rest of us. While it is vital to respect these MP's private views, Australia suddenly felt like a theocracy not a pluralist democracy. Nitschke, who was easing the suffering of the terminally ill under the NT legislation, found his practice and his advocacy, outlawed. So we continue to sentence the terminally ill who want the only relief possible — to die, to a form of life that is unbearable in its acute suffering. Dr Nitschke's book, *The Peaceful Pill*, has been banned here by the Censorship Review Board. In 2010, a Labour government will censor pornography on the internet, but intends to include Exit International's website (now the only public access) under the banned list, despite public opposition.

the U.S. and work. Beginning just three days later, her mother had several strokes and *'was considered a vegetable'*. It was at this point that she was yelling at God for not ending her mother's suffering. Elisabeth made sure of the best possible care for her mother, and the family visited constantly. Yet it was four years before her mother's release finally came (Kubler-Ross 1997, p.p. 154-5).

An extraordinary and beautiful book by Ken Wilber and his beloved wife Treya Killam Wilber, (2000), records the gruelling *and* precious five years of their marriage, and Treya's fight with cancer, ending in her death. It wasn't a grim death, despite the sound of this-it was utterly joyous. Treya had done everything possible to stay alive; despite her suffering, she had lived courageously and with joy, inspiring everyone around her, and had gone on working successfully for other cancer sufferers. When the cancer kept returning and was finally swelling in her brain; when only deterioration into complete dependency and imprisonment within a non-functioning body lay ahead, she made a conscious decision to die, and accomplished it forthwith, easing the transition with the morphine she'd not touched all through the increasing pain of her illness. Such a decision, involving few then no drugs or other death-dealing measures, will increasingly be possible for the rest of us, not just the very advanced few - as the perennial philosophy in its many branches, tells us. There is exploration of this later in the book through the writings of Alice Bailey.

The challenge to 'material universe' in our intuitive knowledge about death

What would it take to overcome our fear of death? There is a change needed, radical yet not so difficult, to move beyond this fear. We would create this paradigm shift, this change in consciousness, through undertaking a critical scrutiny of our view of the universe.

Twentieth-century science convinced us as a culture that there is nothing beyond death because there is nothing beyond the physical universe. It has become an idée fixe-a deeply rooted belief, which prevents us from seeing what is really there. We are it seems, prisoners of our outdated science construction, this 'material universe' idea. We consider there is no alternative but the mediaeval popular vision of the afterlife, where God sits on a cloud, surrounded by serenading angels and crowds of the deceased. This 'Material Universe' paradigm is destined to become a curio in the History of Ideas Museum, along with 'flat earth' and 'geocentric universe', and every other past construction of the cosmos. The Material Universe idea, belonging to last century, led to the belief that there is nothing at all beyond death; that 'when you're dead, you're dead'. It has been steadily unravelling as a viable premise or useful guide to reality, both at the cutting edge of science, and in ordinary life.

Yet there is still intense resistance to the needed change in every area of science, including this one. Melvin Morse, who pioneered the study of Near-death experiences in children, gives a bizarre example in Closer to the Light, of just how far we-experts in the physical sciences especially, will go to avoid contemplating the possibility of perception by other than physical means. In a fascinating chapter on pre-death visions, he notes that it is not at all unusual for those about to die, and those close to them, to have a vision indicating that death is imminent. However, Morse notes a Swiss study on crib death which scientifically documents a link between mothers' reports of these pre-death visions about their babies, and their subsequent cot deaths. But cause and effect were reversed in the experts' minds, with frightening consequences. They concluded that these mothers, through their unconscious death wish, caused their babies to die! The researchers speculated that this death wish *'leads to an emotional neglect that the child senses and that then causes its death'*, (Morse and Perry, 1991, p. 81). 'Post hoc, propter hoc' –the Latin phrase for the belief that a second event which followed the first one was necessarily caused by it, was applied with an alarmingly uncritical zeal. These scientists dismissed the alternative as unthinkable. This alternative was the possibility that the mothers could have had knowledge of events which had not yet happened.

The visions common around death, and our failure to listen to the dying person

An entire class of events commonly associated with death is cordoned off or consigned to the vaults by our refusal to take these events into account. Science is vital to our understanding of the universe: I appreciate Richard Dawkins' efforts to expose the irrational and delusional in pseudoscience and our thinking, especially in *The God Delusion* (2006) and his television documentaries. But he champions a scientific alternative, one which may be equally irrational. Certainly it is resistant to the possibility that these non-physical events may be anything but dying brain phenomena, delusions, or self-fulfilling fantasies. But are they more than that? Karlis Osis' study, *At the Hour of Death*, (1977) investigates a phenomenon known as the *deathbed vision,* in which the dying person sees partners, family members, and dear friends who have already died: These loved ones have come to 'collect' her or him, exactly as family and friends will gather to collect their patient who is being discharged from hospital. The study is based upon interviews with 1000 doctors and nurses who have some familiarity with this experience in their patients. Osis concludes that these visions cannot be dismissed as delusional.

The deathbed vision

There is apparently, a surprising acceptance of deathbed visions among nurses especially; it is 'professional folklore' in some wards that deathbed visions are an accurate indicator of imminent death. It is not uncommon that hospital staff see and even talk to, someone from their ward who has not long died. Try dropping in on the conversations of nurses on the graveyard shift, if you doubt that these are anything but the hallucinations of grieving relatives!

A typical example of this common phenomenon, the deathbed vision, is related by Kubler-Ross in *The Wheel of Life: A Memoir of Living and Dying* (1997). Not long before the beginning of her pioneering work in thanatology, the study of dying, at a time when Kubler-Ross described herself as against religion, and sceptical about God and any afterlife, she went home to Switzerland to be with her dying father. Elisabeth's father asked her to open his bedroom window so he could hear the church bells:

> *Then my father began conversing with his own father, apologizing for letting him die in that dreadful nursing home.* (Her grandfather had begged to be permitted to go home, and been refused).

> *"Perhaps I've paid with all my present suffering," he said, and then he promised to see him soon. In the midst of their talk, my father had turned and asked me for a glass of water. I marvelled that he was clearly oriented and able to shift back and forth from one reality to another. Naturally I could not see or hear my grandfather (p. 124).*[2]

Years later Elisabeth, bitter at her dying mother's suffering, demanded of God 'Do you even exist?' and was later 'calling him nasty names in Swiss and English' (p. 156). It seems that her father's conversation with his own dead father had been for Elisabeth, a curious

---

anomaly merely; it hadn't changed her thinking about a God who couldn't exist given such suffering. That change came still later.

It has become standard professional practice to work with one set of the experiences of dying: those necessarily subjective experiences which are nonetheless so universal that Kubler-Ross could observe them and systematize them in the now well-known five Stages of Dying. In her study, which became the palliative care handbook, *On Death and Dying (1970)*, she documents the stages from shock and denial, through anger, to bargaining, then depression, to peaceful acceptance. These stages are universal, shared not just by the dying, but also by any one of us who is grieving a great loss. Universal, that is, as long as we are listened to with compassion, and actually *heard*. Kubler-Ross warned that the last stage could be the depressed or bitter *'resignation, which occurs when tears and anger are not shared'* (1997, p. 161).

However, the dying have other subjective experiences, which seem to be just as usual, and are certainly still rejected by the society. I discovered that Kubler-Ross herself had gone on to document a similar set of stages reported by her patients, which took place after physical death:

> 'Up till then I had absolutely no belief in an afterlife, but the data convinced me that these were not coincidences or hallucinations...These remarkable findings led to an even more remarkable scientific conclusion: that death did not exist-not in its traditional definition ...Dying patients went through the five stages, but then after that [their death, there was a further set of four stages]...According to the interviews I compiled, death [itself also] occurs in several distinct phases (pp.188-9).

Although we still tend to regard it as a curious medical phenomenon, we are far more accepting now, of what has come to be known as the Near-death Experience. This acceptance began with Raymond Moody's study *Life after Life*, with a foreword by Kubler-Ross, published in 1975; five years after Kubler-Ross' own NDE work had begun. Yet it remains the case that other experiences that are common around death, are still being denied and treated as evidence of insanity, even by the dying themselves. How many dying people stay silent about their experiences of non-physical phenomena, such as their deathbed vision of a mother or a husband who has already passed, because they themselves regard them as delusional? It is vital that they are seen to be sane and in full possession of their faculties, in order not to have dying taken out of their control, and perhaps a prolongation of suffering, forced upon them.

Post-death visions and bereavement *'hallucinations'*

While those who have had NDE are no longer likely to be dismissed as crazy or senile, this is still not the case with another category of experiences. These (usually) occur to those connected to the one who has died, and are known, mistakenly, as *'bereavement hallucinations'*. Several studies conducted in places as distinct in culture as Japan, Wales and the U.S., agree that roughly fifty percent of us have seen (or heard) someone close to us after she or he has died. These studies have been collected and correlated by D. Scott Rogo (1990, pp. 76-91). This percentage is higher among those who have lost a partner; high enough to say that it is *the usual experience* of someone whose husband, wife or partner has died. It rises again, correlated with the length of time of the marriage or partnership. Yet the experience cannot simply be dismissed as delusional; a product of grief, for two reasons Rogo gives. The first is that it occurs widely among those who are not grief-stricken, and who may have very little personal attachment to the one who has appeared to them after death. The second is that in a small but significant minority of cases, the post-mortem individual was visible or audible to more than one person at the time.

Then there are the cases where the deceased were able to communicate or provide some evidence of their return. A survey of cases of spontaneous contact with the dead was conducted by Julian Burton towards his doctorate in psychology, prompted by his own experience, at forty-two, shortly after the death of his mother:

> *My wife and I were entertaining relatives. I was in the kitchen cutting a pineapple when I heard what I thought were my wife's footsteps behind me to the right. I turned to ask the whereabouts of a bowl but realized she had crossed to the left outside my field of vision. I turned in that direction...and saw my mother standing there. She was fully visible, looking*

years younger ...She was wearing a diaphanous pale-blue gown trimmed in marabou which I had never seen.[3]

When Burton phoned his sister next day and told her, she began to sob. Perhaps she didn't believe him? No, she knew it was true. When mother and daughter went shopping together two weeks before the stroke, she told him, their mother had tried on a gown of that exact description. Although she looked good and loved the gown, she decided not to spend the money (Rogo 1990, p. 87).

Elisabeth Kubler-Ross' own experience falls into this last category, that of the post-death vision providing some evidence (1997). A patient, Mrs Schwartz, had bravely spoken to a hospital seminar about her experience of dying and returning, in what came to be known as the Near-death Experience, - a first for Kubler-Ross. This lady appeared in front of Elisabeth at the hospital lift, ten months after her death, as the Doctor was about to resign, to ask her to continue her vital work on death and dying; *'We will help you'.* Elisabeth insisted that Mrs Schwartz write a note to co-worker Reverend Gaines, to prove that she had returned. Mrs Schwartz took the offered pen, wrote and signed the paper: The writing was as solid as any by a living person-and remained on the paper. Yet reports of this kind from a universally known and respected specialist and pioneer were enough to cause, in some quarters, derision and dismissal of her as having either become, or always been, crazy. Phillip Adams (2008), broadcaster, writer, pundit and Australian national treasure, is one who is guilty of this attitude towards Kubler-Ross. While we continue to treat similar experiences associated with death, as indicators of temporary or marginal insanity, we will never discover how

---

3. I asked someone I had just met (R.L.) about her experiences around death, as I have been doing in order to understand the frequency and nature of contact. (Every second person can report a personal experience of deathbed or post-death so-called 'hallucinations'.) R.L. immediately related her Near-death and Out-of-Body experiences, with the specific and verifiable details I had come to expect about NDE. She next recounted an experience like D. Scott Rogo's, though I had told her none of these contents of the book.

Just after R's mother's death, R's daughter saw her grandmother, and informed her mother that her grandmother had died. R also saw her, wearing a new outfit. It was *'a watermelon twinset [matching jumper and cardigan], and a pleated skirt in cream with a pattern of brown overcheck, almost invisible'.* At the funeral, her father asked did R. know her mother had bought a new outfit the day of her death? Her knowledge of the purchase of this new outfit surprised her father: "*Oh, so she told you about it*", he concluded. His daughter didn't reveal the source of her knowledge; she considered it would only add to her father's distress.

common they are, nor begin to at least incorporate them into grief counselling as something usual and to be expected.[4]

It is fascinating to observe how we deal with our intuitive knowledge in this area. Anyone who has watched or nursed someone loved, to her or his death, will have seen the apparent decline of the selfhood of this familiar person. When we observe this happening simultaneously with the decay of body and brain, it appears that self-hood merely equals body and brain. It leads to the strengthening of the Material Universe idea. Yet those of us who have had this experience are almost invariably struck by those wonderful lucid intervals, when the beloved individual is there again as they always were; just as we have always known them. This is especially the case with the well-known phenomenon of 'rallying', which often surprises us in the days before death. Where this lucidity continues to be interspersed with deterioration, it can't be a result of the sudden (temporary) restoration to health of decaying tissue. Conversely, when these familiar people become silent or comatose we don't ascribe this to their being dead at that moment, especially when it is likely to be succeeded by a lucid moment or by a 'wakening' from coma.

We begin to experience the body and the essential person as separate entities. The throat tumour that has stopped speech, rather than indicating the death of selfhood, merely inhibits its expression. When the terminally ill person struggles to communicate, we realise it is not because they themselves are 'more dead' now, but because the instrument through which they experience, express and communicate is collapsing. We see that they are other than, and more than, the dying body. The essential self is not changed by the physical changes; we witness a clear separation of self and the mechanism of its expression, and begin to have an intuitive appreciation that the self survives the death of matter. Despite this, often that insight is thrust aside as irrational; we go back to the Default Position in our

---

4. At-death and post-death contacts seem increasingly to be made via electronic media from computers to mobile phones. The American Association of Electronic Voice phenomena has been researching these contacts; see www.aaaevp.com, and Tom and Lisa Butler's 2003 study *There is No Death and There are No Dead.* I can add to this anecdotally only. Several weeks after my friend H's brother's death, her other sibling's mobile phone rang. The contact came from the dead brother. She also reported strange (technically impossible?) interference in her attempts to use her own computer. Another friend, M, then told us of the use of her mobile phone to alert her to the death of a friend of hers, via a message with no sender. Such accounts, unverified and possibly highly subjective in their interpretation, could be ignored except that they are becoming quite common, and the Butlers' studies provide some grounds for treating them with respect.

thinking, which is the nothing-beyond-the-physical idea. Yet within science itself, the Material Universe paradigm has had its day; it is beginning to be replaced by a more adequate construction of reality, one which indicates there is indeed life, and a universe, beyond this gross physical dimension.

Material Universe and the Great Heresy of Separateness

What is this better construction of reality? Einstein's discovery of the equivalence of physical mass and energy caused us to contemplate the possibility that dense matter might not be solid, after all. Conclusions of recent research in quantum physics seem inescapable: matter is quite literally nothing but 'frozen light', as David Bohm, the great physicist, proposed (Sogyal 1992, p. 275). The solid mass and inertia of objects in the material world turns out to be an illusion created by the resistance of a high-energy sea of light in which we are immersed: the electromagnetic zero point field, as American scientists Haisch, Rueda and Puthoff discovered (Haisch, 2000). The news is not so much the Zero Point Field but its 'creation' of mass and inertia, and of our experience of the solidity of our world. The implications of this discovery are profound. Bernard Haisch wrote of them:

> (I)f we are right, then 'Let there be light' is indeed a very profound statement, as one would expect of its purported author. The solid, stable world of matter appears to be sustained at every instant by an underlying sea of quantum light. There must be a deeper meaning in these physical facts, a deeper truth about the simultaneous interconnection of all things [my emphasis]. It beckons us forward in our search for a better, truer understanding of the nature of the universe,

of the origins of space and time-those 'illusions' that yet feel so real to us.[5]

Buddhism and Hinduism have always known about this Electromagnetic Zero Point Field. It is called Fohat, defined in Christmas Humphreys' *Dictionary of Buddhism* as: *'Primordial Light. The intelligent vital force of the universe, forming or destroying perishable forms. The power of the One Life of the universe. It has been called* cosmic electricity [my emphasis]. (Humphreys 1928).

The Material Universe idea is the source of almost all our human misery. Stanislav Grof, in *Birth, Death and Transcendence in Psychotherapy* (1985), makes a profound and persuasive argument for the connection; I am indebted to him for the reminder. (He continues to lecture on this critical subject-the urgent need to change our thinking). The greed which seizes for oneself what needs to be shared, the terrible violence inflicted on those not of one's tribe or persuasion, the sense of superiority which denies the rest of humanity what one enjoys apparently by birthright-all these have their roots in what has been called, in the perennial philosophy, the Great Heresy of Separateness.

This heresy is the illusion that we each have, of a separate existence, self-created, hermetically sealed and therefore in competition with every other life on the planet. What will happen if we don't control carbon emissions before reaching the Point of No Return? The experts-Tim Flannery, Gwyn Dyer and Maude Barlow, Al Gore and his team among others, warn that instead of an individual death, we are facing a terrifying collective death as a result of global warming making the planet uninhabitable-and not just for humans. This seems to me to be the result of a mix of overpopulation and the illusion of separate existence; competition instead of cooperation. It's about the crazy delusion that I, as an individual, a

---

5. Bernard Haisch wrote excitedly of this discovery:
'*In fact, the work that Rueda, I and ... Puthoff, have since done indicate that mass is, in effect, an illusion. We publish(ed) in... the world's leading physics journal, the Physical Review, in February 1994... Science and Scientific American ran stories on our new inertia hypothesis. We waited for some reaction... my experience should have warned me that we had ventured into dangerous theoretical waters, that we were going to be left ...to sink or swim...An alternative to having other scientists replicate your work... is to get the same result using different methods. In 1998, we published two new papers that again showed that the inertia of matter could be traced back to the zero-point field. And not only was the approach ...completely different than in the 1994 paper, but the mathematics was simpler while the physics was more complete; a most desirable combination. What's more, the original analysis had used Newtonian classical physics; the new analysis used Einsteinian relativistic physics'.* Extracts from 'Brilliant Disguise: Light, Matter and the Zero Point Field', in *Science and Spirit Magazine* 2001, used with permission of Bernard Haisch.

state, a company or a nation, can survive despite or even because of, the death or demise of those around me.[6]

In daily life right now, we express this illusion of separateness constantly, in treating the other person as a tool, a mere means to our own comfort. Every encounter with the Other becomes an occasion to have my own needs fulfilled, turning the Other into It, instead of Thou, as Martin Buber expressed with such power in *I and Thou* (2002, first published in 1923) and Gabriel Marcel in *Being and Having* (1965, first English edition 1949). It was Einstein who expressed this heresy so beautifully in saying about each member of humanity: *'He experiences himself, his thoughts and feelings, as something separated from the rest-a kind of optical delusion of his consciousness. This delusion is a kind of prison for us...'*

There is a delightful rendition of the release from this prison. Sat-Chit-Ananda, being-awareness-bliss, says Bill Harris[7], repeating the ancient Hindu mantram, is the One energy, the One consciousness, which is what we are in reality. This energy, he says, *'is aware of itself being everything and everywhere and everywhen, and ... as a result of this awareness, it is blissful, happy, peaceful... You are not a separate ego in a bag of skin, but, rather, this Oneness'* (Harris c. 2008, p. 3). This could be dismissed as just Nouveau Hippy-trippy, except for the legion of challenges to the Material Universe idea.

Recent science puts the lie to our illusion of separate material existence. Evidence of the interconnection of all life comes from fields as diverse as biology (Sheldrake's Morphological Fields for instance), psychology, (Carl Jung's work, especially synchronicity, is just one example), and quantum physics (Bell's Theorem for example). Our worldview has been based on the idea that atoms or humans can't possibly affect, or be affected by, each other unless they are in each other's locality. This is known as local causation: two entities, two items or two beings, must be in physical contact to affect each

---

6. What is the responsible choice? China's new pipeline from Tibet diverts water needed for crops in the Asian plains: millions in China will benefit, while millions outside China starve. Similarly, here in southeast Australia, where the rains have failed again, the Victorian State government is diverting water from the dying Murray River and food bowl, to urban industry and households. The rain that the scheme requires for fairness to city folk, farmers *and* the river environment, has evaporated due to global warming. The bushfires of Black Saturday, February 7 2009, were unmatched in their ferocity, as the day was in the intensity of the heat (48 degrees Celsius) and wind. The loss of lives, communities and habitat to this inferno while Queensland drowned in massive floods, should shake us awake about the reality of global warming and our contribution to it. Instead the Victorian government will build a huge polluting desalination plant, partly to deal with the escalating threat of such fires. This just tightens the global warming noose.

7. Bill Harris is the inventor of the cerebral renovation tool Holosync.

other's properties and behaviour. When Bell's Theorem was tested, electrons separated in time and space, seemed to 'know' what was happening with the other electron. They were behaving as a single entity, and demonstrating non-local causation. This means we don't, after all, live as separate material entities, and we don't live in a material universe, or non-local causation would be impossible. There are explanations of the Bell's Theorem tests on the Internet. Yet the book that introduced us to it back in the eighties, still gives one of the best- Gary Zukav's *The Dancing Wu-Li Masters* (1979).

Chance, Design and Suffering

If we grant, (as it seems from the scientific evidence we must), that there is a universe beyond the physical dimension, does it follow that there is a Divine Intelligence, or God, who is the source of everything? Perhaps not, but it certainly takes us into the territory of the raging debate on Chance vs. Design. Can life itself be merely the result of the haphazard collision of atoms in the primordial soup? For the sake of the argument, let the answer be "Yes", however questionable this seems given the very nature of quantum physics. This means we accept for the moment, the hypothesis that Life Arose by Chance-the underlying assumption of materialistic science, and by implication, of Western civilization, despite all of us who believe otherwise.

This hypothesis has in fact, been put to the test in statistical calculations, by more than one famous scientist. Fred Hoyle, with colleague Chandra Wickramasinge, made a well-known calculation.[8] *'The likelihood of the formation of life from inanimate matter is one to a number with 40,000 noughts after it.... If the beginnings of life were not random, they must therefore have been the product of purposeful intelligence,'* concluded Fred Hoyle. Dr Emile Borel, discoverer of the laws of probability, clarified the meaning of these figures. *'The occurrence*

---

8. Dr James Coppedge did a different set of calculations, yet arrived at the same conclusion:
   'The probability of a single protein molecule being arranged by Chance is 1 in 10-161st power. Using all the atoms on earth, allowing all the time since the world began, for a minimum set of the required protein molecules for the smallest theoretical life, the probability is 1 in 10 to the 119,879th power...That is 10-119,831 times the assumed age of the earth and is a figure with 119, 831 zeros.
   Nobel Prize winner Ilya Prigogine commented about the idea that life could have been spontaneously generated:
   It is impossible to accept that such an object could have been thrown together by some kind of freakish, vastly improbable event. Such an occurrence would be indistinguishable from a miracle.

of any event where the chances are beyond 1 in ten followed by 50 zeros is an event which we can state with certainty will never happen, no matter how much time is allotted and no matter how many conceivable opportunities could exist for the event to take place.' The chance formation of the smallest, simplest form of living organism is of this order of probability.

Richard Dawkins (2006), in the chapter *Why there almost certainly is no God,* (pp.113-159), considers that we get into an infinite regress here; what purposeful intelligence created the purposeful intelligence? I loved Phillip Adams' story, in *Adams vs. God: The Rematch (2008)*, of his identification of this Uncreated Creator Conundrum as a six-year-old: He had quizzed his grandmother: *'If God began everything, who began God?* (p. 29).' My answer -- that we don't need a creator of a creator once out of the timebound physical world and its cause-and-effect dynamic, wouldn't satisfy Adams or Dawkins, for reasons including that they don't see any evidence for a universe that is other than purely physical. (Besides, what a cop-out on my part: I invoke God to explain the universe, then when asked to explain God, I take the ball and go home!) Dawkins also calls the argument from improbability *'the Ultimate 747 gambit'* — from Fred Hoyle's statement that the probability of life originating on Earth by chance would be equivalent to the chance of a hurricane in a scrapyard assembling a Boeing 747. Dawkins argues that the issue is not Design vs. Chance, but Design vs. Natural Selection. Dawkins' Design demolition argument is that we need a crane instead of the God skyhook: He looks to the future discovery of a Natural Selection mechanism working on a cosmic, not just a planetary, level.

At this stage, purposeful intelligence, otherwise known as God, still looks to be ahead in the probability stakes by a clear Universe. *'Not such purposeful, intelligent design as you'd **notice'**,* I have been known to rage, in moments of black bitterness at human suffering. This remains the sticking point for most of us --- the appalling level of suffering endured by so many fellow humans. (How desperate I am, we all are, to avoid suffering; to only have pleasure or joy, and how unbalanced it is! And yet-the suffering of billions of humans is unacceptable to me.) For this reason, Pamela Bone famously remarked that she didn't believe in God, *'but if he exists, I don't approve of him'.*

Regardless of her own very long and painful dying, Elisabeth Kubler-Ross came to an acceptance of suffering because she saw it in a much larger, unitive and purposeful context; the one I mean to present in this book. This was a result of her study of dying, and acknowledgement of all, not just some, of the common dying experience. It would help all of us to acknowledge the full range of death experiences, not just those that fit our current worldview. It's something of a detour, but I believe Pamela Bone did have one of these extra-physical experiences, though my conclusions about it may not weigh much as evidence. The second time in the hospital emergency department, very ill indeed and desperate to escape the clamour of the scene around her, she found she could 'hypnotise' herself to a sylvan scene:

> *I imagined myself in a green clearing in a forest, with mossy banks beside clear running water; and a high blue circle of sky above tall trees. There were birds singing and a soft breeze blowing on my face. Somehow, I was really there, instead of in the crowded, noisy hospital ward. How lovely, I thought, this means it doesn't really matter what happens to me because any time I want to I can come back here. But...I have never been able to find it again (2007. p. 73).*

Despite her assertion that there was no consciousness apart from the brain, (and therefore no life after death), Pamela had this experience of consciousness separate from her brain-awareness. That brain-awareness, fed in from her senses and her nerves, was and could only have been, of the awful noise of distress around her in Emergency, and the pain and illness caused by an infection in the Hickman line inserted into her chest to drip-feed chemotherapy.

Unusual states of consciousness-delusional or empirically testable?

Non-ordinary states of consciousness, called NOSC in the US, are explored in later chapters, especially Six and Seven. These states have been regarded as delusional by orthodox science especially, and by most of humanity-seen as something that overtakes the sane and rational person without rhyme or reason, as happened with Pamela Bone. Or we see NOSC as the fabled continents of the mystics; realms of the borderline insane, certainly having nothing whatever to do with ordinary consciousness. Yet isn't it possible that these states of being are as real as each other?

Infantile to transpersonal awareness: The stages of cognition and consciousness development

The progression by which ordinary humans can achieve the highest of these levels of consciousness, known in the East as Enlightenment, *is known*. It can be described-and experienced. There is a clear and well-trodden path from the 'material universe' consciousness of most of humanity, imprisoned within perceptions of the solidity of the physical world, and the ubiquity of time and space, to the blissful 'unified cosmos' consciousness of boundless and unitary Being. (The path leads back to earth, work and service again, say the sages). This path was once taken seriously only as the rites of initiation in secret Orders, or as the stages of meditation or contemplation.

The stages of the path have, in the last decades, been scrutinized by the leading edge of Western psychology, (prompted especially by the research of William James, Carl Jung and Roberto Assagioli) which became aware that *growth in consciousness* was part of human evolution. These expansions of consciousness (applying both to individuals and to civilisations and cultures) have been discovered to take place in fairly sequential steps and stages. These can be documented, categorized, and most of all, worked upon; the higher *states* can at least be encouraged, if not induced. (However, these states, the 'seminar high' or 'contact high' tend to remain elusive until the *stage* is grown into and fully lived.) Thus it is now possible to crosscheck the stages: We can for example correlate those described by a seventh century Zen master, (known as the Five Ranks of Tozan, passed down through the lineage from master to disciple, to Dennis Genpo Merzel (also known as Genpo Roshi), with those discovered by transpersonal psychologists. Genpo Merzel (2007) has combined these to produce the *Big Mind, Big Heart* process he is currently teaching in the U.S., aided by Bill Harris, to assist movement from the personal into the transpersonal domain of consciousness.

The stages given in texts of the perennial philosophy from the ancient world, and the stages described by philosophers, psychologists and sociologists of the modern world, have been correlated and organised into a system of meta-epistemology, or knowledge of knowledges, the Integral theory of consciousness. Ken Wilber, one of the world's foremost philosophers and transpersonal psychologists, has accomplished this. These stages from birth to transcendence were set forth especially in *The Atman Project: A Transpersonal View of Human Development* (1980). A different but related scheme of stages – including all but the highest- has also been empirically derived and tested by Suzanne Cook-Greuter (2007 for example), building on the work of Jane Loevinger and Ken Wilber, and described in Wilber (2000, p. 218 is one instance). The foundations were provided by work such as Piaget's discovery of the stages of cognitive development and Kohlberg's discovery of the stages of moral development.[9] According to the ancient wisdom *and* modern developmental psychology, the changes in consciousness brought about by these stages do eventually *take us to the place where we know there is no death*.

What am I proposing to reveal, to help prompt a change in consciousness that would mean the end of the illusion of death, along with the end of the Material Universe idea? What will extend your knowledge or even change your mind about death? I've summarized the chapters of the book, to give you a quick overview of its contents.

Chapter summaries

Two: Death in our Traditions, Reincarnation ánd the NDE. I begin by looking at our Western attitudes to death, and their origin in Christianity, before a brief look at immortality in our other major spiritual traditions. Why only one life in Christianity, and why resurrection, not reincarnation? What do our traditions teach us about the nature of death, and about its meaning? What do they tell us will happen, after death? While Buddhism teaches us to prepare for this vital event, which will determine our next reincarnation, modern Christianity's idea of Heaven is too vague, too lacking in detail, to be of much help in calming our fears by forming a definite idea of what happens at death. It is necessary to look elsewhere for knowledge about death and after.

Three: The Near-death experience: News from the Other Side or dying brain fog? The arguments for and against the validity of the NDE are considered in the light of the most recent evidence from hospital studies of the NDE, reported in top medical journals such as The Lancet. Conclusions from these studies confound the explanation of Dr Susan Blackmore, champion of the scientific establishment's view of NDE as nothing more than dying brain phenomena, mistake or fantasy. When you're dead (in body) you're well and truly alive elsewhere, it seems! So something like soul must exist.

---

9. Jane Loevinger then described (and tested the validity and reliability of) eight stages of ego development from the infant Impulsive stage through to the mature adult Integrated stage, reached by relatively few of us so far- less than 2 percent in the U.S. Cook-Greuter has added two more stages, culminating in the Unitive consciousness of the spiritually developed, mature human; consciousness of the 'unified cosmos'.

Four: Joy, light, reality: Death and the NDE in Tibetan Buddhism and in the perennial philosophy. Why is there Light and consciousness the other side of death? Can science or spiritual traditions give an account of the cosmos that makes sense of the NDE? What do two sources which admit continuance beyond death, and which tell us something specific about its nature and the process of dying, have to say? The first is Tibetan Buddhism, through *The Tibetan Book of the Dead, and The Tibetan Book of Living and Dying* by Sogyal Rinpoche. The second is the perennial philosophy, which includes all our great traditions under its conceptual and spiritual umbrella. Do these teachings make survival of physical death seem plausible?

Five: Death as Mere Disappearance: Buddhism to Einstein and Hawking on States of Being. Is there any equivalent or explanation, in Buddhism, to the Light reported after death, in NDE? Is there any room in science and the Western worldview, for the continuity of consciousness this entails? A particular application of quantum nonlocality (science's inability to pin atoms down to one spot in timespace, and recognition that they don't have one locality) is investigated to see if it can account for life after death. The seven levels of being of Buddhism and the perennial philosophy are considered. Where do these levels take us? Does quantum physics allow for levels of being beyond the material?

Six: Buddhism's No-soul and the Separation of Body and Consciousness. This considers *our state after death,* the Bardo experience in Tibetan Buddhism, and relates it to the after-death state in other traditions, the perennial philosophy and Christianity especially. Are there a soul and a conscious afterlife in Buddhism? Stages of the dying process are considered, from that prior to clinical death, to the point just after, where we stand amazed that we are still alive and still ourselves. We are told we should try, through the dying process, to retain a clarity and continuity of consciousness that will take us out of the material and transitory realms, into Buddhi, Universal Mind, or the Mind of God. How does it feel, to die? Is the rest of the dying process in these teachings consistent with patients' reports of NDE?

Seven: The States after Death: Heaven, Purgatory, and the Bardo, traces the process, which takes place after death, from the emotional world via the mental to the soul consciousness. It details theses states of consciousness, and the post-death process in a modern presentation of the perennial philosophy, and compares it with the Tibetan tradition. Will Westerners experience the Hundred Peaceful and Wrathful Deities? What is the truth of aspects that terrify many Westerners? Socrates, Jung and Aldous Huxley are three great minds that have given us insights into the post-death states; these tally remarkably with the Tibetan scheme.

Eight: Tasting the Bliss of the Divine Mind. The final stages in the post-death process are the periods spent in the mental and soul worlds; in the most perfect happiness we are capable of receiving. What causes the movement to these higher levels of consciousness, and what is the process undertaken there? Who gets stuck instead, on the emotional (astral) level, and why? It examines whether these states of consciousness can be assimilated to modern transpersonal psychology. Do the higher levels relate to the higher stages of evolution of consciousness, which have been elaborated and systematised in recent decades, in developmental psychology? While these teachings are enlightening, they remain too conceptual to reassure us. There are other sources that do provide this reassurance.

Nine: The Bardo of Becoming; Rebirth considers the Tibetan teachings on rebirth: How and why are we reborn? These are amplified through the Ancient wisdom teachings. Reincarnation in the West is explored in Carl Jung's writings and Morey Bernstein's regression of a 1950's American, to her life as Bridey Murphy, in Nineteenth century Ireland, in *The Search for Bridey Murphy*. Wambach's psychological study of the time before birth, in *Life Before Life*, is considered.

Ten: Drs Whitton and Newton discover the Interlife, discusses exciting studies on the world beyond the physical. Two eminent researchers probe subjects' recollections of the place beyond death and birth, and come to the same conclusions about its true nature. The subjects of both find themselves surviving death, and returning to a state of consciousness marked by timelessness, peace and love. Here they are members of a soul group, bonded by an aeons-long love, working together to advance via successive experiences in a physical body.

Eleven: The Soul's World: Whitton's study vs. Newton's. There is agreement on the nature of the soul world, the soul's task of reviewing the achievements and failures of the finished life, and the metaphysics of the encompassing scheme. Both researchers discover that evolutionary progress works towards enlarging consciousness, and developing the capacity to love and serve the whole, not just a separate aspect of it.

Twelve: The God Argument: Christians vs. Buddhists, Homo Erectus and Evolution. This chapter ponders the Big Questions about the Ultimate. Does God exist? Is there an alternative to Darwinian evolution or Death-of-God Christianity? The difference between the Buddhist and Christian conceptions of the Ultimate or God is discovered to be too minor to divide us.

Thirteen: The great chain of Being, Hierarchy, and Teachers of the Race. Given a Supreme Consciousness, how could mere human creatures be connected to that Being? The chapter considers whether there is anything in the time-honoured idea of the Chain of Being as the fabric of Deity and cosmos, and what might be the nature of those higher in the chain than humans, and their relationship to us. It considers the nature and reality of the Being of Light encountered by those who have undergone a Near-death Experience. This is the being apparently referred to in our religious traditions-variously, as the Christ, the Imam Mahdi (the Great Teacher, the Coming One in Islam), Krishna (in the Hindu tradition), the Messiah (in Judaism), the Bodhisattva and the Maitreya Buddha in Buddhism. Is there any objective reality to this individual, or to the role of World Teacher seemingly played by the one known under these different names?

Fourteen: Soulmates: Just a Myth? The timeless and enduring love for which we search, does have a basis in reality after all. When death takes someone we can't live without, it is not the end of the relationship. But what is the nature of the separation? Can the gap be bridged from our side? Our attitudes to funerals and mourning have changed for the better, but we still behave as if death is the end of our beloved when, given all the evidence in the previous chapters, death is not the end of anything but a cycle. Death is merely the great illusion that holds us captive!

I am presenting the evidence for our survival of death and the argument for a new and positive, even joyful, attitude towards it, as simply as possible. But it necessarily goes into some difficult places, because it proceeds by logical argument and can't be clinched just by handing you a chunk of moon-rock in a specimen jar. The choice is yours–to follow the argument or to skip the more demanding chapters and move on to something more congenial. (You might decide to take their conclusions as read!)

My investigation of death and discovery of greater life

What caused me to investigate Eastern philosophies about death? At any crisis such as serious illness or severe pain or loss or depression, we are brought up sharp at the finiteness of our term. We are forced to confront the inevitability of death –and that the reality of it is now, since it may strike at any time.

When a moment arrives to look into the abyss of death, it creates great loneliness and even terror... a sense of separation from the rest of humanity who are vital and healthy and oblivious to the threat of death, or so it appears just then. It seems too weak and cowardly to carry this fear and loneliness even to a beloved partner, family member or friend. That person will have (along with the rest of humankind) her or his own death to face; my fear or depression or despair may be an impossible extra burden for that person to carry. It would only be worse, if my mother or sister or lover or close friend greeted my fear and need for comfort and reassurance with incomprehension or impatience, or treated it as the nightmare of a seven year old. Yet any fears about death are likely to be met by the insistence that there is nothing to worry about–at least not just yet. The powerful taboo in our society works to actively discourage us from considering the prospect of death.

Earlier on in my life, before my original family of five was reduced to three by deaths of cancer, and looked as if it might be reduced to two, I had ignored this taboo, and done as others have, in their search for meaning and for a hand stretched out across the abyss. I began to learn about the traditions that appeared to offer something not so much alternative to, as additional to, my own–Christianity, which hadn't satisfied all my needs. (Often we go to alien and exotic traditions not so much as a complete rejection of our own, but because they offer something extra, something we don't already have or know.) These were also the traditions which did actually give some definite idea about what lay beyond death.

The Hindu teachings, Cabbalistic Judaism, Spiritualism and Theosophy and Anthroposophy and Buddhism, offered a depth of perspective on this one little life, and new hope. I began to understand that apparently separate and conflicting religions were aspects of the tradition, which was said to be the source of them all, generally referred to as the perennial philosophy. I discovered the modern rendition by The Tibetan abbot, Djwhal Khul, (often referred to simply as DK, in this book as well) in collaboration with Alice Bailey, where the tradition is called the Ageless Wisdom. This offered a wonderfully expanded conception of the universe and the meaning of existence, along with a precise description of the dying process from a kind of super-medical perspective, containing startling details about this process and about the phases of the journey beyond the grave. Still there was nothing concrete about the nature of the life Beyond, the life of my soul or my spirit or some attenuated part of me, the aspect that supposedly survived death.

It all continued to sound at the best, deeply unsatisfying. I attempted to fill this still rather sketchy picture in further with Tibetan Buddhist teachings especially. They weren't much help to this state of mind, of fear, either. They seemed to be saying that all of us who weren't sufficiently evolved to escape to Nirvana, wandered around in the Bardo after death for a short or long time, struggling to free ourselves from delusions, cravings and other earthly burdens. Then when we failed, as we must have done over and over to be here on earth at all, we were drawn back into yet another life, and had to return to earth. How dismal a prospect this was!

The one who eventually got to experience eternity certainly didn't seem much related to this one–me. It was the Immortal Mind or Soul, who spun a fine thread and unravelled it, throwing it out, till the little separate spider-self parachuted out over the abyss and landed back on earth. And was drawn up again, just the skeleton, and a fresh line and new spider spun out and unreeled the next time, the next life. Until one got to the point where no more spider-lives were necessary, when 'I' and the Immortal One become one and the same, until 'there be no more going out'. What was promised, even by The Tibetan's Ageless Wisdom teachings, seemed nothing better than a series of partings and transitions, separated by periods of half-existence. So I feared death, as leading to a state more temporary and fragmented even, than this earthly one.

The fear was sufficient to cause me to lie awake after midnight, even before my sister's cancer diagnosis. I realized that even though I knew more about death than the majority of intelligent and well-read people, enough to put this crisis in perspective to help both my sisters and me in our coping with it, I was actually powerless to offer them reassurance.

How would I have it be for all of us? What did I want? I wanted beauty, light, and peace; all the things we are promised by our spiritual traditions. I wanted to be beyond my cold little separate self. I wanted the end of partings; of the aching within the core of me, of us, for a love that cannot be found on earth. I've felt all this much less urgently since my daughter's arrival in my life. Yet I believe it remains the source of the deepest anguish for most of us. The yearning is for belonging: for the joy of being permanently together with all those who are loved, in a sharing and merging impossible under earthly conditions. Ultimately it is for union with the Divine Beloved, with the One Life.

So has that longing been satisfied, even just in prospect? Have my further journeyings into the place beyond the moment of death, opened any vistas that could calm and reassure that midnight fear? Yes, they have. I am in absolutely no doubt now about the reality of our continuance as our quintessential selves, more alive and complete than ever, and the reality of great joy at the least, and communion and love as a natural state of being, beyond the physical life. I hope I can show you why. Please bear with me as I put logical ladders to the Beyond in place. It is first necessary to convince you that Mind, Soul, Spirit and similar ideas are not just the flights of fancy of medieval theologians, or of New Age nuts. First-hand accounts, for example those of travellers who have returned and told us of their Near-death experiences, are full of light and warmth and a sense of palpable reality, which is exactly what I want to convey about the place beyond death. But to go straight there simply wouldn't work. You would be likely to dismiss this as fable or delusion because I had failed to gain your intellectual assent, at best to the reality of life after death, or failing that, your assent to keeping an open mind.

How does it feel to die –according to the reports of those who've returned?

Here is a typical account:

> I was feeling no pain. I felt wonderful. I felt like an observer, not a participant. I was just floating there between two worlds. One world I knew very well; the other I didn't know existed. To my right and above me the ceiling had given way to a path paved with blue-white clouds. The atmosphere seemed to be sprinkled with gold dust. It was very, very bright, and the light was blinding. I didn't see them, but I sensed the presence of many

> *others and they were joyous. I, too, was joyous with anticipation of joining them.*

This Near-death experience is reported by Leon Rhodes, a respected investigator of the NDE phenomenon, in Tunnel into Eternity (1998)[10]. It was contained in a letter to Rhodes written by 'Maggie, an acquaintance', obviously an intelligent and educated young woman. She describes her experience of an O.O.B, the Out Of Body element of the Near-death experience, which occurs with some NDE:

> *Two doctors had arrived and they were with two nurses who were looking intently at a body on the bed. I took a long look at the body. It was a young woman in a yellow gown. She had very long hair, and it was damp, spread out on the pillow. Her eyes were tightly closed and drawn together. The lips were slightly opened and a smoky blue in colour. She was not struggling to breathe and did not move at all.*

Rhodes also gives us some of the considerable, but not atypical, detail of the NDE reported by Maggie:

> *Maggie saw another nurse and could read her thoughts; "It's too bad. She was only twenty-five"; and saw her leave the room, shaking her head to Maggie's husband, saying, "I'm so sorry". Maggie heard further sad conversation and said, I felt great sympathy for them. I tried to tell them I wasn't in pain. I wished they could be there with me." She could hear and see people in her room and in another room, wondering why "all of these people wanted me to come back and leave this wonderful place that I had found." She tried to tell them where she had been and made the decision to go back. "I gave a wistful look at the beauty of this other existence and started down, hovering over the body for a moment, thinking, 'I will go back up there another time'." Returning, she immediately felt all the pain, felt the doctor pounding her chest with his fist, asking her how she felt.'* (Rhodes 1998, pp. 66-7.)

There are thousands of accounts similar to this now on record, most of which report seeing and hearing things those who report them shouldn't know about while clinically dead. Can they so readily be dismissed as sceptics like Dr Susan Blackmore do, as dying brain phenomena or embroidery of the truth plus imaginative filling-in on the basis of past knowledge?

This question is considered when the latest research into the NDE is reviewed in Chapter Three. The next chapter (Two) ponders Life on the Other Side according to our spiritual traditions,

---

10. Excerpts from Leon Rhodes 1998, *Tunnel into Eternity,* published by the Swedenborg Centre, Sydney, Australia, are used with the permission of the Swedenborg Centre; info@swedenborg.com.au

which shape or considerably influence, the attitudes of society and culture, and thus our own attitudes, to death and the hereafter.

Chapter 2

Death in our Traditions, Reincarnation and the Near-death Experience

Summary Points

- Monty Python and our desperate courage in the face of death
- **The Christian afterlife and the history of resurrection**
- *Asleep in Christ until the Resurrection*': Then where does the soul go after death?
- **The Heresy (Pelagianism); separate soul with inbuilt immortality?**
- The perennial philosophy in Gnosticism and Christianity
- **The Church's position, Christ as the first to defeat death**
- **Life and death in the major religions especially Buddhism; one life or many?**
- Responses of science and religion to the Near-death Experience
- Moody's *Life after Life* (1975) opens the floodgates of accounts of NDE

- The NDE confirms key elements of Christian teaching about life after death
- **The Being of Light; nothing more than a collective fantasy?**
- The perennial philosophy, Buddhism, Advaita Vedanta and Hinduism.
- **Will the reality of life after death reconcile the views of our major traditions?**

Death in our Traditions, Reincarnation and the Near-death Experience

The not-Christ film by British comedy's Monty Python team, cheekily titled *The Life of Brian*, is about an ordinary man who is mistaken for Christ by the crowds and the Roman authorities in pre-Christian Jerusalem. At the end there is an instant of pure black comedic genius, a sly backhanded celebration of the human spirit. The song *'Always Look on the Bright Side of Life'* is rendered by Brian and the two other men who are hanging from crosses on Calvary Hill. *'...So always look on the bright side of death, When you come to draw your terminal breath...'* they sing with desperate bravado, swinging from their crosses. No Christ, no Divinity, no Resurrection, just Brian and his mates being defiantly brave in the face of the human condition and cosmic indifference -- defining in the moment of negation, Christ, Divinity and Resurrection as part of the human preserve. I laughed and cried together at this dark, hopeless, brilliantly funny moment. Of course, it was just a film; no one I thought, would be capable of it when facing death, especially such a death as crucifixion.

Then, in 1982, at the height of the conflict between Britain and Argentina over the Falkland Islands, a ship of the British Royal Navy was bombed by the Argentine forces, caught fire, and began to sink. Most of the crew were imprisoned below decks. In the open radio contact they could be heard singing that same line: *'...So always look on the bright side of death...',* as the fire burned ever fiercer and closer, and they were faced with death by burning, drowning, or a bit of both.

What brilliant comic insouciance, what stark courage! And yet it seemed to be the courage of ordinary human beings, observable at many, perhaps most, deaths. My mother could not talk to my father about his death from cancer until it was imminent, in company with many of us in that situation. Holding his hand as he lay on his deathbed, she teased him *"Hurry up, Douglas dear, or you'll be late for your own funeral"*. He managed to laugh back up at her. It was two days until his death. Seven months later, she too, was diagnosed with terminal cancer, yet stoically kept it from me for six weeks. Is the Church right, are our great religions right, that there is something beyond death after all? Is there a resurrection to eternal life, and meeting with those we love, or is it only this great dignity and courage of ordinary humans, despite their bewilderment about what death is, which bestows meaning on the void? *All of this is a snapshot of our Western beliefs and bewilderment about death, around 2000 C.E., and after two millennia of Church doctrine.*

We display the same courage in the face of the unknown or the cosmic emptiness, when we lose someone dear and necessary to us. This is even when, regardless of our spiritual convictions, it seems that they really have ceased to exist. Some may own that they feel the presence of the beloved individual after death, as Prince William did about his mother Diana guiding and helping him. Such a statement usually arouses skepticism. Although we are likely to comfort each other by implying that there is an afterlife, we know what death is like: the personality we knew no longer exists, except in memory. There is no body, no voice, no hand to reach out and take our empty, slack hand. Why reassure us as the Church will do, raising false hopes about the joyous meeting to take place after our own death? All that is left is the grief, and the painful but precious memories. How can it comfort us to be told that the beloved has "gone to a better place"? If it exists, that place and condition can only seem inhuman and without relevance to us in this life-the only one we know. It scarcely matters where, we reflect, they are gone, lost to us forever.

The Christian afterlife and the history of resurrection

Yet, when grief becomes a little less poignant, the community's spiritual beliefs do provide a measure of comfort to all but convinced atheists-because without final proof, there is room for hope. The Christian Church's beliefs about the nature of death have their origin in the teachings and example of Jesus of Nazareth about the relationship between God and humanity, (or at least as much of that as has come down to us). It was all very mysterious and difficult to comprehend. He rose from the dead, and on the first Easter Sunday dawn, walked out of the sealed and guarded rock tomb where his body was laid after his crucifixion as an enemy of the people. Deep in their grief, His disciples at first failed to recognise Him when he met them on the road to Emmaeus some days after. Later He gathered them to witness his Ascension, telling them that he was going now to return to the Father in Heaven, where in due course they would follow Him.

The context, the setting, of this core experience of Christianity was the Judaeo-Greco-Roman civilization, and its contemporary beliefs about the afterlife. The common cosmology was of a triple-decker universe, with earth in the middle, heaven above and the underworld beneath: the Greek Hades, the Judaic Sheol. Pre-Christian Judaism had added (though it had not invented) first Paradise, then Purgatory, says Professor Geddes MacGregor, in a wonderfully scholarly and insightful discussion in the first chapter of *Reincarnation in Christianity* (1978). Sheol then became the place of punishment for the wicked, while the virtuous went to Paradise, linked to the Garden of Eden by the Hebrews, a state to which they longed to return. It is important to note that the other key idea introduced into pre-Christian Jewish thought was that of resurrection from death to eternal life *'abundant in Jewish literature just before Christ, apocryphal, apocalyptic and deutero-canonical'* [i.e. the idea appears in Deuteronomy, in the Old Testament]. (MacGregor 1978, p. 91). In *Omens of Millennium*, Harold Bloom traces the resurrection of the dead and the triple universe back to Zoroastrianism, and says *'It is ironic that Christianity always has regarded Islam as a heresy, and Zoroastrianism as an exotic remnant, while owing much of its spirituality to both traditions'*. (Bloom 1996, p. 9).

Thus Christians came to believe that the spiritual part of us, the 'true person' leaves the physical body at death, is judged (in the Individual Judgement) and undergoes a cleansing process in Purgatory, then is *'asleep in Christ'* until the Day of Judgement. If the soul is found worthy, it regains the body and ascends into the Presence of God for Eternity. Those are worthy who have led a virtuous and compassionate life, and sincerely attempted to live in imitation of Christ. The thoroughly unworthy end up in Hell, in the netherworld ruled by Satan, the incarnation of Evil.

There is a text which is central to Christian belief: *"I am the Way, the Truth and the Life; no man cometh unto the Father but by Me"*; John 14: 6. Christians perhaps naturally understood that only those who followed the teachings of the man Jesus of Nazareth, and believed he was the sole Son of God, would be permitted into Heaven, to enjoy eternal life. There are other interpretations that do not drive the sword of contradiction through the very heart of this great faith in the way that the canonised literal interpretation has done. God is Love, Christ taught and Christianity holds; it is simply not possible that the intention of this compassionate God could be to condemn to utter futility, and finally to damnation or annihilation, the lives of the rest of humanity for the rest of time. Even contemporary interpretations, in the teachings of those Christian schools and sects which did not survive to become the official voice of the Church, cast a very different light on these words; one which is inclusive of humanity, not exclusive of everyone else but those who are baptized into the Christian Church[1] . There is further discussion of this later in the book.

Geddes MacGregor also makes an objection to Hell, before revealing the state of confusion of the doctrine about death and beyond, in his argument for the reasonableness of a scheme of many lives to achieve 'moral and spiritual evolution':

> *Even the crassest form of the doctrine of Purgatory suggests moral and spiritual evolution. Surely, too, even countless rebirths as a beggar lying in misery and filth on the streets of Calcutta would be infinitely more reconcilable to the Christian concept of God than is the traditional doctrine of everlasting torture in hell...Indeed, even apart from the notion of everlasting punishment, traditional Christian doctrine about "last things" (the destiny of humankind) is so notoriously confused that vast numbers of people, even habitual churchgoers, have given up believing anything about the subject at all. Christian eschatology (as that branch of theology is called) is by any reckoning the most unsatisfactory area of the Church's concern. A sitting duck for the Church's adversaries, it is also an embarrassment to thoughtful Christians* (MacGregor 1978, p. 12.)[2]

Where does the soul go after death?

We are used to the standard gravestone phrases - 'Gone to God', 'Rest in Eternal Peace', 'Gone to her Reward', and 'With the Angels

---

1. Dion Fortune's explanation of the Crucifixion is helpful in moving us away from this belief that no-one gets eternal life except professing Christians. '*There is known to occultists a method of healing by substitution, in which, by extreme compassion with the suffering of a beloved one, the suffering is experienced in the very self, and then, by the appropriate reaction and realisation, is expiated upon a higher plane. Such a process is extremely dangerous...(and) extremely painful.... Now that which is sometimes done between two individuals is performed between the Saviour and the group-soul of the world when an Atonement is made at the end of a phase of evolution. In the few short hours of the Crucifixion the sin and suffering left over from a phase of evolution were realized and abreacted. Little wonder that, in anticipation of this ordeal, the Lord...prayed, "Let this cup pass from me"*'. Dion Fortune n.d., The Esoteric Orders and their Work, Rider, London, p. 34.

   Elisabeth Kubler-Ross' experience in her night of a thousand deaths, may have been an example of this substitution healing, this atonement. '*...I could barely breathe, and I bent over in agony and pain so overwhelming that I did not even have the strength to scream or call for help...[E]ach time a death was completed another one began...One thousand times.*' It was followed by a dawning of Light. (1997, pp 218-223). This healing via substitution and exceptional compassion for suffering, is the principle behind the Buddhist practice of Tonglen.

2. Reincarnation in Christianity © Geddes MacGregor, 1978, published by Quest Books, see <www:questbooks.net>. Quotes from MacGregor printed by permission of the publishers.

in Heaven' and the jokes about the sheer boredom of such an un-varying condition of bliss. The Church tells us that the soul reinhab-its the fleshly body at the Resurrection... a very strange and I sus-pect, uncomfortable idea- where is the soul in the meantime? We are supposed to somehow be asleep in our graves or in some inter-mediate but non-heavenly realm, until the clarion call of the Last Trumpet is sounded. It doesn't add up, and it isn't particularly com-forting - certainly not the lifeline we long to throw to a distressed friend about the essential person who has just disappeared from their life.

The Church and the Pelagian heresy; separate soul with inbuilt immortality

Difficulties arise for the Church where it continues to insist on im-mortality as a state that can only be gained via 'the resurrection of the dead', at the end of time, and in the physical bodies that have lain decomposing in the grave for aeons. And in fact a separability of body and soul, which allows the soul to find its way immediately into a place of love and peace, is the more natural and intuitive position[3] that has developed in popular thinking about the state after death. It is essentially a Platonist position. The doctrine of the ability of the soul to shed the body and rise to an immortal state has been known as *The* Heresy, since Bishop Pelagius propounded it in the fourth century and St Augustine, a founding scholar among the Church Fathers, denounced it. A separate soul, which is naturally immortal, has no need of being raised from its mortal condition to eternal life by God, assisted by the priesthood. The Church is di-minished in relevance and importance. I am indebted to Frank J. Tipler (1995) for his discussion of this issue; he devotes a chapter to it, in his controversial book *The Physics of Immortality: Modern Cosmo-logy, God, and the Resurrection of the Dead.* (Tipler proposes immortal-ity via uploading of the contents of our brains onto computers. It is a complex and quite brilliant thesis, to which this sentence of sum-mary does no justice.) Dion Fortune (n.d.) traces the ancient Mys-tery teaching or perennial philosophy, through its Christian incarna-tion. She notes that the Church attempted to annihilate it, because in its Neo-Platonist teaching of a reincarnating and naturally

---

3. This is the position supported in folklore-the lore of the folk, as a result of personal experiences of those who dared talk about it-of visitors to and returnees from the Beyond, being passed down orally.

immortal soul, priest and Pope became, if not redundant, at least inessential.

It is hard to see how to make sense of a position that has been bequeathed to us mainly by various historical conjunctions, plus numerous anathematisings and persecutions, such as the ones cited by Dion Fortune and MacGregor. Why would the Creator of all this *need* the mortal remains to recreate us? And why would we ourselves want any kind of physical body? Our souls are supposed to be connected to or coexistent with these bodies which have become dust or ashes. Are these souls asleep in the grave with our bones, or hovering above them? Obviously they have a kind of inbuilt immortality anyway. Really, none of it makes sense! It's time for a rethink, given that it is not a doctrine based on any indisputable foundation.

MacGregor explores the ideas of immortality of the pre-Christian civilisations, that the soul could be ensnared in a lace veil, or needed a chimney or an opening in the coffin or urn, to escape and rise to the place of souls. He finds them to be 'primitivistic' in their notions of soul and body as being like yolk and egg-that neither can exist (except in the culinary sense) without the other. It becomes clear that essentially, this is the origin of the Church's present-day teachings about life after death-that we need a *physical* body to have or house a soul; the psyche cannot exist by itself. Yet the virtually inescapable conclusion of the scientific studies in the upcoming Chapter Three, is that the psyche does indeed have a separate existence.

Professor MacGregor's reconciling of reincarnation with Christianity also attempts to deal with this difficulty along with the others. Modern scientific understanding ends the need for this notion of soul-body dependency; the one which drove the Church's charge of heresy against the Albigensians, who thought the soul naturally immortal and therefore separable. In countering this heresy, the Lateran council declared that *all shall rise with the bodies they now have*. MacGregor comments:

*For today we see no "soul" and "body" to be so connected,[4] so that the import-
ance formerly attached by Christian theologians to this question can be eliminated. In any case, such very Latin teaching about a carnis resurrectio
[resurrection body] does not seem to fit Paul's teaching in the New Testament, which is that the body is to be of a new order, the perfect instrument of
...the spirit...The curious notion of the revivification of the material particles
of the body does not arise in St Paul."* (MacGregor 1979, p. 84).

Yet Professor MacGregor notes that there was a different reason
for the Church's neglect of the idea of the soul travelling through
lives in many bodies, (common at the time and taught especially by
Gnosticism). While this provided no doctrinal difficulty for the
early church, its members, during the first century, were eagerly
awaiting Christ's Return and the Day of Judgement, which they understood to be imminent. Ideas about consequences of actions in
this life, the karma, they were making for their next life were
irrelevant -- there wouldn't be one. Yet the Church had originally
embraced and assimilated ideas, including reincarnation, of every
culture it touched.

---

4. MacGregor cites Gilbert Ryle's critique in *Concept of Mind*, of this as a 'category
mistake' made by the Church Fathers (and repeated by Descartes), that body and
soul were distinct kinds of 'stuff' or categories of existence, (which could perhaps
live separately, as the Gnostics thought, or not, as the Church Fathers concluded).
Modern science, he says demonstrates this: there is no distinct soul-stuff vs. body-
stuff; we should think in terms of Teilhard de Chardin's radial energy.

True, we now understand from relativity theory that matter is energy in a different
state, and from quantum physics that the basic quanta of energy 'disappear' from
the concrete world, and 'reappear' there. This however, can be made into an argument for the soul as nothing more than an emanation of the brain, or a construct of
the personality. This solution only lands us back again in the old dilemma of
Cartesian dualism, where there is no possible connection between mind or soul,
and body (or brain and its emanation). What McGregor is saying is more than this,
but not sufficiently distinct. God, he argues, transcends entropy, and by the fact of
becoming human, by divine grace and our connection with God, we do too. (Our
understanding of entropy has altered since then; there is now no need to rescue us
by any extra-thermodynamic agency).*The difference between the ancient "soul-stuff" notion of personal immortality and the one I am proposing is enormous. On the ancient view, I
am an immortal soul temporarily clothed in a human body: On my view, I have become a
soul through millions of years of evolutionary development and struggle, and the "soul" I
have become is capable of immortality.'* p.84

In my own view, both positions are correct and easily reconcilable, as I hope will
become obvious in the rest of the book. Reincarnation in Christianity © Geddes
MacGregor, 1978, is published by Quest Books; see <www.questbooks.net>.
Quotes from MacGregor are reprinted by permission of the publishers.

Examination of the Church's position; Christ as the first to defeat death

Thus the Church's inevitable position became that Jesus of Nazareth was the first one in history to have risen from the dead. This substantiated his apparent claim to divinity, and he became for the church, the only son of God, and the only one able to confer immortality and divinity on members of the human race-that is, those who became Christian. *Yet at the very time that this became the canonical reading, there was an alternative view.* Christ was stating a spiritual truth. Although it was not accessible to ordinary humans of the time, this truth was commonplace among its sects, esoteric orders and teachings, and was background to the thinking of many great minds of the age.

Christ's appearance to the disciples after his death was a miracle only to the limited material consciousness. His teaching was completely consonant with the teaching of these sects and orders. This was that *every one of us* has the capacity to 'rise from the dead' and 'ascend to heaven'; to transcend the consciousness trapped within materiality, through discovering the divine Self within, or "Christ within us, the hope of glory"-the immortal principle, the Christ energy. This teaching was that all of us have the capacity to ascend to heaven as distinct from 'descending' to a relative hell or returning immediately to another life on earth- the alternatives of the materially limited consciousness, explored in Chapters Eight and Nine. Jesus' statement "I am the way, the truth and the life; no man cometh unto the Father but by Me" thus has a different light cast upon it.

Richard Tarnas (1991) in *The Passion of the Western Mind*, ponders the historical twists and turns of establishing the Christian church in his brilliant book, surely already a classic:

> *As early as the second century, Justin Martyr first advanced a theology that saw both Christianity and Platonic philosophy as aspiring toward the same transcendent God, with the Logos signifying at once the divine mind, human reason, and the redemptive Christ who fulfills both the Judaic and Hellenic historical traditions (p. 152).* However, these theological variants such as Justin Martyr's, *'and religious innovations-Gnosticism, Montanism, Donatism, Pelagianism, Arianism, [which] controverted matters close to the heart of Christianity, were therefore viewed as heretical, perilous, and requiring effective condemnation. (p. 153).* Tarnas concludes that by the end of the classical period, the *'exultant and inclusive religious spirit visible in primitive Christianity had taken on a different character: more*

inward, otherworldly and philosophically elaborate, yet also more institutional, juridical and dogmatic' (p. 154).[5]

The difficulty for modern Christians has always been the disparity between the rational and scientific understanding of a world hung together by cause and effect, and this seeming Biblical fantasy which apparently only ever happened to one individual-Jesus of Nazareth, and which seems to have no rational or scientific basis whatever. Belief seems to require an immense leap of faith, or of what might be seen by sceptics as a silly credulity, over the yawning chasm between doctrine and our present knowledge and experience. The view of the Life After, for twenty-first century Christians, is vague and unsatisfactory in the extreme. Perhaps the prospect of death and the afterlife is more comforting or more reasonable in the view of other religions? Or is it very little different? *What is living and dying about, according to the world's religions?*

The meaning of life and death in the major religions; one life or many?

Christianity, Judaism and Islam teach that there is indeed an afterlife, and a relationship between the way we live now on earth, and the nature and quality of that afterlife. What exactly happens, though, when a virtuous life is over? Heaven (Christianity and Judaism) and Paradise (Islam) are enjoyed by those who have shown themselves worthy of its blessings. The nature of this heavenly or paradisal life is very vague, apart from the assurance that those chosen will spend eternity being blissfully happy contemplating God.[6]

These three faiths are mono-incarnational religions (in their popular and exoteric forms, though not their esoteric or uncanonised forms-Sufism in Islam, Kabbalism in Judaism, and the various forms of esoteric Christianity still extant). A single life is all we have to make and perfect the soul, and to reach Heaven or Paradise. This 'one life' idea is the shape that each religion has taken as a result of the kind of historic accidents and decisions by its leaders, already outlined in the case of Christianity. Both the Bible and the Koran

---

5. Excerpts from Passion of the Western Mind by Richard Tarnas, published by Harmony Books, (originally published by Ballantine) a division of Random House, Inc, and Copyright© 1991 by Richard Tarnas, is reprinted by permission of Random House.

6. Chapter Eight explores the nature and experience of this place through historic accounts and some traditions.

have what seem to be unmistakable references to reincarnation. I would agree with Church authorities that *'Except a man be born again, he cannot enter the Kingdom of God'* (John 3: 3) may not refer to reincarnation (why make a point of it when it is going to happen anyway?) Yet the dissenting view, that it does talk about needing many lives to perfect the soul, is also reasonable. But how else (bar reincarnation) to interpret the answer to Jesus' question *'Who do ye say that I am? They answered saying, "Some say Elijah, some say John the Baptist."* Both were known to be dead, Elijah long since, though John's life overlapped with that of Jesus, whom he baptised in the Jordan. In other words, the people thought that Jesus was the reincarnation of Elijah or John the Baptist. Jesus does not tell them that reincarnation is nonsense, and no part of God's design. He seems to accept it as a perfectly reasonable assumption, that he might be the reincarnation of one or the other-and that therefore, reincarnation is a reality. He doesn't correct the principle, only the specific application of it to connect these prophets to him.

This is perhaps the most important difference between these religions and Hinduism and Buddhism. It is important because the Eastern belief that each of us requires a long series of lives to reach that Heaven or state of blessedness, Moksha, Nirvana, creates a dramatically different perspective, and requires a different evaluation of the nature of reality - specifically the relation of 'Heaven' and 'Earth', of body and soul or mind, of physical, incarnate reality and discarnate, non-physical reality, and their relationship.

The time between lives also assumes a significance far beyond the idea of the Afterlife as merely the place where we get our well-deserved rest. It is a time for spiritual digestion of the experience of the just-finished life, for extraction of the lessons, and preparation for another return to incarnation for a different set of experiences and different lessons, and to continue the work of building and perfecting the Self. We are (only) finally able to experience the Buddhist Nirvana or Moksha, the Hindu heaven, when we have attained to such a state of grace that there is no need to incarnate further in the earthly system, and such a state of consciousness that we have completely transcended the earthly, material view. Meanwhile, modern branches of the perennial philosophy such as Theosophy and the esoteric philosophy of Alice Bailey, are more explicit that the state of bliss is itself only an oasis on the long trek to greater Being, and greater responsibility in an incalculably vast universe.

Curiously enough, the credulity gap is possibly even greater for a Westerner contemplating the 'weird' Eastern idea of reincarnation. It looks to us even less rational and plausible than the idea that we live and die only once. It requires a totally different construction of the nature of reality than the one most familiar to us and perhaps most sympathetic – that of modern science.

Reports of the Near-death Experience, and our responses

It's no wonder that we were curious and excited by first the trickle, then the flood, of accounts of individuals who had apparently survived their own deaths to tell us of the experience! These floodgates were opened in the mid nineteen-seventies by Dr Raymond Moody's publication of his informal study, *Life after Life* (1975). After hearing two accounts of the Near-death Experience, Moody, struck by their similarity, set out to discover if any of his philosophy students would report anything similar, which to his amazement, they promptly did.

These people insisted to Moody and researchers since, that their experiences were more real and memorable than 'yesterday'; that they had gone through death and expected to be non-existent, only to find themselves hovering around ceiling height, looking down on their own inert bodies, and trying to tell grief-stricken people at the scene that they weren't dead, they felt more alive than ever, and were experiencing a wonderful, joyful peace. But no one was able to hear them.

The common elements of the NDE; my sister's NDE

Researchers discovered that there were common elements. Near-death experiencers travelled down a tunnel towards a very bright light, and emerged into a beautiful scene of a celestial city or fields or gardens. A great Being of Light appeared-occasionally seen as God or Christ or an Angel, and asked did they have something of the just-past life to show? A life review followed; every single act was seen in crystal clarity in its benevolent or malevolent intention and its outcomes and effects upon others. Finally either the Being of Light, or people they knew who had already died came with the message that they had to return to earth and their life, it was not yet time for them to leave it. Or they were given the choice, after reviewing the significance of that life and the finishing of it, and chose to return. None of them really wanted to leave such beauty, harmony, all encompassing love, and joy, to return to the suffering of earthly life. When they did so choose, it was out of compassion for those still living it, especially family members, and obligation to them and to unfinished life tasks.

This quick summary is of course a composite of the typical elements in a Near-death Experience. As every investigator from Raymond Moody on points out, no two experiences are exactly alike, nor are all the elements present in all NDE, nor in the same order. Yet the surprise is that they are essentially the same experience, with variations. My sister Meredith's NDE was quite typical, though at the time she knew nothing of the NDE phenomenon. She felt herself travelling out of her body:

> 'It was not a narrow, tunnelly tunnel but a broader one, with light in the distance. When I got into the Light, it was very bright and universal; all worries and concerns, all pain and distress, were gone, and I felt blissful, and wanted to keep going. Everything about the life you've been so involved in is suddenly irrelevant, and even though I had a husband and two young daughters who needed me, I didn't want to go back, because this was Life! That, back there, was suffering and obligation and huge effort. Then God asked me what I chose to do with my life-whether to return or go on into the Light.'

This involved a contemplation of her life and its values and goals, in which she was made to realise that the things she was focused on and striving to achieve, such as her painting, were less important; what mattered was her family–her two daughters and her husband. She answered that she would go back, in order to be there for them. *I felt as though I had given the correct answer to the question-as though it was a test, and I had passed it'*, she concluded.

My sister gave this feedback when I read her what I had written about her experience:

> "It's an urge, like a huge magnet. You're irresistibly drawn towards it-you don't have any other possibility or feeling. It's like the reverse of being born. It's a very formless experience; the beingness that you're in is full and realized. There's no thinking 'Isn't this lovely?' It's a being state, not a thinking state, it's a feeling state, but there is no emotion-none at all-it's way beyond emotion."

It's worth noting that whenever I talk about this book at parties or gatherings, someone can report a Near-death Experience.

Responses of science and religion to the Near-death Experience

The reports of investigations into NDE by Raymond Moody and others tended to have one of three effects upon readers. Either we responded as many in the scientific community responded, and Dr

Susan Blackmore (1993) so famously did, concluding that all Near-death Experience day-trippers to Paradise were hallucinating or caught up in a fantasy produced by their own cultural conditioning. Or these reports excited curiosity, and gave some of us hope. Perhaps we did live on; there was a soul after all. For some of us there was a prospect of other lives, as well.

Those who already believed in the Christian vision of life after death, like the Catholic school community in which I taught, and where there was a class set of copies of Moody's book, *Life after Life*, often regarded the Near-death Experience as a fleshing-out of the bones of truth about the life after death and the experience of dying. The cumulative experience of the NDE appeared to add up to a confirmation of some key elements of Christian teaching about life after death (putting aside the Church's confusion over whether our souls are 'sleeping' until our bodies are revived in the general resurrection at the end of time, or whether they go to Heaven after our individual deaths). These elements are:

1. That there is an afterlife,
2. That those who have died before us are indeed 'gone before us' to that heavenly place, and may come to meet us on our arrival there,
3. That we are put into the charge of great superhuman beings of a nature that is clearly divine-The Christ, angels, or other messengers of God,
4. That these great beings are omniscient...certainly they know every detail of our lives, however insignificant, and they know our hearts and our thoughts intimately and without any communication about them.
5. That we really are asked to account for every action and its good or evil effects.

Who is the Being of Light? Do Muslims see Him? Can Buddhism help explain NDE?

Did some in the Islamic and Judaic communities, perhaps in Western countries where Moody's book was in currency, respond in the same way as these Christians, to the idea of the NDE? Those Muslims who undergo the NDE are likely to identify the Being of Light as The Imam Mahdi or the Prophet Mohammed or Allah/God. So Muslims coming across the NDE may conclude that it was a purely Christian experience, because of the Christian terminology sometimes used by NDErs. Even though most of those who experienced NDE reported in a non-specific way about a great Being of Light, or an Angel, many others in the published accounts responded to this Being as Christ, because the accounts come from overwhelmingly Christian countries. If they had said 'the Imam Mahdi' 'The Messiah', 'The Lord Maitreya' or 'The Lord Krishna', the relevance for other branches of religion, other faiths, would have been seen.

Sceptics are likely to point to this as evidence of the origin of NDE in cultural conditioning, a charge that will be explored in Chapter Three. They would assert that the NDEr's identification of the Being of Light depends purely upon which deity or divinity they had been taught to imagine in the imaginary heavenly realms. Is there any reply to this? Yes. Years ago, there was an excellent book in public and school libraries -*'One God and the Many Ways we Worship Him'*. Simply because I refer to the Being of Light as Christ and you refer to the same Being as 'The Imam Mahdi' or 'The Messiah' does not reduce that great Being to a fantastical production of cultural conditioning, any more than a woolly four-legged grass-eater is reduced to a fantasy simply because I call it *the sheep*, you, if you are French, call it *le mouton*, while an Italian speaks of *il pecorino*.

At this point, caught between our modern materialistic and scientific skepticism, and growing interest in a phenomenon which shows no signs of disappearing or being explained away, many of us have turned to the wisdom of the East, made accessible to the West by scholars from the later Nineteenth Century onward. (It is fascinating to note that here in Australia, there are now more Buddhists than Baptists, according to the 2006 census. This is due at least as much to Australians of non-Eastern background becoming Buddhists, as it is to immigration from the East.) All branches of Buddhism are finally traceable back to the same great source in the body of teachings we know as Hinduism. Prince Siddhartha, the Gautama Buddha, was a Hindu, if he can be said to be anything so limiting. His teachings were not a denial of or rewriting of his religion, they were instead an updating of it; the extension and clarification of what became Advaita Vedanta, the localised version of the ancient teachings. It is referred to now under the generic heading of Hinduism.

In *The Secret Doctrine*, Helena Blavatsky, (1888a, p. xxi) clarifies this point with authority in her Introductory. It was she who with Colonel Olcott, revived Buddhism in Ceylon (now Sri Lanka), where her contribution is still celebrated annually.

> Readers are asked' *to bear in mind the very important difference between orthodox Buddhism -- i.e. the public teachings of Gautama the Buddha, and*

his esoteric Budhism (wisdom). His secret Doctrine, however, differed in no wise from that of the initiated Brahmins of his day [i.e. initiated into the ancient Wisdom Religion]. *The Buddha was a child of the Aryan soil; a born Hindu, a Kshatrya and a disciple of the 'twice born' (the initiated Brahmins) or Dwijas. His teachings therefore, could not be different from their doctrines, for the whole Buddhist reform* [that is, the reform undertaken by Gautama the Buddha], *merely consisted in giving out a portion of that which had been kept secret from every man outside of the 'enchanted' circle of Temple-Initiates and ascetics. Unable to teach all that had been imparted to him-owing to his pledges-though he taught a philosophy built upon the ground-work of the true esoteric knowledge, the Buddha gave to the world only its outward material body and kept its soul for his Elect.*

The division of the Ageless Wisdom into separated and exclusive faiths, into 'isms', could be seen as a result of geographic isolation. This division was later reinforced by the clash of cultures, and the necessity to defend one's own version of the Ageless Wisdom as the only one, against the view of other traditions that theirs is the true faith. Such apparently contradictory positions cannot all be true together (or so we inevitably reason in defence of our own position). Either there is One True Faith, Islam or Judaism or Christianity or Buddhism or Hinduism and all the rest are nonsense, or the atheists are right: God does not exist, and all religious traditions asserting that God does exist are myths and fantasies of humans desperate for escape from a harsh reality.

There is a third alternative, something which even the Roman Catholic Church, post John XXIII, has not yet seen, or admitted at least (in the good company of the official positions of most major religions). The adherents of any faith but Christianity in its approved Papal version, were anathematized until very recently. Perhaps that was to be expected. The Roman Church is the only one given Divine Authority to issue and stamp one's passport to Heaven. What, back then in the Middle Ages? No, right now, in the early twenty-first century! Jews most recently, and Muslims slightly earlier, have been given rights of admission. Jews who died prior to the ministry of Christ, who simply had no chance of hearing of Him, have always been admitted into the presence of God by the Vatican. Now even post-Christian era Jews are deemed eligible to enter into Eternal Life if they have lived virtuously.

The Roman Church is not alone in this exclusivity; it simply exemplifies the position of religions with long traditions, each convinced of its preeminence as God's representative institution on earth. Christ said 'I have other flocks that ye know not of.' What other flocks can these possibly have been, but those of other great

45

religions? They do indeed know Him under other names- the Lord Krishna (Hinduism), the Lord Maitreya (Buddhism), the Messiah (Judaism), the Imam Mahdi (Shia Islam).

What, then, is this third alternative? It is of course, that God or the Ultimate does indeed exist; that all traditions contain some glimpses into this great truth, and that these glimpses are flawed, incomplete and apparently contradictory because of the 'mere' humanness of their adherents and per-petuators.[7] If God does exist, then it follows that the third alternative is true. A Creator big enough to be responsible for even the little reality we know about, and the 'embodiment' of Divine Love, would not give the keys of the Kingdom to just one group of His creatures. Blavatsky had already made it clear that the Hindu tradition was a branch of the one Secret Doctrine, or Ageless Wisdom. Two paragraphs before, she wrote:

> '...Esoteric philosophy reconciles all religions, strips every one of its outward, human garments, and shows the root of each to be identical with that of every other great religion...(T)he records we mean to place before the reader embrace the esoteric tenets of the whole world since the beginning of our humanity, and Buddhistic occultism occupies therein only its legitimate place, and no more. Indeed, the secret portions of the 'Dan' or 'Jan-na' ('Dhyan') of Gautama's metaphysics-grand as they appear to one unacquainted with the tenets of the Wisdom Religion of antiquity-are but a very small portion of the whole. (Blavatsky 1888, vol. i, p. xxi).

Will the reality of life after death combine and reconcile the views of our major traditions?

This view of Christianity's relationship with Christ, and with our other great faiths, will I hope, remove the tallest barriers to a

---

7. The ABC's (Australian Broadcasting Corporation) leading television religious affairs programme, *Compass*, considered atheism and scepticism through some famous proponents (The Atheists, Compass, Sunday March 29, 2009). They included Philip Adams, Richard Dawkins and Michael Shermer, who appears in the next chapter. I loved Shermer's title for Dawkins and his like: *'evangelical atheists'*! Shermer, and Adams in his mellowing years, belong to a more mature order of scepticism; they see it as unhelpful to force atheism on creatures who still have a need to give life meaning in this way, and harmful to stir up further sectarian conflict. My problem with all sceptics is that they aim too low: They are too busy demolishing God as the tribal patriarch of an infant or barely adolescent humanity, a God each tribe claims while denying the other's claims; a God, as they rightly point out, who is too small to exist. If they adjust their sights, will they catch a glimpse of a Presence vast enough to contain the galaxies in the night sky, which are as countless, Adams reminded us, as the grains of sand in the Sahara?

reasoned consideration of the validity of the Near-death Experience, and the possibility of a life after death that is more rational
and consistent, more lively and recognisable, than the vague and
conflicting ideas often presented in Christianity. Perhaps life after
death will look more like the Buddhist idea of it, or combine elements of the teachings of all our faiths-Judaism, Hinduism, and
Islam especially. But that is to be explored. This understanding of
God, Christ and the Church also makes possible a more dispassion-
ate consideration of the medical and scientific evidence about The
Near-death Experience, which is discussed in the next chapter.

Chapter 3
Science and Near-death Experiences

Summary Points

- **Plato to Moody-NDE out of folklore and into the paranormal**
- Studies to investigate or disprove NDE as conscious survival of bodily death
- First scientific study of the NDE by Dr Michael Sabom
- **Scientists and the 'delusional' NDE; Ken Wilber and the Four Quadrants of knowledge**
- Dr Susan Blackmore explains NDE as dying brain sparks or fantasy
- Dr Serdehaly's report of dead Jimmy observing his rescue
- **Kenneth Ring and Cooper's Mindsight: visual NDE in the blind**
- First hospital studies of the causes of NDE
- Parnia and Fenwick's U.K. study discussed in interview

- **The Parnia-Fenwick study: NDE not caused by drugs, hypoxia or other brain affectors**
- **The 'Lancet study' – Van Lommel's ten-hospital Dutch study**
- Does NDE take place before or after the period of clinical death, instead of during it?
- **Blood supply insufficient for NDE as merely a brain event**
- Shermer in Scientific American--NDE only a brain product
- **NDE more than dying brain; indicators of conscious survival of physical death**

Science and Near-death Experiences

We have an idea, a firm conviction even, that our senses provide us with reliable perception of everything in our world, even in the face of the evidence that we are in fact, aware of only a limited range of phenomena. So those of us who have not had a Near-death Experience may dismiss reports of NDE as fantasy. Yet Near-death Experiencers report an entirely new range of phenomena 'known' through different apparatus of consciousness and perception than any they used when in a physical body. Are we dismissing the Near-death Experience as fantasy mainly because we ourselves have not had the experience? Is there any evidence to weigh in the balance of either possibility: fantasy or extra-physical perception?

Plato to Moody-NDE out of folklore and into the paranormal

In the last two decades or so, it has become at least acceptable if not exactly respectable, to have had a Near-death Experience. We are indebted for this change of attitude to Raymond Moody, the American lecturer in philosophy and medical doctor who was the first to collect data on the Near-death Experience and report on it in *Life After Life*, (Moody 1975). Reports of those who had died and returned to life had been around at least since that most famous, supposedly true account in Plato's *Republic* (Jowett 1942, p.503), of the soldier Er the Pamphylian, who after what the translator Jowett describes as *'a brief visit to the lower world'*, returned after twelve days, to life and to his body, to find it laid on a funeral pyre. Yet before Moody's pioneering work, almost no modern reader would have read this as anything but a good drinking story, with currency then as now, when mates gather round the amphora of wine or beer tap at the local pub or tavern. Twelve days! And his body didn't even have holes where the vultures had put him to the taste test? Meantime, those who had gone through these remarkable Near-death experiences often lived the rest of their lives telling no-one, fearing they would be rejected as deluded or even insane.

'Irritated' scientists and conflicting evidence

Moody's work opened the floodgates. Medicos everywhere discovered that Moody's patients were not peculiar: some of their own patients also reported NDE (if asked sympathetically, by the right person). The scientific and medical communities were nonplussed by this news. Inevitably they set about to explain the Near-death Experience to fit with the assumptions of their disciplines about the nature of the universe, and the sceptical and materialistic temper of the times. There had to be a rational explanation! This meant exposing life after death as just a myth. In her scholarly and groundbreaking study *The Fire in the Equations*, Kitty Ferguson quotes the American scientist Robert Jastrow on scientists dealing with evidence or experiences that are in conflict with science's assumptions:

> *I am an agnostic in religious matters. However, I am fascinated by some strange developments going on in astronomy--partly because of their religious implications and partly because of the peculiar reactions of some of my colleagues...Theologians generally are delighted with the proof that the Universe had a beginning* [after the investigations in quantum physics showed that the universe had not always existed] *but astronomers are curiously upset. Their reactions provide an interesting demonstration of the response of the scientific mind--supposedly a very objective mind--when evidence uncovered by science itself leads to a conflict with the articles of faith in our profession. It turns out that the scientist behaves the way that the rest of us do when our beliefs are in conflict with the evidence. We become irritated, we pretend the conflict does not exist, or we paper it over with meaningless phrases.* (Ferguson 1994, p. 75).

Ferguson then notes Einstein's response to the emerging evidence of an expanding universe. *'This circumstance irritates me'*, he wrote. He was 'irritated' by the implication that the universe, rather than having always existed and being self-created, must have had a beginning – in the Big Bang. That meant its cause lay beyond the universe itself. In the opening sentence of *The Eye of the Spirit*, Ken Wilber remarks: *'The Big Bang has made idealists out of anybody who thinks. First there was nothing, then in less than a nanosecond the material universe blew into existence (1997, p. 2)*. Idealists are those who see the material world as a product of mind, unlike the materialists, who reverse that position. For Einstein, there was an implied conflict between his Relativity Theory and quantum physics. Amused or bemused about the reaction of some scientists to the Big Bang theory, Ferguson comments *'For reasons entirely apart from scientific objectivity, the Big Bang pill was a bitter one to swallow, and a few still have it hiding behind a tooth'* (Ferguson 1994, p. 75).

The Near-death Experience came out of the fogs of implied insanity and began to take on an objective and recognized existence, thanks to Raymond Moody's discovery of this quite common phenomenon. Yet even now, several decades later, I hardly dare suggest that there could be a parallel between Big Bang and NDE in the abrasiveness of the irritant presented to the scientific mind. The Big

Bang is respectable science, isn't it; theory proposed by eminent scientists –some of the greatest minds on the planet? How could it be in any way comparable to what we still have a tendency to regard as the twilight tales of the moribund? How then, *has* science dealt with NDE?

Dr Michael Sabom and Dr Susan Blackmore were two of the most notable of these who set out to produce a scientific and supposedly rational explanation of the Near-death Experience. *So what did they discover by way of an answer?* And are we as a civilisation, able to deal objectively with the implications of these discoveries, and not *'paper [them] over with meaningless phrases'*, as Jastrow found of scientists?

First scientific study of the NDE by Dr Michael Sabom

Dr Sabom is cited as an eminent cardiologist, who admits he found it impossible to give any credence to the notion of life after death, and who though a churchgoer, saw the church's myths about death and beyond merely as *'guiding proper behaviour'* and *'relieving anxieties about death and dying'* (Sabom 1982, p.15)[1].

In 1976, while Dr Sabom was in his first year of cardiology at the University of Florida, the congregation of the Methodist church he and his wife attended was suddenly stirred by the accounts of life after death in Moody's newly published book, *Life after Life*. As a result of Sabom's training in the scientific ethos, he *'couldn't relate seriously to these "far-out" descriptions of afterlife spirits and such'* (1982, p.15). The presenter, Sarah Kreutziger, asked for Sabom's help with a second presentation to 'a churchwide audience'. He was to deal with any medical questions from the audience. Both he and Kreutziger (a psychiatric social worker) were working with critically ill patients at the time.

Prior to the church address, Sabom decided to question some of his own patients about any experience they'd had while hovering between life and death, expecting to report to the congregation that he'd tried and failed to find any evidence corroborating Moody's assertions. Kreutziger did the same. Sabom was shocked to discover a patient who spoke about his out-of-the-body experience in a similar way to Moody's subjects. This challenged him to apply scientific methodology, to find the flaws in Moody's work, which originally he couldn't accept as *'non-fiction'*-that is, factual. Together he and

---

1. Excerpts from Michael Sabom and Sarah Kreutziger, 1982, Recollections of Death, published by Harper & Row, are used by permission of Dr Sabom.

Kreutziger designed a study, building in the more rigorous methodology that was missing from Moody's *casual, unsystematic* approach. This study sought to answer vital questions including the following:

How common is the near-death experience? A prospective study design was used. Study subjects were not chosen, like Moody's subjects, because they admitted to having had a subjective Near-death Experience, but because they were known to have survived a medical near death crisis. That is, they had died on the operating table or elsewhere, and been resuscitated.

What were the educational, occupational, social and religious backgrounds of those reporting a Near-death Experience? Did the occurrence or content of the NDE vary with these factors? Perhaps the only people who had NDE were the uneducated or those deeply indoctrinated by their religion. Were plausible accounts of resuscitation techniques only given by the educated and medically informed?

Did medical matters such as the type of near-death crisis event, the duration of unconsciousness or the method of resuscitation influence the occurrence of the near-death event? Perhaps the NDE only occurred in patients who had received electro-cardiac shock treatment to resuscitate them, and was a side effect of that treatment.

Did survivors' fear of death decrease because of the content of their experience, or merely the fact of their survival?

No simple explanation of NDE found by Sabom

Sabom and Kreutziger failed to find any 'ordinary' explanation of NDE. This was despite their systematic collection of data in a scientific study of the Near-death Experience. Instead they became occupied in documenting more precisely, and categorizing, the *content* of the NDE, which came across as powerfully real, an experience resistant to all attempts to reduce it to physical or psychological phenomena. Sabom provides a summary, in answer to the questions posed in the study design, along with a full set of tabulated data and statistics, with explanations:

> *The data presented... indicate that the NDE is a common experience encountered by persons during a near-death crisis event [ie the medical crisis which takes the patient to the brink of death or beyond]. In this study, it was found to occur in approximately 40 percent of prospectively interviewed near-death survivors. A person's age, sex, race, area of residence, size of home community, years of education, occupation, religious background or frequency of church attendance did not seem to affect whether he or she would or would not encounter an NDE during a near-death crisis event'* (Sabom 1982, p. 89).

Even the original cause of the near-death crisis (accident, cancer, heart disease or other) was found to be without bearing on the likelihood of NDE. Sabom did however find that *Reports of NDEs were more common... following in-hospital near-death crisis events associated with unconsciousness for longer than one minute and involving some type of resuscitative measure'* (Sabom 1982, pp. 89-90).

No significant difference was discovered between groups regarding the content of the NDE. Age, sex, religious background, and education made no difference except that women and blue-collar workers more often reported *'element 9, encountering others'* (p. 90), than men and professionals. Those who'd undergone an NDE reported a decrease in death anxiety and an increase in afterlife belief which was found to be due to the content of the NDE, as survivors who did not experience an NDE reported no such decrease in anxiety merely as a result of surviving a death crisis.

Sabom set out to *disprove the reality of the NDE*: he expected to reduce it to a side effect of physical or medical conditions of the near-death crisis event. If these weren't conclusive, then most probably NDE was the result of a demographic factor such as education level or religious conviction. He ended the study unable to account for his subjects' experiences by any of the tested medical and scientific explanations, and *personally convinced of the reality of the NDE*. Dr Kenneth Ring and Dr Bruce Greyson, also pioneers of NDE research, conducted other studies and designed somewhat different NDE scales. However, their findings are in general agreement.

Scientists and the 'delusional' NDE; Ken Wilber and the Four Quadrants of knowledge

The optimistic assumption built into the scientific method is that everything that exists is potentially discoverable by scientific theorizing and testing in the 'real world'. Therefore, (according to the scientific view) anything we can't even theoretically observe or test, has no substantial reality and therefore doesn't exist except as, at best, an idea. While blows have been dealt to this view, for example by

Heisenberg's Uncertainty Principle[2] and its implications, science continues with it as an operating assumption. The typical response of the medical and scientific community to the NDE is that it must be fantasy because it cannot be reduced to the purely physical; it does not fit within the 'material universe'[3] paradigm I mentioned in Chapter One. A strong challenge to this paradigm comes from Ken Wilber's systematisation of knowledge. He puts this simply in A Brief History of Everything:

> [W]e have four different quadrants, each with a different type of truth, a different voice. And each has a different test for its truth-a different validity claim... They are all falsifiable in their own domains, which means that false claims can be dislodged by further evidence from that domain. (So let us gently ignore the claims of any one quadrant that it alone has the only falsifiable test there is, so it alone has the truth worth knowing!) And, over the centuries and millennia, humanity has, by very painful trial and error, learned the basic procedures for these tests for truth (Wilber 2007, pp.177-8).

These four quadrants are laid out in Diagram 1 in the Appendix. Wilber calls them the four faces of truth; the Subjective, the Objective, the Intersubjective and the Interobjective (Wilber 1997, pp 12-13). *Quadrant denial* occurs when we deny the validity of a statement based purely on its quadrant, as when the Swiss researchers decided that mothers could not have had visions of their babies' cot deaths. They believed that such visions are unscientific, and to accept them would mean the impossible; that there's something beyond the material universe. We also commit *quadrant denial* when we decide post-death visions like Julian Burton's of his mother, must be imaginary. *Such visions*, we reason, *cannot give rise to valid data about*

---

2. Quantum behaviour confounds scientific principles. Elementary quanta seem to have no definite location, and show up in a wave form or a particle form when we look for them in that mode. Are they inseparable from the rest of the universe, or aren't our instruments sophisticated enough? Or in the micro world, is there really no division between observer and observed?

3. Kitty Ferguson in *The Fire in the Equations: Science, Religion and the Search for God*, gives us the state of the debate between science and religion over the origin of the universe. Science has not ruled God out, she says (Stephen Hawking made a similar observation). It is possible to have a brilliant scientific mind and still believe in God. Leading theoretical physicist Reverend Dr John Polkinghorne is a good example. He wrote in The Cambridge Review: *'Those who essay a quantum cosmology are necessarily skating on intellectual thin ice, however pretty the arabesques they perform. Needless to say, Stephen Hawking is well aware of this problem. He believes that sufficient of the lineaments of an eventual theory of quantum gravity can be discerned to make at least general sense of the cosmological programme. Doubtless Steve's speculations deserve to be taken more seriously than those of many other practitioners, but they remain speculations nevertheless.'* 'The Mind of God'?, *Symposium: Hawking's 'History of Time' Reconsidered. The Cambridge Review*, March 1992: 1. (Quoted in Ferguson, Kitty 1994, p. 134).

reality; otherwise the dead aren't really dead. These are cases of those viewing from the Objective, science and technology quadrant, denying the validity of data from the Subjective quadrant of consciousness; the interior realm whose data may be validly gained through meditation or introspection. It's not the case that false claims will be 'passed' just because they come from an untouchable quadrant. If they are false, they will be invalidated by further evidence from that same quadrant. Subjective claims are not valid simply because they are subjective. They must be submitted to the validity testing applicable to that quadrant.

Evidence is produced by what Wilber calls the *'community of the adequate'* performing the experiments and scrutinising and comparing the results, just as the scientific community-that is, of the adequate in science, does. I am using validity claims from different quadrants as appropriate throughout the book, but this chapter concentrates on the objective, scientific evidence. *I make a criticism of our treatment of that evidence; our apparent inability to accept the evidence presented by science itself where it conflicts with our beliefs, at the end of the chapter.*

Blackmore explains NDE as dying brain sparks or fantasy

Dr Susan Blackmore is a respected academic who has risen to prominence as a result of her explanation of the NDE. Blackmore's book *Dying to Live; Science and the Near-Death Experience* (1993), is both typical of science's response, and exemplary of the arguments put forward against the validity of the NDE.

So what has Blackmore to say about the scientific validity of the Near-death experience? Most elements of the NDE can be accounted for, without accepting them at face value, and concluding that they indicate a life beyond the physical body, according to this academic. They are merely *dying brain phenomena*, with no reality other than a purely subjective one, she argues.

The appearance of objective reality of some NDE, in the way that patients seem able to report events and conversations taking place around them while clinically dead, is misleading, she says. These reports have never been verified, and are likely to prove just as subjective as the other aspects of the NDE.

> *It is my contention that there is no soul, spirit, astral body or anything at all that leaves the body during Near-Death Experiences and survives after death. These like the very idea of a persisting self, are all illusions, and the NDE can be accounted for without recourse to any of them. If so, then we*

should not expect people to have access to any information other than that already available to them through perfectly normal means.... The first thing to remember is that if the brain is still functioning, even if very poorly, it will be capable of sustaining imagery... (W)here does the information come from to construct these images?

The answers include prior knowledge, fantasy and lucky guesses, and the remaining operating senses of hearing and touch. Add to this the way memory works to recall accurate items and forget the wrong ones, and we have the basis for an alternative account of why people 'see' what is going on.... So imagine two people talking about their recollections of a hospital resuscitation. The patient says "I could see you there down the hall, you were wearing that green coat and skirt and your favourite pearl necklace..." What if she were wearing the coat, but not the skirt and necklace? She would be caring more for accuracy and less for the sick patient if she bothered to go into detail on all of this.' (Blackmore 1993, pp 114-116).

Dr Serdehaly's report of dead Jimmy observing his rescue

A typical NDE survivor's Out-of-body account is more detailed, more easily verifiable and just plain accurate, than this 'what if' scenario put forward by Blackmore. Melvin Morse, who studied NDE in children, gives one such example:

Dr William Serdehaly at Montana State University told us the remarkable story of an eight-year-old boy named Jimmy, [who] was fishing from a bridge when he slipped from his perch on the railing and hit his head on a rock in the water below. The doctor's report says that Jimmy had stopped breathing and was without a pulse when a police officer pulled him from the deep water in which he had floated facedown for at least five minutes. The policeman performed CPR for thirty minutes until the hospital helicopter arrived, but he reported that the boy was dead on the scene when they started the rush to the hospital. Two days later, he [Jimmy] told Dr Serdehaly: "I know what happened when I fell off that bridge". "He proceeded to describe his entire rescue in vivid detail, including the name of the police officer who tried to resuscitate him, the length of time it took for the helicopter to arrive on the scene, and many of the life-saving procedures used on him in the helicopter and at the hospital. He knew all this, he said, because he had been observing from outside his body the entire time.' (Morse 1991, pp. 120-121)[4] .

Dr Blackmore's argument is that the hallucinations of the dying brain plus memory, fantasy, lucky guesses and prior information fully account for the Near-death experience. Sabom had already

---

4. Excerpt from Melvin Morse & Paul Perry 1991, Closer to the Light, acknowledged by the publisher, Random House, to fall under fair use .

discounted prior knowledge, by comparing the knowledge of medically educated patients with medically unsophisticated patients who'd had an NDE. Twenty-three of the twenty-five knowledgeable control group patients made major mistakes in describing the resuscitation procedure. Significantly, all the NDE patients described their own resuscitations accurately, without mistakes. Apparently this failed to satisfy Dr Blackmore. In her argument, she goes on to examine a number of typical NDE, to check whether any have been independently corroborated. A tape made of a lecture by Elisabeth Kubler-Ross, the pioneer whose work in supporting and caring for the dying, and in understanding bereavement set the benchmark, is quoted:

> 'We asked them to share what it was like when they had this near-death experience. If it was just a dream fulfilment, those people would not be able to share with us the colour of the sweater we wear, the design of a tie, or minute details of shape, colour and designs of the people's clothing... (T)hey were not only able to tell us who came into the room first, who worked on the resuscitation, but were able to give minute details of the attire and the clothing of all the people present' (Blackmore 1993, p. 33).

Blackmore doubts Kubler-Ross; NDE memory just endorphins in the temporal lobe

Dr Blackmore challenges Kubler-Ross' conclusions. Though Dr Kubler-Ross concludes that even those who are blind can, once released from their bodies, see perfectly well, Blackmore pointed out that there was no evidence other than anecdotal, for this claim. She does note, however, that the evidence of NDE in blind individuals where there was a visual Out-of body experience might challenge all this. If blind patients could see, not just in the post-tunnel stages of the NDE when it could still be argued that they were only dreaming or fantasizing, but also in an Out-of-body experience, then the sceptics' explanations would no longer hold water. If these blind NDErs could give accurate visual descriptions of the scene around them after their clinical death, then neither they nor sighted NDE survivors could be said to be dreaming or fantasizing.

For years no such evidence was available, though Blackmore certainly looked everywhere for it. Her conclusion was that the images that occur during the dying process are made to seem both coherent and familiar by aspects of the dying brain process. Stimulation of the temporal lobe via endorphins released in the process produces a sense of familiarity. The Life Review, says Blackmore, is produced in the same way. Regardless of the seeming truth of this 'review' of life memories, we are unable to go back and check on the accuracy of these memories. *'We can only accept the person's word that these felt like memories and were convincingly realistic and vivid,'* she says. *'The ... abnormal activity in the temporal lobe causes the flashbacks and associated feelings of familiarity and meaningfulness.'* (Blackmore 1993, pp 213-4).

The difficulty remains for this position: NDE is occurring after clinical death and before resuscitation, when there is no brain activity of any kind to produce flashbacks like this, as the studies quoted later in this chapter demonstrate.

Kenneth Ring and Cooper's Mindsight: NDE in the blind

Six years after Blackmore published Dying to Live, Dr Kenneth Ring and Sharon Cooper produced the evidence that blind individuals do seem able to see the physical scene around them after their clinical death and before resuscitation. The authors investigated the NDE and OOB experiences of 31 blind and sight-impaired people. The majority of them reported being able to see once out of their bodies. This by itself wouldn't satisfy Dr Blackmore or any other serious critic. The blind subjects had to have reported accurately on visual details of a real physical scene in order to invalidate the sceptics' claim that they were merely dreaming. The cases are carefully analysed to try to discover whether what they reported seeing was objectively real. Where independent witnesses are available to corroborate or deny the claims, their evidence is included. (I have quoted one of Ring and Cooper's cases in Chapter Thirteen; that of Vicki Umipeg, blind from birth, but able to report visual details of the scene around her after her clinical death in a car accident.)

The authors conclude that there is vision taking place without involvement of the visual organs, the eyes, in these cases. *Mind sight: Near Death and Out of Body Experiences in the Blind,* by Dr Kenneth Ring and Susan Cooper (1999), was published as part of its transpersonal study program, by the William James Centre for Consciousness Studies.

First hospital studies of the causes of NDE –just dying brain?

There is much to be said in rebuttal of the standard argument of scientific sceptics that the Near-death experience is nothing more than phenomena produced by the dying brain. Blackmore's main argument revolves around the question as to whether the patient's brain is able to use residual electrical activity taking place during the apparent death phase, to reconstruct some sort of account of what happened during the time the patient was unconscious. Two unrelated research groups set up prospective studies of the NDE, with the *specific intention of discovering if it was just a production of the dying brain or body*. These were a thirteen year study by a Dutch team in ten hospitals, led by Dr Pim van Lommel, with Drs van Wees, Meyers and Elfferich, and a smaller study by cardiologist Dr Sam Parnia and London neuropsychiatrist Dr Peter Fenwick, in the U.K.

The Fenwick-Parnia team chose to work in the Coronary care unit of their hospital, since coronary arrests would be a common occurrence, and it was likely that a percentage of patients would be resuscitated. Some might report having one of these still-mythical Near-death Experiences, which was what the team intended to study.

Parnia and Fenwick's U.K. study discussed in interview

A critical reason for choosing a cardiac or coronary unit, was in order to test out and either definitely prove or conclusively disprove, the argument that the Near-death Experience is a function of phenomena produced by the dying brain. Dr Peter Fenwick spoke of this rationale to Tony Jones of the Australian Broadcasting Corporation, on the TV Channel 2 Lateline programme (Jones 2000).

Fenwick explained:

> *Well, that's why we did it in a coronary care unit, because remember what happens when you have a heart attack. You lose consciousness immediately. Then there's a period when you recover consciousness slowly. Also when you are fully unconscious, you show the signs of clinical death, which is no respiration, no cardiac output, fully dilated pupils showing that your brain stem is not functioning and that is the clinical criteria of death.*

The type of unconsciousness Dr Fenwick is indicating here, is obviously different from the unconsciousness of someone who has fainted or someone in a coma. This is the absence of consciousness of the body without vital signs, and not the temporary dimming or loss of consciousness of someone still breathing, as in a faint or a coma. There is no discernable difference between the (lack of) vital signs of those who do return and those who don't, in the phase shortly after cardiac arrest, while the resuscitation team works to bring them back to life. No relevant physiological difference separates them. It is not the case that those who return to life were displaying different vital signs to those who do not, and that the ones who are revived had never really died after all- which is an argument implied or stated by those scientists who attempt to disprove the possibility of a valid Near-death Experience.

Is the brain still functioning? Tracking brain activity during NDE

Dr Fenwick explained to Tony Jones that his team is intending to use electrodes attached to the scalp to connect the patient to an EEG machine (Electroencephalogram) *'to measure the electrical activity of the brain'* of patients during the critical interval between cessation of heartbeat and restarting of heart function, where that is successful. Dr Fenwick mentions that it is already known *'that during a cardiac arrest there is no electrical activity'*. He obviously expected, from his knowledge of brain electrical activity, that it will be possible to produce hard data to show that the brain of any given patient resuscitated after a fatal heart attack (regardless of the experience or lack of it, of NDE), displayed no electrical activity during the critical interval, and was therefore incapable of recording anything of the events and conversations taking place during that interval. He stressed earlier in the interview, that more studies were necessary:

> *'We need ... a number of other studies on the table that have found out the same sort of thing that we have. Let's not make any assumptions until the data is there and clear.*

> *And we need to do what was one of the key experiments and that is to look at people who say they leave their body and have targets in the room that only can be seen from the ceiling, which is where people usually report their viewpoint...*

> *If they can see the targets and nobody (else) in the room knows what they are, but yet (the arrested patient) can bring back that information, then one has to seriously consider that brain and mind may be different things'*, Fenwick concluded.

Tony Jones had earlier asked *'How can you apply any kind of scientific criterion to those sort of experiences?'* - the common experiences of Dr Fenwick's subjects, of *'peace and calm, going down the tunnel, meeting a being of light, going into a garden,* [undergoing] *a life review...'* Peter Fenwick's answer was that it was necessary to show that these experiences do happen, and then to apply scientific techniques to discover why they occur.

'So, our question was-- if people have these experiences, when do they have them? Now, they couldn't have them as they are going down, because we know from the way you lose consciousness, that the memory circuits all go immediately...so could it be as you come back? ... If you come round from an anoxic episode like that, then it's confusional, so you get no clarity in your experiences. So, we were left then with the only other alternative and that is that they actually occurred during the episode itself and that is a difficult one because neuroscience would say it wasn't possible.'

Jones clarified this: *'Because you're saying effectively that people are having an experience while their brain is dead, while they're effectively dead?'* Fenwick replied *'Absolutely, absolutely...'* before Jones asked *'Does your scientific study ... conclude that there is a fundamental separation between the organic thing which is the brain- the machine of the brain, and the individual consciousness that inhabits it?'*

Fenwick's answer was that it is too early yet to say, however there is now plenty of evidence that people in NDE *'get information that they couldn't have got just lying unconscious on the floor...(It's) very detailed and suggests that the mind may have separated from the brain... So, two possibilities. One is that mind and brain are not the same thing and the other is that it's a sort of quirk of looking back ...on the period of unconsciousness, (when) you see these things in the brain.'*

Jones asked in summation: *'If it were the former, if the mind and the brain are different things, would you conclude that such a thing as the human soul might be proven to exist?'* Fenwick's reply was a careful but excited *'We'd be getting close to that'*.

The Parnia-Fenwick study: NDE is not caused by drugs, hypoxia or other brain affectors

Just weeks after this interview, the Parnia team published their first results, in a paper titled *A qualitative and quantitative study of the incidence, features and aetiology of near death experiences in cardiac arrest survivors*, in the medical journal *Resuscitation* (Parnia et al 2001, pp 149-156)[5]. It was a one-year prospective study of cardiac arrest survivors, who were all interviewed within a week of that event. There were 63 arrest survivors, and of those, four reported an NDE. The study incorporated the elements (such as use of EEG to check for brain activity, and placing objects where only a patient viewing the scene from around ceiling height could see them) that Dr Fenwick had discussed in the ABC interview. This last-mentioned element of

---

5. Excerpts from this study by Parnia and Fenwick in *Resuscitation*, and other excerpts from the work of Dr Sam Parnia and team, are used by permission of Dr Parnia.

the study was frustratingly inconclusive, since none of the patients who'd experienced an NDE had also had an Out Of Body experience, which would have enabled them to observe the objects if it was a genuine experience.

The results of the study were as Fenwick had foreshadowed with Tony Jones. No evidence was found that drugs, hypoxia, hypercarbia or electrolyte disturbances played any role in the causation of NDE. Therefore, there was *no evidence to support the view of NDE as a hallucinatory response to an alteration in cerebral mediators*--substances like endorphins that are 'go-betweens' in cerebral or brain responses. Nor was there any evidence that it was wish fulfilment fantasy in response to facing death.

The 'Lancet study' – Van Lommel's ten-hospital Dutch study

Shortly after, the scientific establishment was agog with the news of a Dutch study carried out by Drs Pim Van Lommel, Ruud van Wees, Vincent Meyers and Ingrid Elfferich, reported in one of the world's most esteemed medical research forums, the British journal *The Lancet*[6]. This study, much larger and longer (up to four years in some of the hospitals), was concluding at the same time as the U.K. study. What exactly did the Van Lommel team set out to discover? What did their hospital study attempt to prove or disprove? What were their findings?

Careful screening of all the supposed causes of NDE

The Dutch team set out to discover *'the origin of the Near-death Experience' (Van Lommel et al, 2001)*. The prospective study was set up in ten Dutch hospitals. Any patient who underwent cardiac arrest during the time of the study became a subject. This gave the NDE team the opportunity to set up a study design to check for the occurrence of the factors that were said by an understandably sceptical scientific establishment to be the cause of the NDE – anoxia, intense fear, or hallucinations following drugs administered prior to NDE. The team could also screen for a range of other possible factors such as prior knowledge of cardiac arrest procedures (which Blackmore asserted was a basis of the apparently accurate reports of arrested

---

6. Excerpts from *The Lancet* study and other studies of his team are used by permission of Dr Pim Van Lommel.

patients about events around them while they were clinically dead), and demographic factors such as age, sex, and education.

Drugs, anoxia, fear, prior knowledge, religious beliefs ruled out as causes of NDE

If it were the case that anoxia was the real cause of NDE, then it would be confined to patients who had suffered anoxia. If NDE were a hallucinatory state caused by drugs, only those patients to whom drugs had been administered, would report an NDE. If the fear of death caused patients to imagine an alternative ending, the study would clearly show that. Only patients who had experienced fear prior to their cardiac arrest, would be able to report an NDE. The study attempted to design for every possible explicable cause of NDE, and rule it definitely in or out of contention.

So, what were the results? The study showed, just as the Parnia study had done, that anoxia was not the cause; drugs were not the cause, neither was fear the cause of NDE. Other possible factors such as prior knowledge of just what an NDE was, religion (or lack of any), sex and education level were also ruled out: there was no statistical relationship, let alone a clear causal connection. This was now established fact- established by Sabom, the Parnia-Fenwick team, and the Van Lommel Dutch team. There were other interesting results though: women and younger people were more likely to have (core) NDE; a deep or core experience of NDE was a predictor of imminent death at a probability of 0.0001, that this could occur by chance alone. That is, there was a possibility of 1 in 10,000 that this could occur by chance.

'You must have missed something': – the scientists' response

The scientific and medical world was still expecting to discover some ordinary cause for the NDE. In reply to the general stir caused by the Lancet study, Christopher C. French (2000), wrote a Commentary on the state of play regarding NDE in *The Lancet*; titled 'Dying to know the truth; visions of a dying brain, or false memories?' In it the author considered the likelihood of the NDE occurring, not when patients are clinically dead, but rather as they *'rapidly entered or gradually recovered'* from the clinical death episode.

French wrote that the authors of the Dutch and UK studies consider this unlikely. This was due to the reports from medical staff, of patients who were able to recall, accurately, *'events that took place during the actual cardiac arrest'*. French notes the failure of the Dutch team to corroborate with the patient an apparently impressive anecdote from a nurse. (This nurse had taken the dentures of a cardiac-arrest patient out during resuscitation procedures. She had placed them in the drawer of the 'crash car'. A week later when the nurse entered the ward where the cardiac-arrest patient was recovering, he identified her, saying *'Oh, that nurse knows where my dentures are'*, giving accurate details about the event.)

French comments *'On many previous occasions such attempts at corroboration have revealed that the evidence was not as impressive as it initially seemed'*. However, his sole justification for drawing this conclusion turns out to be Susan Blackmore's critique in *Dying to Live; Science and the Near-Death Experience (1993),* which was by then eight years old. The quote to which French refers, in order to corroborate his comment, is Dr Blackmore's writing that NDE had to be due to *'information available at the time, prior knowledge, fantasy or dreams, lucky guesses, and information from the remaining senses. Then there is selective memory for correct details, incorporation of details learned between the NDE and giving an account of it, and the tendency to tell a good story'* (Blackmore 1993, p. 115).

But all of this is, as French suggests in the article, only speculation by Blackmore as to *'why people may sometimes seem'* to describe accurately the events occurring during an NDE. Blackmore wasn't drawing conclusions from hard evidence: There weren't *'many previous occasions'* where the evidence didn't stand up to scrutiny; there were *no occasions at all,* but simply Blackmore surmising that this is what *might be discovered* when accounts of NDE were investigated. It is curious, and unsettling, that Blackmore's list- 'prior knowledge, fantasy or dreams, lucky guesses', and so on, seems to be shifting into the realm of accepted science, instead of being identified as informed guesswork, about the Near-death Experience.

Can the sceptics take any comfort?

While the story of the dentures should have been corroborated, there is no evidence in these more recent studies to give any traction to Blackmore's 1993 explanation. Nearly all heads of her attack have been shown to be invalid – the NDE is not triggered by drugs, hypoxia (oxygen starvation) or hypercarbia (oversupply of carbon); it isn't related to intense religious conviction, nor to fear of impending death. There remain the psychological charges – that patients are dreaming or fantasizing or telling a good story. Surprisingly perhaps, in all the accounts and studies we have now--three decades of data, there is *no evidence* for this assumption. This deserves to be stressed. It is not the case that there is contradictory evidence, or that there is some evidence which is counterbalanced by the weight of opposite evidence. ***There is absolutely no evidence that patients are dreaming or fantasising or telling a good story.***

Yet the sceptics' view had not been completely discredited. Though every other possibility had been struck off; every other Blackmore-style explanation invalidated, there was still the possibility that subjects were experiencing the NDE, as Christopher French went on to surmise in the *Lancet* article, when they were on the way in to, or out of cardiac arrest, when the brain *was* functioning.

Christopher French's conclusion was an excellent summation of the state of play regarding NDE at that time: '*However, if reports of veridical (true) perception during OBEs were to be forthcoming in future studies, they would represent a very strong challenge to any non-paranormal explanation of the NDE*' (French 2001, pp 2010-11). Reports of veridical perception despite a dead body and brain, if and when verified by medical staff and the medical record, would be more than a strong challenge to NDE as a Material Universe event like any other. These reports would mean the deconstruction, not just of death as the end for individuals, but of the assumptions at the base of the entire scientific and technological enterprise upon which our civilisation is built. We would have to replace it with a more sophisticated version of our contemporary religious beliefs -- something like the perennial philosophy.

Does NDE take place before or after the period of clinical death, instead of during it?

Since there was still scepticism among fellow scientists and medicos, immediately after, in January 2002, Drs Parnia and Fenwick went on to publish a paper reviewing the findings of these recent studies and discussing the implications, in 'Near death experiences in cardiac arrest: visions of a dying brain or visions of a new science of consciousness', in the medical journal *Resuscitation*. Fenwick and Parnia needed to examine the way in which the findings of the recent studies fitted together with the knowledge of brain physiology and function, to clarify the implications for NDE's causes. *When did the NDE take place?* Were patients experiencing the tunnel and the light and the great Being, just before or just after, instead of during, clinical death with its *cessation of vital functions including brain function?*

Is blood supply sufficient for NDE as just a brain event? Parnia and Fenwick say No.

In the paper, the authors particularly consider the extent to which continued consciousness depends upon a sufficient supply of blood to the brain, and its flushing through the brain to retain oxygenation of brain cells, allowing these cells to function. If there is sufficient blood perfusion for good functioning, in the brain just before and just after cessation, then NDE may be just a dying brain event. This cessation occurs about 10 seconds after cardiac arrest. Brain function does not begin again for some time after resuscitation; it can take one or two hours (Parnia 2008).

The paper sets out to discuss the issue of cerebral blood perfusion, given that the authors of both hospital studies of the nature and origins of NDE, Dutch and English, have a serious question. Is it remotely possible that *'lucid, well structured thought processes, together with long term memory formation [as opposed to the short-term modality] that is characteristic of NDEs can arise during a cardiac arrest when cerebral function is impaired and would not be expected to support'* this kind of wide awake, clear cognition and thinking?' (Parnia & Fenwick 2002, p. 5-11). The researchers needed to find out if the residual supply of blood still left in the brain after heart death, was sufficient to support thinking processes.

This is of course, at bottom Christopher French's question also. Parnia and Fenwick proceed to review the present knowledge, discussing 1) how cerebral perfusion is measured; 2) the nature of the relationship, if any, between cerebral perfusion and the maintenance of consciousness and of ordered thought-processes; 3) how cerebral perfusion drops markedly during cardiac arrest; 4) how it remains considerably lowered during intervention measures (CPR and epinephrine) and 5) whether these much lower measures of cerebral perfusion can still support consciousness and rational thought.

They conclude that all the evidence points to a single fact: Cerebral perfusion measures in cardiac arrest are too low to permit any *'lucid, well-structured thought processes with reasoning and memory formation'* (*Parnia and Fenwick 2002, p. 5*). The authors go on to discuss the *'implications for the study of consciousness and its relationship with the brain'* and finally *'the contribution that near death experiences during cardiac arrest may make to the wider understanding of human consciousness'* (Parnia and Fenwick 2002, p. 11).

Now that seven out of eight possible causes for the NDE have been explored and exploded, can Susan Blackmore and like minds take any comfort that there are still unexplored avenues for non-paranormal causation of NDEs?

The last 'ordinary' explanation: Is there any evidence for NDE as fantasy or 'traveller's tales'?

Delusional states have been ruled out. Hypoxia and hypercarbia cannot be causing delusional dying-brain NDE given that studies are clear on the following:

1. There is *no* brain function after clinical death and before resuscitation;
2. There is not enough blood supply to the brain to support consciousness just before or after clinical death; and
3. The reported experiences are *'lucid, well-formed thought processes characterised by memory and reasoning'* (Parnia and Fenwick 2002). This means that regardless of when NDE is taking place, *it is not a brain event*. Perhaps it is still possible to cling to the view that somehow, after their resuscitation, patients are fantasizing or deliberately telling good stories (the eighth possible cause of NDE)?

The final refutation of NDE as fantasy waits upon sufficient numbers of patients 1) being resuscitated, 2) reporting an NDE, and 3) reporting an OOB aspect, that is, out of the body and able to observe the scene from a vantage point usually around ceiling height, and 4) most importantly, having their accounts properly checked and verified, as the report of the dentures in the crash car was not. It would then be possible to ensure exactly when the NDE occurred. If it really were after clinical death, the patient would report what happened at the scene in the interval between arrest and resuscitation, rather than just before arrest, or just after resuscitation. This would eliminate the final retreat for sceptics, which is that patients who were clinically dead and who reported NDE, were only dreaming, fantasizing, or telling a good story.

These accounts of Out-of-Body, such as Jimmy's and the dentures case I've quoted, join a long list. Even Dr Blackmore cannot quote a single case where the NDE or OOB account was found to be false- as distinct from her assumption that it would be if challenged. No one reporting an NDE has ever been 'found out' to be fitting together prior medical knowledge, or fantasizing, or inventing a good story. On the contrary, reports continue to appear from doctors, surgeons, and medical and hospital staff who have been surprised at the accuracy of Out-of-Body perceptions during medical death. Have these reports been properly checked by the community of the adequate?

Some of the more recent evidence comes from the Parnia-Fenwick team. In his address to the U.N. symposium on September 11, 2008, Sam Parnia noted that the problem with concluding that the NDE took place just before or just after, the cardiac arrest, *'is that we have cases where people have ... told us in detail what happened to them twenty or thirty minutes into a cardiac arrest, when all our studies tell us there is no brain activity.* This *'sub-group'* of arrest patients who experienced NDE, *'will also tell us exactly what we were doing and what we were saying.... They come back saying "I was up at the ceiling" and reporting accurately on the scene below them.'* (Parnia 2008). So, these reports were known to pertain to that period, twenty or even thirty minutes after the clinical death, because the details of the OOB accounts given by these patients had been corroborated by hospital staff as having actually occurred at that time. That is, these accounts were found to be true!

This knowledge may be sufficient to open the minds of most of us to at least consider the possibility of life after death. More than that may be required by the scientific materialists and sceptics of the medical establishment, whose science and worldview is predicated upon physical reality as the only kind, and mind as a function of brain. *They* may need to have every last nook and cranny of hiding places for a materialistic explanation, explored and eliminated before conceding the defeat of what Dr Fenwick refers to as a Galilean science and worldview.

The idea that NDErs could be fantasising or telling a good yarn, is very much the sceptics' last refuge. A definitive study of *'what happens to mind and consciousness at the point of death'* (Parnia 2008), which will also test this, was announced to the world at the U.N. symposium to launch it, on September 11, 2008 – the AWARE (AWAreness in REsuscitation) study. This study is to be headed by Dr Sam Parnia, who has become a leading expert in the area of brain and consciousness in clinical death. This study is necessary because we, as a civilisation, cannot accept the evidence before us regarding the survival of consciousness. I say that because this evidence, of veridical post-death perception, is no longer confined to a few isolated and questionable cases where no one checked the details. It is becoming more and more widespread, with greater curiosity about NDE. Patients and hospital staff kept quiet in the past, for fear of being thought insane. Now, we have a series of reputable medical scientists including Bruce Greyson and Sam Parnia, telling us that they know of evidence of veridical perception after the death of heart and brain. Their evidence is even stronger than that collected via retrospective interviews by Sabom and Ring and others- like those quoted above. Will we, though, accept this evidence? We –doctors, scientists and public alike, accept the more mundane conclusions of tests and studies such as Sabom's, Greyson's or Pim Van Lommel's, once we have assessed the adequacy of the research.

When Sabom says '*A person's age, sex, race, area of residence, size of home community, years of education, occupation, religious background or frequency of church attendance did not seem to affect whether he or she would or would not encounter an NDE during a near-death crisis event*', this is accepted as established fact for the U.S. at least. When Parnia and Fenwick say that blood supply in the brain after cardiac arrest is not sufficient to sustain consciousness, we accept this too, as the established outcome of their study. We accept the finding as valid when Pim Van Lommel's team concludes that '*fear was not associated with NDE*' (Van Lommel 2001, p. 9), or that most of the NDE group, as a result of their NDE and regardless of their earlier positions '*did not show any fear of death and strongly believed in an afterlife*' (Van Lommel 2001, p. 9).

However as a culture we seem unable to take the logical next step: We cannot contemplate consciousness as functioning separately from the brain and body. So what is planned in this U.N. auspiced study? It is a longer, wider and more sophisticated version of the OOB study, which failed in the original Parnia-Fenwick study because no one reported an Out-of-body Experience. It will be run in 53 U.S. and European hospitals, and is expected to take about 36 months. Computer screens with randomly changing images will be placed on shelves above hospital beds, where they can only be seen from the ceiling-the reported vantage point in NDE with OOB. There will be a record of what images appeared at what time, to check the accuracy of reports, if patients do actually come back from a near death event, and say they saw these images. '*If no-one* (who has an OOB element to their NDE) *tells us they saw these images, then we know NDE is delusional*' Parnia concluded (2008).

Shermer in Scientific American--NDE only a brain product

Shermer's article *Demon-haunted brain,* in *Scientific American* (2003, pp. 6-8)[7], may have caused readers to consider the debate as good as won for the sceptics. The demons of past times and the aliens of the present are not in our world, but in our brains, he contends.

Shermer argues: *'If the brain mediates all experience, then paranormal phenomena are nothing more than neuronal events'*. But Shermer doesn't proceed to prove that all experience is mediated by the brain. Instead, he takes it as read: *'In reality, all experience is mediated by the brain',* is his additional premise. Where there seem to be exceptions to this, Shermer returns to this premise: All experience is mediated by the brain, therefore this (and every other) paranormal experience is just a 'neuronal event'. This, then, is his argument: *Given that we can show that paranormal events do not refer to anything external and therefore real -- because the experiencer is the only one who can see, hear or feel them, it follows that they must be constructed entirely within the brain,* as there is nowhere else to look for them. Leaving aside the circularity of this argument, Shermer is only left with the question- *how does the brain construct these paranormal events?*

An Out-of-Body experience can be induced via magnetic or electrical stimulation of the temporal lobes of the brain, as neuroscientists Michael Persinger and Olaf Blanke have shown. However, Shermer has already defined this and every other Out-of-Body experience as nothing more than a construction of the brain, because it doesn't refer to consensual reality-that which we can all perceive.

Is the NDE just due to an overstimulated brain?

In the NDE, Shermer asserts, the trauma of dying replaces magnetic or electrical stimulation (which he sees as producing mere neuronal events mistaken for reality). He evidences the trauma of cardiac arrest and dying in the Dutch study of Pim Van Lommel and his team, cited above, to account for the twelve percent of patients who reported Near-Death and Out-of-Body experiences.

The phenomenon of mindsight — blind NDErs who are able to see once out of their bodies, (Ring & Cooper, 1999), is an example of experience apparently not mediated by the brain. But Shermer has

---

7. Excerpts from this article, Demon-haunted Brain in Scientific American, Feb 10 2003, are used with permission of Dr Michael Shermer.

already defined these events as unreal in his circular argument-unreal because they don't refer to consensual reality. The evidence Shermer provides only shows that some experiences falling into the paranormal category, non-consensus events by definition, and therefore unreal according to Shermer, are *triggered by physical causes.* Even the fact that it is possible to induce Out-of-Body experiences with electronic or magnetic brain stimulation does not prove that the experiences themselves are false and meaningless, and have no reference to anything external to the brain, any more than Aldous Huxley's or Timothy Leary's famous experiences after taking mescalin or LSD, can be reduced to nothing more than the effects of the chemical on the brain. The alteration of brain chemistry is a trigger which permits altered and in this case, enlarged, perception. Huxley's experience of this, related in his book *The Doors of Perception* (2004) is considered in a later chapter.

Dr Penfield's brain probe produces replay of real experiences

The original research in this area is that of Dr Wilder Penfield, (quoted in Harris 1970, p. 10). He showed that stimulation of the temporal cortex via an electric probe caused the subject to experience a scene (unrelated to any present scene) in vivid detail. Shermer would have concluded that this was just the brain in a closed loop, *creating* its experience. Instead, these scenes turned out to be minutely accurate recordings of past events and their associated responses, for example, early childhood incidents.

Transactional Analyst Thomas Harris (1968, p. 11) comments on the Penfield data: *'The brain functions as a high-fidelity tape recorder...'* This would seem to support the materialist position that mind equals brain, in the way that memories seem to be located in the temporal cortex. Yet in his chapter 'Can our memories survive the death of our brains?' Rupert Sheldrake points out that *'Penfield, on further reflection, abandoned his original conclusions'* (that the memory record was actually located in the cortex) (Sheldrake 1990, p.119).[8]

Harris also notes that *'Recollections are evoked by the stimuli of day-to-day experiences in much the same way as they were evoked artificially by Penfield's probe.'* (Harris T. 1968, p.7) This is something with which we're all familiar –an example is the tune that evokes a strong emotion, even when you can't work out its association. It is not possible

---

8. Sheldrake (1990, p. 119) goes on to quote Penfield: *'In 1951 I had proposed that certain parts of the temporal cortex should be called "memory cortex," and suggested that the neuronal record was located there...This was a mistake...The record is not in the cortex'.*

to argue that every stimulus which produces an Out-of-Body experience similar to the brain-probe one, (such as the trauma Shermer cites as the stimulus for the OOB experience of cardiac arrest survivors), therefore produces an unreal experience. I am not arguing that everything that falls into the paranormal category refers to reality. I am saying that at least *a significant number and category* of paranormal experiences cannot be reduced to brain events.

On present evidence, NDE is more than an aberration of the dying brain or psyche

This only provides a very small fig leaf (if even that) over the nakedness of the argument of Shermer and others, that the *'fate of the paranormal and the supernatural is to be subsumed into the normal and the natural'*, as Shermer argued in the Scientific American article. It is all too reminiscent of Ferguson's revelation in *'The Fire in the Equations'* quoted near the beginning of this chapter, that scientists react as irrationally as the rest of us when faced with evidence which conflicts with the prevailing assumptions about the nature of reality.

Regardless of the conclusion of this argument, it becomes irrelevant anyway once we have even a single example of a subject having an experience that is not mediated by their brain. What is the evidence of this? It is the results of the Dutch and British studies, which showed that patients were known to be brain-dead or thought-impaired at the time of their NDE. The brain has been shown not to be functioning during cardiac arrest, and not to be capable of lucid thought before or after brain death in arrest situations. The only argument left is that the experiences must be, not lucid, but confused or imaginary, since the Out-of-Body experiences haven't been definitely proven to refer to external reality – in the scene around the patient during the arrest phase. Yet their lucidity is a primary factor in NDE and OOB. As I have stated, we do have evidence. Research groups, particularly IANDS (International Association of Near-Death Studies) IONS (Institute of Noetic Sciences), and The Scientific and Medical Network have massive data bases of evidence; enough to prove the case ordinarily. But we obviously need more to satisfy the sceptics. The results of the U.N. auspiced AWARE study mentioned above, will be eagerly awaited in many places around the world, and are likely to have a profound effect on our worldview. Hard evidence of conscious survival of death will test the rationality of our best minds, including the likes of Richard Dawkins. So will we reject the evidence, *and choose instead to dangle precariously from the crumbling materialist construct?* It's obvious where my bets are placed: I fully expect that if patients have an OOB, they will be able to accurately report what is on those screens.

Chapter 4
Joy, Light, Reality

Death and NDE in Tibetan Buddhism and in the Perennial Philosophy

Summary Points

- Is death something other than an ending?
- The joy and light after death...just a personal state of mind, or reality?
- **Buddhism and the Ageless Wisdom: Death is an illusion of the earthbound**
- Two Tibetan Buddhists shed light in a dark place
- A tradition of direct knowledge via spiritual practice, on the experience of dying and beyond
- What is the meaning of living and dying, according to Tibetan Buddhism?
- **The Near-death Experience in the Tibetan Book of Living and Dying**
- Does the NDE 'fit' with Tibetan Buddhism and the Ageless Wisdom? Comparison of key elements

- **The Tunnel. The Life Review – a modern Judgement?**
- **The Near-death Experience;** what causes it? Placing it in the sequence of events of dying

Death and NDE in Tibetan Buddhism and in the Perennial Philosophy

Benjamin Franklin, as a printer aged twenty-three, composed his epitaph, comparing his dead body to a gutted book: *'But the work shall not be lost, For it will, as he believed, appear once more, In a new and more elegant edition, Revised and corrected by the Author'*, he wrote.

Is death something other than an ending?

The notion of life after death tends to incur the same dismissive attitude from the society in general, as the Near-death Experience. Most of the evidence for survival after death is either anecdotal, or part of psychological case studies. It would be more reasonable to reject this evidence as lacking reliability, if these accounts were rare, and if they were idiosyncratic - if one survivor's incredible story were not remarkably like another's. Yet if the sheer weight of the evidence - its enormous volume, were sufficient, the case for survival of death would be proven.

As a society, we behave as if we expect death to be the end, despite individual spiritual conviction or religious belief in some of us. So it would be instructive and quite fascinating, to spend some time contemplating the alternative hypothesis – that death is not the end of individual human persons and lives except in a limited sense. It will mean travelling into some interesting places and states of mind, foreign to the Western worldview, and therefore difficult for us to even contemplate.

Religion and science both warn that the nature of the mental and psychic place into which we project ourselves (whether considered the result of actually exiting the dying body, or of suffering 'hallucinations' because of being near the point of death) is due to our state of mind at the critical moment.

The joy and light after death...just a personal state of mind, or reality?

It is amazing that the evidence from NDE actually contradicts this idea-at least, the idea of a momentary state of mind of joy or terror (as distinct from a more habitual one), landing us in a similar place of joy or terror after death. Leon Rhodes points this out in *Tunnel into Eternity* (1998, first published 1987), a lucid and objective commentary upon the NDE phenomenon: *'Under many circumstances the conditions leading to the point of the NDE involve terror, severe suffering, or frantic efforts to escape the disaster'* (*p. 21*). All of these are likely to have been the case with most of those who died in the World Trade Center infernos of September 11, and elsewhere in the world, from London to Bali, and with those who died via tsunami or hurricane, earthquake, volcano or fire such as the 2009 Victorian bushfires.

Rhodes continues:

> *In other situations, such as during major surgery, an NDEr might be under sedation or simply rendered unconscious by a physical injury. Nonetheless, the first awareness of dying is the most striking part of the experience because it is almost invariably described as peaceful, painless, and calm. People try to convey the experience of those first moments using words such as 'unconditional love', 'ineffable joy' or even 'ecstasy'* (Rhodes 1998, p. 21).

This wonderful peace and joy is noted by every researcher into the NDE experience, even Dr Blackmore herself. NDE researcher Dr Peter Fenwick, originally a sceptic, later deeply impressed by his patients' experience of it, says in the ABC interview quoted in Chapter Three: *'You must remember that at this point in the experience you are surrounded by universal love...'*

Death comes in a variety of ways. We may be calmly waiting for death, or dreading it; we may die over weeks or months, or in seconds. We are likely to die of cancer or heart attack, less likely to die by terrorism, or by misadventure, encountering a stingray, (as 'the crocodile hunter' Steve Irwin did), or by smashing a rally car into a tree as Australian racing legend Peter Brock did. Yet whether we die of old age, or in the bombing of World Trade Centre One or Two, extrapolating from the NDE, the experience seems to be similar. *Contrary to what we may expect, joy, peace and love are experienced the other side of the stopping of the heart.* NDE survivors so similarly report the elements of the experience as to build up a good picture, which, as a result, has a certain claim to objectivity.

Peace and a powerful reality

This peace, as has been established in Chapter Three, is *not* the result of universal effects of the phenomena of the dying brain. The similarity of the experience regardless of the way death comes *must therefore* be due to the nature of the reality which awaits us beyond the physical realm. Rhodes points out:

> *No two experiences are the same; however, NDE's seem to follow a familiar pattern...We know that the near-death experience for most is an ineffable*

experience and that it is something that will not be forgotten. It has none of the qualities of a dream, hallucination or fantasy, and it has powerful effects on the lives of those who return (Rhodes 1998, p 47).

This conclusion, too, is borne out by other researchers, for example Dr Michael Sabom, whose NDE study was discussed in Chapter Three. Typically, experiencers like my sister Meredith, whose NDE appears in Chapter One, will say that it was 'something I will never forget, even though I can't remember yesterday'. Or 'It was the most real experience of my life'. Rhodes reports one woman who as a child of seven, *'got caught in the surf and was thrashing around in panic when suddenly she felt total calm, a great feeling of peace. She said "The next thing (the NDE) is the most incredible and vivid memory of my life"'* (p. 69).

Near-death Experiences reportedly have a quality of totality and absoluteness about them that makes even the reality of our conscious lives pale by comparison. The NDE tends to be experienced as more real than anything we see as reality in earthly life.

Buddhism and the Ageless Wisdom: Death is an illusion of the earthbound

The teachings which are most likely to easily accommodate the Near-death Experience phenomenon are these of the East, particularly Northern or Tibetan Buddhism, with its explicit instructions about dying and the after-life. What does it teach about death and dying, and the time after death? Does it have anything to say about the NDE?

Tibetan Buddhism considers that expert guidance through the passage of death, through what Christians know as 'The Valley of the Shadow of Death', is part of making the right connection between the present life, and the one to come. The ideal is an aware and un-afraid death, where we are able to make the right choices because of our knowledge of reality. We are not submerged in the illusions of ignorance, and are in a position to escape the round of birth and death altogether, or to make a good choice of our next incarnation. Death is, therefore, not a final mysterious and unexplained chapter before oblivion or eternity. It is a phase in an orderly sequence, which illumines the existence of what we in the West term *soul* or *psyche,* and the relationship between it and personality. Many of us in the West are deeply grateful for the preservation of Tibetan Buddhism, and for its new accessibility to Westerners who turn to the East for enlightenment about life and death. It is so much more specific about death than Christianity, Judaism or Islam; it gives guidance and preparation for that great event, to its followers. Preparation for a good death is a cornerstone of its teachings:

As the Tibetan Book of the Dead teaches, the dying should face death not only calmly and clear-mindedly but with an intellect rightly trained and rightly directed, mentally transcending, if need be, bodily suffering and infirmities, as they would be able to do had they practiced efficiently during their active lifetime the Art of Living, and, when about to die, the Art of Dying.

This is the summation of Evans-Wentz, the remarkable scholar and pioneer interpreter of East to West, in his preface to the first English translation of the *Bardo Thodol*, 'Liberation through hearing on the after-death planes', whose English title is *The Tibetan Book of the Dead* (©1927 by W.Y. Evans-Wentz and published by Oxford University Press. All excerpts in this book are used by permission of Oxford University Press; see website at http://www.oup.com).

Evans-Wentz continues:

But in the Occident, where the Art of Dying is little known and rarely practiced, there is, contrastingly, the common unwillingness to die, which, as the Bardo ritual suggests, produces unfavourable results. As here in America, every effort is apt to be made by a materialistically inclined medical science to postpone, and thereby to interfere with, the death-process.

The term 'bardo' will be familiar to readers of *The Tibetan Book of the Dead*, and of *The Tibetan Book of Living and Dying* as a stage or passage in the cycle of life. *The* Bardo is the passage between death and a new birth. Liberation from the Bardo and reincarnation may be achieved with the help of the reading of the Bardo Thodol. Tibetans read the text to the one passing through physical death, to help her or him to avoid the pitfalls of the after-death planes. Guidance is needed especially in the Bardo of Becoming, the passage just prior to reincarnation, to achieve liberation. So is there any evidence that the NDE traveller to death and back, crosses into this Bardo place?

Two Tibetan Buddhists shed light in a dark place

When Sogyal Rinpoche, a Tibetan Buddhist initiate of the Dzogchen order wrote *The Tibetan Book of Living and Dying* (1992), a commentary and explanation of *The Tibetan Book of the Dead* and of Tibetan Buddhism, especially for Westerners, the intended audience snatched it up hungrily. It became a bestseller. Sogyal Rinpoche didn't just spend a couple of decades reading sacred texts; he sat, as Tibetan disciples do, at the feet of masters, and received the wisdom teachings transmitted from master to disciple going all the way back to the Primordial Buddha, Samantabhadra. He was initiated into the spiritual practices and meditations which gave him *direct experience* of death and beyond. How then, does Sogyal Rinpoche regard the experiences of those who have gone through NDE, in the light of the Tibetan Buddhist tradition? And more importantly, what does this tradition of direct experience through spiritual practice, have to say about the experience of dying and what lies beyond?

What is living and dying about, according to Tibetan Buddhism?

This wonderful book recognizes the validity of other religions, in particular Christianity (mentioned often because of its target readership), and is in fact something of a trailblazer in the consciousness of Westerners not much exposed to the attempts of the leadership in all faiths, to promote interfaith dialogue. Sogyal Rinpoche is to be credited with deliberately setting out to promote this dialogue, with a careful placing of the teachings of the faiths alongside each other, to draw out their common elements. Another major triumph of the book is the way in which it recognizes the work of Kubler-Ross and Raymond Moody, thus creating the channel for a *mainstream view* of death that unites not only East and West, but also science and religion. It takes the views we obtained in the West from Kubler-Ross' assistance to the terminally ill and Dr Moody's collection of experiences of those patients who died and returned to tell of the experience, and considers them alongside Tibetan Buddhist teachings.

As a result, the views of Kubler-Ross and Moody are no longer odd recountings of weird paranormal phenomena; they are placed in an overall context which begins to make a much larger sense of them, and which connects them to spiritual wisdom and practices of all societies in all ages. These are the very practices and wisdom that modern Westerners began to deeply mistrust and to discount, with the advent of scientific materialism in the nineteenth century.

There is another, *further dimension to add* to this roadmap-about the reality of, and details of, life after dispensing with the physical body. The first step in the filling-out of this further reach of the roadmap, is to place alongside Christianity's and Tibetan Buddhism's exoteric teachings and Moody and Kubler-Ross' findings, a *contemporary presentation* of the perennial philosophy. This is the view imparted by the Tibetan Master, D.K., who was occasionally presiding over a Tibetan lamasery *'when my other duties permit'*

(Bailey 1955, p. vii)[1]. He worked with and through Alice Bailey to produce an amazing body of writings, which updates the teachings of esoteric Buddhism for modern humanity.

These books are things of wonder in the vastness of their comprehension, the cosmic extent of their knowledge, and yet the profound compassion and understanding of the human condition and of individual human lives and struggles and suffering, they offer. They hold out a deeply reviving hope and promise to weary humanity.

While it is a fact that the esoteric knowledge imparted by D.K. is recognizably Buddhist, it is also Hindu or Brahman, and it speaks both of the enduring gift to humanity made by the Buddha, and of the vital role of the great teacher of humanity known in the West as the Christ. Esoteric Christianity embraces most of its basic tenets. This is the Christianity that did not become the accepted and promoted form we know today, but that of the groups and interpretations which lost out in the struggle for primacy and acceptance. These include the Gnostics[2], the Waldensians and Albigensians, the Cathars, the Knights Templar and Rosicrucians, and the Christian Neo-Platonists, of which the Anthroposophy of Rudolph Steiner is a modern example. Esoteric Judaism, in Cabbalism, and esoteric Islam, in Sufism, also share these tenets. This wisdom teaching of vast antiquity, which has been handed down from master to disciple over the ages, declares itself to be beyond any and all 'isms'. It may have a common source, which has since branched out to become the separate rivers of the world's great spiritual traditions. It would seem that logically it must have the common source claimed for it: the Self or the Divine Mind. That source tradition has needed no name till now, but for the sake of our recognition of it, is called the perennial philosophy or Ageless Wisdom. Other terms include the

---

1. All excerpts from the books of Alice Bailey, in this chapter and the rest of the book, are reprinted with the permission of the Lucis Trust, which holds copyright. See http://www.lucistrust.org

2. Gnosticism, with its ideas of pre-existence and reincarnation, *'a prevailing mood, ...rather than a specific cult...was a syncretistic, eclectic amalgam of religious ideas.'* It seemed that the Church struggled to permit only the minimum of dogmatic accumulation. *'The Church, in its discriminating attitude toward fashionable Gnostic doctrines, was in no mood to give its approval to any dogmas at all'*. Insightfully, MacGregor points out that if the Gnostic doctrines had been admitted, the Church would not have survived competition with Neoplatonism, in particular, because it was too similar, and because the Church lacked the racial and cultural cohesion of Judaism and Hinduism especially, in the lands to which it spread. MacGregor 1978, *Reincarnation in Christianity*, pp. 36-7.

Great Tradition, the One Teaching, the Initiates' Lore, the Ancient Wisdom, and the Secret Doctrine.

What is the perennial philosophy or Ageless Wisdom?

Ken Wilber, surely one of the great contemporary philosophers, has this to say:

> What is the worldview that led Alan Watts to state flatly that "we are hardly aware of the extreme peculiarity of our own position [scientific materialism], and find it difficult to realise the plain fact that there has otherwise been a single philosophical consensus of universal extent? It has been held by [men and women] who report the same insights and teach the same essential doctrine whether living today or six thousand years ago, whether from New Mexico in the Far West or Japan in the Far East."
>
> Known as the 'perennial philosophy' - perennial precisely because it shows up across cultures and across the ages with many similar features - this worldview has, indeed, formed the core not only of the world's great wisdom traditions, from Christianity to Buddhism to Taoism, but also of many of the greatest philosophers, scientists, and psychologists of both East and West, North and South...(Wilber 1997, pp. 38-39).

Every one of the world's great religions including Christianity, is said by the teachers of that Wisdom tradition, to be a development and adapted local cultural version of the great spiritual truths given to humanity in the distant past by the sages and adepts of those times. These teachings of the perennial philosophy are as universal and all embracing as Christianity (along with other great traditions) in its traditional and popular form has tended to become local and confined. (The Christian universe is centred on humanity and the relationship between God and individual humans. These are presented as the apex and raison d'etre of all creation and of God's plan and purpose.)

A typical statement about the Ageless Wisdom tradition comes from Vera Stanley Alder, a theosophist and renowned spiritual teacher in Britain in the earlier twentieth century:

> [T]he Ancient or Secret Wisdom...is a collection of teachings handed down from the very earliest times, explaining man, his origin, his composition and destiny, and also the purpose of the Universe. The Wisdom has come to us in unchanged form, concealed and taught throughout the world under the garb of many of the ancient religions. [It] is still to be found in the East (Alder 1968, p. 38).

This ancient wisdom tradition corrects Christianity's too-cramped perspective, in its ability to embrace all human formulations of spiritual truths and all human cultures and traditions, along with everything from the great galaxies with their millions of stars, to unicellular life such as that of the amoeba, and to relate it all in one vast scheme created by a stupendous Intelligence and motivated by an immeasurable Love. The perennial philosophy places humans, and their life and death, in a scheme that situates and relates everything and everyone in the universe, including Christianity, Judaism, Islam, Hinduism, Buddhism and every other approach to God and the puzzle of human existence. The older of these significant branches of the Ageless Wisdom, Hinduism and Buddhism, extend this vision further than the newer branches. It is a constantly evolving cosmos, and every element and part of it is evolving too, including humanity and each individual of the group. Evolution is towards a greater wisdom, love and compassion, greater omnipotence and omniscience, greater responsibility towards all lesser lives on the planet, and greater usefulness towards the Whole.

Before looking in detail at the teachings about death in Tibetan Buddhism and in the Tibetan's presentation of this ancient wisdom for modern humanity through the Alice Bailey books, it would be interesting to consider what light they may throw on the Near-death experience.

The Near-death Experience in the Tibetan Book of Living and Dying

How does Sogyal Rinpoche (1992) consider the NDE and (Tibetan) Buddhism, in the chapter 'The Near-Death Experience: A Staircase to Heaven?' Does he conclude that there is something real going on...that these experiences match up in any way, or share similarities, with the experience of dying as Tibetan Buddhism understands it? And does he think that it is possible to take a quick trip to the After-death State and return?

The chapter begins, typically enough for this remarkable book, with the Near-death experience of a Christian saint-the eighth-century English historian, Bede. The Rinpoche goes on to relate the story of a famous Tibetan Delok, one returned from death to teach the living. Perhaps surprisingly after all this- the recognition of the existence of Near-death experiences in virtually every spiritual tradition, he does still warn that it is premature to draw conclusions about the nature of the NDE. He quotes his teacher saying that anyone who returned to the bodily life may have stood at the threshold and glimpsed into the next bardo, that of death, but he or she must still have been in the natural bardo of this life, by virtue of the fact that he or she has not finally died. (Sogyal 1992, p. 332)

He says there are differences-the chief being that anyone who passes through the entire experience does not return. There are also similarities. The dawning of the blackness of Full Attainment is like the darkness and peace of the Tunnel experience; the light after this darkness is like the *'ground luminosity or Clear Light'*, which at the moment of death, dawns in all its splendour.

Similarities with the Bardo of Dharmata are noted by the Rinpoche, and he goes on to examine these. He summarizes them from the Tibetan Book of the Dead as: The Out-of-the-body experience; Helplessly watching relatives; Perfect form, mobility and clairvoyance; Meeting others; Different realms; and Hellish visions. (These latter are actually rather rarely reported among NDE survivors.) *So these experiences are known both in the Buddhist tradition and from recent collections of Near-death experiences!*

Sogyal Rinpoche concludes that the release of the mind from the body in the NDE means that it undergoes similar experiences to those of permanent death. (Sogyal 1992 p. 325).

Does the NDE 'fit' with Tibetan Buddhism and the Ageless Wisdom? Comparison of key elements, the Tunnel and the Life Review

The Tunnel experience or the peaceful black void described by those who have experienced NDE is one contender for the Christian 'Valley of the Shadow of Death'. The other is the Bardo proper, as explained later. The Tunnel may be, as Sogyal Rinpoche considers, the 'Blackness of Full Attainment' phase of Tibetan Buddhism, which is explained in the next chapter. It would make sense for 'Full Attainment' to mean that the withdrawal from the physical body and level is complete. The Tibetan adept, D.K., describes the separation of the vital or life body from the physical body, and withdrawal of the 'dead' person, very much alive and in full possession of a sharpened awareness and capacity for thought and feeling, from the discarded body. This takes place through an opening at the head, heart or solar plexus, according to the degree of advancement of the dying person, as we shall see later.

The Tunnel phase of the Near-death experience is as we have seen, sometimes preceded by an out-of-the-body experience. The NDEr will report the experience of hovering above their body, looking down on it often from around ceiling height, feeling weightless and organless, and aware that they no longer have a physical body. They report being in, or having, a different kind of 'body' altogether. It is at this stage that they report 'helplessly watching' relatives and others grieving over their death, and being unable to communicate to them that the only dead thing is the discarded physical vehicle.

Post mortem, 'helplessly watching' and trying to communicate

Sogyal Rinpoche reminds us that in the Tibetan tradition, the newly deceased can *'see and hear their living relatives, but are unable...to communicate with them'* (Sogyal 1992, p. 326)[3]. The Tibetan, D.K., similarly remarks of this moment that the 'dead' are aware of those they've left behind, and remain close and watching, though not able to make their living presence known. It is, though, surprising how often those close to the supposedly dead will confide, despite their own reservations about life after death, that the Departed appeared to them to reassure them that all was well and the bond between them could not be severed by death. The openly sceptical will not be trusted with these confidences, and cannot know how common this is. Later, the experiencer is likely to be persuaded that it was 'just a dream' or wishful thinking. A recent experience among friends is a good example. Silvia's mother and family watched as this delightful young woman endured the steady deterioration of her faculties along with the ability to use her body, as her disease progressed-a decline similar to that seen in Alzheimer's. Her partner told me after a secular funeral, that the night before she died (hours before, that is, at a time when no-one yet knew that her death was imminent), he dreamed of Silvia. She woke up and got out of bed, fully herself again.

There is a light at the end of the tunnel, literally, NDErs report, and they emerge to peace, bliss, and a sense of eternity. They travel down the tunnel towards a brilliant light, which however, is not painful to vision, and towards a great Being of Light, whose welcoming love and wisdom is engulfing, universal, yet somehow still deeply personal. It is as if this Being knows them more intimately than any human could ever know them, including all their faults and weaknesses, yet accepts them with unconditional love. They communicate with this Being, seen as Christ, God or an angel, but more often simply as a Being of Light, without words, by the instantaneous

---

3. This excerpt and all others from The Tibetan Book of Living and Dying by Sogyal Rinpoche, now published by Rider, are reprinted by permission of the Random House Group.

exchange of thought. Afterwards they are likely to express wonderment that such communication was possible.

The Life Review – a modern Judgement?

The question put by the Being, rendered in words is something like: 'What do you see yourself as having done with your life? Did you accomplish what you set out to do? What are its achievements and its lessons?' Then the just-completed life is seen, not in summary, but replayed as it was lived. The good and positive and the wrong and negative are reviewed; every apparently minor decision and its consequences, every motive for action and its outcomes, and every thought and word and its reverberations and effects in the lives of others and upon the planetary life as a whole, is replayed. Could the universe be such a moral place, after all? NDErs return convinced that it is. What do Buddhism, and The Tibetan D.K., say of this experience?

Sogyal Rinpoche points to the similarity of the Judgement scene in the Bardo of Becoming (the Sipa Bardo). The person who has just died comes before Dharma-Raja, King of the Dead. Evans-Wentz' introduction to the *Tibetan Book of the Dead* calls Dharma-Raja the Buddhist and Hindu Pluto, who as *'a Judge of the Dead, corresponds to Osiris in the Egyptian version. In both versions alike there is the symbolical weighing: before Dharma-Raja there are placed on one side of the balance black pebbles and on the other side white pebbles, symbolizing evil and good deeds...'* (Evans-Wentz 1927, p.35)[4].

This Judgement or Life Review is not a weighing-up according to the personality's sense of the success or failure of the life just finished, as you would expect if this were really just a fantasy. Nor is it objectively about one's accomplishments alone. It is a stocktaking of all the acts of the individual's life. This judging or critical assessment of the deeds, before or by, Pluto, Osiris, Dharma-Raja, Christ or the Being of Light, objectifies them. It becomes clear that they cannot be dismissed as purely private events which meant nothing except to the self. They were either benevolent and compassionate, and therefore, morally good, or they were selfish and negative, and therefore morally bad. Which will predominate? It is a universe where morally good and bad deeds seem to matter – they are in fact of paramount importance, unimaginably to scientific materialism.

---

4. Excerpts from The Tibetan Book of the Dead, © W.Y. Evans-Wentz 1927, used by permission of Oxford University Press.

Earlier, in the chapter titled 'Evolution, Karma and Rebirth' Sogyal Rinpoche (1992, p.97) says that he has been *'moved by how the near-death experience reports confirm, in a very precise and startling way, the truth about karma.'*

The Rinpoche selects some examples from NDE reports, to make it clear why he has drawn this conclusion:

> *"Everything in my life went by for review-I was ashamed of a lot of the things I experienced because it seemed I had a different knowledge...Not only what I had done, but how I had affected other people... not even your thoughts are lost..."*

Another NDEr spoke of reliving every thought, word and deed, and of discovering the effect of each on *'anyone who had ever come within my environment or sphere of influence... plus the effect of each thought, word and deed on weather, plants, animals...'" (Sogyal 1992, p. 97).*

These testimonies are very far from anything that could be produced by fantasy. It would be quite a challenge for the sceptics to attempt to reproduce even just the total replay of the most minute details of a single day of one's life, whether through fantasy or oxygen deprivation, or by any means they believe to be the cause. The idea taught by all great teachers is more than just a theological proposition-in truth we *are* all One!

The Near-death Experience-is it actually a phase of dying?

The Tibetan Master, Djwhal Khul's teachings about the passage through death place the Near-death experience in context, making it possible to position it correctly in the sequence of events of dying. The element of doubt which lingers in Sogyal Rinpoche's assessment of the NDE seems to be resolved in Djwhal Kuhl's statement clarifying that it is indeed a real experience of dying:

> *Occasionally men are brought back again into physical plane existence when at the exact point of complete physical restitution* [restoring the elements of the body to their source in physical substance]. *This can only be done as long as the conscious entity* [one's self, or the conscious person] *is still occupying the etheric vehicle* [otherwise known as the vital body, the next in density to the physical body], *though the discarding of the dense physical body has to all intents and purposes been completed...'* [This return to physical life can happen], *'even where the death of the physical body* [including] *the cessation of all heart activity has been effective and the withdrawal* [of the spiritual being in the etheric body] *is already well under way* (Bailey 1953, p. 460).

What on earth does all this mean? The untangling of it follows, in later sections of the book! The Tibetan Master gives a straightforward explanation as to how it is that someone who undergoes the Near-death experience can apparently die and return, cease existing and then resume existing, disappear and reappear. NDErs do, it seems, actually leave their physical body. Yet they have not gone so far into some other state of existence that they are unable to return and re-occupy the physical body, though it takes pain and struggle. *Could it be that death is in the end only a disappearance from the physical plane, and becoming invisible to those left behind, whose senses are limited to perception of physical plane phenomena?*

The next chapter attempts to reconcile opposite positions: East versus West, three thousand plus years of philosophy versus a century of relativity and quantum physics. The West considers consciousness a mere outgrowth of the physical brain, hence there can be nothing beyond physical death. If the universe and therefore consciousness are not purely physical, what are their nature, according to Buddhism and the perennial philosophy especially? Is there any way of reconciling our Western science idea of the 'merely physical' universe, with our religious traditions? They all teach a universe created from spiritual levels, and a life which extends beyond the death of the body.

Chapter 5
Death as Mere Disappearance

States of being in Buddhism, and Quantum Wave Collapse

Summary Points

- Are there peace and light after death, in Tibetan Buddhism as in the NDE?
- **Why do we go into the Buddhist Mind's light, not nothingness? The bishop, the poet and Stephen Hawking**
- Does Matter make Mind? Or does Mind create the universe? Einstein's No Dice.
- The levels of Being beyond the concrete world
- What lies 'above' the physical level of existence?
- **Is there another existence not produced by the concrete world? The two sides of the coin**
- **Death-defying consciousness via Quantum Wave collapse –does it hold water?**
- Sogyal Rinpoche: Death as *'a gradual... dawning of ever more subtle levels of consciousness'.*

Death as Mere Disappearance

Does death with its associated loss of a physical body, merely render us invisible to those left behind, whose senses are limited? Are we in fact, released into the light and love perceived by those who undergo a Near-death Experience, and into another order of consciousness?

It strikes most Westerners as a novel and surprising idea, that death may be no more than *'an interlude in a life of steadily accumulating experience'* or that it mainly *'marks a definite transition from one state of consciousness into another'* (Bailey 1937, p. 220). Our mistaken ideas about death have led us to fear it, advises the Tibetan, D.K.:

> [W]e have looked upon it as the great and ultimate terror, whereas in reality it is the great escape, the entrance into a fuller measure of activity, and the release of the life from the crystallised vehicle and an inadequate form (Bailey 1922, pp.64-65).

Are there peace and light after death, in Tibetan Buddhism as in the NDE?

What does Tibetan Buddhism, particularly in Sogyal Rinpoche's reinterpretation and rewriting of The Tibetan Book of the Dead, have to say about this amazing experience known to NDErs; the universal light, the joy, the peace, the love? Can it explain this phenomenon, accounted by many scientific experts as nothing but the last flashes and fizzings of the dying brain? Can Tibetan Buddhism offer anything which could make sense of what sceptical Westerners regard as so unreal that, if not these last gasps of brain circuitry, must be hallucination or deranged imagination? (Remember that the NDE studies have shown that there was no brain function at the time!)

The four bardos and The Bardo: Physical life as the opportunity for Enlightenment

What does this tradition of direct experience through spiritual practice, teach about the experience of dying and what lies beyond? What has been discovered about the meaning of life and death? How does Sogyal Rinpoche regard the experiences of those who have gone through NDE's, in the light of the Tibetan Buddhist tradition?

The cycle of life is divided into four bardos, or stages, Sogyal tells us in The Tibetan Book of Living and Dying. Each of these bardos presents us with a priceless opportunity to get clear, not only of the bardos and of incarnation itself, but of the delusion and ignorance in which we exist, to become aware of the true nature of reality, or of universal Mind. This awareness takes us beyond all ignorance, and its fruits of harm to others and suffering to ourselves, and ultimately into the Buddha Nature.

This awareness is characterised by a word which, surprisingly enough, has resonance-and a degree of understanding, well beyond the Buddhist East. A generation of Westerners growing up everywhere from San Francisco's Haight-Ashbury district to Amsterdam to Sydney as long ago as the 'Sixties knew that *Enlightenment was the Word*, the Holy Grail they sought whether they were learning to meditate or smoked marijuana or ingested a tab of LSD, some editions of which were known as Clear Light, after the Buddhist Clear Light state. They even understood that Enlightenment is about entering into the bliss beyond love and joy, the bliss that is Reality. Perhaps they were hazier about enlightenment as being a vast awareness of all life, and a profound love and compassion for all beings. The world's cities were filled with Flower Children and hippies telling us to "Chill out, Man! Realize that everything passes; nothing is Real". Sogyal Rinpoche says that travelling the spiritual path, all our *'old concepts of the world...are purified and dissolved, and an entirely new...'heavenly' field of vision and perception opens up.'* He then quotes the eighteenth century English poet and mystic, William Blake, who wrote a couplet, which became a mantram for the sixties' consciousness revolution:

If the doors of perception were cleansed,
Everything would appear...as it is, infinite...

However most of us, Sogyal says, continue to make the karma which will bring us back to earth and another life, by *'clutching onto happiness and suffering as real... So everything is at risk in how we live now, at this very moment'* (Sogyal 1992, p. 115).

The four stages of life are given by Sogyal Rinpoche as: The 'natural' bardo of life; the 'painful' bardo of dying; the 'luminous' bardo of dharmata; and the 'karmic' bardo of becoming which he says, is what is usually referred to as the Bardo, the stage lasting until rebirth. Other teachers do generally speak of the Bardo as the entire stage between death and rebirth. The Mahayana Buddhist teachings tell us to seize the opportunity presented in the bardo of this life-the time between birth and death. It is presented to us as the neces-sary *'time to prepare for death: by becoming familiar with the teaching and stabilizing the practice'* (Sogyal 1992, p.104).

Just what is this existence for which are we preparing? It can't be simply to Go Gently into that Goodnight-the darkness that the poet Dylan Thomas exhorts us to resist -*'Rage, rage against the dying of the light'*... heralding the non-existence we often expect in the West. Once we have moved through the processes of the death of the physical body, and through what is known as the inner respira-tion, the conscious self moves into the Light, the *'dawning of the nature of mind, what we call the "Ground Luminosity" at the moment of death'* (Sogyal 1992, p. 104).

The light of the NDE and Buddhism's Ground Luminosity-do they make any sense?

Luminosity is about light. So is this stage, marked by the death of the physical body and the end of the 'inner respiration', an experi-ence of dawning light, or of travelling into light? Does it bear any re-semblance to the experience of light of those who died and re-turned? *Is the resemblance sufficient to add weight to the likelihood of the NDE being a real experience?* And if there is a resemblance, how does that NDE experience relate to the Buddhist teachings about the whole nature of life and death -given that here in the scientific West, we suffer from an obvious inability to relate it to anything at all apart from the dying throes of brain cells? Or when thinking of it in a religious context, to anything apart from what we may regard as myths about Heaven being illumined by the glory streaming from the Presence of God?

Is there a coherent explanation of the NDErs' experience of light and love, which makes sense of it in the context of the entire Buddhist philosophy about the nature of life and death? Then there is that arresting phrase: dying culminates in the dawning of the nature of mind. What is this about? Why is this dawning of mind connected with light and love? It is even more important, though, to discover the answer to this question: What could the ***dawning of mind*** *possibly have to do with* ***dying?***

The *'luminous'* bardo of dharmata *'encompasses* **the after-death ex-perience of the radiance of the nature of mind, the luminosity or "Clear Light",** *which manifests as sound, colour, and light'* (Sogyal 1992 p. 104). Here is the Clear Light I referred to earlier as the name of the LSD ticket to one of those impossibly instant trips to enlightenment. The light experienced by NDErs corresponds to the light of the Ground Luminosity, at the 'entrance' to the bardo of Dharmata. It is experienced when and because they travel out of the clinically dead physical body into what Tibetan Buddhism tells us is *the radiance of the nature of Mind*. So there is now a clear connection between the NDE experience of 'Light at the end of the Tunnel', and the Buddhist 'Mind of clear light of death'.

In the chapter *The Near-Death Experience: A Staircase to Heaven?* Sogyal Rinpoche (p. 325) writes about the existence of consciousness after death: *'In the near-death experience, the mind is momentarily released from the body, and goes through a number of experiences akin to [the experiences after death in] the mental body in the bardo of becoming'.*

While there is a specific mental body in the Tibetan or Northern Buddhist tradition, this seems to mean more generally, the 'body' or 'vehicle' we possess when the physical body is gone. In other traditions, it is referred to as the emotional or astral body, or the Kama rupa of the original Indian traditions. I deduce this usage of 'mental body' from the fact that later in the book, Sogyal Rinpoche says people who have passed through death but not been able to resist the pull of the physical world, (and who therefore must have little or no actual mental development and no mental body as such), are in the 'mental' body. The connection between the individual's level of mental development, and their prospects after death, will become clear in the course of the next three chapters.

Why do we go into the Buddhist Mind's light, not darkness or nothingness? Bishop Berkeley versus Dr Johnson

Can realms of light and the dawning of the nature of mind make any sense of the total experience of life and death -- and the NDE? What connection is there if any, between light and mind? Tibetan Buddhism would say that we travel into Mind, (and not, for argument's sake, into an alternative physical universe such as those presented in science fiction), due to the nature of the total cosmos, of Reality. Despite the prevailing Western worldview, (at its zenith only during the last century or so), *the physical world may be only one level and aspect of the total reality, which the Buddhists call Mind*. So when we exit the physical body, we immediately find ourselves in the encompassing reality of Mind. This Mind is the creator of everything, including the 'illusory' physical world. And as Sogyal Rinpoche says, the all-pervasive light is of the very nature of Mind.

There is much misunderstanding about this...it's too close to the position that physical existence is the mere hallucination which is a kind of special, but typical, derangement of the human species. And at times the argument appears to the Western mind as sliding towards this position.

The celebrated reply of Dr Samuel Johnson, eighteenth century English writer, comes to 'mind'. When he heard of the famous philosopher Bishop Berkeley's latest position - that the world and all in it were (merely) the outpicturing of thoughts in the Mind of God, he stubbed his toe on a handy rock and declared *'I refute it thus! [Ouch!]'*. Stephen Hawking, who reminds readers of this famous incident, in his book *"A Brief History of Time"*, writes that Berkeley *'believed that all material objects and space and time are an illusion'*.[1] Hawking also points out that the rock chosen by Johnson was a large one! (Hawking 1988, p. 18). Dr Johnson was demonstrating that thoughts have no physical existence whatever; they are less substantial than air: they have no height, width, depth, weight or dimension in time. It is impossible to stub one's toe on a mere thought of God. Surely insubstantial Mind could not create the physical world and its rocks; Berkeley must be wrong!

Does Matter make Mind? Or does Mind create the universe? Einstein's No Dice

How then, can mind be the preceding condition or the creator of anything? Or be the simultaneous reality of all physical things? Surely it can only be the other way around, as Western thought assumes-that the physical level creates 'mind'? The notion that any substantial body such as a rock, cannot also be a thought in the mind of God, leads straight into a famous moment in twentieth century science. Einstein *'didn't want to accept quantum uncertainty as inherent uncertainty'*. Kitty Ferguson (biographer of Stephen Hawking) recounts and comments on this famous incident in the annals of science, in *The Fire in the Equations* (Ferguson 1994, p. 21).

Heisenberg, Pauli and Bohr's work showed that atoms have what is for the rational Western mind, a very strange and paradoxical existence, which does not have a definite position and a definite momentum at the same time, and which is either a particle or a wave of

---

1. Berkeley is one of the best-known and most quoted of those who belong to the school of thought of monistic idealism; that is, monist not dualist because he believed in a universe made of just one substance not two or more, idealist because that substance was not material, but ideal; that is, of the mind.

energy, seemingly depending on what aspect the scientist is observing. And worse, *'it seems that when an atom isn't being observed it lapses into a state that can be described as ghostlike, with no concrete reality to it at all'*, says Ferguson (1994, p. 21).

The revelation for scientists was that a subatomic particle could disappear and reappear, it could *exist and then not exist* in the physical world. Whatever could this mean? Perhaps the physical world was not the sole real world, nor the creator of all other 'ghostly' worlds, such as the mental?

Is there another existence not produced by the concrete world? The two sides of the coin

Did scientists actually cause the physical manifestation of subatomic life when they observed it? Was it a form of existence dependent on the attention of the scientist? Or alternatively, were the observational instruments simply altering it? Was it somehow still 'out there' and real, though manifesting only when we turn our attention to it and perceive it? Einstein did not like this inherent uncertainty. *'God does not play dice'* that great mind insisted in frustration with these contradictions. *'Albert, don't tell God what he can do!'* came the famous retort from Niels Bohr (Ferguson, 1994, p.21).

It is fascinating that the final referee called in to judge the clash of realities was none other than God! And that Bohr could be found daring to correct the great Einstein, in pointing out that surely, in the Divine Mind a thing and its opposite *could* comfortably co-exist. It is also worth pondering that Einstein was quite comfortable with the idea of individual human consciousness as in the end, an illusion:

> *A human being is part of a whole, called by us the "Universe", a part limited in time and space. He experiences himself, his thoughts and feelings, as something separated from the rest -- a kind of optical delusion of his consciousness. This delusion is a kind of prison for us, restricting us to our personal desires and to affection for a few persons nearest us. Our task must be to free ourselves from this prison by widening our circles of compassion to embrace all living creatures and the whole of nature in its beauty.* (Albert Einstein, quoted in Sogyal 1992, p. 68).

This might have come from the Dalai Lama. Perhaps they share access to higher levels of the One Universal Mind than most humans can reach? Kitty Ferguson reviews these attempts to resolve the clash between Newtonian physics and quantum physics, science and religion, in the way that Bohr resolved the atomic paradox with the idea of the complementarity of both states of atomic life: that is, that each state is a necessary complement to the other, as dependent on each other as are two sides of a coin:

> *The question* [about which worldview is correct; that of science or religion] *can be answered only in a way that would imply 'Both are correct' and 'Neither is correct'. "Together", says [C.S] Lewis, [author of Narnia, that wonderful children's series now on film] "they are more nearly complete than either is alone. Yet both are no more than feeble human perceptions -- or revelations of God dimly understood, or revelations that God purposely made simple enough for human mentality -- of occurrences which are inestimably far beyond our capacity to understand or describe. If we knew what really happened at what we call 'the beginning' we'd find our current disagreement more than slightly embarrassing, regardless of which side of the dispute we're on"* (Ferguson 1994, p. 230).

This antinomian, opposites-together style of thinking, here of Bohr, Lewis, and Ferguson, is almost impossible to Western minds: a statement and its opposite cannot both be true together, a thing and its opposite cannot both exist, by definition. It would make nonsense of the thinking and the approach that has resulted in the triumph of Western philosophy and science in untangling the web of things. It would demolish the careful separation of objective from subjective, of that which is logically related from all that is not, and the delineation of cause and effect which has been so successful in moving us beyond a world where women accused of witchcraft were tested by submerging them in water on the ducking-stool. If they floated it proved they were witches. So they were condemned to death either way.

Death-defying consciousness via Quantum Wave collapse –does it hold water?

Despite the continued mindset of present-day science that there is no 'mind' beyond death; that there is nothing at all because everything begins and ends in the material world, there are dissenters. There is a different resolution of the quantum indeterminacy paradox, and one that is currently popular among scientists. It is that the consciousness of the observing subject 'collapses' the quantum wave from the many possibilities of manifestation held in 'mere' probability, into tangible materiality, and appearance as a discrete particle. This idea is developed by American scientist Amit Goswami, reared in India by a father who was a Hindu guru, or spiritual teacher. It is an understanding of the cosmos he calls Science within Consciousness. In *Physics of the Soul* (2001), Goswami takes us

with him on his expedition to reconcile science and religion. He accounts for the soul, immortality and reincarnation through this
quantum physics-based idea of the collapse of the quantum wave via
consciousness. Goswami's resolution of the paradox is one Bishop
Berkeley might fail to recognise, even though it is still idealistic
monism -- the philosophy that makes consciousness, not matter, the
source of the universe. It is brilliant, but not entirely satisfactory: it
fails to account for all the data even of the Out-of-body experience
Goswami uses to make his case:

> *Clearly, there are no local signals to carry the information [that is, clinically*
> *dead NDErs have no access to 'local signals' of the senses and brain to view*
> *the scene around them]. So how else to explain this information transfer than*
> *quantum nonlocal viewing in conjunction with somebody else's (for example,*
> *the surgeon's) viewing? (Goswami 1993). The most recent data is showing*
> *that even the blind can 'see' in this way; they are not encumbered by the fact*
> *that their own vision is inoperative (Ring and Cooper 1995); they must be*
> *seeing **telepathically** [my emphasis -that is, nonlocally] in synchronicity*
> *with someone else's viewing (Goswami 2001, p. 75)[2] . (The 1995 work by*
> *Ring and Cooper cited here, is their Mindsight; Near-death and Out of Body*
> *Experiences in the Blind, quoted in Chapter 12, and cited in the Bibliography*
> *of Physics of the Soul).*

Thus for Goswami, it requires a physical body and consciousness
within it, to collapse the probability wave; therefore, the NDEr
must be 'seeing' through the apparatus of some still-living person.
This fails to account for a number of OOB experiences, such as the
ability to see through walls and round corridors, or through ceilings,
which are not uncommonly reported. Such a time-and-space-defying
view is obviously not the surgeon's view. In fact, it cannot be the
view of any living person: Clearly it is a super-sensory, superphysical
view. It also fails to account for those who undergo NDE and OOB
experiences, and look down on their own lifeless bodies, when no
one else is present or awake to have that view.

At a meeting with Goswami and three others to consider the science of life beyond death, Kenneth Ring of NDE repute, (whose
own solution to these dilemmas is contained in his book *The Omega
Project*) asked *'If a real disaster hit the globe, could we survive it as disembodied beings?'*

Goswami replied:

> *'We would certainly survive as disembodied beings, just as anybody who dies*
> *does now. But, Ken, there is one problem. According to my model, you cannot*

---

2. Extracts from Amit Goswami 2001, Physics of the Soul, Hampton Roads Publishing, Charlottesville, VA, used with permission of the publishers.

have experience without a physical body. The state of consciousness of a dis-embodied being is [therefore] like that of sleep; the possibility wave does not collapse. So, as a civilization, we could hardly choose this state of limbo and be satisfied.' (Goswami 2001, p. 241).

Goswami was pleased when the Theosophist present, Dick Robb, agreed that according to Theosophy, incarnation was necessary -- without it, there was no resolving of one's karma.

But Goswami is here tending toward something which is always a hazard for the hypothesizing scientist; the attempt to make the evidence fit the theory instead of vice versa. It's hard not to do this; how else can you test a theory than by taking the evidence and see-ing if it fits? In his model, as he says, the possibility wave cannot be collapsed by a disembodied consciousness. His employment of this forcing process is to assume that therefore, the after-death con-sciousness *has* to be 'like that of sleep'.

However, if the consciousness of a disembodied being is *not* 'like that of sleep', but is instead as NDErs and other sources usually re-port it, far more intense and extensive than the consciousness con-fined to a physical body, the validity of Goswami's model would be put in serious question, if not just exploded. Another major prob-lem I have with *Science within Consciousness* is this: If Goswami needs *consciousness* to be the source of the material universe, since no al-ternative materialism works, why does he then resort to a basically materialistic solution? That is, he explains *transcendence of death* as being only possible through the *use of a brain* in a presently incarnate human being! This effectively cancels out the idea of consciousness as the source of all.

Chapters Six and Seven explore the after-death state of consciousness.

David Bohm's 'co-existence' solution to 'ghostlike' subatomic particles

The great scientific mind of David Bohm saw the answer to these contradictions and disagreements in the idea of the physical world as *co-existent* with other levels of being, an extension of Niels Bohr's idea of the complementarity of wave and particle states:

*His ambition was, as he wrote in his notebook, to show that "all the apparent laws of the universe have the same source"... (H)e sought a cosmology, a sci-entific account of the interconnection of all things. In particular, David pro-posed to include the **nature of mind** in his cosmology (Peat 1997, p. 25).*

Bohm's solution to the difficulties presented by the indeterminacy principle was the Hidden Variable theory. This theory implied levels of being, and the understanding that the material state of being was a manifestation of other, hidden states.

Science has evolved ever-finer instruments to detect ever more that we cannot perceive with any of our senses. Yet we still assume, as Einstein seemed to have done, that these phenomena are concrete, physical 'things'. That is the real paradox, that we can have the quantum physics experience, yet assume that there is one basic state of existence: there is concrete physical existence, (and a limited consciousness dependent on it), and no others. This relegates atomic particles to a state that is *'ghostlike, with no concrete existence to [them] at all'* as I have quoted Kitty Ferguson remarking, above.

How do we know of the existence of the solid, liquid and gaseous states -- of water, for example? We have always been able to observe ice turn into water and back again; we have always been able to smell some gases. We discovered how to ignite gases for heating, or use them to anaesthetize a patient before surgery. We can't see gases; we know them through their palpable effects. Our experience of atoms is less palpable than seeing the flame at the end of a gas lighter, yet we accept the existence of both gases and atoms.

Nuclear physicists were expecting atoms to travel through time and space on linear paths that could be tracked by our instruments. Instead, they appear and disappear, and appear again, but not by moving on any linear time-space path: their behaviour gave rise to the formulation known as the Indeterminacy Principle. Do atoms really exist and become non-existent? No, and yes. Is it true that they have no definite concrete existence, until nuclear physicists aim sophisticated apparatus at them? Is it as the result of this 'processing' of them, that they emerge into our experience, and we can perceive them? This is the way that it has been read. But what some scientists have seen as following from this, is that atoms must be observed, in order to exist. And not just by sophisticated instruments, or the physical world would not exist. It's necessary to take a position like that of Amit Goswami: that the very first living cell provided the first consciousness which 'collapsed' the quantum waves to retroactively create the physical universe.

Alternatively, is the appearance of the atom similar to an everyday experience-that something is not there, until I notice it? I've become so used to the tinkling calls of native bellbirds in the bush gully out the back, that the only way I can hear them these days is to decide to listen. *I never hear them otherwise.*

Does this mean they don't exist until I become conscious of them? Of course not, most of us would say. Especially when I'm often reminded to become conscious of their existence when someone on the other end of the phone line, in Auckland NZ or Mumbai, India, hears this delightful birdcall and remarks on it. I haven't heard anything, and wonder what they're talking about -- until I listen for that particular sound. Will this model work to explain quantum nonlocality?

But what about the way that sometimes there isn't a particle, but a wave there? When different methods are used to detect them, they are no longer discrete quanta, but have become a 'wave'. Surely this 'wave' state is further from the gross material state, and closer to the source state of all things, where 'things' exist not even as different energies, but as an undifferentiated whole. It is a subtler manifestation than particles, of the energy which Einstein's revolutionary formula, $E=Mc^2$ equates to mass and therefore, matter.

Isn't it possible that the movement of atomic life from the wave to the particle state is analogous (at a higher level still) to the movement of water, from its gaseous to its liquid state? Just as we don't assume the gas is non-existent when a gust of wind blows out the pilot flame, we could and do understand that the atom doesn't cease to exist, but resumes existing in a state which is beyond our capacity to perceive, even with instruments evolved from nuclear physics itself. Yet while finer instruments will be invented, there are limits. It does become more difficult for science to detect the higher, finer states of life, not just because the instruments of observation and the act of observing alters what is being observed, but increasingly as perceiver and perceived become less distinguished, and finally become a unity. It is only on the more concrete levels of existence, where pure energy resolves into discrete existences or 'things', that a science necessarily based on the separation of subject and object can work.

In fact, quite specific statements about the nature of atomic particles parallel to this have been made by Dr Douglas Baker, English scientist, medico and esotericist. He divides the physical plane, the lowest of the seven planes of Tibetan Buddhism and the perennial philosophy, into seven sub-planes. The solid subplane, that of greatest density, is number seven. The liquid, gas, and ionic subplanes are numbers six, five and four. It is the characterization of the next three levels which is of great interest here. The first of these he gives as the Third etheric, which is constituted of 'matter of the order of Protons'. The Second Etheric consists of 'matter of the order of Neutrinos'. The First Etheric is made up of 'matter of the order of Electrons'. Baker says:

> The material of these subplanes becomes rarer and more electromagnetic as they proceed upwards...The material of the first subplane is made up of ultimate physical 'particles' which are not particles at all. They are vortices of energy. They receive, transmit, and transmute energies from higher planes. They provide, therefore, the energy and the medium by which many of the phenomena of the continuum occur. These first subplanes of all the seven planes produce the physical, emotional, mental and spiritual phenomena which some are wont to call the miraculous (Baker 1974, p. 44).

While Western scientists wrestle with these great paradoxes of existence, they sit comfortably within Buddhism, and once again, the Western mind struggles to understand the apparent contradictions of Buddhist thinking. Carl Jung, founder of Analytical Psychology, in his Psychological Commentary on the *Bardo Thodol*, or Tibetan Book of the Dead, points to this essential difference -- the West's need to take a stand at one end or its opposite, in the continuum: either *'God is'* or *'God is not'*. He notes by comparison that the *'ever-present, unspoken assumption of the Bardo Thodol is the antinomial character of all metaphysical assertions'*. The opposites-together nature of Eastern philosophy in the Bardo Thodol text, combines both 'ends' of what is an indivisible whole, while it also contains the idea of *'the qualitative difference of the various levels of consciousness and of the metaphysical realities conditioned by them' (Evans-Wentz 1927, p.xxxvii)*.

Jung is of course, here implying that the Western view is an oversimplification, and that reality is better described by the Buddhist 'both-and' position.

The levels of Being beyond the concrete -the seven worlds

In the Buddhist philosophy, Mind is all there is; the solidity of the material world is a temporary illusion of that Mind; the Mind-Matter dichotomy or 'split' isn't a split in the end, because everything is all and only Mind. Yet the various branches of the perennial philosophy, the Vedanta-Hindu especially, teach that although matter is ultimately an illusion from the standpoint of immortal, unified existence, this stuff of manifested existence comes in finer and coarser grades.

This has profound implications for the process of dying and its meaning, and the cycle of incarnation too. The overarching tradition in which the Tibetan, D.K., is a teacher and master, that includes esoteric Buddhism, names aspects of this Mind. So there are separate terms characterizing the ever-higher and more expansive levels of consciousness, which we access according to our degree of evolution. The Ageless Wisdom teaches that our solar system exists in seven levels, the physical level, numbered seven, being that of the greatest density. The emotional or astral level, Kama, is number six, the level above that, five, is the mental or plane of Manas, level four is the Buddhic or intuitional plane, level three is the plane of Spirit or Atman (the 'place' of what might be called the soul's soul), two is the Monadic or plane of the Will, and the first is Adi, the plane of the Logos, or the One in Whom we live and move and have our being. These Sanskrit terms are found in both Buddhism and Hinduism (Humphries 1928); unsurprising given that the concepts derived originally from the common source of both, called here, for a designating term, the Ageless Wisdom. The outstanding correlation and cross-referencing of these levels as they exist in all versions of the perennial philosophy is that of Ken Wilber, first introduced in Chapter One. His representative system contains five levels, Matter, Body, Mind, Soul and Spirit, subdivided into (at least) nine levels (see Diagram 1 in Appendix, from Wilber 2007, p. 208).

Thus the cosmic Mind of the Buddhists encompasses all Reality beyond the concrete physical plane and body- Mind, Soul and Spirit, (including the centauric, the psychic, the subtle and the causal levels of consciousness in Wilber's scheme, as per Diagram 1, in the Appendix). In its own esoteric teachings and in other wisdom traditions, it can be subdivided into other levels, and would seem to cover every level above the physical. If there is a lack of emphasis on these levels in such records of Gautama's teachings as have been written down and passed down, it is in part because the Buddha had his life's work more than cut out for Him in giving humanity the Four Noble Truths and the Eightfold Path.

These were the teachings strictly necessary to enlightenment, and what could be understood and absorbed by humans-the uninitiated, of that time in that culture: *The Buddha himself would not discuss what happens after death, because such questions are not useful in the search for reality here and now. But the doctrine of reincarnation, the six kinds of existence, and the intermediate bardo state between them, refer very much to this life, whether or not they also apply after death'* says Francesca Fremantle, in her Introduction to the Shambhala Classics edition of the original 14th century Tibetan Book of the Dead, translated with commentary by Fremantle and Chogyam Trungpa (1975, p.xix).

More esoteric teachings were to wait till later when humanity was more ready for them, as we are beginning to be ready now. The Buddha's teaching was in any case, part of a long wisdom tradition

which dealt with all these esoteric matters if the student was ready
and searched for the knowledge; a tradition from which Buddhism
has been (only) partially separated in the ensuing centuries. The
Tibetan states that Those Who watch and guide humanity consider
the race ready for the next level of the teaching. These guides of humanity are the Buddha and the Bodhisattva, (known to Christianity
as the Christ, and referred to by that title in DK's writings, and
known he says, by other names in our other dominant traditions)-
and their co-workers and assistants. In his instructions to his own
disciples, published now as Discipleship in the New Age, he notes:
*'[O]ut of the chaos of the world war (precipitated by humanity itself) there
is developing a structure of truth and a paralleling responsiveness of the human mechanism which guarantees ...the rapid unfoldment of the next stage
of the teaching of the Ageless Wisdom'* (Bailey 1955, p. 314).

Where do we go after the physical level of existence?

Evans-Wentz, in his introduction to the 1927 *Tibetan Book of the
Dead*, considers the esoteric significance of the forty-nine days of
the Bardo's duration. He makes mention of the seven levels of being
in Northern or Tibetan Buddhism: that of the Mahayana school,
along with other aspects of esoteric knowledge common to the
Himalayan wisdom schools. The text of the Bardo Thodol is constructed around the sacred number seven and its square, forty-nine:

> *[A]ccording to occult teachings common to Northern Buddhism and to the
> Higher Hinduism which the Hindu-born Bodhisattva Who became the
> Buddha Gautama, the Reformer of the Lower Hinduism and the Codifier of
> the Secret Lore, never repudiated, there are seven worlds or seven degrees of
> Maya* [illusion-as contrasted with the Reality beyond manifestation]
> *within the Sangsara* [Samsara or manifested, illusory world], *constituted
> as seven globes of a planetary chain. On each globe there are seven rounds of
> evolution, making the forty-nine (seven times seven) stations of active exist-
> ence...[I]n both these interdependent embryonic processes, the one physical,
> the other psychical-the evolutionary and the involutionary attainments, cor-
> responding to the forty-nine stations of active existence, are passed through*
> (Evans-Wentz 1927 p.7).

The 'attainments' referred to, are the developments that take place
in a system or an individual, from the original moment of manifestation of a system and its lives, down through the levels of increasing
concretisation, to the greatest point of density of materialisation.
At this point the return cycle begins, and the evolutionary attainments begin to be garnered, via the cycle of increasing spiritualisa-
tion of matter through its imbuing with consciousness -- the divine
consciousness.

There are different schemes, both within the ancient traditions and in modern philosophy and transpersonal psychology, which define and describe the levels of manifestation and of development of consciousness (the forty-nine stations of active existence). These schemes have different numbers, names and descriptions of their phases, but they are in remarkable agreement. Ken Wilber's *Spectrum of Consciousness* (1977), developed in the *Atman Project* (1980) and subsequent books, is the first psychology to so comprehensively unite in itself, and thus demonstrate, the essential union of East and West. It unites all the prior schemes into a single, coherent, and wonderfully comprehensive map of the development of consciousness:

> *Manifest reality consists of different grades or levels, reaching from the lowest and most dense and least conscious (insentient matter) to the highest and most subtle and most conscious (superconscious spirit). Arrayed in between are the other dimensions of being arranged according to their individual degrees of reality (Plato), actuality (Aristotle), inclusiveness (Hegel) consciousness (Aurobindo), clarity (Leibniz), embrace (Plotinus), or knowingness (Garab Dorje)... Sometimes the Great Chain is presented as having just three major levels: matter, mind, and spirit...Other versions give five levels...Still others give very exhaustive breakdowns of the Great Chain...For the time being, our simple hierarchy of matter to body to mind to soul to spirit will suffice* (Wilber 1997, p.39).

The scheme I am using here to describe the stages of death, is narrower and more specific. It includes the physical body, etheric or vital body, emotional or astral body, mental body, soul body and spiritual body. (The correlation of this Ageless Wisdom scheme with Wilber's summary can be seen in Diagrams 1 and 3, in the Appendix.) All above the physical are not, of course, bodies in the physical sense. They are the denser containers or sheaths of the higher principle that vitalises them.

Once the physical level is left behind at death and the vital body has been shed, it is in fact the emotional level, the astral level, where we are likely to arrive first, though this is dependent on our degree of evolution. A Marie Curie or a Stephen Hawking will arrive immediately on the mental level at least, by virtue of having developed their mental apparatus or body, and functioning fully and normally in everyday life, on that level. The majority of human beings instead spend most of their time reacting emotionally, thrashing around in the subjective fog of their feelings and responses to the world, rather than in thought about the objective reality of that world. Attitudes, opinions, prejudices, preconceptions, received wisdom, folklore and traditional responses take the place of true thought for this majority. In between these two poles is a large and growing group of us who have access to the mental plane and the world of ideas. You must be among this group, given that you are reading these words and have come this far in the mind journey that the book presents!

It is likely that a Nelson Mandela or Mahatma Ghandi or an Elisabeth Kubler-Ross is sufficiently developed to leave their dogmatisms and personality flaws behind, travel through the lower levels, the emotional and mental, rapidly, and arrive at the Buddhic plane- the place of the intuitive Mind. At this level Mind is intuitive because the subject who can function on such a relatively high plane, loves with inclusiveness, and has thus stretched the boundaries of selfhood to encompass all other lives. These lives now lie open to that subject's (intuitive) perception in the same way that everything within the domain of one's own ordinary human selfhood lies open to each of us who is a 'possessor' of that selfhood.

So, there is now an answer to the question posed earlier – Why do we travel into light and the mind, not darkness and the gross physical level? It is due to the nature of the whole cosmos, and the relationship between the physical and non-physical levels of being. Once we leave the physical body, we also lose our hold on the physical level, and our ability to move about and communicate in physical ways. The loss of the gross physical component of our being automatically takes us into the subtler realms and levels, referred to generically by Buddhism as Mind. Why do we see the Light? It is due to the further decrease of density and materiality experienced with every higher level, and the corresponding increase in the light from which even the physical level is made. The light reported by NDErs corresponds to the light of the Ground Luminosity, and to the background sea of light of the Zero Point Field which sustains all apparently concrete manifestation, as reported by scientists Haisch, Rueda and Puthoff in Chapter One. It is experienced when and because we travel out of the now-lifeless physical body into the light of the all-encompassing Mind, either briefly or permanently.

Sogyal Rinpoche remarks similarly that the process of dying is: *'a gradual... dawning of ever more subtle levels of consciousness. Each one emerges upon the successive dissolution of the constituents of body and mind, as the process moves gradually toward the revelation of the very subtlest consciousness of all: the Ground Luminosity or Clear Light'* (Sogyal 1992, p. 256).

Again, all this is explained in detail in upcoming chapters on the stages of death in Tibetan Buddhism and the Ageless Wisdom, through the teachings of D.K. in collaboration with Alice Bailey. Chapter Six goes into the **actual stages of the dying process,** firstly according to the Tibetan Buddhist tradition, and then as they are described by D.K. in the Alice Bailey books.

Chapter 6

Buddhism's No-soul and the Separation of Body and Consciousness

Summary Points

- Death is the movement from the physical state and world into another state of consciousness
- P.M.H Atwater's experience of death: *You are not your body...*
- Death in our religions is the separation of body and consciousness
- **Is there an identifiable Self or soul that survives death in Buddhism?**
- The reconciliation of Buddhism and the other faiths on self after death
- Eastern teachings on the true nature of death and the process of dying
- What happens after the death of the physical body?

- **The stages of death of the physical body, and the movement of consciousness into higher bodies according to Tibetan Buddhism and the Ageless Wisdom**
- Cardinal Benson's description of his own dying and after

Buddhism's No-soul and the Separation of Body and Consciousness

Were an Asiatic to ask me my definition of Europe, I should be forced to answer him: It is that part of the world which is haunted by the incredible delusion that man was created out of nothing, and that his present birth is his first entrance into life. Schopenhauer.

How does dying actually feel? Atwater's list of NDE survivors' experience

P.M.H Atwater is a Near-death survivor who searched for the truth about the NDE. This *'led me through ten states to speak with several thousand people and to find two hundred other survivors'* (Atwater 1988, p. 4). She distilled from their various experiences, the common elements, both of the NDE itself, and of the experience of the actual moment of dying. Atwater notes the NDErs' subsequent realization; that death is illusory, and that the reality is ongoing life and selfhood. This distillation of experience of several thousand NDE survivors also demonstrates the truth of the proposition, introduced in Chapter Five, that death is essentially *the shifting of consciousness onto a new plane* with its new conditions of life. Here is her summary of the subjective experience of dying. It illustrates the movement from the physical state and world into another state of consciousness.

What it feels like to die

Any pain to be suffered comes first. Instinctively you fight to live...

It is inconceivable to the conscious mind that any other reality could possibly exist beside the earth-world of matter bounded by time and space...

Your body goes limp. Your heart stops. No more air flows in or out.

You lose sight, feeling, and movement-although the ability to hear goes last...

Identity ceases. The 'you' that you once were becomes only memory.

There is no pain at the moment of death. Only peaceful silence...

The biggest surprise for most people in dying is to realize dying does not end life. Whether darkness or light comes next... the biggest surprise of all is to realize you are still you. You can still think, ... you can still see, hear, move, reason, wonder, feel, question, and tell jokes-if you wish.

You are still alive...more alive than since you were last born.

Only the way of this is different, ...because you no longer wear a dense body to filter and amplify the various sensations you had once regarded as the only valid indicators of what constitutes life. You had always been taught one has to wear a body to live.

If you expect to die when you die you will be disappointed.

The only thing dying does is help you release, slough off, and discard the 'jacket' you once wore (more commonly referred to as a 'body').

When you die you lose your body...

Nothing else is lost.

You are not your body... (Atwater 1988, pp. 10-11)[1].

Atwater underwent several NDE; it is interesting to compare the various NDE I've quoted so far, with the real thing- for example Robert Hugh Benson's actual death, quoted later in the chapter.

Death in our religions is the separation of body and consciousness

Hindus, Muslims, and Christians agree on this central aspect of death: that there is a separation of body and psyche, and that the immortal aspect of us, the psyche, continues. What about Buddhism? Sir John Woodroffe comments on this in his Foreword to The Tibetan Book of the Dead:

The need of some body always exists... and each of the four religions affirms that there is a subtle and death-surviving element -- vital and psychical -- in the physical body of flesh and blood, whether it be a permanent entity or Self, such as the Brahmanic Atma, the Moslem Ruh, and the Christian 'Soul', or whether it be only a complex of activities (or Skandha), psychical and physical, with life as their function-a complex in continual change, and therefore, a series of physical and psychical momentary states, successively generated the one from the other, a continuous transformation, as the Buddhists are said to hold. Thus to none of these faiths is death an absolute ending, but to all it is only the separation of the Psyche from the gross body [my emphasis]. The former then enters on a new life, whilst the latter, having lost its principle of animation, decays. As Dr Evans-Wentz so concisely says, Death disincarnates the 'soul-complex', as Birth incarnates it. In other words, Death is itself only an initiation into another form of life than that of which it is the ending (Woodroffe, in Evans-Wentz 1927, p. lxviii).

---

1. On her website, PMH Atwater gives free permission to quote from her work. See cinemind.com/atwater/FeelDie.html

So Buddhism, along with the other major religions, considers that death is a separation of consciousness from body: an initiation rather than an ending. This paragraph has been very carefully phrased by Woodroffe to deal with the difficulty of the Buddhist 'anatta' or no-soul teaching, which continues to cause misunderstanding and controversy. This is the teaching that there is no permanent and separate entity of selfhood, but rather a series of states of life and consciousness leading one into the other, or skandhas. These *'psycho-physical aggregates'* as the Dalai Lama refers to them, are, as Buddhists are taught, like candles, each one lit from the previous one, with the flame the consciousness emanating from each candlelike psycho-physical vehicle. This *'psycho-physical aggregates'* term means *'psyche combined with physical vehicle as long as there is one, that is, before separation from the body; thereafter the psyche or mind or consciousness, in its various increasingly less physical bodies'.*

Is there an identifiable Self that survives death in Buddhism?

There is much disagreement, and as I see it, misunderstanding, about the nature and implications of this Buddhist 'no-soul' teaching. Followers of Buddhism in East and West often take this *anatta* or no-soul teaching to mean that despite reincarnation, nothing identifiable with the 'I' of this life, survives: there is no continuity of consciousness across the border into post-death states.

Western Buddhists especially, may conclude it means *there is really no one there after death.* For these people, life after death in Buddhism may be reduced to the status of a dream, even one generated merely by the dying brain. It has been taken to mean that there is literally *no superphysical aspect* of us that survives death. One intelligent practitioner, a student for some years, even saw it as casting doubt on reincarnation. *'The Buddha didn't teach that we definitely reincarnate. How can we, when there is no soul?* this friend declared.

Some have abandoned Buddhism in despair at this apparent soullessness. If there is no identifiable self beyond the 'plane of illusion' of the physical world, how then can the individual life or experience really matter? Yet many Westerners are drawn to Buddhism by its no-soul and no-God doctrines, attracted as much by its apparent fit with the scientific and materialistic mindset of the last century or so, as its teachings of universal compassion and individual responsibility. They perceive it as a-theistic, along with Australian intellectual, iconoclast and critic of the Establishment, the broadcaster Philip

Adams (2005), when he said Buddhism was 'not really a religion, as I understand it'.

But what was Buddha's response to the God-question? He maintained the 'noble silence'. In his time there was debate among Brahmin sects about God's nature and even existence, says Chogyal Namkhai Norbu:

> But instead of affirming or denying the existence of a Supreme Being as the first cause, the Buddha advised his disciples to leave aside all doubts and speculation and to strive to attain the state of Enlightenment in which questions disappear and clarity manifests. (Chogyal Namkai Norbu, 2000, p. 90).

In other words, stop sitting around down here arguing about it; meditate until you can go there and find out for yourself!

My own response is that it depends on what you mean by God, whether Buddhism is godless or not. This is further discussed later. Buddha may have changed the emphasis on God because of humanity's wrong attitude. We did not understand that there is no separation; there is essentially nothing but the One Life, the One Self. At the lowest level, there was a childish dependence on the idea of a Big Daddy who would fix everything if we just slaughtered enough goats, gave enough alms or said enough prayers. At a higher level, there was a need to heal the illusion of a separate Creator, and of little helpless humans without connection (except through priestly intercession), with their all-powerful master, and therefore *without responsibility* for creation of and in their own lives and the universe.

Theravada versus Mahayana Buddhism on Soul

Theravada Buddhism takes a more conservative view of the Buddha's teachings than the Northern schools. There is the curious fact that Helena Blavatsky, founder of Theosophy (God-wisdom or study), was the one who, along with Colonel Olcott, revived Buddhism in Ceylon, the present-day Sri Lanka, where Theravada Buddhism has a much more pronounced flavour of no-God, no-soul than Mahayana Buddhism. What does a modern scholar of the world's religions, deeply appreciative of the unity underlying their multiplicity, have to say? Nicholas Coleman's book *The Worlds of Religion* (1999) was written in response to the evidence that so many are adrift, suffering lack of meaning in the absence of God or tradition. The book attempts to satisfy 'the yearnings of the young who want food for the soul.' Does Coleman find himself denying the soul in Buddhism to satisfy the soul of young Australians?:

Buddhists of different schools are still discussing the exact meaning and extent of [The Buddha] *Sakyamuni's denial of the soul. The liberal opinion of the Mahayana (also known as the Northern or Tibetan school of Buddhism) is that the Buddha did accept the existence of the universal or Enlightened Self (which is equivalent to the Absolute Brahman of the Upanishads), and only denied the genuine reality of the individual self, or personal ego. The conservative view of the Theravadins is that the Buddha denied both the individual and the universal self* (Coleman 1999, p. v).

Surely this contradicts Buddha's teaching on reincarnation? There had to be a soul by any other name, for the Buddha to have experienced all his incarnations as part of his Enlightenment under the Bodhi-tree. There had to be something which linked one incarnation to another, and was capable of experiencing them and holding the memory of them. In the quote above, from the Foreword to the Tibetan Book of the Dead, Woodroffe explains that *each of the four religions affirms a subtle and death-surviving element whether soul or skandha.* Woodroffe uses the term 'psyche' to refer to this disputed 'soul' element. He also quotes the book's editor, Evans-Wentz, referring to the 'soul-complex'. The point that must be emphatically underlined, is that they would have no need of any term like psyche or soul-complex if Buddhism had no soul-concept. Woodroffe would be unable to include Buddhism in the religions that affirm a death-surviving element.

Yet there is an obvious need for an English term for the superphysical body states; that is, those states or skandhas which provide consciousness and the sense of coherent selfhood *after the death of the physical body and disintegration of its associated skandhas.* Unless Buddhism denies consciousness and coherent selfhood to the death-surviving element? This cannot be the case. The Buddha's great gift to humanity was to teach us that the suffering of incarnation could be ended by the *release of consciousness* from attachment to and entrapment within that which is material and temporary and therefore ultimately illusory.

Buddha, reincarnation and the soul

There would be no point at all, in ending the suffering of incarnation by obtaining the release of something unconscious or not self-conscious, even if it were possible. Self-consciousness is required to obtain the release, and to realize that it has been obtained. The Buddha taught us that we must strive through successive incarnations to make that consciousness Buddha-like and universal, by understanding the Four Noble Truths and following the Eightfold

Path to Enlightenment. These create a steady evolution and enlargement of consciousness through discipline, compassionate action and spiritual practices. Buddhism is therefore founded on the teaching that a coherent consciousness of a higher Self *does* survive death. It is merely the nature of that higher Self that is in dispute.

How do Tibetan Buddhist teachers themselves refer to the disputed concept when writing in English? They all speak of the *'mind'* or the *'mental body'*. They mean by this the higher sheath or body; *that which encloses consciousness after the death of the physical body* and the loss of the brain which has both enabled consciousness to function, and limited it. (The NDE was shown in Chapter Three not to be capable of reduction to any ordinary, material world explanation. It became clear that brain and mind were functionally quite separate in all the studies of the nature of the Near-death Experience.) Sogyal Rinpoche prefers the terms 'mind', and 'mental body' for this state of super-body consciousness; for example in the quote in Chapter Five when he says of the similarity of the NDE experience and the one known in Tibetan Buddhism, that in the NDE, *'the mind, released from the [physical] body, goes through a number of experiences akin to the mental body in the bardo of becoming'*. Chogyam Trungpa uses the term 'mind', along with 'the person', for example when he is discussing the reading of the Tibetan Book of the Dead to the newly-dead: *Your stability is part of (that of) the dying person...Just relate with him, just open to each other simultaneously, and develop the meeting of the two minds'* (Fremantle and Chogyam Trungpa, 1975, p. 29).

A Westerner renowned for helping to open the doors of the Eastern wisdom is also easily able to reconcile 'soul' and 'anatta', Buddhism's 'no-soul' concept. LSD populariser Timothy Leary's colleague Richard Alpert, later known as Ram Dass, says:

> *'We can refer to that part of the individual that passes through the veil of physical death as the "soul", even though we may understand that this "soul" is itself but a subtler thought form that eventually dissolves as the fullness of the Buddhist term anatta (no-self) is realized* (Ram Dass 1990, p. 161).

The renowned transpersonal psychologist introduced in Chapters One and Five, Ken Wilber, recognised *the identity* of the transpersonal realms discovered in his research, with the mystical realms of the perennial philosophy. He based his resulting scheme upon the stages of the Tibetan Book of the Dead. Yet Wilber, like Ram Dass, uses the term 'soul', along with 'spirit', in his analysis of the dying process, a term neither would use as scholars of Buddhism if it had no soul-concept.

The reconciliation of Buddhism and the other faiths on self after death

Thus what anatta really means is that there is no *separate, eternal, unchanging* self or Soul, but rather Woodroffe's *'series of physical and psychical ... states, successively generated the one from the other, a continuous transformation'*, (Evans-Wentz 1927, p lxviii), just like the lighting of one candle from another. This is quite compatible with the logical need for and belief in, a centre of consciousness that is capable of a panoramic ethical overview of incarnated life. Does it, in the end, matter whether we conceptualise this as a somewhat more permanent unit of consciousness, or a series of skandhas or attributes, leading one into another? Buddhism is focussing on the movement, the process; the other major religions are focussed on that which moves; the content.

Buddhism is correct that there is nothing permanent: that consciousness is always in transition. Christianity, Hinduism, Islam and Judaism are missing this constant transition and renovation of consciousness in focusing on an everlasting, indestructible Soul; Buddhism is in danger of misleading its adherents that there is no overriding consciousness and no coherent selfhood after death, which teaching is the great virtue of the other religions.

The last word surely belongs to the Dalai Lama. The book *The Buddha Nature: death and eternal soul in Buddhism* (Dalai Lama 1997), is a record of the Dalai Lama's teachings to Dr Peter Michel on these topics.

His Holiness says in reply to Dr Michel:

> *When we refute the soul, or atman, theory, we are refuting the theory of a substantial, independent person. There is no independent self that exists substantially, from its own side.* [There isn't a soul existing self-generated, self-perpetuating, separately from the Universal Self.] *However the self, or person, does exist dependent on the psychophysical aggregates.'* [The existence of a self is dependent on there being a 'place' for the Universal Consciousness to separate, centre and focus, which it can only do in a body or sheath of one sort or another, whether physical or more subtle.] *This applies to all beings, from the level of ordinary sentient beings up to Buddha...*[This Buddhist teaching of] *Anatman is the mere negation of a self that is supposed to exist...substantially and independently of the psychophysical aggregates.*

Dr Michel summarises: *'The wide-spread idea that the anatman (notself) teachings negate eternal individuality, has led to misunderstandings, especially among practitioners of Western religions.'* (Dalai Lama 1997, p. 38). The conclusion is that the anatta or not-self teachings do not in fact, negate eternal individuality, or the existence of a self or soul/ spirit in the terminology of Christianity, who continues forever, even when becoming ever more identical with the One Self, the One Life, and therefore ceasing to be our human idea of an individual, separated self; becoming, that is, increasingly No-self and All-Self.

Eastern teachings on the reality beyond death, and the process and stages of dying

Our major traditions agree that body and psyche separate at death. At this point the Western and Middle Eastern traditions diverge from the Eastern. In the East dying does not lead immediately to Heaven and Eternity, but is part of the cyclical process of the Great Wheel of existence, leading (usually) to another incarnation. What, then, does the East believe about the nature of death and its processes?

Many Western seekers of the wisdom of the East have knowledge of Hindu teachings. They have been popularised since the Sixties by such gurus as Yogananda, author of *Autobiography of a Yogi* (1946), one of the first lives of modern saints of the East to be widely known in the West; Maharishi Mahesh Yogi, the Beatles' guru, Meher Baba, Baba Muktananda and others. However, as there is a common source of Hinduism and Buddhism anyway, and since Hinduism is closely identified with the Ageless Wisdom teachings, and still very similar to Buddhism, and Buddhism is currently more popular in the West even than Hinduism, I have chosen not to discuss Hindu beliefs.

There are teachings, texts of Tibetan Buddhism and the Ageless Wisdom which *go into detail about the after-death states and places.* What do these two schools of spirituality, apparently from the same source, have to say about the reality beyond death, and the process and stages of dying? Do they give any checkable or correlating detail; to suggest they may both have access to some truths unknown at present to Western science? *Or do they each appear to the rational Western mind merely as separate and quite fascinatingly elaborated cultural myths designed to ease the pain and fear of dying?*

How to recognise the universal mind or Buddha nature, to avoid reincarnation

Buddhism understands dying as merely the passage into a further stage of life. However, whether that stage is a good or bad experience depends on our approach to it. Tibetan Buddhism teaches that we need to be familiar with the stages of dying and the signs that accompany them, and to keep practising - meditating, through them. It is essential to establish the practice well before death, so we can keep it up right through the dying process, and not become lost in the various fears and illusions accompanying different stages of dying. We can then recognise the vital moment of the dawning of Clear Light or universal mind, and seize the moment to enter into a higher state of awareness. This short-circuits the otherwise unending round of birth and death.

This Clear Light state is the Reality underlying all in the concrete physical world; the cosmic sea of light in which we are immersed, (discovered by quantum physics[2]), is one level of its manifestation. Recognition of this will prevent us wandering in delusion and bewilderment through the Bardo of Becoming to an incarnation that is not properly chosen. Such a life is likely to lead us downward, deeper into the mire of illusion in incarnation, instead of upward into the Buddha nature and release from incarnation. Escape from the cycle of birth and death is the goal; we must seize the moment of dawning of Rigpa to achieve it.

This entire prospect-that we are condemned to delusion and ignorance, unless dedicated and spiritually hungry enough to pursue Enlightenment at whatever cost to our present lives, looks grim indeed to most Westerners who contemplate Buddhism, however briefly. Those of us who struggle with depression especially, (my impression is that the majority of us do at some time), and who may have already decided that we would prefer to cease existing altogether at the end of this life, are hardly likely to find these teachings an encouragement to change our minds. If you find yourself among this group, please keep reading! Tibetan Buddhism as it is often understood in the West especially, does not offer more than a rough and quite dispiriting sketch of the afterlife or interlife period. There is a great deal more to be revealed, particularly through research into recently explored areas of mind and spirit, almost all of it joyful at

---

2. See earlier references to this in Chapter One, in the work of Haisch et al.

the very least. (How much of the depression which is epidemic in the West, could be relieved by a massive injection of hope and positivity, such as could happen with a change of understanding about the nature of reality?)

The process of death of the physical body

This next summary of the Tibetan teachings on physical death sheds light on a process about which most of us would rather remain in deepest ignorance! This is especially the case, as the aspect of death that causes greatest concern to older people, (next to the disappearance of those we love into the Great Silence, and the grief and loss of meaning this may bring), is less likely to be non-continuance, than the pain and suffering which precedes death. However, no account of Tibetan Buddhist teachings on death would be complete without it: the teachings emphasise that it is important to know the stages of the process, and their accompanying signs. They are the signs on the roadmap that help the Driver of consciousness through death, to retain a sense of control.

Tibetan Buddhism teaches that dying is a process of dissolution of the elements which make up our body and our mind, in order from the *grossest to the subtlest*, Sogyal Rinpoche explains (1992, p. 250).

Chogyam Trungpa says that the Tibetan Book of the Dead *describes the death experience in terms of the different elements of the body, going deeper and deeper.'* (Fremantle and Chogyam Trungpa 1975, p. 4).

Ken Wilber calls it 'dissolving the Great Chain of Being':

> That is, [in the Buddhist system] upon death, the body dissolves into mind, then mind dissolves into soul, then soul dissolves into spirit, with each of these dissolutions marked by a specific set of events (1990, p. 176).

The first major stage in the Tibetan tradition is that of the Outer dissolution: the senses and the elements (Sogyal p. 251ff.). Our senses cease to function -- first hearing, then sight, and then smell, taste and touch. (P. M. H. Atwater, in the quote near the beginning of this chapter, says hearing is the last to go. I have no explanation for this discrepancy-though it could be cultural). This begins the first phase of the dissolution process. There are four more phases, each due to the dissolution of one of the elements, and each with its characteristic secret sign, recognition of which aids the dying person. The first of these is the Earth element. Its dissolution, of the aggregate of form, means that our body loses its strength, as the earth element is withdrawing into the water element, which takes over in its ability to support consciousness.

The dissolution of the Water element, with the aggregate of feeling, manifests in loss of control of bodily fluids and bodily sensations. Here the secret sign to the dying person is the vision of a haze with swirls of smoke.

The Fire dissolution stage follows. We lose bodily warmth. The aggregate of perception is dissolving, and we no longer recognize familiar people.

The fire element dissolves into Air. During this stage we struggle to breathe, and our mind becomes bewildered with the dissolution of the aggregate of intellect. Its sign is known as 'fireflies', as fire dissolving into air creates momentary sparks. This next passage tells of a dying experience worrying to Western students of Buddhism. However it ends in reassurance from Sogyal:

> [I]f there has been a lot of negativity in our lives, we may see terrifying forms. Haunting and dreadful moments of our lives are replayed, and we may even try to cry out in terror. If we have led lives of kindness and compassion, we may experience blissful, heavenly visions, and 'meet' loving friends or enlightened beings.
>
> **For those who have led good lives, there is peace in death instead of fear** [my emphasis. The air element dissolves into the higher, subtler element from which it is derived: mind or consciousness. Then the winds or pranic life energies collect in the heart, along with three drops of blood]. 'Then, suddenly, our breathing ceases...
>
> All vital signs are gone, **and this is the point where in a modern clinical situation we would be certified as 'dead'** [my emphasis] (Sogyal Rinpoche 1992, p. 253).

Yet, in this process of concentration, extraction and dissolution, which will result in the release of consciousness or the psyche from the physical sheath, the inner 'respiration' continues for approximately twenty minutes according to Tibetan masters.

This is death as the Western world understands it: the victim lying lifeless on the bed, the body stiffening into rigor mortis. Now the Tibetan Book of the Dead depicts the individual moving into the After-death States, and consciousness shifting out of the physical body and into subtler centres or bodies of expression and experience.

Death and birth as movement between the universal and the concrete levels of being

Stephen Levine (1990) writes about death and this shifting, from the experience of assisting dying patients with his wife Ondrea. He had become close to Robin, who was dying of bone cancer. She encouraged him to go to his retreat though her death, they both knew, was close. Deep in meditation at the retreat, Stephen began to feel pain, and pressure preventing him from breathing. He managed to stay open to the experience, through intensifying pain and increasing difficulty drawing breath:

> *Then, about ten minutes into the experience, I heard Robin's voice saying, "We've been so close, we've shared so much, and there is really nothing I can give you. But I know you want to know what it's like to die, so I am sharing my death with you."...The effort to breathe was becoming even more difficult, and I watched my body starting to vibrate with a sense of emergency... I felt fear arising as I watched the body trying to hold on, contracting almost as if it were involuntarily trying to encapsulate or contain the 'fire', the life force inside itself, trying not to let it out...(The description of this 'dying' continues.) Perhaps twenty-five minutes into the experience, I felt as though I was being evicted from my body by the pressure in my lungs. I continued to watch the body trying to hold on, even more on 'alert' than before, with the mind trying to think its way out of the situation. But there was no room for control...I felt like a tube of toothpaste being squeezed with its top still on* (Levine 1990, pp. 226-7).

At this point in his death, my own father, Douglas Shore, became frightened, and was calling "Help me!" I didn't know enough then, to be of very much use, except to squeeze his hand and repeat that I was there with him and would stay. The solution to this suffering is revealed below by Stephen Levine: cease to identify with the body. "Don't fight to breathe, Dad. Just let go into the next stage of living", I should have told him.

Levine continues:

> *Finally, however, the mind said, "Stay in? Why?" No answer came. And suddenly there was great peace... It was as though I had remembered something that I had forgotten a long time before, perhaps since birth...Death was no longer a threat, but became another inconsequential bubble in the flow of change and the sense of joyous expectancy...I felt a pervasive sense of knowing that everything was as it should be, and the certainty of this knowing converted the pain and pressure ejecting me from my body into an ally, instead of an enemy...And again I heard Robin's voice, this time saying, "It's time to stop being Robin and become Christ dying"...Then I no longer*

identified even with "someone" dying-and just experienced the process itself in its perfect unfolding...And I knew that dying was just another part of living (Levine 1990, p. 226-7).[3]

Levine had no way of knowing, in the middle of his retreat, that his experience coincided exactly with Robin's death. Despite this, conventional psychology and psychiatry would interpret this experience of another's death, and of dying as just a stage in the ongoing process of life, as mere fantasy. Given our culture shaped by science, we are likely to regard any transpersonal elements of death, including the sense of survival, as imaginary. Otherwise, why, at birth, don't we experience a similar process in reverse; descending from transcendent realms, to the concrete and physical, via a process whose stages are commonly recognized if not remembered, like those of the Near-death Experience?

Stanislav Grof's research over seventeen years beginning in Prague in 1956 shows just such a process, in birth as in death:

Clinical observations from LSD psychotherapy suggest that the human unconscious contains repositories or matrices, the activation of which leads to the reliving of biological birth and a profound confrontation with death. The resulting process of death and rebirth is typically associated with an opening of intrinsic spiritual areas in the human mind that are independent of the individual's racial, cultural and educational background (Grof 1985 p. 3)[4].

Consciousness does not begin post-natally, as our science has assumed; Grof discovered that being born is a traumatic and terrifying experience, involving the struggle to survive the several stages of this process, of an individual *in whom consciousness is already well established*. It's not unlike being trapped in an earthquake or tornado- just ask a neonate! It seems to have some parallel in the dark tunnel of exit from the body, and in the earthquakes and tornadoes reported by Tibetan Buddhism, of the lower Bardo experience.

Grof's work with patients led to the discovery of the critical nature of our experience of the birth process in our personal psychology, and to the development of his pioneering transpersonal psychology:

Transpersonal experiences have many strange characteristics that shatter the most fundamental assumptions of materialistic science and the mechanistic worldview... On the one hand, they form an experiential continuum with biographical and perinatal experiences [that is, with known events. Many

---

3. 'What Survives?' by Stephen Levine, copyright© 1990 by Stephen Levine. Extracts used by permission of Jeremy P. Tarcher, an imprint of Penguin Group (USA) Inc.

4. Extracts from Stanislav Grof's *Beyond the Brain, 1985*, are used with permission of Dr Grof.

specific details of clients' birth experiences correlated with their medical records]. *On the other hand, they frequently appear to be tapping directly, without the mediation of the sensory organs, sources of information that are clearly outside of the conventionally defined range of the individual.* [Grof was struck by the accuracy of instances of these phenomena, some of which he was able to verify.] *They can involve conscious experience of other humans ...microscopic and astronomic realms not accessible to the unaided senses, history and prehistory, the future.... Perinatal experiences seem to represent ...a frontier between the personal and transpersonal-a fact reflected in their connection with birth and death, the beginning and end of individual existence⁵. Transpersonal phenomena reveal connections between the individual and the cosmos that seem at present to be beyond comprehension,* [and which involve] *the superconscious mind* (Grof 1985, p. 127).

Birth, then, involves the experience of moving from the cosmic unitary level of consciousness, through stages to the concrete, separate bodily experience, just as death involves the reverse process.

What happens after the death of the physical body? Inner Dissolution

This next phase is an important element in Tibetan Buddhist teachings about the passage through death. Practitioners are taught to identify the stages of Inner Dissolution; which are Appearance, Increase, and Full Attainment, leading to the dawning of Ground Luminosity; Clear Light. They learn to recognise the accompanying signs, so as to seize the moment of the dawning of Rigpa, the Clear Light state, and be set free from the cycle of rebirth:

> *Then, as we become slightly conscious again, the Ground Luminosity dawns, like an immaculate sky free of clouds, fog or mist. It is sometimes called "the mind of clear light of death". His Holiness the Dalai Lama says: "This consciousness is the innermost subtle mind. We call it the buddha nature, the real source of all consciousness. The continuum of this mind lasts even through Buddhahood"'* [my emphasis] (Sogyal 1992, p. 254).

We have now travelled through death, from the stages of demise of the physical body and its discarding, moving into higher and subtler

---

5. Ken Wilber makes an important criticism of the logic of Grof's consequent claim that access to the transcendent realm is through the reliving (via LSD or breathwork) of these perinatal experiences. Wilber says that this is the backdoor (or involutionary) route to the transcendent, as opposed to the route taught for millennia in the perennial philosophy, which gives access through meditation. Grof's work also '*demonstrates that all deep perinatal experiences involve intense life-and-death issues; it does not in the least demonstrate that all life-and-death issues are perinatal*' (Wilber 1997, p. 171).

levels of consciousness, through Inner Dissolution, into the Ground Luminosity of Rigpa, the buddha nature, the real source of all consciousness. It is worth reiterating and extending the quote of Ken Wilber on 'dissolving the Great Chain of Being':

> 'That is, upon death, the body dissolves into mind, then mind dissolves into soul, then soul dissolves into spirit, with each of these dissolutions marked by a specific set of events. Buddhists see us moving from the individual embodied consciousness bounded by one's personal self and life-history, through gross, intermediate and subtle mind, to a merging of the separate self with the One Self, the buddha nature (Wilber, 1990, p. 176).

Death is freedom from the illusion of the physical world

Padmasambhava, the great teacher and founder of Tibetan Buddhism, said of the ignorance that sustains this illusion: *All beings have lived and died and been reborn countless times. Over and over again they have experienced the indescribable Clear Light. But because they are obscured by the darkness of ignorance, they wander endlessly in a limitless samsara [cycle of birth, physical life and death]* (Sogyal 1992, p. 261).

We overcome death permanently when our consciousness is sufficiently developed to recognize Universal Mind, the Buddha Nature, and to 'see through' the illusion of physical life.

The Tibetan sage, Djwhal Khul, explains that our usual idea of death is erroneous. He characterises death for most of us as:

> the cataclysmic end, involving... the severing of all signs of love and of affection, and the passage (unwilling and protesting) into the unknown and the dreaded. It is analogous to leaving a lighted and warmed room, friendly and familiar, where our loved ones are assembled, and going out into the cold and dark night, alone and terror stricken, hoping for the best and sure of nothing. (Bailey 1934, reference edition 1979, p. 494).

Yet this is not at all the reality of death. Just as Buddhism teaches, the experience of death is essentially about where, and of what, we are conscious. It is about achieving release from the consciousness trapped in the illusion of the body and material world as the beginning and end of existence. Westerners are likely to feel that this is something we will only accomplish by retreating to a monastery or a mountain cave for a lifetime. Yet it is not that difficult; it is a matter, at least initially, of consciousness, of understanding, of a renovation of perspective and attitude.

The Tibetans, says D.K., refer to the process of death as "entering into the clear cold light". Death is merely the experience which frees us from the illusion of form. *'Death, in the last analysis,*

*and from the standpoint of the average human being, is simply **disappear-**
ance from the physical plane – the plane of appearances' [my em-
phasis] (Bailey 1960, p. 309). It is implied here, that we travel in
death, from that foggy illusion into the clear cold light of reality, of
Rigpa.

Dying is something we practise frequently, D.K. reminds us. We
have died, and shall die again many times. His next assurance is perhaps the most comforting of all. Death, for us as conscious individuals, is not about what happens to the body, it is about what happens
to the psyche. It is not about a slow and terrible material decay into
non-existence, it is about a swift movement in consciousness: *'Death*
is essentially a matter of consciousness. We are conscious one moment on the
physical plane, and a moment later we have withdrawn onto another plane
and are actively conscious there.'

Death is similar to sleep

Elsewhere, he reminds us that we practise a form of dying every
night, when we withdraw consciousness from the sleeping body, and
'go abroad' onto the astral plane for a few hours. We are unable to
bring back any clear recollection of this into the sleeping brain, so
we fail to see the similarity of death and sleep. There is one critical
difference. A current of energy or magnetic thread, sometimes
called the Silver Cord, joins the emotional-astral body to the
physical body via the etheric body. In sleep this cord remains intact,
making it possible to return to our bodies. In death the cord is
snapped, and there can be no return to that body. The cord is still
intact in those who have undergone clinical death and returned in a
Near-death Experience.

Once we have grasped this identity of sleep and death, our consciousness is no longer identified solely with the physical world:

> *Just as long as consciousness is identified with the form aspect, death will*
> *hold for us its ancient terror. Just as soon as we know ourselves to be souls,*
> *and find that we are capable of focussing our consciousness or sense of aware-*
> *ness in any form or on any plane at will, or in any direction within the form*
> *of God, we shall no longer know death* (Bailey 1934, reference edition
> 1979, p. 22).

It is this development of consciousness that is referred to in the
Tibetan tradition, when we are urged to seize the moment of the
dawning of Rigpa, the universal Mind-essence, so as to be free of the
physical realm and the necessity to reincarnate.

How amazingly simple is this idea! Yet how liberating it proves to be! This is regardless of the difficulty and steady, concentrated effort -- in meditation chiefly -- required to put it into practice and thus know its truth from direct experience. It is not necessary, however, to have this direct experience of higher states and worlds. It is possible to grasp the concepts of these teachings, and simply understand that there is no death because the material world contains only a part of ourselves, and a very limited and finite part at that. The Tibetan practices traditionally and potentially offer Enlightenment, and freedom from reincarnation. The freedom offered by simply grasping the idea is not as great, but it is a measure of real, vital liberation, which is our goal.

Lama Kazi Dawa-Samdup, the great Tibetan scholar, worked with W.Y. Evans-Wentz to translate the Bardo Thodol into The Tibetan Book of the Dead, the first English version. Another great Lama responsible for making the Tibetan teachings accessible to the West, Anagarika Govinda, wrote in his Introductory Foreword to that book:

> *This illusoriness* [ie this illusion] *of death comes from the identification of the individual with his temporal, transitory form, whether physical, emotional, or mental, whence arise[s] the mistaken notion that there exists a personal, separate egohood of one's own, and the fear of losing it.* [This is the essence of the no-soul doctrine of Buddhism-the doctrine of Anatman or Anatta-the denial of the 'mistaken notion' of a permanent separate egohood.] *If however, the disciple has learned, as the Bardo Thodol directs, to identify himself with the Eternal, the Dharma, the Imperishable Light of Buddhahood within, then the fears of death are dissipated like a cloud before the rising sun* (Lama Anagarika Govinda, in Evans-Wentz 1927, p. lxii).

It is true; it is not the personal self that reincarnates. Susan Shore will come to an end with my death. This is not however, the same as saying that there is nothing beyond that temporary body-personality of any one of us. P. M. H. Atwater (1988) in the quotation' *What it feels like to die'* near the beginning of this chapter, draws our attention to the same paradox: *The you that you once were has become only memory*, versus *The biggest surprise of all is to realise you are still you.* This is the paradox of identity that becomes apparent at death. Atwater's first 'you' refers to the personality, the second to the enduring Self.

The process of physical death in the Ageless Wisdom

An 'Extract from a Statement by The Tibetan, D.K.,' prefaces each of his books, written through and with Alice Bailey. He is a Tibetan disciple 'of a certain degree' as are *all from the humblest aspirant up to, and beyond, the Christ Himself.* [The Buddha is a disciple 'beyond the Christ Himself'].

The Tibetan explains:

> *I live in a physical body like other men, on the borders of Tibet, and at times (from the exoteric standpoint) preside over a large group of Tibetan lamas, when my other duties permit. It is this fact which has caused it to be reported that I am an abbot of this particular lamasery [i.e. the head monk]...I am a brother of yours, who has travelled a little longer upon the Path than has the average student, and has therefore incurred greater responsibilities ...My work is to teach and spread the knowledge of the Ageless Wisdom wherever I can find a response, and I have been doing this for many years...*

> *The books that I have written are sent out with no claim for their accept-ance... It is for you to ascertain their truth by right practice and by the exer-cise of the intuition. Neither I nor AAB [Alice Bailey] is interested in...having anyone speak of them...as being the work of one of the Masters.*

The sequence of events at a deathbed

So what enlightenment on the subject is to be found, in the two ac-counts of death of these sources emanating from Tibet? Sogyal Rin-poche and Chogyam Trungpa describe the equivalent phases of death in their respective books, as the dissolution of the senses and the elements as we have seen, into space and consciousness. D.K speaks of death as the process of separation of *the inner person* from the physical body, and that body's subsequent disintegration into its component elements so that restitution may be made of them to the reservoir of substance of which all forms are made. This corresponds with the processes described by Sogyal Rinpoche, of dissolution of the elements which compose the body-personality. Both teachers also speak of the nadis, the channels of vital force underlying and in-terpenetrating the physical body, and of the energy that flows through these channels to vitalise the entire body.

However, the physiology of the dying process seems clearer, to the Western mind at least, as the process and its stages is described by D.K. (Bailey 1953, pp. 472-8). The vital element of dying is explained by D.K. – the governing role of the soul or subtle mind, under the direction of still higher elements of the One Self, in the timing, the instigation and the process itself, of dying. This is a perspective that is gained more obliquely, from a Westerner's reading of the Tibetan accounts, in their reference to the hour of death being karmically determined, for example.

'The soul sounds forth a "word of withdrawal" from its own plane, and immediately an interior process and reaction is evoked within the man upon the physical plane.' The quotes in this section and elsewhere, on the sequence of events in the dying process, have been gathered out of the works of Alice A. Bailey and published in Death, the Great Adventure (1985), where they appear on page 66 and following pages. The quotations below are taken from Bailey 1953, Esoteric Healing, pp. 472-478.

> 1. This brings about *'certain physiological events'* at the seat of the disease and in the blood stream, the nervous system and the endocrine system. These events are well documented in the pathology of death, says D.K.

The soul has called, quite literally. The first part of the response involves the higher bodies of the 'dying' individual organizing to separate from the physical body. This takes place by disentanglement of the etheric body (containing the emotional and mental bodies) from the physical body, which it has vitalized since gestation of that body in the mother's womb. These separating events prompted by the soul's call begin in the etheric nervelines, the nadis.

> 2. *A vibration runs along these subtle nervelines or nadis:*
>
> *The nadis are... the etheric counterpart of the entire nervous system, and they underlie every nerve in the entire physical body. They are the agents ... of the **directing impulses of the soul** [my emphasis], reacting to the vibratory activity which emanates from the etheric counterpart of the brain. They respond to the directing Word, react to the "pull" of the soul, and then organise themselves for abstraction',* D.K. explains.

The word from the soul has been registered, and the higher aspects or bodies of the individual must extricate themselves from the physical body, which has finished its job and must now be left behind. The physical is that sole element and aspect of ourselves which truly dies. The extrication cannot take place until the physical body has been prepared for the separation and its death: if possible, the etheric body should not be ripped out violently from a still-living physical body.

The next step requires **the preparation of the physical body for its death** and disintegration. D.K. reveals an occult process which is the real cause behind the stopping of the heart -- the final cause of death:

> 3. ...*The glands, in **response to the call of death**, inject into the blood stream a **substance which in turn affects the heart**. There the life thread is anchored, and this substance in the blood is regarded as "death-dealing", and is one of the basic causes of coma and of loss of consciousness. This substance and its effect will be questioned as yet by orthodox medicine, but its presence will later be recognised.*

The heart has now been stopped, and can no longer anchor the life-thread, which is freed from the physical body. Once the heart has stopped, as became clear in Chapter 3, the other systems and the organs will also cease functioning.

> 4. The psychic tremor resulting from the vibration in the nadis of Step 2 breaks the connection between the nadis and the nervous system, which detaches the etheric body from the physical body, starting in the eyes.

> 5. There is often a pause, to make the loosening process as gentle and painless as possible:

> *This is the stage in which-the fear of death once and for all removed from the racial mind, the friends and relatives of the departing person will "make a festival" for him and will rejoice with him because he is relinquishing the body.*

The Tibetan here indicates the changed attitude to death which will result from knowledge of its true nature.

> 6. The etheric body, containing the integrated energies of the emotional or astral body and the mental body, gathers itself together prior to separation and exit. It withdraws to the exit point of solar plexus, heart or head, awaiting the final "pull" of the soul.

There are three usual points of exiting the physical body: the head *'for disciples and initiates and also for advanced mental types; the heart for aspirants, for men of goodwill, and for all those who have achieved a measure of personality integrity and are attempting to fulfil, as far as in them lies, the law of love; and the solar plexus for the undeveloped and emotionally polarised persons'.*

This same stage of exit through one or another point is expounded by Sir John Woodroffe in his 'Foreword; the Science of Death' in *The Tibetan Book of the Dead* (Evans-Wentz 1927, p. lxx). He mentions the pressing of the arteries, as the Tibetan, D.K., also does, as the means of assisting the exit of the life force through the Brahmarandra, the fontanel or Foramen of Monro, and into a higher state after death. This idea is, as he says, common to many cultures:

'A good exit is one which is above the navel...the best is through the fissure on the top of the cranium called Brahmarandhra...' Chapter 7 further explores the exit points and their corresponding destinations.

Consciousness separates from the physical body, and the etheric body

This moment begins the final separation of consciousness from the physical body.

The Tibetan sage, D.K, continues his delineation of the 'dying' process beyond the point where science and medicine stop, and even belief and imagination tend to falter, with an amazingly precise and plausible description. (Bailey 1985, pp. 68-70.) He details the pull 'upward' drawing the indi-vidual in his or her[6] subtler bodies out of the physical body and realm, and now a pull 'downward' on the physical body:

> *All has been proceeding under the Law of Attraction up to this point-the magnetic, attractive will of the soul. Now another "pull" or attractive impulse makes itself felt...The dense physical body, the sumtotal of organs, cells and atoms...begins to respond to the attractive pull of matter itself... Restitution of the commandeered matter of the form occupied by the soul during a life cycle consists in returning to this "Caesar" of the involutionary world (the physical plane life force or "spirit of the earth") what is his, whilst the soul returns to the God who sent it forth.*

While the vital body is being prepared for exit, and the physical body is responding to dissolution, the 'dying' individual is withdrawing the consciousness, steadily and gradually, into the astral and mental vehicles, in preparation for the complete abstraction of the etheric body when the right time comes.

There is another pause, when the physical elemental can regain its hold upon the etheric body if the soul desires, (the point at which NDErs return to their bodies) or if the physical elemental is powerful enough to postpone death. This is a major cause (though not the only one) of coma, and of some long, lingering deaths where the conscious self has left some time before, but the body struggles to hold on:

> *When, however, death is inevitable, the pause at this point will be exceedingly brief, sometimes only for a matter of seconds. The physical elemental*

---

6. There is no physical division into masculine and feminine once beyond the physical level, though there are the astral reflections of sex; yet we continue to identify for a time, with the sex and orientation of the life just finished.

has lost its hold, and the etheric body awaits the final "tug" from the soul, acting under the Law of Attraction.

The etheric body emerges from the physical body gradually via the chosen point of exit. It is still under the influence of the physical body, and remains close for a time, when clairvoyants may be able to see it 'hovering' around the deathbed or coffin.

D.K. continues: *'Still interpenetrating the etheric body are the integrated energies which we call the astral body and the mental vehicle, and at the centre there is **a point of light which indicates the presence of the soul'** [my emphasis].*

The etheric body is dispersed. After the loss of the physical and etheric bodies there is now nothing to respond to the attractive pull of matter. The discarnate individual in the astral body, is freed for the time being, from the material body and material world. But who is it who has survived death? Is it anyone those left behind, mourning the loss, would recognise? We can no longer identify this beloved person through familiar physical features, and we are likely to cling to the lifeless body, as though that is all that is left of them. Yet D.K. assures us their individuality is not lost, and that the person we knew is still present upon the planet:

> *Only that has disappeared which was an integral part of the tangible appearance of our planet. **That which has been loved or hated, which has been useful to humanity or a liability, which has served the race or been an ineffectual member of it, still persists,** is still in touch with the qualitative and mental processes of existence, and will forever remain-individual, qualified by ray type, part of the kingdom of souls, and a high initiate in his own right [i.e. as a soul].*

The individual stands in the subtle bodies, ready to begin the process known as 'The Art of Elimination'. The conditions into which s/he now moves depend upon three factors. They are a) how highly developed is the astral or emotional equipment; b) how highly developed is the mind of the individual, and the quality of the mental condition 'in which he habitually lives'; and c) whether the voice of the soul and soul influence is unknown or familiar and loved.

Torn between Church and Truth-Cardinal Benson's account of death and beyond

I came across a well-known example of life on the astral plane after death, *'Life in the World Unseen'* as told to Anthony Borgia. It contains an account of a conscious travelling through death, which correlates well with Atwater's and Levine's accounts, above. Originally, this book was too briefly reassuring because I still didn't have all the facts to be able to 'place' it in the context of the correctly arranged stages and sequences of the journey, so until I knew more, it seemed to be at odds with other versions.

This book is the account of Robert Hugh Benson, son of an Archbishop of Canterbury, Edward White Benson. Robert Hugh Benson became a cardinal in the Roman Catholic Church, and died in 1914. His reason for communicating his story, post-mortem, to Anthony Borgia, is an example of DK's *"non-fulfillment of a recognized and urgent duty"*, mentioned in Chapter 9 as a reason for remaining earthbound for a time: Benson had to correct untruths about the after-death state, written to conform with and placate the Church.

Benson had, for years, been troublingly psychic, able to see and hear things that were non-existent to others:

> *As happening to a priest of the Holy Church they were looked upon as temptations of 'the devil'...The great barrier to any further investigations of these faculties was the Church's attitude towards them, which was-and is-unrelenting, unequivocal, narrow, and ignorant...*

> *Many of my experiences of psychic happenings I incorporated into my books, giving the narratives such a twist as would impart to them an orthodox religious flavour...In a larger work I felt that I had to uphold the Church against the assaults of those who believed in the spiritual survival of bodily death, and that it was possible for the spirit world to communicate with the earth world. And in that larger work I ascribed to 'the devil'-against my better judgement-what I really knew to be nothing other than the working of natural laws...To have followed my own inclinations would have entailed a complete upheaval in my life, a renunciation of orthodoxy, and most probably a great material sacrifice, since I had established a second reputation as a writer...The truth was within my grasp, and I let it fall. I adhered to the Church (Borgia 1954, pp. 10-11).*

What drove the former Monsignor Benson to communicate his story in a book-length letter back to Earth, was a sensed moral obligation to set the record straight. In the process of doing this, Benson gives us a first-hand account of *the process of dying both before and after the exit from the physical body*.

Cardinal Benson's description of his own dying and after

Benson is in agreement with D.K. that the "actual process of dissolution is not necessarily a painful one." He continues:

> *I had during my earth life witnessed many souls passing over the border into spirit. I had had the chance of observing with the physical eyes the struggles*

that take place as the spirit seeks to free itself... from the flesh. With my psychic vision I had also seen the spirit leave, but nowhere was I able to find out-that is, from orthodox sources-what exactly takes place at the moment of separation, nor was I able to gather any information upon the sensations experienced by the passing soul. The writers of religious textbooks tell us nothing of such things for one very simple reason -- they do not know. [And if they did, they would probably do as Benson himself did-lie about it to suit the Church's orthodoxy. Or give up writing religious texts!] The physical body many times appeared to be suffering acutely, either from actual pain or from laboured or restricted breathing. To this extent such passings had all the appearance of being extremely painful. Was this really so? -- was a question I had often asked myself...

I had a presentiment that my days on earth were drawing to a close... There was a heaviness of the mind, something akin to drowsiness, as I lay in my bed. Many times I had a feeling of floating away and of gently returning... During such lucid intervals as I had I endured no feelings of physical discomfort. I could see and hear what was going on around me, and I could 'sense' the mental distress that my condition was occasioning. And yet I had the sensation of the most extraordinary exhilaration of the mind. I knew for certain that my time had come to pass on, and I was full of eagerness to be gone. I had no fear, no misgivings, no doubts, no regrets-so far-at thus leaving the earth world. (My regrets were to come later...) All that I wanted was to be away.

The account which follows is in complete agreement with earlier quoted teachings on the passage through physical death, and it also amplifies those briefer general descriptions:

I suddenly felt a great urge to rise up. I had no physical feeling whatever, very much in the same way that physical feeling is absent during a dream, but I was mentally alert, however much my body seemed to contradict such a condition. Immediately I had this distinct prompting to rise, I found that I was actually doing so... I saw my physical body lying lifeless upon its bed, but here was I, the real I, alive and well. For a minute or two I remained gazing, and the thought of what to do entered my head, but help was close at hand. I could still see the room quite clearly around me, but there was a certain mistiness about it as though it were filled with smoke very evenly distributed. I looked down at myself wondering what I was wearing in the way of clothes, for I had obviously risen from a bed of sickness and was therefore in no condition to move very far from my surroundings. I was extremely surprised to find that I had on my usual attire...

All of this is very reassuring, and fleshes out the teachings of DK and Sogyal Rinpoche about the dying process. But what happened after that?

Benson was met by a priestly colleague who had passed over some time before:

I ... was waiting with excitement for all manner of pleasant revelations of this new world, and I knew there could be none better than my old friend to give them to me. He told me to prepare myself for an immeasurable number of the pleasantest of surprises, and that he had been sent to meet me on my arrival (Borgia 1954, pp. 11-12)[7].

All the subsequent detail-of a beautiful place and its agreeable inhabitants and occupations, much too long of course, to quote, suggest that Benson had arrived as 'the majority of humans' according to D.K., on (a higher level of) the astral plane. He becomes aware in time, that there are higher and yet higher levels of consciousness, and that he as others must grow spiritually in order to access these. For the duration of the book however, he is on the astral plane, carrying out his urgent obligation to set the record straight for those still on earth. Curiously though, the book denies reincarnation. This seems to throw light on the puzzle of the great eighteenth century Swedish scientist and mystic Swedenborg's clear knowledge of much about the after-death states, yet his rejection of reincarnation. As the Tibetan, D.K. tells us, and as Buddhism also teaches, there is a moment of contact with the soul, and in that light we know who we are and understand the true nature of the scheme including that this is an interval between incarnations, not the end of the journey. But after the moment of soul contact, what follows is what Mahayana Buddhists call the 'swoon'; we next come to consciousness usually, somewhere on the astral plane-the plane ultimately, of illusion. As Swedenborg himself told us, this will be among our own kind, who may as yet have no self-discovered knowledge of reincarnation, and who have forgotten their epiphany in the soul's light, because their consciousness is as yet too little developed to be able to retain that memory. There is resistance, too, from an entrenched Christian worldview which denies the one soul, many lives. Benson demonstrates this lack of more complete knowledge at the early stage of the full process of dying to the physical world.

Peter Richelieu's book *A Soul's Journey* (1996, first published 1953) contained the best description I have yet found, of the relationship between the physical and etheric bodies, and physical and astral spheres.

Richelieu went into shock and profound grief on the news that his brother Charles had died in an air battle, a 'dogfight' as they were known, while defending London from German bombers during World War Two's 'Blitz'. The writer, who refers to himself as

---

7. All extracts from Life in the World Unseen by Anthony Borgia, published by Psychic Press, are reprinted by permission of the publishers.

'Henry' in the book, received a mysterious visitor who knew everything about him and his brother, and had come to comfort him by teaching him the truth about death. *A Soul's Journey* is Richelieu's account of the teaching he received from the Indian sage who was known to him just as Acharya, (or teacher). This entire event is bound to seem incredible to many readers, especially at this early point in the development of the knowledge in the book. If this is the case, please just regard it as fiction. The point of its inclusion is, as I have said, to illuminate the relationship between the physical and other higher bodies, and the movement from one to another in death.

A fighter pilot's death in war

It is 1941, and Richelieu ('Henry') and Acharya, who is teaching him how to remain conscious through the passage onto the astral sphere, once asleep, go astral travelling in wartime London. They 'dine' at the Trocadero, and walk down Piccadilly in an air raid after. Henry's teacher suggests they help if possible:

> *We glided about amidst the inferno that was raging, the bombs and machine-guns being audible [on the astral level, where they were] the whole time. For the first time I saw what the life of a fighter pilot actually was... I saw flames appearing from the engine, [of a downed plane] which gradually enveloped the whole aircraft...*

> *'Now you will see how those who have knowledge can help' said my Indian friend, and as we came to rest on the ground we saw that, although the body of the airman was terribly burnt and hardly recognizable as a human being, the real man in his astral body (presumably) was standing by the body on the ground, looking frightened and intensely miserable.... I saw what looked like a cloak of dense matter attempting to wind itself round the astral form that was standing before us... I was told later... that the etheric double, which is forced out of the physical body at the moment of death, winds itself round the astral body in its effort to retain some form of life, for the death of the physical body means also the death of the etheric double...* (Richelieu 1996, pp. 54-56)

Henry's teacher explains his new situation to the frightened boy who is watching as the paramedics put out the fire, then carry his body to the ambulance. He succeeds in reassuring the young pilot, and telling him how to free himself from the clinging etheric body, which begins to fall away:

> *[T]his was effected by the boy being told to make an effort of the will to disconnect himself from it. After a little time it all dropped to the ground and*

seemed to evaporate into smoke and dust...because the etheric matter... is rel-
atively... fine, compared with the dense part of the physical body...
(Richelieu 1996, p. 56)[8].

The teaching of D.K. is demonstrated with remarkable clarity in this experience of a death as witnessed by Richelieu. The life force is delivered to the physical body by the nadis, the nervelines in the etheric body, as explained earlier. We have a graphic description of its separation from the physical body when the young airman's body is burnt in the aircraft wreck. His etheric body with its nadis is suddenly wrenched out of that body, and in a reflex action of the will to live, wraps itself around the astral body. The suddenness of the death has meant a lack of preparation: The soul is unable to take its incarnated aspect through a more gradual passage out of the physical world.

The theosophist and student of the Ageless Wisdom, Annie Besant, in her book *A Study in Consciousness: a contribution to the Science of Psychology*, brings her higher knowledge and the clarity it affords, to the whole issue of consciousness and its relationship to the physical body. In this extract, Besant (1959, pp. 31-32) is explaining the relationship between the physical brain, the etheric aspects of it, and consciousness on the physical and astral levels:

The ordinary waking-consciousness of a man is the consciousness working through the physical brain... conditioned by all the conditions of that brain, limited by all its limitations... checked by a clot of blood, silenced by the decay of tissue.

While the brain constantly hinders the manifestation of consciousness, it is also the only physical instrument through which consciousness can work:

When... turning its attention away completely from the physical world and shedding its fetters of physical matter, [the psyche of the sleeper] roams through the astral world at will, or drifts through it unconsciously....it receives many impacts from that astral world, which it ignores or accepts according to its stage of evolution or its humour of the moment. If it should manifest itself to an outside observer-as may happen in trance conditions-it shows powers so superior to those it manifested when imprisoned in the physical brain... that such an observer may well regard it as a different consciousness... (Besant 1959, pp. 31-32)

This chapter considered the experience of death of the physical body, and the movement of consciousness into first the etheric and

---

8. All extracts from A Soul's Journey © 1953 Peter Richelieu, are reprinted by permission of the publishers, HarperCollins.

then the astral body according to Tibetan Buddhism and the Ageless Wisdom. But what happens next? What is the Tibetan Bardo? Do we hover on the astral or higher planes until we go to Heaven proper and meet with God, as Benson and Swedenborg thought? Or is it only until we return to a new life? The next chapter, Seven, considers this. Does the Christian Heaven exist? Who goes there? Or do we all just melt into the nothingness of Nirvana? And is there a Hell or a Purgatory?

Finally, Annie Besant is worth quoting to help clarify the relationship between the many aspects of self discussed in this chapter:

> ... the consciousness of each man is a Unit, however separate and different from each other its manifestations may appear to be; secondly... all these Units themselves are parts of the consciousness of the Logos, (the Word, or Divine Self, the Christian God) and therefore react similarly under similar conditions. We cannot too often remind ourselves that consciousness is one; that all apparently separate consciousnesses are truly one, as one sea might pour through many holes in an embankment...Yet truly our consciousness is a Unit, and the variety is due to the materials in which it is working (Besant 1959, pp. 31-32).

Chapter 7
The States After Death

Heaven, Purgatory and the Bardo

Summary Points

- **Degree of consciousness determines our exit point and our destination**
- **The perfect dying (and preservation of the body) of the Enlightened**
- Lost in the Bardo-just a Tibetan myth?
- **The hidden process of death; peeling away the layers- etheric, astral and mental**
- Subtle mind and Buddha mind
- The stages of ascent from body to soul
- **Heaven or Devachan vs The Astral, the Bardo, or Purgatory**
- Plato, Schure and Aldous Huxley on Heaven and Hell
- A fighter pilot in the Bardo
- **The terrors of the Bardo**
- The delusions of the bardo -- emotional phantoms?

- Letter back to earth: Sister Frances Banks to Helen Greaves
- **The emotional rubbish-deal with it now, in life; or on the astral after death?**

The States After Death

Our response to the Light of higher levels of consciousness, or the Buddha Mind, determines our fate. Will it be immortality or rebirth? Will we merge with the One Life, immediately or in time, or react against it and recoil into the separate self-sense in the Great Heresy of Separateness? Or simply fall into unconsciousness?

The bliss of Nirvana, the end of reincarnation, is the goal of every Buddhist. While only the enlightened attain it, there are other states of great beauty, bliss and love. The highest of these, mentioned but not detailed in the *Bardo Thodol*, the Tibetan Book of the Dead, is the plane of lesser Nirvana, called Devachan. *This is the Christian Heaven*. Only those of us who have a degree of mind development and soul contact, or in Buddhism, consciousness in the subtler mind realms or sheaths (developed mainly through meditation), can awaken after physical death, or be reborn, on this plane. The rest of us make contact with the source of our life, the Buddha Mind, the rough equivalent of the Western soul, but can't remain conscious there. When we recoil out of the great, inclusive Self into the personal self, or become unconscious, we 'awaken' in the pleasant[1] or unpleasant regions of the Bardo, which is the astral realm. Sooner or later, according to Buddhism, we find ourselves back in a body on earth.

Degree of consciousness determines our exit point and our destination

The 'dead' person (more alive than ever, as will become increasingly clear) leaves the physical body, as we have seen, through one or another aperture. In Mahayana Buddhism, for example, it is one of nine openings, and the exit point decides:

> '*exactly which realm of existence we are to be reborn in. When it leaves through the opening at the fontanel, at the crown of the head, we are reborn, it is said, in a pure land, where we can **gradually proceed** towards enlightenment*'. [My emphasis. The true Nirvanee who succeeds in reaching

---

1. A pride defined as '*an instinctive self consciousness which arises when faced with the impersonal nature of the luminosity*', is the response which propels us back from the Buddha Mind into the 'realm of gods'. (Judy Arpana 2009, in notes for her seminar *Facing Death, Embracing Life,* a Spiritual Care Programme of Sogyal Rinpoche's Rigpa Foundation). Judy, an Australian, is a senior student of Sogyal Rinpoche, and has studied under Kubler-Ross. The Formless God realm is the first of the Six Realms; it is said to be reached via exit from the top of the head, not the crown.

the final Nirvana, achieves this instantly, not gradually, as I explain more fully below] (Sogyal 1992, p. 233).

This 'reborn' of the quote does not necessarily mean 'reincarnated', which carries the extra meaning of rebirth in a physical body. These other rebirths take place in the movement from one body or sheath of consciousness to another. Rebirth is a fair term for any struggling movement of the nascent consciousness out of an old body or sheath, to create or organize and occupy a new one. In Buddhism this may be from the gross mental body to the subtle mental body, for example. In other, theosophical, systems, the equivalent would be *ascent* of consciousness from the emotional body to the mental body. Then, rebirth also refers to *descent* from a higher to a lower sheath, as when the soul or subtle mind consciousness descends through the planes of increasing density on the way to incarnation in a physical body.

I apologise to readers for the difficulty of this chapter, perhaps the most demanding of the whole book. The ideas presented here were originally the obscure teachings given to initiates into spiritual orders from esoteric Christianity to (Hindu) Advaita Vedanta and Buddhism. It has taken some years for me to be able to correlate them so that I was sure for example, that there was a Buddhist equivalent of the Christian Heaven or the Islamic Paradise, and what its name and description were, or what the Six Realms were; where they sat in the levels of consciousness, and how they were accessed after death.

These ideas have, in the past, been beyond the understanding of ordinary intelligent humans; it is a measure of our evolution in recent centuries that they are now accessible to the more intelligent and aware Westerners of the upper levels of consciousness examined in the next chapter, Eight. This is the mountain peak of the book! It is all a downhill run, from here to Chapter Fourteen, Soulmates -- an easy read by comparison. There are diagrams in the Appendix to assist in comprehension. I've referred to Diagram 1, Ken Wilber's *Four Quadrants*, in earlier chapters Three and Five. Diagram 2 is Ken Wilber's *The basic levels or spheres of consciousness*. Diagram 3 is *The seven planes of our solar system*, from Alice Bailey, with some additions made by me to map the concepts in this chapter such as Nirvana, Devachan/Dewachen and Purgatory, into their correct positions in the scheme of the *seven planes*, which are also the *spheres or levels of consciousness.*

The perfect dying (and preservation of the body) of the Enlightened

The best dying practice, the best way to die, is to have already *'made real the wisdom mind of the buddhas'* within oneself (Sogyal, p. 230). Enlightened practitioners have already before their deaths, reached the highest levels of Western developmental psychology, through their spiritual practices, and their service to all life. The body is no longer a sarcophagus, imprisoning the consciousness within flesh, bone and the material world; it is a tool merely. Consciousness does not exist within the body; it is the reverse case for the highly evolved: body exists within consciousness. These highly evolved ones are able to consciously dissolve the physical elements drawn together to form the vehicle of manifestation: they may choose not to leave behind a dead container for others to disintegrate using burning (the best way) or burial. Sogyal Rinpoche tells of one instance of many, the death of Sonam Namgyal, in Tibet in 1952. He asked that his body be wrapped and left undisturbed for a week. In that time, the lamas, monks and family noticed the mass in the wrappings shrinking. When unwrapped for burial, only his hair and nails remained (Sogyal pp. 167-168). Great rainbows (and other phenomena) mark the assumption of the Body of Light or the Rainbow body, by such saints.

Alternatively, these evolved or holy ones may choose that their bodies remain in a state of perfect preservation for centuries, like that of St Teresa of Avila[2], or for as long as needed, as with Jamyang Khyentse, Sogyal Rinpoche's master, whose body showed no signs of decay for six months during the Indian summer while inspired teachings were given in its presence (Sogyal p. 270). *Impossible!* will be the reply of many developed, educated Western minds. So which will be challenged and even rejected? The plain fact of these 'miracles' (they aren't really, just manifestations of a higher consciousness, a higher world not ruled by the physical laws)—or the limited understanding of reality of the Material Universe thinking which marked the science of the twentieth century? The

---

2. The body of this sixteenth century Spanish saint, exhumed several times over years, showed no decay. Her heart 'incorrupt' (on display in a reliquary) and body are (mainly) at the Carmelite convent at Alba de Tormes. Teresa, to her consternation, used to levitate at Mass; the community and locals thought her devil-possessed. She was basically told to 'get a life' – meditate less, spend more time out in the community!

'miraculous' or the materialistic? When the soul is fully incarnate at last, *'the disciple passes out of the control of the universal, natural law, and uses or discards the body at will...the spiritual will'* (Bailey 1985, p. 98).

The head exits, common in the West by now: Where do we go as a result?

The highest exit is, as we have seen, through the crown chakra, the top *back* of the head. This is Brahmarandra, the fontanel; eight finger-widths back from the hairline. This exit is said to (at least) guarantee rebirth in the realm known in the West as Heaven. This in Buddhism is *'Dewachen, the western paradise of Amitabha'* the Buddha of Limitless Light, says an ancient text (Sogyal 1992, pp. 233 and 400). This paradise is also known as Sukhavati, as the Happy Land, and as the Pure Land; Dewachen/ Devachan, says Buddhist teacher Rob Nairn, is *'rather like heaven'* (2004, p. 95). It is a Buddhist equivalent.

There is a specific practice, success at which will ensure rebirth in this blissful place, according to the Mahayana text *The Provisional and the Final Nirvana* (Saddharmapundarika V, 59-83).[3] This is the practice of Phowa/Pho-ba: *'Pho-ba is part of the pure Land practice...By means of it the yogin learns how to shoot his consciousness up through the crown of his head into a visualized image, and at death he is able to direct it to the dharmakaya realm'* (Fremantle and Chogyam Trungpa 1975, p. 33); the causal or formless state, and thus achieve the Pure Land consciousness.

When Phowa is successful, says the Bardo Thodol, it is not necessary to read this Liberation through Hearing text to the dead person, as they have recognised the Limitless Light, and attained to a degree of enlightenment.

In the descriptions of the Near-death Experience, and others of actual death, the usual report is of the consciousness departing through the head. It needs to be remembered that, among those who die and are resuscitated, only a minority report a Near-death Experience. NDErs, for whatever reason, perhaps including a more advanced level of consciousness than some other clinical death

---

3. Dharmakaya/Dewachen is the provisional Nirvana. The final Nirvana is what D.K. describes later in this chapter, as the *'Nirvana of the soul.'* Devachan/Dewachen is *'the abode of Bliss'* says Blavatsky, but she also notes *'the false bliss of Devachan'*. It is false in that it is not liberation from incarnation, but just *'a little rest on [the] threshold'* before passing to another life on earth (1888a, p. 39). It is also false because it is still a separate consciousness, and not yet the world-including Nirvana of self and Self as One. See Diagram 3 in the Appendix for the 'location' of Dewachen.

returnees, seem able to make the transfer from the physical body in full consciousness—the skill taught in the phowa practice. Or is this just a feature of the NDE in that etheric nervelines to the brain remain intact as they do not in actual death? Frances Banks, the ex-nun whose experience of dying is quoted in Chapter Fourteen, and extract from her 'letter back to Earth' is quoted in this chapter, would certainly have gone into the Light, but did not recall it after the unconscious period which preceded her 'waking up' on the higher astral level.

NDErs, like most of the rest of us, may either just go unconscious during the transfer to non-physical being, or after their contact with the soul or Mind. Including, no doubt, now deceased Australian media magnate Kerry Packer, who informed the rest of us on his earlier return from a clinical death episode: "There's *nothing there!*" No, there wouldn't have been for Kerry Packer, in a mere clinical death episode. Even if momentarily conscious in higher realms, he would not have been able to retain any memory.

Given that there are other head exits—the brow and the 'top of the head' (Sogyal p. 399), four finger widths back from the hairline, a head exit may not necessarily be through Brahmarandra, the crown. But many of us have now evolved to the point where we exit through the head, and not even through the heart which, as DK indicated in Chapter Six, was the usual route for ordinary good humans attempting to fulfil the law of love. This is fascinating! If you know someone who has had NDE, or an OOB experience, do ask which exit they used! The sister whose NDE was quoted in Chapter Two, thinks she exited through the brow.

This common head exit is a good indicator of how far evolution has brought us, even though this is not the mass of humanity, but a smaller group of Westerners of considerably more advanced consciousness. According to Mahayana Buddhism, *head exits lower than the crown chakra* will still take us into higher places than the dreaded aspects of the Bardo. Sogyal Rinpoche quotes Lama Lodo (p. 399), that if consciousness escapes through the top of the head not the crown, we will still be reborn in '*the formless god realm*', (formless because without a material form or body, god because beyond the human condition, in the realm of higher beings, even if they are ourselves discarnate, is my understanding).[4]

---

4. In this case, our consciousness is not centred in Buddhism's 'mental body' (the psychic body usually dominated by emotion), but in the higher 'body of light' or 'subtle body', which confusingly I know, is called by D.K. the manasic or mental body.

The highest stage is that of the *permanent assumption* of the body of light in the Nirvana of the soul (as distinct from the temporary sojourn in Heaven/Devachan before return to the soul and then incarnation). D.K. describes it thus:

> [D]esire for individual experience is lost and only the longing to function as a conscious part of the greater Whole remains. Then...can the conscious soul appropriate the body of light and of splendour, the expression of the glory of the One which, when once assumed, makes all future incarnations in the three worlds impossible, except as an act of the spiritual will (Bailey 1942, reference edition 1971, pp. 332-3). The emphasis is mine.

Buddhist Rob Nairn, author of the enlightening book *Living, Dreaming, Dying: Practical Wisdom from the Tibetan Book of the Dead* is asked by an audience member "What happens if you get it right and become enlightened?" He replies:

> "You will be finished with the whole cycle of birth and death. You preempt any karma that can force you to rebirth and you go to what is called a pure realm, a pure land. Then you are able to send your consciousness back into a chosen form [D.K.'s 'body of light and of splendour' often called the Light Body] to help beings on many planets..." (Nairn p. 114).

'Pure land' seems to be being used by Nairn in a relative sense here, since the Pure Land practice is said to lead not to Nirvana or Enlightenment, but to Devachan, the 'lesser Nirvana'. The Devachanee, while able to make a conscious choice, not a forced or automatic incarnation, is not yet able to create and use the Light Body to help 'beings on many planets'.

Liberation from reincarnation is the result of reaching Nirvana or enlightenment. However, as both D.K. and all the Buddhist sources tell us, one who has seen the light, and attained this bliss, is likely to choose to return for humanity's sake. In Buddhism, those who do return from Nirvana are the Boddhisattvas. In each major religion, there is a tradition of at least one great Return—Krishna, the Messiah, the Christ, the Imam Mahdi, the Maitreya Buddha. Chapter Nine considers the more ordinary return to physical life of a cross-section of humanity, along with the reasons in Helen Wambach's study, given by those who consciously chose to return. (These are devachanees, not nirvanees). Reincarnation in these cases, is actively chosen by the higher consciousness, rather than just grabbed at by the personality, or unwillingly suffered by it.

Thus, the consciousness released from the body, moves through the tunnel or the darkness of Full Attainment, into the Light, which is that of Universal Mind or Buddhi. If the Light is not recognized or proves unbearable (as Huxley describes below), other, lesser states of consciousness in lower realms await. The Bardo Thodol does not go into much detail about the bliss of higher realms or states of consciousness such as Dewachen or beyond that, Nirvana; it is too busy concentrating on getting us through the Bardo safely, and thus on grim descriptions of the phenomena of each separate day in the Bardo. I did not at first find the Buddhist teachings very reassuring! It was some years before I could discover how to 'translate' the Tibetan teachings: to locate these same Tibetan elements and stages, when they were being described in what I realized were parallel or similar terms in Western sources. In the first, the Bardo of (physical) Dying, the Chikhai Bardo, we must become conscious of the Light.

A dying person who recognises the Light, and who can bear the shattering of ego-boundaries and the loss of ego of this merging with the All-Self, says Evans-Wentz, is sufficiently evolved to enter this state. If this state goes unrecognised, it is due to the *'pull of worldly tendency (Sangskara)... He is then presented with the secondary Clear Light, which is the first, somewhat dimmed to him by the general Maya* [illusion of the solid reality of the material world] (Evans-Wentz 2000, p. lxvii).

The discarnate individual may not register either Clear Light, because consciousness is not sufficiently developed. He or she is still too attached to, or defined by, the material existence; this draws the psyche back to earth, and to familiar people, scenes, habits and passions. The mind of this individual may wander restlessly in the lower levels of the dreaded Bardo. The case of Nineteenth Century Irishwoman Bridey Murphy is discussed in Chapter Nine; she is an excellent example of this situation. Poor Bridey finds herself after death in a world scarcely more exciting and stimulating than the one she had just left.

Is oblivion preferable?

Even after reading the authoritative Tibetan works, and the Tibetan sage DK's teaching in the Alice Bailey books, my midnight terrors were not yet put to sleep.

The Tibetan's teaching of the previously secret lore seems to carry enormous authority. There is the amazing detail, the facts to which no ordinary human has access, the complete consistency of the atomic and cosmic levels of consciousness in a vast scheme, not just planetary and solar, laid out for us in the Alice Bailey writings. The scheme, far beyond the elaboration of any other spiritual or scientific source of knowledge, is powerfully convincing. But after becoming acquainted with both these writings and the Tibetan Book of the Dead, (a decade or more before reading Sogyal Rinpoche's book) I was more unsettled than ever about the prospect before us in death.

Christianity, at least as known to the ordinary worshipper down the ages, has been more about avoiding a terrifyingly depicted Hell, the eternal damnation of unrepentant sinners, than seeking and discovering a Heaven which was by contrast, the palest wisp of half-life, threatening us with the alternative of eternal boredom. So, whether it is Heaven or Hell, Nirvana or the Endless Wheel of Rebirth, being described in our spiritual traditions, the prospect of life beyond the mortal realm has seemed less than enticing all these centuries.

> *It all sounded so abstract in DK's account, and so frightening in Tibetan Buddhism.*

I wasn't sure that oblivion was not, in the end, preferable. Was this really all there was? I had turned with anticipation to the Tibetan Book of the Dead, and to the explications and commentaries on it, especially Sogyal Rinpoche's in The Tibetan Book of Living and Dying, to discover if the picture of life *after* the death of the physical body, was there more vividly depicted and more realistic. Was it more just plain human, more an experience I could imagine as following life on earth as an ordinary, limited human being? The answer at that time was a resounding No.

Lost in the Bardo-just a Tibetan myth?

The experience of roaming through the Bardo in solitude is the stuff of nightmare:

> *Yet all the experiences of this bardo arise only from our mind, created by our karma and habits returning... Trying to escape* [these psychologically created apparitions; storms of wind, water and fire] *in the terrifying darkness, it is said that three different abysses, white, red and black, deep and dreadful, open up in front of us. These, the Tibetan Book of the Dead tells us, are our own anger, desire, and ignorance... Consumed by fear, blown to and fro like dandelion seeds in the wind, we roam, helpless, through the gloom of the bardo* (Sogyal 1992, p. 290).

Reading passages like this, I simply became more confused and fearful. Despite some knowledge of esoteric teachings on the after-death state, I could make little sense of the Tibetan Buddhist version of them; or at least, nothing that gave perspective or reassurance about this terrifying Bardo experience. I suspected many or most Westerners responded similarly. Even when I had been lucky enough to hear the teachings from a Tibetan monk of the Dalai Lama's order, nothing changed. I remember being filled with admiration and appreciation of the Buddhist wisdom about the true nature of life, and its proper uses-how not to waste it on the ultimately trivial, or allow oneself to be sidetracked by any supposed good which would disintegrate at death, because this life determined the whole future. Yet I spent much time puzzling over the stages and states of the transition, and the accompanying signs which identified the stages- whiteness like a pure sky struck by moonlight, redness like sun shining in a pure sky, blackness like an empty sky shrouded in utter darkness. It still sounded like the passage into a cosmos constructed by and for, Tibetan Buddhists. *None of it appeared to line up with anything known in the West.*

When I read the tentative identification of the NDE by Sogyal Rinpoche (quoted in Chapter Five) it had some real use in identifying similar stages in Western and other Eastern systems. But finally, the NDE traveller returned to the physical body and life; what lay beyond that point of return was still hopelessly obscure. It was seven years before I began to identify the parallel terms in Western sources, and work out how to 'translate' the Tibetan teachings- to locate these same Tibetan elements and stages, when they were described in Western sources.

The hidden process of death; peeling away the layers- etheric, astral and mental

The complete dying process as described by D.K., is similar to that required to peel an onion, or undo the nest of Russian dolls or eggs given to children. Each layer or body is peeled off to reveal another, inner one, which looks like the substance or core until it too, is pulled off or peeled away, until we get to the innermost egg or self (or that which is presently for most of us, the innermost—the soul).

The understanding of the nature of the self in Buddhism; that is, self and soul not as definite entities, but as no more than passing states with no fixed address, must be kept in mind.[5] Yet once this is

---

5. However, there is the permanency of the indestructible seed or drop or essence of a causal realm nature, says Ken Wilber (1990), which Tibetan Buddhism describes as departing from the body in death. This essence is described by D.K. as *'the manasic atom (which) is the nucleus of the future causal body in which the individual passes from life to life'* (Bailey 1970, p. 169).

noted, the process as described in these two traditions along with others of the perennial philosophy, is similar. In Buddhism we see the Light, or not, then move through the peeling process rapidly or slowly, into the bliss of the greater or lesser Nirvana.

The six realms of Samsara-Hell, Hungry Ghost, Animal, Human...

If we fail to see it we get stuck in one of the six realms of Samsara, in the astral states of our major negative emotions (as happens constantly in life, not just in the transition after physical death). Anger it is said, will take us into the Hell realm, greed into the Hungry Ghost realm, ignorance into the Animal realm, desire into the Human realm, jealousy into the Jealous god realm, and pride into the God realm. This is pride not in the ordinary sense, but *'intoxication with the existence of ego'* (Fremantle and Chogyam Trungpa 1975, p. 10); the recoil into the separate self I've mentioned above. These 'realms' should be seen more as symbolic descriptions of the kind of existences into which we wil l be helplessly pulled, and reborn, as a result of our identification with and entrapment within, one or other of these emotional states. Thus we find ourselves catapulted back into incarnation.[6]

It is important to remember that the Buddhist term translated into English as mind is a general term, taking its meaning from its context. It often indicates, as in gross or lower mind, all consciousness that is not strictly physical, but still limited to the world of Samsara; that is to conditioned, ultimately illusory existence. It includes, and in the mass of humanity is limited to, the emotional consciousness, called the astral in other schemes. In more advanced humans the Buddhist gross or personal mind includes the lower, concrete mental level, the first of the true spheres of mind development. The Buddhist 'mind' is equivalent to 'psyche' or 'consciousness'. 'Subtle mind' and 'buddha mind' refer to states beyond Samsara,--manifested and conditioned existence.

---

6. *[F]or most of us the moment of death is a blank and a state of oblivion, for we have neither encountered nor evolved any way of recognizing the Dharmakaya reality when it arises as the Ground Luminosity. Nor do we have any hope of recognizing the Sambhogakaya fields as they appear in the bardo of dharmata. Because our entire life has been lived out within the realm of the impure perceptions of the Nirmanakaya manifestation, so at the moment of death we ...awaken, frantic and distracted, in the bardo of becoming in the mental body...stumbling helplessly, propelled by past karma, towards rebirth'* (Sogyal 1992, p 344).

The stages of ascent from body to soul

Ken Wilber (1990) gives us the stages of death: 'Buddhists see us moving from the individual embodied consciousness bounded by one's personal self and life-history, through gross, intermediate and subtle mind, to a merging of the separate self with the One Self, the buddha nature.' This makes five stages in all, of the passage from incarnated consciousness to the merging of the separate self with the Universal Self or buddha nature.

Wilber begins this paragraph with a Westernised list of the stages in that by now familiar quote: 'That is, upon death, the body dissolves into mind, then mind dissolves into soul, then soul dissolves into spirit, with each of these dissolutions marked by a specific set of events (Wilber 1990, p. 176).

D.K's enumeration of the stages is similar to both the above lists. As detailed in the last chapter, there are four stages, and, as in Buddhism, five states or bodies covering the dying process of most of us. In the first stage, the life force and consciousness of the 'dying' one, enclosed within the etheric or vital body, withdraw from the physical body, which then begins to disintegrate. In the second stage, the life force and consciousness, contained in the astral body, withdraw from the etheric body, and that body also disintegrates. In the third stage, the life force and consciousness, contained within the mental body, withdraw from the astral or emotional body, and this body disintegrates also.

The fourth and 'final stage *for the human being is its withdrawal from the mental vehicle. The life forces after this fourfold abstraction are centralised entirely in the soul'* (Bailey 1953, reference edition 1975, pp. 414-5. Extracted in Bailey 1985, p. 66).The human soul returns to the spiritual soul and the world of souls, to the Place from whence it came, refocusing the life forces to become once more a radiant point of light upon the third level of Manas, the mental plane where souls have their dwelling place. The part returns to the whole and the consciousness comprehends the true meaning of the words of Krishna, *'Having pervaded this whole universe with a fragment of myself, I remain'*. For the most highly evolved, who have attained enlightenment and reached Nirvana, there need be 'no more going out'; no more incarnations. For all but these few of the billions of us, the soul will at this point, prepare for a new incarnation.

Heaven or Devachan vs The Astral, the Bardo, or Purgatory

The nature of this stage of 'reward and rest', and who goes to Heaven, Paradise or Devachan, will be explored in more detail after consideration of stage two, the astral or emotional world, and its connection with the Tibetan Bardo. Briefly for now, in stage three, when we move from the astral body into the mental body, there is conscious work to be done by the *'liberated spiritual man'* before stage four, returning to the soul. This work is known as **Restitution**. However, before this time on the mental plane, in the (blissful) re-flective state known in Eastern writings as Devachan or Dewachen, also known as the Heavenworld, most but not all of humanity will spend some time in stage two, in their astral body, in the emotional sphere of the inner worlds. Age at death is a critical factor in our re-lationship to the emotional world and astral plane after death, writes medico and esoteric scientist Douglas Baker.

> *When a very elderly person dies, his subsequent occupation of the astral body is a brief affair. His desires have been spent in the long life-the dynamo that drives the astral vehicle is at low ebb. The opposite is true of a young person, with his full complement of emotional energy still extant after he has been torn out of his physical body. So powerful is he in the astral, post-mortem state, that he may even avoid the gentle passage into sublimer regions* [ie the mental plane or Devachan] *reserved for the older man. He may be drawn back into incarnation within a decade or less. The impact of emotional ener-gies of the young man, even after death, could have powerful effects on those he had loved or desired-on his wife, his children, his parents and even on his pets-which would not cease even after he reincarnated-say within that dec-ade* (Baker 1979, p. 25).

This is also an example of someone who doesn't get past the peeling of the two earlier layers before returning to a physical body. Some of us will be confined for a time in the lower levels of this astral or emotional sphere. This is the place which corresponds to the dreaded aspects of the Tibetan Bardo. It took several years of study and research to be sure of this. At the far end of the process I found a description of this same place, in what was for me a totally unex-pected source: the mystery traditions of Ancient Greece.

Plato, Schure and Aldous Huxley on Heaven and Hell

In Plato's Phaedo, Socrates says that after the death of the body, when it begins to disintegrate, the soul *'departs to the invisible world-to the divine and immortal and rational* [Heaven or Devachan or beyond]:

*thither arriving, she is secure of bliss and is released from the error and folly of men...and all other human ills...*The Tibetan tradition would agree that the souls who arrive in 'the divine and immortal and rational' are those who have seen and recognised the Light, literally, of Universal Mind, which Socrates calls the 'rational', and been able to move beyond the spheres of inevitable, forced or self-propelled incarnation. Socrates continues:

> *But the soul which has been polluted, and is impure at the time of her departure... and is in love with and fascinated by the body and by the desires and pleasures of the body, until she is led to believe that the truth only exists in a bodily form...is held fast by the corporeal... And this corporeal element, my friend, is heavy and weighty and earthy, and is that...by which a soul is depressed and dragged down again into the visible world...Yes...these **must be the souls, not of the good, but of the evil, which are compelled to wander about such places** [emphasis mine]...until, through the craving after the corporeal which never leaves them, they are imprisoned finally in another body. And they may be supposed to find their prisons in the same natures which they have had in their former lives.* (Socrates gives the example of lives of gluttony, wantonness, and drunkenness). (Plato 1942, p. 116).

It is not until this Socratic scheme is put in a context like this, that its striking similarity with the Tibetan tradition is seen. There is another truly remarkable passage, echoing the Bardo Thodol, in a book written some years *before the publication* of The Tibetan Book of the Dead. In *Pythagoras and the Delphic Mysteries,* Eduoard Schure (1906; quote from 1912 edition, p. 121) elaborates on these teachings of the wisdom initiation schools of Orpheus and Pythagoras and their successors.

He begins by saying that as death approaches, there is a 'presentiment' of the separation from the body that is about to take place.

> *When the exhausted life stops in the brain, the soul becomes perplexed and altogether loses consciousness. If it is holy and pure, its spiritual senses have already been aroused by gradual detachment from matter* [hence the emphasis laid on the practice of Detachment]. *When the soul finally leaves the cold corpse, rejoicing in its deliverance, it feels itself carried away **into a glorious light, towards the spiritual family to which it belongs*** [my emphasis].

Here in a Western source, not directly influenced by Tibetan Buddhism's Bardo Thodol, (though influenced and informed by Eastern traditions as known to Theosophy) are both the 'glorious light' of which every tradition seems to speak, and the *spiritual family*, of which more is revealed later in the book.

The Bardo-like passage is the following, in which Shure excepts the 'ordinary man' who has a deep attachment to the physical state, from this bliss. Those whose conception of life is limited to the material, are likely to awake only half-conscious in this gloomy place:

*...Darkness is all around, chaos within...This state may be prolonged for months or years. Its duration depends on the strength of the material instincts of the soul [my emphasis]. Once free from its body, it will escape into the abysses of the terrestrial atmosphere, whose electric streams carry it here and there, and whose many-shaped inhabitants, wandering about more or less like itself, it is beginning to perceive... There begins a desperate, vertiginous struggle on the part of the soul... to free itself from earthly attraction and reach, **in the heaven of our planetary system**, [my emphasis], the region proper to it and which friendly guides alone can show it.... This phase [ie the purgative] of the life of the soul has borne different names in religions and mythologies. Moses called it Horeb; Orpheus, Erebus; Christianity, Purgatory, or the Valley of the Shadow of Death'* (Schure 1912, p. 121).

This description sufficiently resembles that of the Tibetan Bardo, that it could have been drawn from the commentary on one of the translations. Yet that is impossible: the first translation from the original text of the Bardo Thodol, edited by Evans-Wentz, appeared twenty-one years later, in 1927. It is another testament to the shared experience and/or the common source, described in these separate writings. (This also explains why there is no mention of the Tibetan term Bardo in Shure's list of the names given to this place in different traditions.)

Theosophist Charles Leadbeater, in his book The Life After Death, refers to the entire experience in the astral realm as the Purgatory equivalent, since even when it is pleasant, as it usually is for most of us, we are still working to shed the lower bodies and elements of our nature in order to return to the soul. In the chapter 'The Heaven-World' he says:

*'A man decides for himself both the length and character of his **heaven-life**...He had made himself an astral body by his desires and passions during earth-life, and he had to live in it during his astral existence, and that time was happy or miserable for him according to its character. **Now this time of purgatory is over, for that lower part of his nature has burnt itself away** [phrases in bold text are my emphases]: now there remain only the higher and more refined thoughts, the noble and unselfish aspirations that he poured out during **earth-life*** (Leadbeater 2004, p. 41).

It is these higher elements only, of the last life that are taken into the blissful Heaven or Devachan phase of the inner life.

What about Hell?

So by the time of fitting these pieces of the puzzle together, I was increasingly sure that I had located the common geography and ontology of the Bardo/Purgatory/ Horeb/ Erebus/ Gehenna. What about 'Hell'? The word is used in the title of Aldous Huxley's book *Heaven and Hell* (2004) originally published together with his *The Doors of Perception* in 1954, from both of which I quote later in this chapter. Westerners sometimes say that Buddhism is more sophisticated than Christianity; there is no Heaven and no Hell. In fact, there are both, if we trust the English translations. Ryuho Okawa is a popular and influential spiritual teacher and interpreter of Buddhism for the modern world, whose books are bestsellers in Japan, and who heads its Institute for Research in Human Happiness. The word he uses, in the English version of his book *The Laws of Eternity* for this lower bardo-state, is 'Hell'.

Ryuho Okawa (1998, p. 15) says that any one of us who has expressed our true spiritual nature while on earth, doing good and refraining from evil, *'will be able to ascend to heaven, and the more fully he manifests his true nature the higher he will rise. If he does not awaken to his true nature as a child of Buddha ...he will be doomed to hell and will be inflicted with severe ordeals.* (He examples a lascivious person doomed to search for sexual satisfaction in the Hell of Lust, and says those who cheat others will end up, foxlike, in the Hell of Beasts. These hells are versions of two of the six Samsara realms of the Bardo Thodol, mentioned above.)

It became clear that all major traditions spoke of a separate place for those who find their only satisfaction or reality on the material plane, who are held captive by their desires for earthly things- luxury, sex, money, fame or power, or, worse, who have by evil thoughts and acts, created suffering for others. Lacking the capacity to move higher, they will awake in the place populated by desires and fears; the self-created nightmares of their own poisonous atmospheres.

It is in the soul's *'struggle... to free itself from earthly attraction'* (Schure, as quoted above) that the purging process takes place for which the Christian Purgatory was named. (The Vatican has recently 'abolished' both Purgatory and Limbo; they are no longer part of the Church's scheme of life, death, and the hereafter. They continue to be recognised in other branches of the Christian church, the Russian Orthodox for one. This will, of course, make no difference to their actual existence or otherwise.) The purpose of the

Bardo Thodol, the original Tibetan Book of the Dead, was to assist the soul in this process, so that it is no longer *'compelled to wander about such places'* (Plato, as quoted above) but is enabled to rise out of the *'abysses of the terrestrial atmosphere'* (Schure, as quoted above) into the Light, to *'ascend to heaven'* (Ryuho Okawa, as quoted above) to the regions proper to the soul.

I puzzled over the use of the term soul and its cognates in Tibetan Buddhism. Why did it seem so contradictory even in DK's teachings? The reason is that it is a rather vague term, used broadly for several stages of evolution, including the human soul (the egoic or causal body) and the spiritual soul (the Buddhic permanent atom). The soul, mind, individual, human, astral or mental entity, are all problematic terms, because they suggest things about the post-death entity which don't apply to everyone. For example, DK some-times refers to the 'soul' after death in order to distinguish that en-tity from the physical body-personality. However, there is no soul involvement to speak of, and certainly no soul presence, in many in-dividuals in earlier stages after death, any more than there was for those individuals before death. Soul when used in this context, means psychic aggregate-all that did not die with the body. It does not refer to the 'spiritual' soul, the One which can say, with Krishna: *"Having pervaded the worlds with this fragment of Myself, I remain, immortal..."*

At other times DK may speak of 'the individual' or 'the man'. While this term is sexist, (women exist only as a special case of male humanity in all these older writers, as I'm sure you've noticed), it has a meaning in esoteric science that 'human' does not carry.

Aldous Huxley in the Bardo

All of these discoveries of the parallels that made 'translation' of the Bardo Thodol's states possible for me, were exciting enough. I next discovered Aldous Huxley actually journeying consciously into the Bardo; undertaking an empirical investigation of that state in the presence of two deliberate observers, and recording his experiences in *The Doors of Perception*. This was important evidence! Huxley made fascinating and illumining discoveries after taking mescaline, a hallucinogenic drug chemically similar to LSD. After the ecstatic ex-perience of *'the Dharma-Body as the hedge at the bottom of the garden'*

(Huxley 2004, p. 21)[7], he found himself peering over the edge of the Bardo's abyss. He explained to the colleague whose research he was assisting, and his wife, who were present during the whole experience:

> *'If you started in the wrong way, everything that happened would be a proof of the conspiracy against you. It would all be self-validating. You couldn't draw breath without knowing it was part of the plot.'*

> *'So you think you know where madness lies?'*

> *My answer was a convinced and heartfelt, 'Yes'.*

> *'And you couldn't control it?'*

> *'No, I couldn't control it. **If one began with fear and hate as the major premises, one would have to go on to the conclusion'** [my emphasis].*

Huxley was quite consciously identifying his experience under mescaline, as the self-projections encountered in the Tibetan system, in the Bardo.

> *'Would you be able,' my wife asked, 'to fix your attention on what The Tibetan Book of the Dead calls the Clear Light?'*

> *Perhaps...I could - but only if there were somebody there to tell me about the Clear Light... That's the point, I suppose, of the Tibetan ritual - someone sitting there all the time and telling you what's what....*

> *'O nobly born, let not thy mind be distracted.' That was the problem-to remain undistracted...by the memory of past sins, imagined pleasure, by the bitter aftertaste of old wrongs and humiliations, **by all the fears and hates and cravings that ordinarily eclipse the Light** [my emphasis.] (Huxley 2004, pp. 34-5).*

The Bardo in my Nightmare

My immediate response on reading this was *'fears and hates and cravings...that isn't me -- I'll be okay!'* Many months later, I had an experience which quite starkly illumined Huxley's words and his meaning. It was delivered in what we call a nightmare, and think of as completely unreal. In my dream, my daughter, then barely seventeen, had come to me and told me *'I'm moving out tomorrow - W. and I are getting a flat together.'* The effect was devastating. My baby-the one

---

7. Extracts from Aldous Huxley, © 1954, *Doors of Perception and Heaven and Hell,* published by Chatto and Windus, are reprinted by permission of The Random House Group Ltd. Permission granted for the UK and Commonwealth. Permission for the US and the Phillipines granted by HarperCollins Publishers.

real and living being with whom my life was entwined, but beyond that, my dearest companion, the Other who grew love in me, who caused it to blossom in my barren world, whom I loved utterly, was leaving me. It was the tearing of half of my body and life out of me. I was now to be alone once more, non-existent; worse, I was to be *without her.* How could I survive? I was devastated-my heart was broken, my life was shattered; I was completely undone by grief and pain.

And yet it was doubly, and soon to be triply, unreal. I awoke from it into the daylight world where the terrible grief slowly evaporated. It was quite unreal in that my daughter had already left home to all intents and purposes, by moving in with her father and returning to me only on weekends for what she regarded and I increasingly accepted, as visits. I had been adjusting to this reality for eighteen months. I shed real tears about it, not nightly, weekly, or monthly, but just twice in the first fortnight. After that, I got on with the business of coming to terms with it and getting on with my own life. I'd much rather it wasn't like this, but she must grow up and separate from me, and, painful as it is, I must let her go.

The third layer of unreality to the dream was provided the very next day. My daughter came home for the weekend. *'Mum, is it okay if W and I get a flat together after I finish my Year 12?'*

'Yes, darling, of course it is; I expected you would want to' was my unhesitating and completely unfussed response. And when we'd pondered together, the cost for weekly rental, I pulled out three local newspapers and found the Flats and Houses to Rent section for her perusal, with no sign of distress.

How could I make sense of this? Was one 'real', but the other 'illusory'? If so, which was which? I still find it possible to be identified wholly, with either state, either universe. It was a powerful experiential illustration of a truth stated by more than one teacher and writer on the subject, including Sogyal Rinpoche and D.K., that the physical body provides a very welcome damping-down and muffling of the intensity of our emotional life and world. When that body is gone, these emotions have overwhelming potency; they can engulf us. We can experience ecstasy or heartbreak or wild anger, and be caught up in the apparently ineluctable rationale of a particular emotional universe, in what we think of as the dream state, and find that we have no control; it devours us, just as Huxley experienced. It is the state without access (either briefly or more lengthily) to the mind and rational (and supra-rational) processes, and to the self-awareness which is the hallmark of the soul.

Yet the moment we are conscious in our bodies once more, the entire episode may seem quite irrational and unlike ourselves. To be caught in this way, in a negative emotional or astral state after death and unable to recognize it and thus free oneself, is to be trapped in the dark places of the Bardo. *This is why the practices of self-awareness, of emotional control, of meditation and contemplation*, at the heart of Buddhism, found in fact, but not necessarily practised, in all religions, are so essential. They give us the capacity to know, even while immersed in this state, that it is unreal. Thus we will not be trapped in the lower Bardo. For this reason Rob Nairn (2004) tutors us to practise becoming aware in our dreaming, that this is just a dream, and that we have the power to alter its progress and outcome. My sister Meredith, whose NDE is quoted in Chapter One, calls this 'learning to become the Dream Master', which she taught herself to do as a child having nightmares: *"This is my dream, and I say what happens next!"*

Any intense negative emotional state can bring about this same entrapment for a period of time, even while in the physical body. Probably all of us have experienced depression at one time or another, and for so many of us, it is a constant threat, or worse, our familiar incubus. We have become too well acquainted with this dark and terrifying place that the Tibetans call the Bardo: we know well that despite being in a body, surrounded by three-dimensional space filled with a world of people, objects and relationships, depression can still overcome our connectedness to the exterior world, and block our perception of it (and of the light and love of Reality) till we crawl into bed and stay there, prisoners of the dark lower Bardo state.

Dion Fortune, the English esotericist, confirms this Bardo place of monsters of the unconscious for many when under the influence of drugs. The action of the drugs on one under their influence can *'put in abeyance the higher faculties of the mind, thereby enabling the primitive powers of direct psychic perception (possessed by all humans in an earlier stage of our development) to function unchecked; he would indeed penetrate to the astral plane, but would find himself in its limbo, or purgatorial aspect* (Fortune n.d., p. 106). This limbo aspect is the bad Tibetan Bardo. Fortune adds that when the proper initiatory methods of the development and extension of consciousness are used to open the astral senses, then access is obtained onto other (and higher) levels of the astral plane. Later, when the initiate can move around the astral plane with full consciousness and mastery, s/he is also able to descend into its hells to contact and help 'the spirits in prison'.

This next quote from the Tibetan Book of the Dead is teasing, yet it is at the heart of Tibetan Buddhism: 'Recognizing the voidness of thine own intellect to be Buddhahood, and knowing it at the same time to be thine own consciousness, thou shalt abide in the state of the divine mind of the Buddha' (Evans-Wentz 1927, p. 96).

Will Westerners meet the hundred peaceful and wrathful deities, or be devoured by earthquakes and wild animals?

In Buddhism we achieve liberation from the cycle of rebirth only by being fully conscious in this new state: by recognising its true nature. If we have been unable to stay conscious in the dawning of the Ground Luminosity, we must strive to recognise and stay conscious in Rigpa, the radiant energy of Mind. Hopefully we will be capable of recognising *the appearances of the hundred peaceful and wrathful deities, which occur in the second phase of this bardo... All emerge amidst the brilliant light of the five wisdoms*' (Sogyal 1992, p. 280).

It is an essential part of Tantric Buddhist practice particularly, to visualize the protective buddhas and deities, and to utilize their aid to identify and transmute the negative emotions which would otherwise take us down into one of the six realms of Samsara or conditioned, illusory existence. They are visualized according to the ancient formulas used by generation after generation of monks and lay people, and thus have become visible and concrete to those practitioners. They have become embodiments and expressions of the 'brilliant light of the five wisdoms'. This also means that Westerners will not see them, unless initiated into the Tantric practices. We may see some Western equivalent, though.

Again, the individual who can recognize this secondary Clear Light, which is indeed the soul-light or buddha light 'somewhat dimmed to him by the general Maya', is capable of functioning on that level and will naturally pass rapidly through the third stage mentioned by D.K. This third stage is that of the shedding of the emotional body, to move into and become centred in the mental body, in the state or 'world' of Devachan, or what Christians know as Heaven. *The name Sukhavati, borrowed from Tibetan Buddhism, is sometimes used instead of that of Devachan'*, says Annie Besant (1893, p. 52). The Tibetan Book of the Dead, being written for the average human of those times, concentrates upon the techniques and spiritual development needed to avoid The Bardo. There is little mention in it, of the place between lives for those whom Djwal Khul would describe as proceeding to a more or less conscious union with the soul.

Those who do not recognize this secondary Clear Light will, as the Tibetan Book of the Dead warns, remain for the time being in the emotional or astral body, confronting their phantoms and projections.

Woodroffe summarises the process in Mahayana Buddhism in his introduction to the original Tibetan Book of the Dead. He uses the term 'soul-complex' to get around the difficulties of the no-soul idea in Buddhism, and the necessary but restrictive use of the one term for individuals at different stages of evolution. As we have seen, after exiting the defunct body, the 'soul-complex' will emerge into the Clear Light. If the Void, the Buddha mind or Divine Ground is not recognized, he/she will fall into a swoon of unconsciousness, followed by a return to the state of mind, or psychic life, which existed for that individual before the swoon. The 'swoon' is the temporary loss of consciousness following separation from the physical body and its normal channels of consciousness, the brain and the sense-organs. This state of mind, he says, is one like a dream, and will only end when a new body is occupied- that is, with reincarnation. *'Life immediately after death is, according to this view, as Spiritists [ie Spiritualists] assert, similar to, and a continuation of, the life preceding it (Evans-Wentz 1927, p. lxxiv).*

Huxley on Heaven and Hell

Huxley's experience of the Clear Light under mescalin, caused him to reflect on the after-death state, and how such an intense experience of the Divine Ground or the Void would be handled by individuals with differing development of their mental and psychological equipment:

After having had a glimpse of the unbearable splendour of ultimate Reality [which is what he'd glimpsed under mescalin], *and after having shuttled back and forth between heaven and hell, most souls find it possible to retreat into that more reassuring region of the mind, where they can use their own and other people's wishes, memories and fancies to construct a world very like that in which they lived on earth.*

*Of those who die an infinitesimal minority are capable of immediate union with the divine Ground [Nirvana], a few are capable of supporting the visionary bliss of heaven [Devachan, the lesser Nirvana], a few find themselves in the visionary horrors of hell and are unable to escape; the great majority end up in the kind of world described by Swedenborg and the mediums. From this world it is doubtless possible to pass, when the necessary conditions have been fulfilled, to **worlds of visionary bliss**, [Devachan] **or the final***

enlightenment [my emphasis]. (Huxley 2004, pp. 92-3) This final enlightenment is of course, Nirvana.

Spiritualists have, as Huxley says, given us extensive descriptions of
the life of the astral plane, *'that more reassuring region of the mind',*
where most of us can, after death, retreat to *'use...wishes, memories and
fancies to construct a world very like that...on earth.'* Those whose mental
and higher bodies are undeveloped, as D.K. states and Huxley implies, will find themselves in this place of wishes, memories and fancies, for some length of time, along with those who died young and
still have powerful emotional energies, as Douglas Baker explained
in a quote above. It is worth noting that not everyone who dies
young fits this category. Those who have developed consciousness
on higher levels, and for whom an early death was soul intention
rather than personality accident, may move rapidly through the
emotional level to higher states of being.

A fighter pilot in the Bardo

The following excerpt is another from Peter Richelieu's book *A
Soul's Journey* (1996, first published 1953). This is an unusually enlightening yet completely typical description of the lower middle astral plane, and illuminates the situation of someone (Roy Chapman)
who is busy on the astral constructing a world like that he knew on
earth. Yet my former caveat is still in force. Please regard this as fiction if it is too difficult to credit; its inclusion is to clarify the relationship between the physical and the astral planes, and to cast light
on the nature of the reality, yet ultimate unreality of the astral plane,
where people do indeed *'construct a world very like that in which they
lived on earth'* as Huxley says.

To set this extract in context, readers are reminded that 'Henry',
Peter Richelieu, from whose recollection in *'A Soul's Journey'* (1996),
extracts were taken in the last chapter, has been helped by his teacher 'Acharya' to rendezvous on the astral plane, with Charles, his
fighter pilot brother. Charles has not long died in an air battle over
London, and Acharya has been dealing with Richelieu's grief by
showing him the unreality of death. Richelieu and his brother have
come to the Trocadero to 'dine', at his brother's suggestion. Charles
hails a young man in air force uniform:

> *Charles... introduced him as Roy Chapman, a pilot who had been killed in
> the Battle of Britain the previous autumn. He was a good type, and when I
> asked him how he liked living under astral world conditions, his reply was
> enlightening: "It's all right, he said, but boring after a time. At first of course*

it's rather nice being able to get everything you want without paying for it, but the novelty wears off and, frankly, I would far rather still be with the old squadron.".

Roy tells Henry he is waiting for his dinner date to arrive. *'I asked him if the girl was dead or alive. He said: "Oh dead of course: if you still want to use that old fashioned expression. It's useless making dates with people still living in the world, as just when you are in the middle of something interest- ing, they have to go back to their bodies" (p. 50).*

I have certainly had that experience, and expect it will be known to my readers too- of being rudely dragged back into one's wakened body, from 'the middle of something interesting'-a long-awaited de- claration of love, a first kiss, or something a bit more physical. However, on the astral level of dreamland, surprisingly, it isn't; it's more like essences melting together. But as Douglas Baker (c. 1974, n.p.) reminds us: *'A man has to come through to physical wakefulness to complete his sexual experience'.* We are likely to find ourselves jolted back into the body after a sexual encounter on the astral level, be- cause consummation isn't possible except through that physical body.

Richelieu discovers that Chapman had *'tried all the usual games and found them pretty boring'* since, under astral plane conditions, it is only necessary to think or wish; to see the game going in the right way, to direct it towards a win. He began to see that his teacher, Acharya *'was indeed right when he said that life on the astral plane could be boring for those whose interests were entirely dependent on physical plane conditions'.* (Richelieu 196, pp. 50-1).

This is completely consistent with the facts according to both the Bardo Thodol and D.K. When we emerge from the swoon of temporary loss of consciousness on separation from the body and brain, and find ourselves in the emotional body, in the Bardo of Dharmata, we are back in a familiar place. The psychic life is indeed taken up and continued from the point prior to the swoon; the 'soul- complex' does *emerge from its experience of the Void into a dream-like state*, just as Evans-Wentz tells us. It is the state of the individual confined to the emotional level, and without access to a physical body. It is also necessarily true that this state is *'similar to, and a con- tinuation of the life preceding it'* – that is, the life before this particular death, as we have seen in the case of Roy Chapman, quoted above.

The Tibetan, D.K., refers to these events in similar terms:

For the unevolved, death is literally a sleep and a forgetting, for the mind is not sufficiently awakened to react, and the storehouse of memory is as yet practically empty. For the average good citizen, death is a continuance of the living process in his consciousness and a carrying forward of the interests and tendencies of the life. His consciousness and his sense of awareness are the same and unaltered. He does not sense much difference, is well taken care of, and oft is unaware that he has passed through the episode of death (Bailey 1934, p. 300; extracted in Bailey 1985, p. 37).

The terrors of the Bardo

Sogyal Rinpoche explains '*how to understand*' these peaceful and wrathful deities of the Bardo. When for example, we experience desire:

> *[I]f its true nature is recognized, it arises, free of grasping, as the "wisdom of discernment". Hatred and anger, when truly recognized, arise as diamond-like clarity, free of grasping; this is the "mirror-like wisdom".*' Sogyal 1992, p. 280).

Does DK's description of the astral plane have anything in common with Sogyal Rinpoche's description of the Bardo of Dharmata (the Chonyi or Chonyid Bardo in Sanskrit)? The answer will test out the truth of the proposal that they are the same experience:

> *Just as the dancing rainbows of light scattered by a crystal are its natural display, so too the dazzling appearances of dharmata cannot be separated from the nature of mind.* **They are its spontaneous expression.** *So however terrifying the appearances may be, says the Tibetan Book of the Dead, they have no more claim on your fear than a stuffed lion*' (Sogyal 1992, p. 279).

The Tibetan Master instructs that at a certain stage of spiritual development, it is vital to learn about the astral plane, its nature and its workings – to understand how it is constructed of the energies of human desires and emotions, and how this unreality can be dissipated in order '*to learn both to stand free from it and then to work on it...The appearance of the astral plane when first definitely 'seen' by the 'opened eye' of the aspirant, is one of dense fog, confusion, changing forms, interpenetrating and intermingling colours, and is of ... a kaleidoscopic appearance*' (Bailey 1934, reference edition 1979, p. 221).

This description fits well with Sogyal Rinpoche's of the dazzling and terrifying appearances in Dharmata, experienced by those who, without the practices for dying, mistake self-creations for reality. The '*energies of the nature of mind released in the bardo state can look overwhelmingly real.... They seem to inhabit the world outside of us...Once we mistake the appearances as separate from us, as "external visions", we respond with fear or hope, which leads us into delusion*' (Sogyal 1992, p. 280).

This is just as Aldous Huxley has explained it in the quotes from The Doors of Perception.

The delusions of the bardo- astral phantoms?

D.K. puts it thus:

> 'The astral plane is the plane of illusion, of glamour, and of a distorted presentation of reality. The reason for this is that every individual in the world is busy working in astral matter, and the potency of human desire and of world desire produces that constant "outpicturing" and form building which leads to the most concrete effects of astral matter... Add to these forms that persistent and steadily growing scenario we call the "akashic records", which concerns the emotional history of the past, add the activities of the discarnate lives which are passing through the astral plane, either out of or towards incarnation, add the potent desire, purified and intelligent, of all superhuman Lives, including those of the occult [that is, hidden] planetary Hierarchy [including the Buddha and the Christ] and the sum total of forces present, is stupendous...' (Bailey 1934, reference edition 1979, p. 221).

It is not difficult to recognize that when 'every individual in the world' works in astral matter, creating part of the records of 'the emotional history of the past' -- the akashic records, what is built up is a major content of Carl Jung's Collective Unconscious, which erupts in and through all of us. Elsewhere the Tibetan notes that for those in incarnation and not treading the Path of Discipleship, the astral plane is intensely real and vital:

> After the first death [the death of the physical body] it still remains equally real. But its potency slowly dies out; the mental man comes to realize his own true state of consciousness (whether developed or undeveloped) and the second death becomes possible and takes place, [taking the discarnate individual into the third stage, into Devachan]. This phase covers the Process of Elimination' (Bailey 1953, p. 409).

This all means that the bardo of Dharmata takes us into the Astral level if we do not recognize the Intrinsic Radiance; it is a bardo whose energies, when experienced negatively, take us into the lower Astral level.

Some insight into the time taken by different individuals to undergo the first and second deaths is gained in the observations of Frances Banks, in the book Testimony of Light, which she wrote through Helen Greaves (1969). Frances Banks was for twenty-five years an Anglican nun in the Grahamstown community of South Africa, teaching at the Teachers' College, until dissatisfaction with the conceptual narrowness of the religious life made her leave to search elsewhere for the truth. Back in England, she began to work with the Churches' Society for Spiritual and Psychical Research; she and her friend Helen Greaves were part of a group experimenting with thought transfer between members. They must have been out-standingly successful: to Helen's surprise, the communications from Frances continued after her death! Interestingly, though there is no overt statement to this effect in the book, Frances and Helen appear to be students of the Tibetan's teachings. References to his teaching are scattered throughout the book even just in the terms she employs. Her quoting of the Great Invocation, the ancient pray-er said to be reconstructed by the Christ and given out to humanity by the Tibetan Master, is the main evidence for this observation.

Sister Frances is nursing in an astral psychiatric ward after her own death:

> 'Our Nazi patient is still the same; inert, motionless, shut up in the shell of himself...[Sister Frances is speaking about a famous Nazi, not Hitler however, who after his death by suicide had, she said, begun to feel great re-morse for his earthly crimes.] Father Joseph tells me that the poor creature might be like this for what we would say on earth, many years. He has already been held in the dark bondage of the hell of his own making since the end of the last war, and that is over twenty years ago... Things 'happen' here, souls or entities at all the lower stages of progress come and go; we either leave or we stay; but we do not reckon these events in time. We live, or we exist, according to the level of our thought-life, [that is, live vibrantly and joyously as Sister Frances herself, who has advanced rapidly as the 'mental man' who 'comes to realize his own true state of consciousness', or merely exist as do some of those she is nursing back to health in the astral infirmary]; some are content to stay, thinking no doubt that this is the final stage. There must, of course, come a time in the soul's awakening when that belief is proved false, but Father Joseph tells me that some souls settle down in one stage for years-even centuries! While others persist in their former earth surroundings for ages!' (Greaves 1969, p 64)[8].

Despite being ultimately unreal, much of the life to be found on the astral plane in its highest levels has a great beauty to it, as evidenced in Carl Jung and his friend's experience at the tomb of Galla Pla-cidia, which is examined for its meaning, in Chapter Nine.

---

8. Extracts from Testimony of Light by Helen Greaves 1969, published by C W Daniel. Reprinted by permission of The Random House Group Ltd.

The emotional rubbish-deal with it now, in life, or on the astral after death?

Desire and the 'wisdom of discernment'...beware of your thoughts!

Recognition of our negative emotions, or of 'what manifests in our ordinary mind as a thought of desire' brings self-awareness – the 'wisdom of discernment'. That is to say, we turn the spotlight of consciousness on what was previously unconscious, something driving us without our awareness of it, and this action immediately changes its very nature. It is no longer unconscious. We are no longer controlled by it, but are capable now of a deliberate choice among alternative behaviours.

Some years ago, I became unhappily aware of my own unconscious racism. I had thought that since I was actively working for the rights of Indigenous Australians, I could be counted among the non-racists. Consciously, that was the case. But I caught some of my subconscious dialogue and feelings, when Aboriginal Australians or African Americans appeared on TV. When I turned on the American NBC News, the Weather Man, Al Roker, who is African American, was sitting chatting to presenter Katie Couric and a white guest-was it Hillary Clinton, or am I making that bit up?

"Why is that member of an inferior race, that Black man, being permitted to socialize with those nice white people?" went the subliminal chatter. Who *was* this shockingly primitive creature within me? I felt deeply ashamed, yet realized that for my generation, this was probably normal. We were reared this way. The Collective Unconscious of our generation was racist. I find myself doing what Philip Adams also describes in his encounter with his inner beasts; monitoring and censoring them to make sure they are not reflected, but replaced, by conscious humanity and recognition of equality, in my speech and behaviour. (Adams is quoted in James, 1981).

What about my and our response to the phenomenon who is Barack Obama? He is the most loved person on the planet, I'd say, writing in the upsurge and outpouring of joy and hope worldwide, inspired by his inauguration as 44th President of the United States of America on January 20, 2009. The hope is for a spiritual renaissance not just for the people of the U.S.A., but also for humanity. The hope and its global upsurge may themselves help to bring about that renewal.

Right now, he is our Prince on a white charger, come to slay the evil dragons-racism, war, poverty, terrorism and the destruction of the planetary environment. Can he carry out even a portion of these millennial expectations-enough to survive and be elected to a second term? Our hopes may be an impossible burden -- but we are, I think, trusting the right person. The man has grace. And gravitas, and caritas, among other statesmanlike qualities. He seems to already be quite practiced at implementing his conscious choice- his principle, in fact, of including and harmonising opposing views and factions. And meantime, we are steadily seeing past, or discounting, or forgetting to notice, the colour of his skin. Presently, as we know less about her, we notice what Michele is wearing, (that elegant Inauguration ensemble in delicious chartreuse lace brocade). Yet we are attending to what her husband is saying and the quality he is emitting as he gives his first Presidential speech.

There is a tribal dynamic at work here. The more we know about someone, the closer we get and the less we attend to exterior aspects, as this outsider becomes included within our tribe. Meantime, our definition of our tribe's characteristics is expanding and becoming steadily more inclusive. It will eventually include all of humanity.

When the Buddha exorts us to practise harmlessness, it is also the mental kind of harmfulness we need to become aware of, and learn to control: the harm done on subtler levels, where 'thoughts are things', and as concrete as a sledgehammer used on denser levels of being.

What change occurs when I recognize all this? I turn the light of consciousness into a previously dark place, and immediately alter not just the content, but also the substance of this negative emotion. I believe this is what Sogyal Rinpoche means when he writes about this thought of desire; *'if its true nature is recognized, it arises, free of grasping, as the "wisdom of discernment".'* I am no longer controlled by it, but capable of a critical attitude towards it; of seeing it 'out there', and knowing it for what it is. I can now choose alternative behaviour. Even if I decide still to act upon it, I do so in full awareness of its nature. The battle with these harmful thoughts isn't over as easily as that though; I have to keep waging it, unfortunately! The battle is worth winning: it is this consciousness which brings about the disintegration of the astral body which DK explains, can take place while in incarnation, for those who have some degree of mental awareness and soul contact.

Otherwise, the work remains to be done after physical death, on the astral level, which is where we individually, as generational and cultural groups, and as humanity as a whole, have constructed these forms of emotional response and ingrained attitude, and where they must be confronted and destroyed. This has become a truly urgent task for all of us.

In the Introduction to the Evans-Wenz Tibetan Book of the Dead, it is stated that the Bardo experiences will reflect the religious and cultural programming of the individual seeing them-the Buddhist, Hindu, Christian or Muslim. The vision of a materialist will be '*as negative and empty and as deityless as any he ever dreamt while in the human body.* (Evans-Wentz 1927, p. 34)

There are, we are told, whole cities or realms created by the believers in a certain dogma or set of beliefs, places that are to these believers, Heaven or Paradise. It may be a long time before they encounter the real Heaven and know these realms to be mere human creations and ultimately unreal. The God worshipped by fanatics of any description, can only be found in these places. This is true of the God worshipped by fundamentalists, and by the closed or restricted cults, even the apparently innocuous ones like the Melbourne cult, (an exclusive sect centred around a Presbyterian church, drawing members from the moneyed and educated suburbs of Camberwell, Kew, and Hawthorn), exposed by Morag Zwartz in her *Fractured Families* (2004). Perhaps this is true of the God worshipped by most of humanity through most of time? Certainly, the tribal god of the credulous and dogmatic, one unpicked to non-existence by Richard Dawkins in his witty and erudite book *The God Delusion* (2006) belongs here. Of course, Dawkins' argument is against the existence of *any* kind of God; he argues that they all belong in the cultural museum with our other unscientific delusions. Wilber would point out that he is denying the validity of other quadrants of knowledge.

The astral or emotional level is the plane largely created by humanity's fantasy and wish life: we have created a whole world, beautiful in the extreme at one end, and ugly and terrible at the other, through the operation of the emotions, foremost desire and fear. It has a compelling reality to anyone unlucky or undeserving enough to be trapped in the lower and darker strands of the astral plane. But its only reality is this - it is the place created by the outpicturing, for good or ill, of all of us combined - Jung's the Collective Unconscious. But the terror that is occasionally encountered there, is attested to in stark terms by the Tibetan Book of the Dead, and has rather come to haunt Westerners as the dreaded Bardo. Yet Blavatsky writes of the astral plane as '*that state which is known in the Arhat esoteric doctrine as Bar-do. We have translated this as the "gestation" period (pre-devachanic)*' (Besant 1893, p. 38). Thus the entire astral plane is the Bardo, the place of the purgative experience, as Leadbeater says above (2004, p. 41). Yet most of its reaches are pleasant, even delightful, and the experience of this Bardo place is positive for most of us. The next chapter attempts to reassure us that there is something better and more purposeful awaiting us after the experience on the astral level. It discovers more about the wonderful higher stages and states of the after-death experience, and about who, according to the Ageless Wisdom, goes to these places in full consciousness.

Chapter 8

Tasting the Bliss of the Divine Mind

Summary Points

- Illusion, the Void and Tibetan Buddhism
- Suffering- and suicide-is it wrong?
- Developmental Psychology, the science of personality, and beyond- mind and soul
- **Piaget, Maslow and Kohlberg and the stages of growth to soul consciousness**
- Beyond self-actualisation to levels of self-transcendence
- **The levels of psychological development, with their colours, in Wilber's scheme**
- **What does this mean for post-death consciousness?**
- Transpersonal developmental stages to ultimate consciousness
- **Who are we after death? Beyond astral to mental and soul worlds**
- Devachan and the soul world
- **Ego domination and the nirvana of the soul**

- **Contact with the Soul -- the climaxing stage of the after-death process**
- Ascending the levels of consciousness -- Richelieu's account

Tasting the Bliss of the Divine Mind

The prospect beyond death as depicted in these Eastern systems is far more elaborated than that of the Abrahamic religions, Judaism, Christianity, and Islam, and yet a certain panic or even despair may be our main response to it. We earthlings think of physical existence as the only kind and find anything else quite unimaginable.

The illusion of earthly life or the Void of the spiritual life-are they the only choices?

Tibetan Buddhism regards the life beyond the wheel of death and birth and suffering, as the only real life. Nirvana, the Infinite, the Bliss that is Nothingness awaits us, and are finally all there is. So there is no need to worry about it. We should concentrate instead on the purpose of living in the body. Once we get incarnation right, and of course death -- a good death, then the rest -- Bliss, Eternity, will follow. If you meditate properly, you will gain personal knowledge of the discarnate state. Meantime however, we poor benighted Westerners may continue unenlightened by proper meditation practices, due to the overwhelming demands of this most material of all phases in the material realm. Unenlightened, and afraid. Of what? We may not be afraid of dying and of personal non-existence. Yet this ending, and more painfully, that caused by the death of those we love and of our relationship with them, along with the general ending, often generates a sense of futility. Our personal fulfilment and happiness, even when we find it, can look pointless in the face of this ultimate lack of meaning.

However, it may only add to our distress, to hear Buddhist teachings that this existence is an illusion, yet that we are condemned to return and repeat it over and over, until we fully recognise this. It seems at the least, arid and repetitive; at the worst, a hell beyond even human invention.

Suffering- and suicide-is it wrong?

So we may continue in our dark place, enduring great suffering often at this stage of the journey. Although we may be frightened, depressed, lonely and even sometimes suicidal, there doesn't appear to be any way out, since what awaits us out of incarnation is little more than the dreaded Bardo. And if we do succumb to despair, and take the quick way out of this body and life, there may be a heavy price to pay for that too. Christianity and Buddhism agree on this point, along with the world's other major religions. And many New Age texts concur. Suicide is a sin, a negative action which will land us in an even worse position than the one we escaped. It will generate massive bad karma. This degree of sense of entrapment is bitterly cruel, and surely unnecessary, given the reality. My researches suggest that we may incur some debt in suicide. However it ranges enormously in its moral weight, and therefore its consequences. At one end are (for example) the embezzling financiers who suicide to escape the consequences of their own misdeeds. Other deaths are at something like a polar opposite. There are the Afghan women who set fire to themselves to escape intolerable treatment, and the virtual imprisonment and slavery condoned by the society. There are those who make the decision to die a little sooner via euthanasia rather than drag out intolerable pain, or worse still, lose all control over one's body, life and circumstances.

It appears that those who end their lives thus, will usually make the decision as souls, to return to face and conquer a balancing situation. It will depend on the lesson which still needs to be learnt -- if there is one. But that is the worst of it. When I wrote this, a couple of years ago now, it was an intuitive statement backed up only by the feeling from a handful of texts. And the understanding that the opposite also occurs -- a dying process dragged out for weeks or months longer than is desirable, because of a desperate battle put up by the body-personality frightened of death and of non-existence. I have now found some evidence: in U.K. psychotherapist Andy Tomlinson's study *Exploring the Eternal Soul* (2007). It is quite clear from the case study of Liam Thompson, who resorted to suicide in several lives to solve his problems, that there is no terrible retribution, no punishment or overwhelming suffering of karmic consequence, following from this action. It seems that we ourselves, as souls, decide what we need to do to correct this weakness and balance the account. I give some detail in Chapter Eleven.

What separates us from the soul-our own, and the souls of those we love who have died?

If either or both spiritual systems, Eastern and Western, are correct, (and I hope to convince you that they are, particularly insofar as they agree that there is a life after physical death), then there is some real comfort -- that of the knowledge of the existence and nature of this soul or eternal Self, or Knower, as the conscious subject is termed in the Introduction to the Tibetan Book of the Dead. This is no comfort at all for us, where it is the embodied personality of the beloved individual who has died, that we loved and for which we grieve. That temporary manifestation has gone, and will never return.

However, if it is the essential individual, in youth or old age, with long glossy hair or a skimpy white fuzz, that we love and long to be with once more, the core being we would recognize in a totally different time and place and physical guise, then there is no death and no loss. Even the separation, such as it is, is temporary. For most of us, it is of course, a mixture of the two that we love and long to rejoin. So, to the extent that it is the physical being we love, our loss is complete. But to the extent that it is the essential individual, then it seems there is no loss whatever -- just separation due to our imprisonment in a body, and not to the beloved's ceasing to exist.

All that divides us is the sheath, the cloak of materiality and physical existence, as the Tibetan assures us. If this is true, then it is we who have died to them; the inability to continue relating exists only on our side of life. It is due solely to the physical barriers to pure (or purer) perception, which hamper us while in the material realms, but which are left behind at the moment of exiting the physical body, as the NDE research indicates.

C.W. Leadbeater answers the inevitable question about reunion with our loves after death:

> 'But of this be sure, that those whom you loved are not lost; if they have died recently, then you will find them on the astral plane; if they have died long ago, you will find them in the heaven-life, but in any case the reunion is sure where the affection exists. For love is one of the mightiest powers in the universe' (Leadbeater 2004, pp 30-31).

This is an age where fear and anxiety have created a great cloud around the planet, a grey smoggy blanketing which can actually be seen by those able to function on super-physical levels. And how much greater must that smog be, since entering the twenty-first century through Kofi Annan's *'gates of fire'* -- the threat of personal and racial extinction via terrorism, nuclear war or (much more likely, and worse because we have all contributed) environmental destruction? At least that part of the astral smog that relates to the business of death and dying, could be removed or lessened.

At such a time especially, it would help to explain that there is more to life than the pain and suffering of being born and living, whether just once or continuously. There is a serene perspective that makes it all worthwhile, or potentially. It is a perspective that instils joy and hope once it is within our grasp: it becomes unnecessary to hide in the minutiae of daily life from our anguish of living and our fear of dying. Or from our grief over separation from those we love. It is something that causes the elusive fragments unearthed by our searching, to form a pattern at last. *It is the revelation of the true nature of the soul, and of the soul's journey.*

Developmental Psychology, the science of personality, and beyond -- mind and soul

The study of the super-conscious must be undertaken, and not simply the study of the self-conscious or the sub-conscious. Through this study...modern psychology will eventually arrive at a recognition of the soul (Bailey 1936, reference edition 1970, p. 100).

D.K. made this prediction before the Second World War. The personality's idea of the Nothingness beyond this life, will eventually be discovered by each of us, to be the soul or Self's Bliss. This is now being recognised, in the transpersonal realm of developmental psychology. A century plus of research in psychology, into the structure and dynamics of the personality, from a surprising number of different and quite independent approaches, has come to concur on the existence of a superordinate, synthesising centre of awareness which is generally called the higher Self. This *superconscious* is, at the beginning of the development of awareness, outside the circle of consciousness; exactly as the *subconscious,* with its fears and prejudices, its complexes and neuroses, and the *collective unconscious* with its psychic structures which are the legacy of the race to each member of it, are outside the circle of consciousness. But slowly -- or more rapidly with deliberate work such as meditation, or with methods like Roberto Assagioli's *Psychosynthesis* (1965) or Jung's analytical psychology, the circle expands until it includes the higher self, as it includes the personal and collective unconscious.

According to Tibetan Buddhism and to the Ageless Wisdom, as well as Hindu philosophy, the nature of discarnate life depends on the consciousness of the one regarding the prospect beyond the flesh; upon where the consciousness is centred. When the integrated, synthesised self ponders life out of form, it is supremely blissful. When the personality ponders life out of the physical body, it will necessarily appear to be rather bleak, since the personality can be said to survive only temporarily, and in an altered or attenuated form. The lesson we need to learn, says D.K., and are beginning to learn, is that death, pain, sorrow and loss only exist because of our misunderstanding:

> [M]an, as yet, identifies himself with the life of the form and not with the life and consciousness of the soul, the solar angel, whose awareness is potentially that of the planetary Deity, Whose greater awareness (in His turn) is potentially that of the solar Deity (Bailey 1942 , reference edition 1971, p. 94).

For 'long ages' in the evolutionary process, D.K. notes, the soul is a factor which scarcely enters in to the life lived out on earth. So the view of all of us while at that stage, is necessarily confined to the more limited round of birth, death and rebirth -- as Tibetan Buddhism emphasizes. The consciousness is centred in the physical body and personality, not the mind or the soul or higher levels -- spirit and beyond. Even when out of incarnation, between lives, there is little awareness. It is however, slowly growing, as the relationship between soul and personality develops.

Piaget, Maslow and Kohlberg and the stages of growth to soul consciousness

The Western science which tracks these changes, called precisely *developmental psychology* - the study of the development of the psyche through all its stages of consciousness, *including the transpersonal*, was mentioned in Chapter One. Three well-known contributions, which provided foundations of developmental psychology, were those of Piaget in cognitive development, Kohlberg in moral development, and Maslow in development of the Hierarchy of Needs and the process of self-actualisation. Appendix Diagram 4 is Ken Wilber's **Some examples of ladder, climber, view,** which lays out, in a tabular comparison form, the developmental stages according to Maslow, Loevinger (to whom I refer below) and Kohlberg.

Frenchman Jean Piaget discovered the stages through which we progress in our cognitive growth, from infancy to adulthood, and from immersion in the world as pure sensation in earliest infancy, to the world as symbols -- images with meaning, during the preoperational stage of development. He found that we next move into the concrete operational stage of being able to mentally manipulate the concrete qualities of these things in the world. For example, we develop from thinking that there is more water in the tall glass than in the squat, broad glass into which we saw the same quantity being poured, to realising that they must hold the same amount, regardless of appearances. Then begins the formal operational stage, at which we can 'do sums in our heads', and other clever things with quantities and properties without having to physically manipulate them or even see them; we arrive at the point in early adulthood where most of us can understand mathematics, and some of us can do symbolic logic, grasp Plato's philosophy, or do calculus. (That's not me! My daughter has just passed her first calculus exams at university. I do my calculus with a toothbrush). Ken Wilber's scheme (2007, and see Appendix Diagram 2, Levels or spheres of consciousness), tracks the development of psyche through these stages (physical, biological, mental, subtle, causal, and ultimate) and across many lines of endeavour and ability. These different lines, in different individuals, progress at rates which are quasi-independent: artistic or aesthetic development is independent of mathematical or moral development, for example.

Lawrence Kohlberg studied and systematised the moral dimension of the development of our psyche, discovering Preconventional, Conventional, Postconventional (and higher) phases of growth. These are further differentiated into Stage Zero, morality as the infant's magic wish; Stage One, the very young child's obedience resulting from threat of punishment, *'what's wrong is what I will be punished for doing'*; Two, the young child's naïve hedonism; Three, middle childhood's right and wrong bound up with the approval of others; Four, the adolescent's conventional understanding of morality as Law and Order; Five, the postconventional stages of late adolescence and early adulthood, not reached by all of us -- morality understood as individual rights; into Six, the adult understanding of morality as individual principles of conscience. Kohlberg suggests a universal-spiritual stage beyond these.

In the early stages of Abraham Maslow's Hierarchy of Needs, individuals (and cultures at that level, hunter-gatherer or subsistence-farmer cultures) are focused on basic survival needs such as food and shelter. Children and adults at Maslow's next, 'belonging' stage, the rough parallel of the Concrete Operational level of Piaget, and the Conventional level of Kohlberg, are meeting the need to belong and have a recognised role in a social group. Self-esteem is the self-need of the next level, before that of self-actualisation, at which we are able to use our talents and capacities to deliver rich meaning to life, to gain an abiding sense of satisfaction and self-worth, while serving the society. There are no cultures or societies functioning at this level yet, though there are some communities. Beyond self-actualisation lie levels of self-transcendence. These are the levels the yogis, saints, mystics and sages of every tradition speak about as their lived reality -- the dismantling of the small personal self and the merging with Self; God, the One Divine Reality (without loss of individuality, as the Dalai Lama said in Chapter Six). Eckhart Tolle's Now moment -- above past, beyond future, the Eternal Present, as described in The Power of Now (1999) is a modern teaching of this transcendence.

The studies of Loevinger and Cook-Greuter, and Ken Wilber's AQAL Integral scheme

These transcendent levels can no longer be dismissed as just fantasies, or at best, non-ordinary states of consciousness which humanity proper can never expect to know. They are increasingly experienced briefly, by those in the middle and upper levels of psychological development. The movement towards these levels comes to be understood rationally as the next step or steps that must be taken in one's own natural psychological development. And the tendency to dismiss them because they are subjective and unscientific is put in place in Wilber's AQAL scheme -- All quadrants, all levels (2007) of his Integral Theory. (See Diagram 1 in the Appendix). This classifies our knowledge according to its quadrant, and makes clear that each has its appropriate validity test: It is not only inappropriate but useless, to dismiss one quadrant – in this case, subjective knowledge of the interior of the psyche, by its failure of the test applied to another quadrant, that of scientific object-knowledge.

As all the theorists point out, our responses as individuals come from all the levels up to our own present leading-edge level, the reach which is presently beyond our firm grasp. We are likely to have a centre of gravity, a fully consolidated, lived awareness, lower than that level.

Description of the levels and their colours in Wilber's scheme

A defined percentage of any population will live from a particular level. A consensus of researchers gives us the figures (Wilber 2002). Before going into these, I believe a caveat is in order. This classification, as presented here, is skeletal. It is more accurate applied to populations than to complex, multi-faceted individuals; more accurate about those at lower levels than those at higher ones. Think of an individual like Radovan Karadzic for example-poet, philosopher, working for years as a spiritual healer when finally tracked down. Wanted for trial by the international community for crimes against humanity, he was the Bosnian Serb leader who did everything possible to get rid of non-Serbs, including the genocide of 8000 Muslim men and boys at Srebrenica -- the worst in Europe since Hitler and Stalin, in the Balkans conflict of 1992-5. A great deal of extra information and other approaches are needed to map the consciousness of such an individual. That said, there are estimated to be 8 percent of us at or below the Preoperational, Preconventional, and naively hedonistic level, **Wilber's Fulcrum-3,** assigned the colour **Red'.** The largest percentage -- 40 percent in the U.S., is at the next, Concrete, Conventional, Group-Membership stage, which is Wilber's **Fulcrum-4, Blue,** Rule-role mind. The next largest percentage, 30 percent in the U.S., is at the Formal (operations), Postconventional, Individual rights stage, **F-5 Orange.** *These two groups form at least a massive seventy percent of the world's democracies.* Meantime the Reds (with addition of a pathological brutality) are the militias who torture and rape in places like the Congo, and the dictators. Examples are Hitler and Stalin of course, Robert Mugabe in Zimbabwe, Slobodan Milosevic in the former Yugoslavia, Pol Pot in Cambodia; men happy to maintain their power by assassination of their rivals, and ethnic cleansing (the term devised by Radovan Karadzjc to sanitise genocide) of any groups in the way of their state's dominance.

The preconventional Reds 'my way or you're dead' are also a central force in the mainly Red-Blue groups engaged in intertribal, intercultural or interreligious warfare in Africa and the Middle East. The Blues among us and within us can be persuaded that all groups deviating from Our Way, the One True Way, must be driven out, if not exterminated. So what about Osama bin Laden and Al Quaeda and its brother groups -- Jemaah Islamiah for one? Is bin Laden pure Red, or is he more Blue? I leave that to you to ponder. There is a consequence of all this in world affairs! The civilisation, along with the planet itself in its survival, is largely in the hands of the Reds, Blues and Oranges. Why? Their members dominate governments either because they muscle or murder their way in (Reds), or they are voted in, (all three). At seventy-eight percent of the total population, (hence their ballot-box power) *when they agree* they 'have the numbers', and can 'call the shots', for good or ill. I see terrorism as

---

1. Wilber originally adopted the colour coding assigned to Clare Graves' values development stages by Spiral Dynamics theorist Don Beck. Wilber has rethought this by Integral Spirituality (2006) and now uses the wisdom tradition's natural rainbow. This for example, alters the Blue of F-4 to Amber, (not Red-orange or Flame). Blue and yellow are now absent; strange rainbow indeed! But it was an attempt to integrate the original colours where possible with a more intuitive scheme.
The new scheme now runs Red, Amber (in place of Blue), Orange, Green, Teal (in place of Yellow), Turquoise, Indigo, Violet, Ultraviolet, Clear Light. I have left the original colours in place for this discussion, in part because Don Beck and Spiral Dynamics teachers continue to use the original colours.

the lesser threat than environmental devastation, to the future of the human race. However, discussing the different responses to this other very real threat more easily elucidates these differences of developmental psychology. My thinking on all of this has been informed by Ken Wilber's online articles, in particular *The Deconstruction of the World Trade Centre* (Wilber c. 2002) -- a witty and telling title for Wilber's considered response to the psychology, morality and reality of 9/11.

Warfare is a more usual resort of the Reds and Blues particularly; -think of George Bush's response to the terrorist attacks of September 11, 2001. His Blue rhetoric divided the world into two camps-'Good vs. Evil' and 'You're either for us or you're against us'. This response is in marked contrast to the refusal to fight of the postformal, poststructuralist, pluralistic-values **Greens** at **Fulcrum-6**, Suzanne Cook-Greuter's Individualists, (twenty percent of the population). Then there is the strongly contrasting value of the more advanced group, the **Fulcrum-7 Yellows**, the Strategists. They can see that it may not be possible to reason with the terrorists; we may need to despatch them before they despatch the rest of us. This is war, but only as a last resort to save humanity,

At any stage below Postconventional, it is possible to persuade or manipulate us into rape, torture, and killing of unarmed innocents because a leader orders it or because they belong to an opposing racial or religious group, as in Sudan where the Arab Janjaweed militia were armed by the government and ordered to wipe out the African population. Men and women in the Orange, formal operations, postconventional morality stage, who would agree with strikes against the terrorists of 9/11 because they attacked the foundational values of society, may not be persuaded to kill civilians even if their own lives were under threat if they refused. But it is in the following stage, **Wilber's Fulcrum-6 Green**, early Vision-logic (2002), where people no longer *want* to fight. These are Jane Loevinger's Individualistic and Autonomous stages of the self-sense (Wilber 2002), and Suzanne Cook-Greuter's (2007) Individualist, the go-my-own-way postmodernist. This is the stage of the pluralist mind which sees *morality as individual rights, all equally valid*. Which group are the force driving events in the world more than any other at this time? Whatever your answer, we need to understand the psychology of all the groups if we hope to survive. Will evolution take us as a civilisation, beyond our present stage of conflict and environmental devastation in time? Before we destroy the planet and wipe ourselves out?

Something has changed in the U.S.

It is all the more surprising, and hopeful, that an elevation of the national consciousness seems to be taking place in the U S -- in the face of (or as a result of?) the worldwide economic crisis triggered by the subprime mortgage debacle of 2008. The most obvious sign is the election of Barack Obama: the majority of the Blues and Oranges had to have voted for him to make that possible. The election of a black President would surely not have been possible at any previous time. Another interesting indication is that Oprah Winfrey, who is herself African American, and one of the most powerful women on earth, a remarkable force for good and for change (she campaigned for Obama), has chosen to put funds, energy and promotion behind an online course in Eckhart Tolle's The Power of Now. The response has been huge, despite the fact that the concepts involved require a mature spirituality to understand, one beyond the Blue level of obeying rules and accepting the dictates of a superior authority -- to understand but perhaps not to attempt to follow.

Blue F-4 teenagers and the Cronulla beach race riots

Teenagers, once largely invisible, now have huge and disproportionate political and cultural power, and the vast majority are functioning from a Blue level of consciousness. They go through tough times negotiating this stage. Even while they need to rebel in order to develop an independent self, they may be in conflict between the values and mores of family and school or church, and those of their new membership group, which may insist that they take drugs, steal, have underage sex, binge drink, or immolate themselves in suicide bombings. It's especially hard for teens who, as a result of family immigration, are caught between cultures, and conflicting demands about roles, duties, and what's right.

The infamous race-riots at Sydney's Cronulla beach in 2007, occurred between teens who were members of the majority culture and its surfing subculture, who demonstrated their cultural allegiance by wearing the Australian flag, and teens from Middle Eastern, mainly Muslim backgrounds, who, after being made to feel unwelcome on the "Aussies'" beach, attacked surf lifeguards. The rift has been somewhat healed, partly by recruiting Muslim teens, girls as well, to the surf lifesaving culture and getting the beach-culture teens to initiate them. And by sending one young Muslim man who had torn the Australian flag from its RSL (Returned Servicemen's League) pole, to hike the jagged, jungle-covered vertical inclines of the Kokoda Track in Papua New Guinea. There he learnt about the service, suffering and courage of Australian soldiers fighting the invading forces of Japanese Emperor Hirohito, in World War Two, and came back with a new respect for the culture to which his family had immigrated. The journey gave him cultural heroes, role models and rules for his current stage of consciousness (Wilber's Blue Rule-role mind), along with a new place and role in his adopted culture. This new role was strengthened by the recognition and applause for his change of attitude, of his peers, the group of young men on the Kokoda trek. The documentary of his journey on national television both mollified and educated the rest of us. It was a clever, and wise, application of the insights of this same developmental psychology.

The F-7 Integrated level vs. F-6 Poststructuralist Greens and their cultural effects

These foundations of developmental psychology already pointed to, or included, levels beyond the postconventional, formal operational, mind. The existing, but rather sketchy, *transpersonal* stages (Maslow's self-transcendence and Kohlberg's universal-spiritual stage) were about to be solidified. Further studies of higher stages, by Carol Gilligan, Jane Loevinger and Suzanne Cook-Greuter especially, led to empirical data on the Integrated stage of development. This stage is identified as one of a cognitive, moral and self-sense autonomy, and a sophisticated integration of previously conflicting or unrelated ideas and systems into coherent wholes, (Wilber's Vision-logic). Previously, there was confusion when all values were seen as having equal rights to exist, whether democratic or terrorist, in the postformal moral relativity (no good, no bad, all equal) Green stage. (The Greens are, though, the first level able to recognise and respect, the values of cultures and groups not their own.) It was this postformal, post-structural relativism that drove the Demolition Derby of deconstruction, which says Wilber (2001), left cultural roadkill all over the halls of academia. However, he says, the events of 9/11 in the U.S., the terrorist plane-bombings of the World Trade Centre and the Pentagon, dealt the death-blow to poststructuralist notions of cultural and moral relativity; 'This *is* bad' was the Greens' reaction.

The Integral is the first level capable of giving respectful yet *stage-appropriate* treatment to different people and cultures at different stages. F-6 notions of relativity, Wilber pointed out, suffer from an inherent performative contradiction: there are no absolute truths; all truths are equal. Yet some are more equal than others, because we declare the foregoing to be true -- thus constituting ourselves as superior and our position as the only absolute truth in a world where there are no absolute truths.

Relativity is replaced in this next, **F-7, Yellow, Integral stage**, by a clear understanding of the *value ranking of all elements*. This Integral mind is the first that is capable of moving beyond exclusive identification with one side of the equation, without getting stuck in the paralysis of *'all values are equal and thus purely subjective'* position of the Fulcrum-6, Green individual. The Integral mind begins to be aware of the dialectical movement identified by the nineteenth century German philosopher Hegel, the shift from identity with a conscious position -- an idea, a value, a belief, a self-sense, a worldview (the thesis) through the conflict of its opposite (antithesis), to transcendence and resolution in a third, higher position (synthesis). Wilber (2001) describes such a process as *identification* with a level and type of consciousness, *dissociation* from it so it becomes an object in awareness, no longer the self-subject, followed by *transcendence and inclusion* of the level in a higher one. He identifies this process as the mechanism driving all changes in consciousness. This dialectical process is about to become deliberately used, a tool of the mind, in **Fulcrum-8**, which has been allotted the colour **Turquoise** by Wilber. Here opposites are united; they are seen as complementary aspects of the whole. The mind itself is becoming an object in consciousness, used by a subject no longer identified with that mind -- the consciousness of the next level of self/Self, which is that of the soul or psyche.

Finally, when the entire sweep of developmental psychology in its vertical and horizontal achievements, was systematised by Ken Wilber, a relatively complete picture of the evolution of consciousness emerged. We now know that there are prerational /preconventional, conventional, postconventional and post-post-conventional stages, and that these span from the earliest, of self not differentiated from world, to the highest stages previously delineated, of mature personality integration and beyond. What lie beyond are several stages of increasing soul control over personality, and integration of the personality into the soul, (and of soul into spirit) in the stages of transcendence of body-personality bounds. *The Integral stage is identified as the critical transpersonal border*-the transfer from personality-centred to soul-centred consciousness. It is also the highest stage currently identified in an empirical way (by Suzanne Cook-Greuter), through psychological study and testing. Here we shift from identification with the ego to identification as the Witness, aware of the personal self and watching from a higher perspective, and developing towards transcendence even of the Witness, in the consciousness as and of the Whole, the Divine Self, God.

What does this mean for post-death consciousness?

It means that since Heaven and Hell, and all places above, below and between, are levels of consciousness, there is a direct correlation between the psychological development level from which you normally function at the end of your life, and the 'place' towards which you gravitate after death. The highest point of consciousness we reach in this lifetime correlates, as we have seen, with the point of the body from which we exit at death, and our fate after death. It is possible to correlate all these stages with the post-death levels particularly described in the last chapters, and thus to predict in a more precise, Western-approved way, the post-death state for any one of us.

There is agreement that at the upper stages, heading towards the Witness point of evolution, when the soul ('subtle mind' in Buddhism) considers life outside of form, it is affirmed as the overriding reality. It is the glorious experience of true Life, (in contrast with the shadow-lands of the material consciousness), as the personal self merges with the Ground of Being. All apparent contradictions of Bliss and Nothingness are quite simply resolved. We may not be consciously aware of this in our waking, earthly lives, except as a lack of fear of or concern about, death - and this is likely to be exchanged for a massive fear, as we shift back into the perspective of the mortal personality.

When we remain in ignorance of the true nature of our own being and the existence of our divine nature, our Eternal Self, we are totally identified with the personality, or ego, and therefore with the strictly physical, mortal aspect. We must strive to unmask the ego, the sleazy politician, says Sogyal Rinpoche. *'To end the bizarre tyranny of the ego is why we go on the spiritual path'* (Sogyal 1992, p. 131).

It is in Ken Wilber's Yellow stage where we are first able to see beyond the perspective of my egocentric self, my personal group, creed, race or nation (my country, right or wrong) and even mine and yours -- equal in value, to the 'our world' perspective of the world citizen. The perspective of the Witness begins to arise. This is a direct result of the shift of identification/identity from the personality and its confined, egocentric perspective to the view of the group-centred soul, who has been the inner teacher all this time.

Sogyal Rinpoche discusses the role of the Inner Teacher, the enduring aspect of ourselves, and the relation of that Teacher to the Master, who is, he says, the spokesperson of one's own inner Teacher. This spiritual Master is the one who is the conductor of *'all the blessings of all the enlightened beings.... He or she is nothing less than the human face of the Absolute'* (Sogyal 1992, p. 134-5). The very fact of Tibetan Buddhism's recognition of the existence of this Inner Teacher, this Higher Self, is the end of the debate about whether there is a soul in Tibetan Buddhism. This is indeed the soul by another name. The existence of the Master on superphysical levels can be recognised and become a fact in consciousness, in the transpersonal developmental stages, which take us into soul or subtle, then spiritual or causal, and on to ultimate, consciousness.

Who are we after death? Beyond astral to mental and soul worlds

'I speak about Death as one who knows the matter from both the outer world experience and the inner life expression: There is no death' asserts The Tibetan. *'There is...entrance into fuller life. There is freedom from the handicaps of the fleshly vehicle'* (Bailey 1934, reference edition 1970, p. 300).

What is the state of consciousness of those who have died? The less evolved will spend most of their time asleep or in a dim state of consciousness. Now that such an individual has no brain, the loss of the body leaves only undeveloped faculties. These are likely to be the individuals of egocentric, Preoperational, Preconventional consciousness only: Fulcrums One, Two, and Three, of Ken Wilber -- Beige, Purple and Red. Others more awake (the majority of Westerners, Fulcrums Four and Five in Wilber's scheme- Blue and Orange) will travel out onto the astral level, and are likely to find themselves in beautiful places. They may see ethereal cities or pastoral views: the Australian bush, for example. Most of us will spend our time here, in pursuing our more refined passions and interests. Leadbeater gives examples of science, art, music, travel and philanthropy:

If his fancy turns towards science or history, the libraries and laboratories of the world are at his disposal...His comprehension of processes in chemistry and biology would be far fuller than before, for now he could see the inner as well as the outer workings, and many of the causes as well as the effects...The man who is kindly and helpful learns much in many ways through the work which he is able to do in that astral life; he will return to earth with many additional powers and qualities ...' (Leadbeater 2004, pp. 26 and 31).

Those of real intellectual or rational development, Fulcrums Six, Seven and Eight, Green, Yellow, and Turquoise, may see nothing which has any identifiable form or appearance. They may move immediately or fairly quickly, to Devachan, where the nature of reality is now mental; there will be no physical aspect to it. Jung's own experience of the Near Death phenomenon, some years before his actual death, and recorded in *Memories, Dreams, Reflections* (1963), is a case in point, as is P.A. Atwater's, quoted in Chapter Six. These individuals of greater mind development of F-7 and F-8, may even reach 'the Devachan of the soul' as D.K. calls it. They will have an increasingly stable capacity to enter into, or live in and work from, the Clear Light of Universal Mind while in incarnation: they are likely to incarnate quickly to get on with work and service on a desperately needy planet.

Who ascends to heaven, who gets stuck on the lower astral, earthbound, longing for another body?

D.K. details what happens to each category of those who have died:

'For the wicked [the tyrants and dictators who imprison, enslave, and murder] *and cruelly selfish* [whether at an international level or within the family -- those all over the world who indulge themselves while those for whom they are responsible suffer], *for the criminal* [the Mafia mobster or the embezzling financial tycoon like Bernard Madoff] *and for those few who live for the material side only, there eventuates that condition which we call "earth-bound". The links they have forged with earth and the earthward bias of all their desires, force them to remain close to the earth and their last setting in the earth environment.'*

What do all these groups have in common in their after-death state?

They seek desperately and by every possible means to re-contact it and to re-enter (Emphasis mine, Bailey 1934, reference edition 1979, p 301*).*

This description tallies perfectly with all the Mahayana Buddhist sources. However, it only applies to a limited group of humans, the evil and cruelly selfish, the criminal and those whose consciousness does not extend beyond the purely material. It is possible to be at a formal or postformal level cognitively, yet morally preconventional: a Hitler or Pol Pot or Mugabe. The reverse is very rare: a low cognitive level and a high moral level. There is a gap in DK's categorisation, between this materially bound group and the next, the 'good and beautiful'. This gap is in fact filled with the largest group of ordinary human beings, whose horizons are limited to themselves, their families, their local communities and survival in the here and now. If they live in a democracy, they will choose leaders who will benefit them personally or advance their particular cause, regardless of that leader's other policies. These average human beings will spend quite a time in the lower or middle astral levels. (There is really nothing 'average' or 'ordinary' about most of us, even when our consciousness is thus limited: it is merely the quickest way to characterise this group.) They are at the F-4, Blue stage and lower F-5 Orange stage.

What of the 'good and beautiful'? These are likely to be advanced Fulcrum Five (Orange) and into Six (Green). They ascend through the levels of consciousness to places of great beauty, as Plato and Schure and Aldous Huxley have attested, and sooner or later, find themselves in the bliss of Devachan. After this, in the fourth stage of the 'dying' or disincarnation process as DK gives it, there will be a time, longer or shorter, of contact or union with the soul. Then they will return to incarnation.

What of those aspiring to live a spiritual life and consciously working to be better human beings, more useful to humanity? These may be later Fulcrum Six, (Green), and Seven, (Yellow). The higher Fulcrums Eight, (Turquoise), and Nine, Coral, now Indigo, have moved on from aspirant status to become disciples and initiates:

> *For the aspirant, death is an immediate entrance into a* **sphere of service** *and of expression to which he is well accustomed [emphasis mine] and which he at once recognises...In his sleeping hours he has developed a field of active service and of learning. He now simply functions in it for the entire twenty-four hours (talking in terms of physical plane time) instead of for his usual few hours of earthly sleep* (Bailey 1934, reference edition 1979, p. 301).

This fits with Sister Frances Banks' experience, reported in *Testimony of the Light*, from which I quoted in Chapter Seven. Return to incarnation appears to be a soul decision, for the members of this group, as the next chapter explores.

Devachan and the soul world

The astral life, says C.W. Leadbeater, will have been happy or un-happy for us according to the preparation we have made during earth life, but the next stage, Devachan or heaven, is always the most perfect happiness each of us is capable of receiving:

> *On this plane we find existing the infinite fullness of the Divine Mind, open in all its limitless affluence to every soul ...small or large, every cup is filled to its utmost capacity; the sea of bliss holds far more than enough for all. All religions have spoken of this bliss of heaven, yet few of them have put before us ...this leading idea which alone explains rationally how for all alike such bliss is possible...the fact that each man makes his own heaven by selection from the ineffable splendours of the Thought of God himself. A man decides for himself both the length and character of his heaven-life by the causes which he himself generates during his earth-life. Now [his] time of purgatory is over, for that lower part of his nature has burnt itself away: now there remain only the higher and more refined thoughts, the noble and unselfish aspirations that he poured out during earth-life. All the highest of his affection and his devotion is now producing its results...all that was selfish or grasping has been left behind in the plane of desire...'* (Leadbeater 2004, pp. 41-2).

Progression through the levels of consciousness is a natural and normal part of the shedding of the physical body and higher bodies and returning to the Source. D.K. summarises this progression and its stages, including the first and second stages, which we considered earlier. This progression is the 'peeling' of the onion skin or nest of eggs referred to earlier (Bailey 1953, pp. 497-9, extracted in Bailey 1985, pp. 42-3).

The Tibetan goes on to describe what happens at the third stage. This is the death of the astral body, in the process known as Attrition, and the movement of consciousness into the mental body, and into Devachan or Heaven. There are *four categories* of psyche or soul development with their four different experiences of the life after death in this third stage. It is important, I believe, to spell out these stages rather than simply generalizing about them, for one reason: The readers of this book are all by definition, at least 'kama-manasic' (emotional-mental), and are most likely to be 'manasic' (mental) or in the higher category still of 'the disciple' (the server of humanity with some soul contact). Since your experience of this third stage will not be that of the generality of humanity, it should be elaborated further for your understanding.

The *kamic* or strictly emotional individual is one at or below the Concrete operations, Conventional, Conformist stage, Wilber's fulcrum-4, Blue, Rule-role mind. The stage below is purely emotional: it is that of the pre-operational, pre-conventional, egocentric self who is a slave to passions and desires. These souls may wander in the Hungry Ghost realm, one which is occupied by those not matured past attachment to experiences of the senses. By contrast, the *kama-manasic* consciousness is that of F-5 and F-6, the Orange, formal operations, postconventional morality level, (Cook-Greuter's Achiever) and the Green, Postformal and Post-postconventional (Cook-Greuter's Individualist). *Manas* or mind, increasingly active in Orange and Green levels, emerges clearly at F-7, the Yellow, Integral stage.

The post-death stage of Attrition is *'relatively easy to understand'*, says D.K. The astral body is fed and kept alive by desire for aspects of incarnate life. Once there is no call from physical substance to evoke this, *'the kamic body (the astral or emotional body) dies out'*. The strictly emotional human being, the kamic individual, after a long time of this process of attrition on the astral plane, in the after-death bardo, *'is left standing free within an embryonic mental vehicle'*. This *'period of semi-mental life'* is brief because of the lack of the mental faculty to utilize a time in Devachan. The kamic individual passes rapidly from the third stage to the fourth stage, reunion with the soul, which will be unconscious for such an individual. Then the soul *suddenly "directs his eye to the waiting one" and by the power of that directed potency instantaneously reorients the individual kamic man to the downward path of rebirth'*. It is clear that the kamic individual has no input into this decision, as a result of the lack of requisite consciousness.

The emotional-mental or kama-manasic individual is capable of a more deliberate withdrawal, in response to *'the "pull" of a rapidly developing mental body'*.

Succeeding incarnations and further mental development produce the probationary disciple. This withdrawal becomes *'increasingly rapid and dynamic, until it reaches the state where the probationary disciple-under steadily growing soul contact-shatters the kama-manasic body, as a unit, by an act of the mental will, implemented by the soul'*. Less time is needed in Devachan by the steadily evolving one; this is due to the fact that *'the devachanic technique of review and recognition of the implications of experience is slowly controlling the man on the physical plane so that he... learns constantly through experience whilst incarnating'*. This means that continuity of consciousness is slowly developing, so that *'the awarenesses of the inner man begin to demonstrate on the physical plane, through the medium of the physical brain at first, then independently of that material structure. I have here conveyed a definite hint on a subject which will receive wide attention during the next two hundred years'* (Bailey 1953, pp. 497-9; extracted in Bailey 1985, pp. 41-2). An aspect of that 'wide attention' is of course, the research into, and huge popular interest in, the Near-death Experience.

The mentally polarized or manasic person has become an integrated personality, who is working towards integration with the soul. It is telling that this is the same term used by researchers: the Integral or Integrated stage. There are two levels of associated development. The lower level is that of the integrated personality, who is *'focused in the mind and is achieving a constantly growing rapport with the soul'*. The manasic person may refuse to be ruled by astral desire because of *'selfish ambition and mental intention'*. We are aware by this stage of our development, that desire is a trap.

The higher level is the *'disciple'*, who may be an evolved practitioner of some religion, or a secular humanist. This developed person practices an inclusive and effective goodwill towards all humanity, and lives by a high moral code centred on harmlessness, love and service. The personality has been integrated so it functions as a conscious whole, and this is now being rapidly absorbed by the soul. *'In this stage of mind development and of constant mental control...the earlier processes of the destruction of the astral body ...are carried on whilst in physical incarnation. The incarnated man refuses to be ruled by desire; what is left of the illusory astral body is dominated now by the mind'*.

The highly evolved human being is refusing to be ruled by desire because of acting under *'the inspiration of soul intention which subordinates the mind to its purposes...'*(Bailey 1953, pp. 497-9 extracted in Bailey 1985, p. 42).

This consciousness has crossed the great ego-Witness, personality-soul divide into Wilber's Fulcrum-8, Turquoise, Witness consciousness; Cook-Greuter's Magician, which she says is a total paradigm shift. Such a consciousness is capable of resolving the great black/white polarities of existence: No longer separate and opposing forces, they are recognised as interdependent aspects of the whole. It is sometimes referred to as the 'paradoxical mind'.

What happens in Devachan?

The location of Devachan is on the fourth mental sub-plane, D.K. goes on to tells us; one below the sub-plane of the mental plane where 'souls have their dwelling-place'. It is here in Devachan/

Dewachen that the life's experience is worked over by the human psyche, so as to be distilled into an essence which is the gain of the life's experience. This will be stored in the permanent atoms, to be the 'seed' or essence or tigle/tikle, in Buddhism, of the future incarnation:

> *'When the life of the personality has been full and rich, yet has not reached the stage wherein the personal self can consciously co-operate with the Ego [the soul], periods of personality nirvana* [in Devachan} *are undergone, their length depending upon the interest of the life* [ie how much it contains to reflect upon], *and the ability of the man to meditate upon experience. Later, when the Ego dominates the personality life, the interest of the man is raised to higher levels, and the nirvana of the soul becomes his goal. He has no interest in Devachan. Therefore, those upon the Path (either the Probationary Path, or the Path of Initiation) do not, as a rule, go to Devachan, but immediate incarnation becomes the rule in the turning of the wheel of life; this time it is brought about by the conscious co-operation of the personal Self with the divine Self or Ego* (Bailey 1925, p. 737. Reference edition 1979).

This means that when either (lower) mind or soul dominates the emotions and the personality as a whole, the astral body is being chipped away during incarnation, so there remains only the stage of the shattering of the mental body after the end of an incarnation, before reunion with the soul.

Contact with the Soul – the climaxing stage of the after-death process

The discarnate one has moved through two processes, Restitution and Elimination. In the process of Restitution, the soul has withdrawn from the physical body and the etheric body, its two phenomenal aspects. The process of Elimination governs the life of the psyche or human soul in the astral and mental worlds, the other two worlds of strictly human evolution. (Beyond this point, we enter the 'kingdom of souls' of the spiritual stage of our evolution.) The essence of the life-experience is extracted by the spiritual soul, first from the astral body, then from the mental body, and these bodies are then eliminated. The soul is then *"ready to stand free within its own place"*.

The third process is that of Integration, *'dealing with the period wherein the liberated soul again becomes conscious of itself as the Angel of the Presence and is reabsorbed into the world of souls, thus entering into a state of reflection. Later, under the Law of Karmic Liability or Necessity, the soul again prepares itself for another descent into form'* (Bailey 1953, reference edition 1975, extracted in Bailey 1985, p 82). These two laws are discussed in the next chapter. There is a distinction made in this passage between the human soul, the soul aspect projected into incarnation, and the spiritual soul, in deep meditation in the world of souls while its projection is embedded in the physical world.

From the moment of death we become aware of past and present. Then after Elimination, when *'the hour of soul contact'* has arrived, and the mental vehicle is being destroyed, we become *'immediately aware of the future, for prediction is an asset of the soul consciousness and in this the man temporarily shares. Therefore, past, present and future are seen as one.'* This achievement of a secure soul contact doesn't stop here: it carries over into the incarnated life as a radical change of consciousness and understanding about the nature of life, and a consequent change of being in the world. It means that *'the recognition of the Eternal Now is gradually developed from incarnation to incarnation and during the continuous process of rebirth'* (Bailey 1953, pp. 496-7). This recognition is called by D.K. the 'devachanic consciousness.' It is a reason that disciples lose interest in Devachan; increasingly they have access to the devachanic - - and higher, states of consciousness, while incarnate.

All of this was, as I have said, still too theoretical and just plain difficult to translate into experiential terms. Everything I'd read till then seemed to be describing only the astral plane; who is to be found there; how they spend their time; the nature of the astral world. I had assumed the lack of information about any higher level was due to the near-impossibility of anyone functioning at that level being able to communicate with those still stuck in the gross physical world. Or was it just that the astral sphere was a dream world, simply an imaginary extension of physical reality-and the soul was non-existent; death was the end after all? A friend came through my garden gate bearing books to help with the manuscript.

Greater understanding arrived with these two books -- Greaves' *Testimony of the Light,* and Richelieu's *A Soul's Journey,* both already mentioned. They contained information that bridged the gap in knowledge between the astral world and soul levels. Here was some sort of confirmation that astral and mental worlds were real; that they were consciously accessible from earth to the more highly evolved, those of 'devachanic consciousness' among us. Henry's (that is, Peter Richelieu's) teacher, Acharya, who taught him to exit his sleeping body in full consciousness and travel in the astral world, takes his pupil onto each level of the astral plane, and finally higher, into the mental levels of consciousness (Devachan /Dewachen or Heaven):

I shall now talk to you about the mental world. I told you that after a period of time it became necessary for all of us to drop our astral bodies and leave the astral for the mental world. ...A man who has had about fifty lives will spend much longer in the astral world and shorter in the mental world than will one who has lived five hundred lives in different bodies and in environments where he has had opportunities for intellectual pursuits... When death occurs at the physical level, this corresponds to dropping the overcoat (the physical body), when it occurs at the astral level, it corresponds to dropping the suit of clothes (the astral body); this leaves the man garbed in his underclothes (the mental body) and it is in this vehicle that he enters the mental world.

As I have said, the mental body is the first body the ego draws round him in his descent from the causal level. It is fashioned of even finer material than the astral. Actually, it is the thought-form of the individual. As you could not yet comprehend a description of this wispy, cloudy form which appears to lack all density, I shall only give you a physical comparison of the mental body of an unevolved human being, say one who has had about fifty incarnations, with that of an evolving human being, say one who has had about five hundred incarnations, by likening them to a wicker basket as seen in two stages of the making...In the early stages you see a basket take shape, but it has only a few strands of cane fixed to its base...The finished article is blended together of many hundreds of wicker strands... Each of these strands may be thought of as representing a particular subject of mental development which has been more or less mastered by that individual.

When a person has finished his life in the astral world, he passes to the seventh sphere of that world; when it is time for him to move on from there, he becomes sleepy, loses consciousness, and awakens almost immediately in the mental world. When, after his physical death, a man becomes fully conscious in the astral world, his first sensation is a feeling of well-being and buoyant health. When, after his astral death, he becomes fully conscious in the mental world, his first sensation is that of profound bliss and a feeling of being at peace with mankind. In the early stages he may not even realize that he has passed to the mental plane...In due course he realizes the change in his surroundings and once more he has to be taught by those who wait to welcome him, the difference between the conditions under which he must now live and those relating to the world he has just left.

The mental world is the world of thought. Thoughts are the only realities; they are things just as much as chairs and tables are things...[I]f we could take any of our astral or physical matter into the world of thought, it would not exist for the people there. Such things would be more or less the same as thought-forms in the physical world; they surround us all the time but we cannot see them-although they influence our minds...At the mental level you do not see other people as individuals, nor as astral counterparts of physical forms, but as thought-forms of the individual concerned, and these thought-forms accord with the mental development of the individual.

Acharya likens the individual functioning on the mental level to a two-way radio set, whose channels or frequencies are the number of subjects understood by that individual. At this level, we can pick up the thoughts of others if we can tune in to that subject's frequency, and when we reply in thought, others interested in the subject can pick up those thoughts:

> *At the astral level you saw the intellectual giants creating beautiful music, pictures, etc., and teaching others in the arts and sciences. When they pass from the astral to the mental world, they continue to help others... but at the mental level their tuition takes the form of technical and theoretical lectures sent out in a perpetual stream of thought... You can only grasp as much of the thoughts as by your own intellectual activities of the past you are able to comprehend* (Richelieu 1996, originally published in 1953, pp.171-2).

The next stage, contact with and absorption by, the soul, and the experience of the even superior bliss of the world of the soul and our soul group, (for those of us who have consciousness sufficiently developed) is succeeded, for virtually all of us, by a return to incarnation. The very few of us who have completed the cycle of incarnation inhabit the Nirvanic consciousness permanently, and work and serve from that high place, in a physical body or out of it as seems most needed for the service to be rendered. They pass onto the Higher Way of evolution, as seen in Appendix Diagram No 3. This appears to be misunderstood by Western and Eastern Buddhists alike, in what I think of as the Nirvana-melt conception of immortal life. Upon reaching Nirvana, the enlightened individual is believed to merge into the Universal or God-consciousness, and not to retain existence which is individually conscious. This idea is exemplified in the ending to the wonderful book I mentioned in Chapter One, Ken and Treya Wilber's *Grace and Grit*. As she is dying, Treya insists to Ken that he must find her again, as he had found her earlier in the life she was now leaving. Ken interprets this as meaning something else than the apparently obvious meaning. This part reads to me at least, as though he expects Treya to reach the Nirvana state, but then to disappear into the impersonal whole of the divine Consciousness. *But this is not what happens to the Nirvanee!*

The subject of the next chapter is reincarnation: the return to physical life -- in all its variations.

Chapter 9

The Bardo of Becoming

Rebirth

Summary Points

- Jung vs. The West on the 'non-existent' psyche, the Self and rebirth
- The all-containing archetype of the Self, the guiding principle of personality growth
- **Jung, Yogananda and disappearing saints and teachers-magical infantile thinking?**
- Jung and the vanishing Ravenna frescoes
- Reincarnation in Buddhism- the Bardo of Becoming
- **New parents and a new body**
- Reincarnation in the West
- **Is reincarnation impossible in Christianity?**
- The Bridey Murphy reincarnation phenomenon
- **The research of Bernstein, Cannon, Fiore and Wambach**

- Can researchers produce 'reincarnation' memories from any hypnotised subject?
- Wambach's studies of the time before gestation and birth-choosing a new life
- **Hasty Return, Unwilling Return, Reluctant but responsible return, Willing return**
- Karma, place, sex, parents, and other aspects of a new life
- Reincarnation a group project- Rudolph Steiner's Reincarnation lectures

Jung vs. the West on the 'non-existent' psyche, the Self and rebirth

It was a surprise to read Jung's Psychological Commentary to the Evans-Wentz edition of The Tibetan Book of the Dead. That pioneering mind had arrived at clarity about what was always implicit in his work and his territory. This is the fact of individual consciousness as being quite separate from and independent of, a body, and as being situated in a state not touched by the death of the body.[1] He writes in the *Commentary*, that psychoanalysis has provided the *'rationalizing'* Western mind with the bridge that has taken us into the essentially neurotic Sidpa or Rebirth state (neurotic in the same way as the rest of the Bardo or lower emotional levels, as seen in previous chapters).

We come to a dead stop there, Jung says, halted by the assumption that the *psyche* has no objective existence, and is therefore unreal. Jung is struck by the identity of the Sidpa or Rebirth Bardo-its psychological structure and contents, with part of this *psyche*, especially the Collective Unconscious as it revealed itself through his researches.

The Western mind, having reached into the Rebirth state, has been blocked there, Jung says, due to the *'uncritical assumption that everything psychological is subjective and personal. Even so, this advance has been a great gain, inasmuch as it has enabled us to take one more step behind our conscious lives'* (Evans-Wentz 1927, p. xliii). The West will remain stuck here, at its 'standstill' until we learn what Jung tried to teach us, what he learnt in such extraordinary researches-a lifetime of dedicated effort and unflinching exploration, attempting to illumine the darkness of the unconscious psyche.

What is that lesson we must learn before it is too late, and we, with our Material Universe carelessness, destroy the planet and ourselves, as I worried in the opening chapter? It is that *the psyche and the Self are indeed real.* The psyche is objective, not purely 'subjective and personal'. It is not a nothing simply when and because it is partly constructed out of our dreams and desires and fears. We think of it as dependent on a body and brain for its (separate, purely subjective) existence. It is not so dependent-it has an existence prior to and independent of, any physical life.

---

1. He had also, through entirely empirical research, discovered the religious or spiritual function of the human psyche, the subject of his 1938 Yale lectures (Jung 1938).

Jung states: *'The collective unconscious consists of pre-existent forms, the archetypes... which give definite form to certain psychic contents'* (Moacanin 1986, p. 30).[2]

The psyche, the Buddhist Mind, is also prior to and independent of all subjective earthly lives added together. It is a universal existent, unifying all apparently separate human consciousnesses; or rather, it is the unified field from which all units of consciousness emerge, imagining themselves separate and self-created. It is timeless and deathless, as Jung discovered. It is ruled by laws as ineluctable as any which operate on the physical level. It is the domain, in fact the very *being* of the eternal, immortal Self, the Archetype of archetypes.

Jung came to understand that the archetype of the Self contained all other archetypes, as the guiding and uniting principle giving the personality direction and meaning in life. He wrote:

> *Intellectually the Self is...a construct that serves to express an unknowable essence which we cannot grasp as such, since by definition it transcends our powers of comprehension. It might equally well be called the 'God within us.' The beginnings of our whole psychic life seem to be inextricably rooted in this point, and all our highest and ultimate purposes seem to be striving towards it* (Moacanin 1986, p. 33).

We in the West, with our 'rationalizing mind' cannot grasp this reality, even many who are dedicated disciples of the genius Carl Jung, working out and fleshing out his insights to assist humanity. We can understand to a degree, the independent life of the psyche. We advance just so far, and then we revert to our Default position. So still in the end, we reduce this life to some soupy mix of the psyches of individual humans. Our inevitable blindness and hubris leads us to claim that we humans as embodied individuals, are somehow, either separately or all together, the only creators of the Self.

We return to the idea of the Self as arising from mere outpicturings, dream and fantasy contents, produced by the physical level. Yet the Self is not some accidental and inert conglomeration, without consciousness except for our own dim lights. It is the consciousness of our entire cosmos, at the least. We are not the creators of the Self; it is the Self who created us. It is not we who own the Self, but the Self who owns us. Jung kept discovering this, to his amazement, in the way in which that vast consciousness kept

---

2. There is a lack of distinction in Jung, says Ken Wilber, between the understanding of archetypes as primitive forms of the undeveloped mind, the Collective Unconscious, and Archetypes as enduring Forms, in the Platonic sense (ie of Plato's philosophy), of the higher levels of the Divine Mind (Wilber 1997).

intruding into his own more confined psychic spaces, drawing him as a result, into greater light and consciousness for humanity as a whole. The further we travel into the higher interior reaches of the Self, the more we realize that we are encountering, not an unconscious Thing, however vast, but the very opposite- the Supreme Consciousness.

For Jung, this was the One identified in all traditions as That in whom we live and move and have our being -- that is, God by that name or any other. Our encounters with the Self eventually teach us the purposive, supremely wise and loving nature of that Consciousness, who possesses all the qualities so fitfully present in us, and to which we individually and as a civilization, aspire. There is the problem of the intense suffering of billions of us-the majority. I don't find it acceptable except in the greater scheme-but who am I to judge? We expect, and demand, not to suffer. Jung himself saw the East attempting to cast off suffering, while the West tried to *suppress suffering with drugs. But suffering has to be overcome, and the only way to overcome is to endure it. We learn that only from him (the Crucified Christ)'* (Moacanin 1986, p. 85).

Jung, Yogananda and disappearing saints and teachers

Even Jung, the pioneer of this psychic territory of the collective unconscious and the psyche's governing archetype, earlier had a tendency to regard himself as the source of the Self's manifestations. This was evident in his vision at the tomb of Galla Placidia (discussed below), and in his original understanding of the nature of being of his teacher, whom he called Philemon. He and his teacher would walk together in Jung's garden and talk in the manner of Socrates and his pupil Plato: This is the measure of just how objective and tangible this teacher was. Jung originally regarded Philemon as an aspect of his own psyche. He later credited this preceptor with having taught him the objectivity of the psyche, and thus the reality of Philemon himself. Douglas Baker has commented that such teachers are assigned to those doing great and vital work for humanity...These workers are, like Jung, sufficiently evolved to perceive beyond the physical level, and thus register the presence of a teacher not in the physical state. Kubler-Ross also had such a teacher, as she is brave enough to reveal in *The Wheel of Life; a Memoir of Living and Dying* (1979).

Yogananda's *Autobiography of a Yogi*, (1946), was the first life of an Eastern saint to be published and widely read in the West. It made an indelible impression upon Western consciousness. This great yogi also had gurus who could take on physical form at need, and disappear – return to less concrete levels of being, at the end of that task.

One amusing story is of the saint Trailanga, who went innocently naked everywhere, his great consciousness occupied on much more universal levels than his appearance. The *'harassed'* police of Benares jailed him for indecency. *'General embarrassment ensued; the enormous body of Trailanga was soon seen, in its usual entirety, on the prison roof. His cell, still securely locked, offered no clue as to the mode of his escape'* (pp. 227-8). This time, a guard was posted outside Trailanga's cell. It made no difference, again the swami was found *'in his nonchalant stroll over the roof'*. At this point the police knew they were beaten; they gave up. There are 'three miracles to every page' (I'm not being literal here) in this extraordinarily inspirational and beautiful text, to which most of us who know it keep returning.

Bill Harris, one of a powerful group of conspirators for an enlightened and unified humanity, whom I introduced in Chapter One, is one of the many evolved servers of humanity who don't yet fully understand the relationship between the physical and subtler levels. In a blog of Bill's early in 2008, (debating the reality behind Rhonda Byrne's 2006 bestseller *The Secret* with his clients and correspondents), Bill acknowledged his respect for Yogananda but insisted that this great teacher was mistaken –somehow imagining it, when he wrote of his own teachers suddenly appearing and then vanishing again, and other miraculous happenings. Bill Harris, like so many scientifically educated Westerners, seemed to have no choice but to reject the Autobiography and its worldview in its entirety, or succumb to 'the magical thinking of the infant'. The missing link seems to be the esoteric knowledge which makes sense of what otherwise can only register as fairytales. What would Harris and like-minded colleagues make of Jung's experience in the Baptistery of the Orthodox? Would they accuse Jung of infantile magical thinking?

Jung and the vanishing Ravenna frescoes

At Ravenna, Jung visited the tomb of Galla Placidia. He went on into the Baptistery of the Orthodox. 'Here, what struck me first was the mild blue light that filled the room...the wonder of this light without any visible source did not trouble me.' This is the first clue as to where Jung is-the level of perception to which he has penetrated. 'I was somewhat amazed because, in place of the windows I remembered having seen on my first visit, there were now four great mosaic frescoes of incredible beauty, which, it seemed, I had entirely forgotten.' He and his companion stopped in front of the fourth-Christ holding out his hand to Peter, who was sinking beneath the waves, and talked about it for twenty minutes:

> *I retained the most distinct memory of the mosaic of Peter sinking, and to this day can see every detail before my eyes: the blue of the sea, individual chips of the mosaic, the inscribed scrolls proceeding from the mouths of Peter and Christ, which I attempted to decipher...I went promptly to Alinari to buy photographs of the mosaics, but could not find any...I thought I might order the pictures from Zurich'* (Jung 1963, pp 265-8)[3]

This is intriguing! A language unknown to Jung, on a mosaic that ceased existing when Jung and his companion walked away! Jung had mentioned the mosaics in a lecture before discovering they didn't exist- not on the concrete level at least.

Jung's own interpretation of this paranormal event is given in a footnote on page 267, by his writer and editor, Aniela Jaffe: *Jung himself explained the vision as a momentary new creation by the unconscious, arising out of his thoughts about archetypal initiation. The immediate cause of the concretisation lay, in his opinion, in a projection of his anima upon Galla Placidia'*-the highly cultivated noblewoman yoked for her lifetime to a barbarian prince. All of this would have helped, but I doubt that it was the source of the vision.

I might accept this interpretation if Jung had experienced the frescoes as a visual projection, overlaid on what was actually there, or if he had seen them but his woman companion had not. Instead both were temporarily transported in consciousness into another dimension-the clue as to which dimension, is given in the mild blue light described by Jung as filling the space. This is the (higher) astral light-always described this way by those who see it, soft, bluish, ubiquitous, and sourceless. Such magnificent art as these frescoes did not arise out of the unconscious aspect of the Self, but out of the superconscious instead. That Jung was experiencing a transcendent moment of the kind available to those whose consciousness is developed beyond the Integral stage, is obvious. But that only takes us so far. These were the works of a master, it is clear -- but which one?

Jung speaks of the original basilica built by Galla Placidia as having been destroyed by fire-the simplest explanation is that he was viewing the frescoes of that church-remembering that time and destruction are features of the physical plane, and that the frescoes may exist for the duration of the Manvantara, on the inner planes. It

---

3. Memories, Dreams, Reflections © CG Jung 1963. Excerpts reprinted by permission of HarperCollins Publishers Ltd.

may not be the case, though. Ravenna may have been the perfect atmosphere to grace Jung with an epiphany which would, it was already known, be received in due time by humanity generally, in the West at least.

I suspect it would have required the powers of a consciousness higher than Jung's, to 'transport' both Jung and his companion – perhaps the consciousness of Jung's own teacher and master, perhaps that of the subject of the frescoes, the Christ, of whom Jung wrote 'Christ, like Buddha, is an embodiment of the self' (Jung 1963, p 261). This is indeed the true nature of both. Has anyone else understood this as clearly? This is very different from seeing the Christ as a homocentric projection of the individual, or of Christians as a group, upon the universe, as do critics of Christianity, and even some apologists.

Jung did not at first accept reincarnation, but later came to its inevitability and logical necessity, as is clear in his foreword to the translation of the Bardo Thodol by Evans-Wentz. His acceptance has been a powerful influence in the West, assisting us to regard reincarnation seriously, not just as a primitive Eastern myth. It was vital in helping to prepare our Western consciousness to receive the East's teachings, especially Buddhism.

Reincarnation in Buddhism- the Bardo of Becoming

What then, does Buddhism teach about the nature of The Bardo of Becoming, the longest of the stages between death and rebirth? What is its essence? It is the phase of preparation for a new earthly body and existence. How is the new life chosen, and what is the nature of the preparation for it? How do we arrive at the moment of contemplating the new birth, from the point of exiting the old body and life? Does Buddhism give a coherent explanation of all this?

Sogyal Rinpoche tells us that it is necessary to be able to exercise mental control over our thoughts; a task made very difficult by the fragmentation of consciousness in this Bardo:

If in life you have developed the natural reflex of praying whenever things become difficult ...then instantly you will be able to invoke or call to mind an enlightened being, such as Buddha or Padmasambhava... Christ or the Virgin Mary' (Sogyal 1992, p.261).

These 'enlightened beings' are not our projections or inventions, they are embodiments of (the archetype of) the Self, which, we need to remember, exists prior to and independent of, human consciousness.

In this bardo, '*you crave more and more for the support of a material body, and you search for any one that might be available in which to be re-born*', says Sogyal, (1992, p.295).

This recalls D.K.'s words on the search for a new body: '*...for those few who live for the material side only, there eventuates that condition which we call "earth-bound"... They seek desperately and by every possible means to re-contact it [the physical level] and to re-enter*'.

Sogyal Rinpoche continues:

> '*Lights of various colours shine from the six realms of existence, and you will feel drawn toward one or another, depending on the negative emotion that is predominant in your mind*' (Sogyal 1992, p. 295).

Each of these six realms is linked to an overwhelming or obsessive emotional state. The form god realm is that of pride and ambition, the demigod is of jealousy, the human of desire, the animal of 'ignorance' or perhaps a coarse and sluggish consciousness, the hungry ghost of greed, and the hell realm is that of anger. Given the lack of higher states of soul or mind that would have enabled us to avoid this bardo, we are drawn to one of the six realms by the predominance of that emotion in our personality, and therefore the underdevelopment of other, positive emotions. We will be drawn downward towards another birth (not deliberately chosen by the aware self, but impelled by the lower nature) in one of the six realms of existence. One cause of the gross overpopulation of the planet is this rushing back into incarnation of these emotionally directed humans. It is these realms, especially the lower, which terrify Westerners who are exploring, or attempting to live the (Tibetan) Buddhist way. Yet, as I have quoted Sogyal Rinpoche reminding us, '*A good life means peace in death and not fear....*'

Transition or rebirth into the 'animal' realm does not actually mean becoming an animal, but instead taking on 'bestial' characteristics. Reincarnation of any human soul into an animal body is not possible at this stage of evolution, according to the exponents of the perennial philosophy. Jung also favoured a metaphorical interpretation.

New parents and a new body

The mechanism of rebirth, as described in the Tibetan Book of the Dead, operates via karmic connection to one's future parents, drawing the reincarnating psyche towards them as they make love. Strong emotions are aroused as a result of those connections:

'Attraction and desire for the mother and aversion or jealousy for the father will result in your being born as a male child, and the reverse a female...' (Sogyal 1992, p. 296).

This is part of what caused Jung to refer to the 'neuroticism' of the Sidpa Bardo state. It is fascinating that this recognition of the fundamental nature of the sexual drive in shaping personality, and the sexual attraction of children to parents, so shocking to Europeans when announced by Freud a century ago, has been known and accepted in Tibetan culture for many centuries!

Our gender is thus said to be due to our intention to become the opposite sex of the parent for whom we feel attraction and desire. Where such a desire is an overwhelming force driving reincarnation, it makes sense as a reason for having to take on the body of one sex or another for the next life. However, this teaching covers only one of the possible reasons for the choice of a male or female body, and only 'the six realms': the lower levels of the gamut of reincarnation scenarios. Those stages or Wilber Fulcrums are, once again, past for most of those who are the readers of Sogyal Rinpoche's book, or this one. It must be remembered that the Bardo Thodol is a text of great antiquity: Its teachings were relevant to the vast majority of humanity at an earlier stage of our development. This reminder is intended for everyone who feels disturbed by the prospects ahead of them in the Bardo, as I also felt.

So, in the Tibetan Buddhist accounts, we then land back in a body on earth.

Reincarnation in the West

The position of Christianity (and Judaism and Islam) that there was a single life, followed by Heaven or Hell, left too much unexplained, I felt; too much that was the business and goal of doctrine, to explain. There really is no way, short of the doctrine of many lives, to reconcile the immense disparity in the nature and conditions under which different lives are lived, with any slightly humane or even rational scheme of divine or cosmic management. How could a crippled beggar girl, born under a scrap of dirty paper on the streets of a teeming Asian city, suffering from all the effects of malnutrition on her ability to think about anything, with no access to even the first opportunity requisite for spiritual growth, be held responsible for any outcome of her life? How could a just scheme deprive her of everything, even that she needs simply to survive, while giving that party animal and porn star Paris Hilton, heir to the hotel fortune, every opportunity available to anyone on earth? How could a just Creator, or the consciousness of an ordered cosmos tending ever towards good, base one's desserts for all Eternity on such an impossibly small and rickety and totally unfair foundation? It doesn't make any sense, and it's time we stopped pretending that it did. The idea that we continue to evolve during many lifetimes, becoming through karma, increasingly the masters and makers of our own destiny, makes more sense.

Yet though I had long accepted reincarnation as a working hypothesis at least, was I in fact being gullible? The round of birth and death and birth all sounded so endlessly difficult and painful, that occasionally I decided along with a good many thoughtful people, that it would be better to be properly dead at the end of this one little life. But then the great hunger for meaning would reassert itself, along with a certain curiosity and excitement about the journey, the ride, and I would want to continue. On the occasions of wanting oblivion, I suspected I might be suffering the reaction Kitty Ferguson describes, as Einstein's reaction to the Big Bang Theory of the origins of the universe. The facts were at odds with my feelings and desires-with what I would *prefer* to be true. Or were they? It required further research. This research, however, turned up masses of material in support of life after death and reincarnation, and nothing at all reliable to counter it. Sceptic after sceptic went into one field of research or another on survival and reincarnation, expecting to explode myths, and had to admit defeat –and personal conviction about our continuance. One of these was Colin Wilson, author of the influential book *The Outsider* (1956). His editor set him projects on the Near-death Experience and on Reincarnation, which resulted in his book *The Occult* (1971). He says he expected it to be quick and easy: a matter of debunking myth and uncovering fraud. Confronted with a mass of unassailable evidence, he became convinced of the reality of the perennial philosophy's position (Wilson 1990, p. 11).

Is reincarnation impossible in Christianity?

Research also uncovered the rather arbitrary nature of Christianity's doctrinal choice against reincarnation. For example, Gnosticism, which was widespread and very popular in the 1st Century Roman Empire, context of early Christianity, taught reincarnation as a central tenet. Christianity risked being outflanked or swallowed up by Gnosticism if it also accepted reincarnation, according to

Professor Geddes MacGregor, whose study on the subject was introduced in Chapter Two. McGregor proposes reincarnation as fulfilling all the requirements, doctrinally as well, of purgatory, observing that each life would then progress the long upward struggle of *'evolutionary moral growth that purgatory must surely be by any reckoning. One must be born again in the flesh or in some other embodiment in order that the birth of the spirit may be gradually achieved. Otherwise, why are we born in the flesh even once?* (McGregor 1978, p.162).

(He is questioning why we descend into incarnation at all, unless birth in the flesh achieves birth of the spirit. And it is a descent from Self or Mind, as demonstrated already in this chapter.)

MacGregor concludes:

> *I see myself drawn forth in the course of my present life from the amorality of self-centredness to a much deeper sense of the love of God... I remember vividly the prison of that self-centredness and know so well how far the grace of God has taken me in my struggle for freedom. Yet for all the vast progress I see, I know I have farther to go than I can hope to go in this life...I need, therefore, another embodiment, and it seems to me that the more progress I make through such re-embodiments the more need for them I shall see...Each reincarnation is, of course, a resurrection. The resurrection that is promised to those who are made partakers of the resurrection of Christ is not only preserved as the Christian hope, it can now be seen as a continuing process in which every rebirth gives me new capacity for walking closer and closer with God....*

> *We may conclude that there is nothing in biblical thought or Christian tradition that necessarily excludes all forms of reincarnationism [my emphasis]. We have seen many historical reasons why it has been suppressed both officially and at the popular level...We have seen no reason why it must be in conflict with the historic teachings that have come to us through the Bible and the Church. We have seen, above all, that some form of reincarnationism could much enhance the spirituality of the West...* (McGregor 1978, p. 172-3).

Our Western view of the reality or unreality of Life, and further lives, after death may be the same story as with the Near-death Experience. Scientists, and the rest of us, tend to dismiss anything which isn't perceivable by our senses, or which is contrary to the assumptions of our worldview (as Kitty Ferguson was pointing out in Chapter Three) as delusory or invented. This is still the case, even in the twenty-first century, and despite the *enormous* weight of evidence supporting the conclusion that death is not the end. If you are unaware of these mountains of evidence, it is partly or chiefly due to the stakeholders of the materialist position, ignoring or suppressing them.

What is the status of this evidence? Most of it is either anecdotal, or part of psychological or psychiatric case studies. It is therefore, reasonable to reject this evidence as lacking reliability, if these accounts turn out to be rare, or if they are only produced under conditions that are unique or unusual. This seemed to be the case earlier in the West's encounter with reincarnation. When the Bridey Murphy phenomenon broke via *The Search for Bridey Murphy* (Bernstein 1956) back in the late fifties, it made its way into the public consciousness as unique. Harry Houdini could get out of a locked steel box; Ruth Simmons (the pseudonym of Virginia Tighe, as originally used by Bernstein) had an even more bizarre talent. She could, under hypnosis, recall details of another life and time, the life of someone called Bridey Murphy.

So Bridey Murphy/Ruth Simmons was a freak, we decided. Yet what if the only reason nothing was known about this phenomenon and its rarity or otherwise, was simply because regression back beyond birth was never tried? *Perhaps this regression was never tried because the mindset of the researchers made it impossible for them to contemplate life before birth?*

The Bridey Murphy Reincarnation Phenomenon

The Bridey Murphy story came about as follows: Morey Bernstein was a successful young businessman who began dabbling in hypnosis in his spare time. He was a complete sceptic about life beyond the physical, including reincarnation. A series of surprising events pushed him to investigate further, and he encountered the work of Dr Sir Alexander Cannon. Bernstein recounts the experience:

> *Turning quickly to this part of the book (Reincarnation outflanks Freud), I observed that the doctor had for many years been conducting age-regression experiments with hundreds of subjects. But instead of stopping when the subject's memory reached back to infancy or birth, the doctor had kept right on going, probing still farther back, investigating the mystery of memories before birth...*
>
> *I had conducted age-regression experiments with dozens of subjects, but naturally I had always stopped when the subject returned to infancy. That was the end of the line, I had figured... I had some excellent subjects who were capable of age regression under hypnosis. What was I waiting for?*
>
> *There and then I decided to find out about this pre-birth aspect of the memory for myself* (Bernstein 1956, p. 114).

Bernstein chose Ruth Simmons, as she was capable of deep trance and would remember nothing afterwards. Under hypnosis, this ordinary American woman leading a typical mid Twentieth Century existence with husband, children and domestic duties, relived her life as the Nineteenth Century Irishwoman Bridey Murphy.

Once Bernstein had regressed Ruth through infancy and back beyond birth, Ruth began recounting the story of the life of Bridey Murphy, an Irishwoman who lived between 1796 and 1864, and who loved to dance. She spent her childhood in Cork, then married and moved to Belfast. Over a series of sessions, the details were filled in. The reporter who had become deeply interested in the story, William J. Barker, feature writer for the *Denver Post's* Sunday magazine *Empire*, later went to Ireland to try to either corroborate or disprove the Bridey story. Most of the definite details, questioned or outright derided by media reports attempting to debunk Bridey and reincarnation, were either verified or found to be consistent with the time and place and local culture. These included the dating of the practice of kissing the Blarney Stone, the nature of the custom of the Irish wake, the use of the term 'ditching' for burial, and the existence of two long-vanished Belfast grocery stores named by Bridey – John Carrington's and Farr's. Much research went into Bridey's use of contemporary terms (she spoke under hypnosis in a pronounced Irish brogue); terms no longer extant such as tup and brate, and a particular use of the word linen. Some details could simply not be checked, a century later. However, *no detail was found to be definitely false.*

There is a fascinating, though rather gloomy, account of time Bridey spent in the Bardo, on the lower astral level, after her death. Her consciousness is too limited to give her access to greater light, life and joy even on the higher astral levels.

What happened after you died? ... Did you watch them bury you?

Oh, I watched them. I watched them ditch my body.

...And you saw Brian (Bridey's husband)...?

I went home. I stayed in the house and watched Brian...

While you were in the spiritual world did you hear anyone call it the astral world?

Yes, I've heard that...

In this astral world did you have any feelings or emotions?

You were just satisfied; you weren't...you... I felt bad when...when Father John died, but he came to me and we talked, and it was not like the grief you have here.

[Bridey is still identifying as someone in incarnation; grieving over Father John leaving the physical world she was hovering around in her astral body, even though she knows that there is no death, and she sees him become discarnate like herself, and talks to him.]

.... You said that you went from your house at Belfast in this astral world; you drifted back to Cork. How did you get from Belfast to Cork?

...I just willed myself there.

Willed yourself there. How long did it take you to get from Belfast to Cork?

I don't know. It wasn't any time' (Bernstein 1956, pp 154-7).

I recalled reading the book as a teenager, and pondering this quirk in Ruth Simmons' brain. Nothing like that would come out I was sure, if I, or anyone I knew, were hypnotised. I recalled a number of other books I had read in the interval; the public response to each book was that they were bizarre exceptions; almost certainly fantasies or outright fabrications.

By the time I was writing this book, my searches were a little more rigorous. It became obvious that accounts of life after death, of the between-lives state, and of rebirth, are everywhere. It was only a matter of directing one's attention to them. Are they replicable? Are they repeatable under repeated instances of the original conditions? *Is it possible to trigger or arouse a memory of surviving death in any one of us, more or less at will?* Does anyone who is hypnotised successfully, and directed to go back before their birth, to something that they remember in some earlier time, recall another lifetime? What would Morey Bernstein have to say on this subject? Or Peter Ramster, the Australian psychologist who has been working in this area for three decades or so?

The research of Bernstein, Cannon, Fiore and Wambach

Morey Bernstein, who had no interest in any 'paranormal' area, was finally driven by his discoveries into active research, as we have seen. He went to the New York Public Library, and began tracking down everything on the subject of reincarnation. It was then that he came across the mentioned book by Dr Sir Alexander Cannon. 'This knighted scientist, the holder of an imposing list of degrees', as Bernstein cited him, wrote as follows:

For years the theory of reincarnation was a nightmare to me, and I did my best to disprove it and even argued with my trance subjects to the effect that they were talking nonsense, and yet as the years went by one subject after another told me the same story in spite of different and varied conscious beliefs, in effect until now, well over a thousand cases have been so investigated I have to admit that there is such a thing as reincarnation.'

Bernstein also observed that it was not the case that other doctors and psychiatrists had never run into this phenomenon; it was only that their researches were not generally known:

'*Nor does this man stand alone. There are, indeed, a number of scientists whose experiments have led them to the same conclusion …[S]ome specialists have been publicising their findings. For some reason, however, their reports have never been as widely circulated as they might have been'* (Bernstein 1956, p. 225).

Can researchers produce 'reincarnation' memories from any hypnotised subject?

Apparently this is dependent only on whether a subject can be hypnotised, and whether the trance induced is profound enough, according to the professionals working in this field, who have tried it on a range of subjects. Peter Ramster, the Australian who has become an acknowledged expert, noted:

'*It is becoming increasingly apparent that anyone capable of deep trance is capable of remembering a past life, in much the same way as a person can remember his or her childhood. Some people can remember details easily, and others only with great difficulty. There are some areas of childhood we often don't wish to remember, and some areas we do. The memory of past lives seems to follow a similar pattern'* (1980, p.139).

That still leaves the question of the real source of these accounts. Perhaps they were merely pastiches of present memory; things read or heard or seen in this life? Only if one does not bother to look at the vast accumulated evidence, is it possible to go on believing these accounts are the fantasies, rare in occurrence in the population as a whole, of the temporarily deluded or gullible or marginally insane.

Dr Edith Fiore was one of the early psychological researchers who discovered the benefits of delving into past lives when all else had failed to resolve a patient's problem. She found that the origin of present illnesses and problems could often be located in lives prior to the present one. It would remain merely an interesting hypothesis if the therapist, Dr Fiore, had been the one responsible for deciding what experience caused what symptom, and if Fiore had suggested to her subject that she would now be cured of the headache caused by a gunshot wound to the temple in a previous life. But that was not how it worked. Symptoms would not be resolved unless the supposed cause was the true cause. Dr Fiore's client had to return for hypnotic sessions until the true cause, in whichever lifetime, was unearthed.

Is Fiore the first researcher yet mentioned, who started out believing in reincarnation? In the Introduction to *You Have Been Here Before*, (1978) she notes that her religious background is important in her journey to acceptance of reincarnation.

> *My family always lived in the country and we went to the church (Protestant, from Dutch Reformed to Episcopal) nearest our farms... While I was a deeply religious child...I radically altered my beliefs during my freshman year at Mount Holyoake College when I was first exposed to agnosticism. It fitted with my scientific bent and I remained an agnostic until I began to encounter past lives through my patients' regressions. Since then I have been gradually changing most of my religious and philosophical viewpoints. At this point I am neither a staunch believer nor non-believer in reincarnation. However, each day as I watch more and more patients and subjects explore past lives, I find myself increasingly convinced that these are not mere fantasies* (Fiore 1978, p. 12).

So, reports of reincarnation are everywhere.

Do we want to return to earth; that is, reincarnate? It certainly seemed preferable to me, to wandering in the bardos, and I didn't see myself as a candidate for Enlightenment just yet. Yet I continued to feel less than thrilled by the repetitive nature of reincarnation. I remembered a book by the psychologist Helen Wambach, which, once again, at the time I couldn't place in the overall context because of missing pieces. Her subjects reported choosing a new life and body, and its sex.

The Western reports of the experience of reincarnation: Wambach's studies of the time before gestation and birth

Groundbreaking studies of the business of *choosing a new life* were carried out by American psychologist Helen Wambach, and reported in *Life Before Life* (1979). She had already written a book '*Reliving Past Lives: the Evidence under Hypnosis*' on her explorations in that field. Wambach regressed 750 subjects to the time before their birth, and recorded their responses to her questions about its nature.

I had thought at first, when told about the book, that Wambach used a standard 'rebirthing' regression; that is, a reliving of emerging from the womb and travelling down the birth canal into the world. She took her subjects back further than that, however. It might still be possible to assume that they arrived on earth from some ortho-dox Christian idea of the pre-birth state: a pristine paradise of souls dwelling with God until incarnation. But Wambach's questions eli-cited responses that either assumed previous bodily existence, or ex-plicitly stated it.

Wambach's subjects report on the Bardo, returning to earth and a physical body

How did the experience of earth, in her subjects' judgement, com-pare to their existence in the pre-birth state? Was one preferable to the other? Where were they after dying and before being reborn? Were they wandering in the gloom of the Bardo? Were they happy to be coming back to earth or was it a grim prospect? Although it isn't the focus of Wambach's book, (which is more the choices made and the reasons for choosing, and the process of getting ready for a new body and life) what is it possible to glean about the pre-natal, pre-conception existence through her subjects' accounts?

Were her subjects prompted by the phrasing of Wambach's questions, to assume they'd lived before? The questions she put to several groups of subjects she'd placed under hypnosis and regressed to the time before their birth, remained the same over a period of years. They were: Are you choosing to be born? This was asked dir-ectly after 'I want you to go now to the time just before you were born into your current lifetime'.

The questions continue

> *Does anyone help you choose? If anyone helps you choose, what is your rela-tionship to the counselor* [i.e. the person helping you choose]*?*
>
> *How do you feel about the prospect of living this coming lifetime?*
>
> *Are you choosing the last half of the twentieth century to experience physical life for a reason? What is that reason?*
>
> *Have you chosen your sex for this lifetime? If you have, why have you chosen to focus as a man or as a woman in this lifetime?* [This is of especial in-terest given the Bardo Thodol's reason: that karmic connections cause us to respond with desire or aversion to each parent, and that the sex of the desired parent then decides our –opposite- sex].
>
> *What is your purpose for coming into this, your current lifetime?*
>
> *Have you known (your mother) in a past lifetime? If you have known her, what was your relationship before?*

This is the first explicit mention of past lives. (I would have pre-ferred the phrasing 'Do you know your prospective mother? If you do know her, what has been your relationship to her?) Wambach asked the same questions about the father (1979, pp. 17-19).

These subjects reported a variety of reasons for returning to earth and bodies, for choosing a particular locale, environment and time, and for the choice of parents. Some of these cases sound just like the situations described by Sogyal Rinpoche, in that they were in a hurry to return, or were conversely, dragged helplessly back into incarnation. Most of Wambach's subjects, though, reported that they chose, usually reluctantly, and with the help of wise advisers and friends in their group, to return, for reasons associated with spiritual growth and service to other humans. I have organized a selection of these accounts of her subjects, into *categories according to the nature of their return* to physical life, and the driving force behind it.

Hasty return, self-chosen or 'pulled'

The following are examples of this first group, who returned hastily:

"Yes, I chose to be born, but it was in panic. It was not a decision made at leisure. When you asked if anyone helped me choose, I was aware of guides that seemed to be large light beams, guiding me not to be born now-but I was determined. My feelings about the prospects of living the coming lifetime were that I wanted it and I knew my mother wasn't ready and this family wasn't right. But I had things to do and three karmic trips to complete" (Case A-493). I will cite the cases as Wambach does, by their case numbers.

"...(S)omeone was trying to keep me from getting born. They were warning me. My feelings about the prospect of the coming lifetime were that I had an urgent desire to get down there to play. But after I was born, I felt that it was so rough. The atmosphere was rude down here on earth. I had expected playing, but it was all commotion, and I longed to be back in the space where everything was light" (Case A-339).

"No, I didn't choose to be born. I felt I had just died in a war, and was looking for some place. Then I felt pulled to my parents. I didn't have anyone helping me choose. My feelings about the prospect of living another lifetime were apprehensive. I did not want to be born" (Case A-148)

These are examples of the kind of experience in the Bardo, and its results in the choice of incarnation, that the Bardo Thodol and its modern versions, warn against. As noted earlier, D.K., the Tibetan, comments on the unhappy results of indiscriminate and uncontrolled sexual practices: souls are dragged into incarnation before they are ready to return to earth. There are several billions more of us on earth in the early twenty-first century, than the earth can sustain, and this may be a major cause.

Unwilling return, 'pushed'.

A separate group of unwilling entrants was made up of those who weren't 'dragged from below', but 'pushed from above', so to speak, as in the following instances:

> *"No, it seemed as though I didn't choose to be born, but was forced by others to be born. It seemed there was someone higher up or others insisting. I just didn't want to be born at all"* (Case A-180).

> *"No, I didn't choose to be born. I had the feeling that something or someone controlled my birth, but I couldn't understand any more about it. I didn't want to go through another lifetime again, but I felt like I needed to learn to love. I felt like it was a recurring lesson and I had to come back again, and again and again"* (Case A-301).

These cases are a reminder of the teaching of the Bardo Thodol: *"O, Son or Daughter of an enlightened family, you must recognize the Light or you will find yourself headed downward to rebirth once more..."*

The individuals in all these cases are, whether willing or unwilling, quite powerless to affect the fact of their reincarnation (as the Bardo Thodol warns will be the case if they have not seized the opportunities of liberation).

If reincarnation occurs as a result of an active decision, not through the operation of forces which overwhelm the personality, that decision is made by the soul. In this group, the soul is most likely to be experienced as a higher power, not as part of oneself, because there is as yet too little soul-contact and soul-control. Helen Wambach calculated that 19% of the total subject group *'resisted the birth experience to the point where they said they either did not choose to be born or were not aware of making a choice* (1979, p. 42). These first two groups-Hasty and Unwilling Returnees, are the groups whose choice to incarnate or not, is contrary to or in ignorance of their souls' intention. They may be the groups to which the *Bardo Thodol*, and *The Tibetan Book of Living and Dying* are most directly and most urgently addressed.

Reluctant but responsible return

The largest group of subjects (67% of Wambach's sample) is reluctant, even profoundly so, yet despite that, they are aware that this was in the end, their own choice. This indicates a greater soul contact, and a higher stage or fulcrum of psychological development than those whose choice to incarnate did not involve the soul. (It is amazing to reflect that this group of reluctant returnees is so large, yet that, once on earth again, we are so *afraid* of the death which is the prelude to release from the flesh, and return to those high and wonderful places we have so unwillingly left!) Here are some examples from pages 42-55 of Life Before Life:

> *"I chose to be born, but I wouldn't say, however, that it was a rational or analytical decision-it was more like an intuition from an oversoul. My feelings about the prospect of being born were that I was a bit anxious and I had a familiar feeling. 'I know I should and I know why I should, and I know I'll be back, and I feel like this one will do its thing"* (Case A-101).

> *"Yes, I chose to be born, but very reluctantly. There were several others around me when I was deciding and they seemed to be just like me. They said they would be around to help me in the coming lifetime. When you asked about the prospect of being born, I did not want to leave the beautiful garden and my friends there" (Case A-482).* This beautiful garden is likely to be Heaven: Devachan, the Pure Land or Sukhavati.

> *"Yes, I chose to be born, and there seemed to be some counselors around me. I felt very depressed and unhappy. Tears ran down my cheeks here during the hypnosis when you asked about the feelings about the prospect of living the coming lifetime" (Case A-55).*

> *"Yes, I chose to be born. It seemed my present husband and I decided. But my feelings about the prospect of being in this lifetime were of anger. I felt shocked and stifled at the prospect of being in a body once more"* (Case A-46).

> *"Yes, it was a difficult decision. There was a group helping me choose. They listened to what I had planned and made some suggestions. My feeling about living the coming lifetime was that I was not happy, but I knew what I was going to do was important enough to push aside my feelings of not wanting to be confined to a physical world"* (Case A-431).

It is fascinating to report that some of this group loved life so much once incarnated, that they could not understand their initial, pre-incarnation reluctance.

Willing return-self-chosen or encouraged

Then there is the 28% of Wambach's subjects, (p. 42) who *'felt enthusiastic about being alive again and felt that they had planned carefully and were ready to begin'*. The following are examples:

> *"I was offered the chance to be born and I agreed at a sort of important con-ference. There seemed to be an old bearded man there who was a big boss. I wanted to have a body again, so I felt happy at the prospect of living a life-time and smiled. I wasn't happy to return as a woman. That sort of put me off, but I still elected to come"* (Case A-316).

Here is someone whose sex was definitely not chosen according to the sex of the parent for whom he felt a previous connection and at-traction; in fact, it wasn't self-chosen at all!

> *"Yes, I chose to be born and a small group helped me choose. We were about six people in the group. My feelings about the prospect of the coming lifetime was a feeling of excitement because I was going to participate in exciting changes that were going to happen on earth. When I chose to be born, I knew I would be meeting up with the people I was with [the six in this subject's group on the soul level] in the future. Some would help guide me.* (Case A-372)

> *"Yes, I chose to be born. I had a very strong sensation of flowing from my ex-panded, dispersed self down into my physical center, and had a vision of it. I think someone helped me choose, but if they did, it was prior to the space I ex-perienced, because I felt my own pressure to enter physical reality. My feel-ings about the prospect of being born were very positive and I was impatient to begin."* (Case A-345)

> *"I did choose to be born and it was all agreed upon by a group of us. My feel-ings about the prospect of living the coming lifetime was that it was okay, kind of business-like. I want[ed] to accomplish something as a group (those who were advising me), and I wanted to expose myself to dissolute living and overcome it."* (Case A-443)

Reincarnation as a group project

Some of these statements from Wambach's subjects identify the im-portant truth about reincarnation: It is a group endeavour and ex-perience rather than an individual one. Many accounts or explora-tions of reincarnation focus exclusively on the path of the individual through her or his lives, as though this is the crux of the matter of reincarnation. This is a mistaken focus, given that it is the group's work and learning and progress, and its contribution to humanity-and the history of that contribution, which is of moment in the final analysis: the self-centred individual will become group-centred even-tually, and his or her contribution to the group work-in-progress will be of vital importance.

D.K. informs us about the way in which this takes place in the case of average humanity. One of the seeds which have been isolated and distilled from the past life's experience, the astral seed: *'through the forces it attracts, brings the man again into relation with those he previously loved or with whom he had close contact....[T]he group idea governs subjectively all incarnations, and ... reincarnated man is brought into incarnation not only through his own desire for physical plane incarnation, but also under group impulse and in line with the group karma as well as with his own (Bailey 1953, p 492).*

There is further exploration of souls' relationships with others in the soul group, in Chapter Fourteen.

Sex and the soul

What about couples? Are they are the smallest group? -- given how deeply we long to be understood, supported, loved, partnered and accompanied; how we finish one unsatisfactory relationship which has failed to provide these profoundly felt needs, and are likely to immediately begin searching for another. (Note the mutual ego-centricity of this need and this searching! And how society is organized around sexual couples in long-term relationships.)

We are vastly uneasy with the thin-sounding 'Love' we seem to be expected to live on once out of the body. There is of course no sex because there is no gender, once beyond the confines of the physical world and its echoes and reflections in the astral world. In that world we continue to identify with the sex of our latest lifetime, since that is the nature of the psyche we have taken with us into the super-physical realms. However, *souls do not have a sex!* They are not subject to this duality, and in the final analysis, not even to separation into "my soul" and "your soul" except in certain contexts, as D.K. explains. There is no sexual relating, but be comforted; *there is love-* a universe of that wonderful, indispensable, life-giving energy!

The dizziest heights of romantic love, with their fainting, reason-mangling hungers for the presence, the voice and the hands, the mouth, the aroma, and the body of the beloved, along with the obsessions which overwhelm any attempt to maintain ordered, responsible living, cannot be compared with the Bliss of Universal Love, and faces decent competition even in the joy of group love as it is experienced right here on earth, and especially between incarnations, on soul levels. Despite this, I wish and hope for all my readers at least one, if not several, doses of this wonderful, terrible Crazy Elixir of romantic love per lifetime!

Karma, place, sex, parents, and other aspects of a new life

There are so many other more complex and inclusive reasons behind the choice of sex, along with the choice of all other aspects of the new body and life, for those at higher stages of the evolutionary spiral. Some of these reasons and choices are discussed in the following extracts.

A remarkable piece of teaching about the karma of rebirth and the origin of important physical attributes is reported in H. K. Challoner's book, The Wheel of Rebirth: An Autobiography of Many Lifetimes, first published in 1969. Challoner's teacher led her through the revisiting of her most important incarnations, in order that she might fully understand the workings of karma and how the results of the choices she made in one life carried over into subsequent lives. One of these lives was led in Ancient Greece:

> *"Can you not see," he (Challoner's teacher) said, "that the life you led in Greece brought as an inevitable consequence a diseased and deformed body? It is curious how difficult man finds it to apply occult truths to the everyday facts of life! As I have told you, by your thoughts and deeds in one life you build the vehicle which will incorporate your spirit in the next. If you impoverish the constitution of your bodies, you will return with similarly impoverished-or almost moribund-atoms and will have to nurture and develop them afresh. Thus an enfeebled mind is often the result of mental laziness or of intelligence wrongly used, and those who weaken their bodies through excess and perversion may reincarnate deformed, epileptic, with some disease, or some fault in the brain, weakness of will, and inherent tendency to their former vices through which any malignant force from their past can more easily manifest. Vanity also reacts upon the physical vehicle; for the man who lives for his body alone will return a slave to it; a glutton for example, might inherit from his past a faulty digestive system, which applies also to one who has deliberately starved himself through foolish asceticism. Thus people are born into families from whom they can inherit the specific weaknesses they have themselves created by past errors"* (Challoner 1976, pp..198-9).

The opposite is also true. For example, Mozart, whose musical genius was already developed before incarnating, needed a family dedicated to music, and with certain unusual physical attributes, to enable him to give the world the gift of his music.

Rebirth and the needs of the soul

It becomes obvious that some agency or agencies higher than the personality are directing and controlling the process of rebirth, and choosing the conditions according to the lessons to be learnt, the talents to be developed and the service to be given to the group or the world. This becomes clearer as Challoner's teacher answers her inquiry-

"'But didn't I come back between Greece and the Middle Ages?" I asked. "It seems such a long interval."

"There is no fixed interval, it is a matter of the soul's needs [my emphasis]. But in your case several attempts were made to build a body strong enough to deal, without too much risk, with those destructive forces (evoked in earlier lives) which still stood in your path; but you were too handicapped by that impoverishment of your atoms of which I have spoken. You incarnated as a Roman, but the body was too weak to serve your ends, so you quickly abandoned it. You made the attempt again several times but each was a failure; you either died stillborn or did not survive for any length of time. At last you sought the East and came through parents who, having studied Hatha Yoga were enabled to render you more assistance (with the building of a stronger body) than any Western parents could have done. You later studied this form of yoga yourself and, although unfortunately the evil forces within were too strong for you and you failed in that life to accomplish your purpose, you did learn enough to enable you to incarnate as Carl, [the Mediaeval incarnation mentioned] *who, despite all his weakness, was yet strong enough to face and grapple with these forces at last"*(Challoner 1976, pp. 198-9).

D.K.'s report card to his disciple SCP, in November 1939, published in *Discipleship in the New Age, Volume I*, focused on her or his soul's present goals in incarnation:

'My aim is to let you know the purpose of your present life activity. It is not the seeking of money [that is, much effort put into financial improvement through study, work, promotion, investment etc] *in order to live rightly and correctly; it is not the full occupation of your time, nor is it place or power. These are not the true incentives. The real aim of your soul is bridging work and the achievement of clear-sighted control over a powerful personality, thus leading you to face yourself as you are and to make the needed changes. When the personality can be appraised justly and its achievements, its faults and its capacities rightly gauged, and when it is then deliberately subordinated to the aims of the soul -- then you will have made a very great step forward.*

And, my brother, you are making it. Your values are truer than they were a few years ago. The small social amenities and the calculated choice of friends no longer entirely govern your attitudes, though ancient habits still per-sist...You are making real progress in overcoming the glamour [ie the astral illusion] *of the social world, of place and position'* (Bailey 1944, p. 341).

Rudolph Steiner's Reincarnation lectures

In Rudolph Steiner's celebrated lectures on reincarnation, given in Dornach, Switzerland in 1924, published in the series *Karmic Relationships* (1983), a very different set of reasons for returning to incarnation emerges. It is the group progress that is being explored in these lectures, not individual reincarnations. Steiner, the founder of Anthroposophy, clearly understood that it is the group that incarnates, not really the individual as such. Part of his intention is to trace the spiritual flow of souls who vivified and created the great movements in Western philosophy down the ages, the *'currents of the whole spiritual life of mankind...'*, and to show us how they brought their contributions to the rethinking and reimagining of the cosmos which was continually going forward in history as human intellect and human understanding developed. So Steiner is not dealing with the reincarnations of average human beings in these lectures, in which he mentions for example, the reincarnations of Plato, of Louis XIV's Cardinal Mazarin, of Haroun al Raschid, of Goethe, and of a nun, possibly Hildegarde von Bingen or Julian of Norwich.

The driving impulses to reincarnation then concern the ability of these souls to contribute to the development of human intellect and spirituality, as the following extract shows:

'Especially in the centuries following the 9th, we see Platonic spirits [those imbued with Plato's philosophy of Ideas as the templates of all things in the material world] *descending on to the earth, spirits of a Platonic trend and orientation. It was they who continued through the Middle Ages a Christian teaching regarded as heretical by official Christianity, but which was nevertheless the truer Christian teaching. Meanwhile the individualities who continued the stream of Christian Aristotelianism remained, to begin with, in the spiritual worlds. For with the given conditions of civilization there was no real point of attachment for their stream down on the earth in the 9th, 10th, 11th, and 12th centuries. On the other hand, those who were more Platonic in character could unfold their spiritual life with remarkable intensity in isolated places, in isolated provinces as it were of the spirit. Interspersed with the Roman Catholic kind of Christianity, which asserted itself more and more officially, we find individuals gathered in schools here and there, carrying on traditions of the ancient Mysteries and illuminating Christianity from these ancient sources. And there was one place where all these streams of old tradition seemed to flow*

together. I mean, of course, the School of Chartres...a school which was spiritual through and through...a spiritual life in which the ancient traditions of the Mysteries were handed down...' (Steiner 1957, p. 58).

He goes on to elaborate on this perception of Chartres.

It is clear that Steiner is addressing, in his lectures, a different group than the readers of Sogyal Rinpoche, who is endeavouring to step down esoteric teachings on death to the understanding of the ordinary intelligent, enquiring Westerner without any particular philosophical or theological knowledge. So of course the view he presents of reincarnation's rationale is bound to be different.

In Chapter IV of *Life Before Life*, 'Choosing the Twentieth Century and Choosing One's Sex', Wambach reports:

"When I asked my subjects if they chose the twentieth century to experience a lifetime for a reason, I had no idea what responses I would get. I was just curious about whether this time period would be regarded as a fruitful time to experience physical life, or if it would be seen negatively by my subjects. The fact that so many of my subjects wished to stay in the between-life state, and reluctantly agreed to be born, suggested that I would get many negative responses... (Wambach 1979, pp. 64-79).

It has become obvious that some agency or agencies higher than the personality are directing and controlling the process of rebirth, once the individual has reached a certain stage of development. Wambach's subjects illustrate many stages of this development, from the individual on the astral plane unconscious of any soul-contact after death, who returns hastily and unadvised, to a new body and life. At the other end of the continuum are the individuals who are aware enough on higher levels to recall being advised by teachers, or to know that the choice they made was one not altogether pleasing to the personality-and that therefore it was a higher aspect of themselves making that decision-the higher self or soul. Then there are those who are sufficiently group-conscious to know that there is work to be done as a group, and say that they have planned it together, as a group of souls, before returning to the physical level.

The next chapter steps back into the Bardo, the interlife period, or 'Intermediate State', as it is titled and therefore officially recognised in the standard-setting Library of Congress cataloguing. The reason for this return to the Bardo is the data we now possess on its nature, through the studies of two eminent researchers, Dr Joel Whitton of Toronto, and Dr Michael Newton of California. Each came quite by surprise, upon this state while working with clients in his private psychological practice.

Chapter 10

Researchers Whitton and Newton Discover the Interlife Period

Summary Points

- **In the clinic: From reincarnation to the discovery of the interlife period**
- Clinical findings challenge the 'one life only' basis of Western psychology
- Psychological researchers Fiore, Wambach, Whitton and Newton go beyond reincarnation
- **Drs Whitton and Newton separately discover the Bardo**
- Could Newton's work be a hoax?
- Newton discovers the place of souls
- Souls-who and what are they? Beyond the astral death
- **Newton's subjects on stages of the round trip from death to 'home' to reincarnation**
- The group life of souls vs. traditional ideas and developmental psychology

- **Teachers, groups and the spiritual classroom: Newton and D.K. compared**

Researchers Whitton and Newton Discover the Interlife Period

The nature of the period after physical death has now been revealed, beginning in Chapter Six with the separation of body and consciousness. The journey has been traced via the 'peeling of layers' process, into the astral world, on to Heaven or Devachan, and finally, to the reintegration with the soul, of Chapters Seven and Eight.

This 'ascent into Heaven' known to the faiths which teach that there is just one life not many, turns out not to be the end or culmination of life. The ancient texts, modern commentaries and recent studies agreed that this was not the end, but the beginning of a new cycle. The rebirth process and its Western exploration were examined in Chapter Nine. That in turn pointed to the existence of the pre-birth state, the Bardo of Becoming in Tibetan Buddhism.

In the clinic: From reincarnation to the discovery of the interlife period

The present chapter tracks the Western discovery that this is something more than a pre-birth condition; it is an *interlife period*, as the East has always known. It examines the Western studies of this entire interlife period and its culmination in, and logical connection with, reincarnation.

Wambach's researches made it clear for the first time that these were ordinary humans, with a consciousness like our own, who were experiencing the interlife period. Their individual responses to their situation at the moment of deciding to reincarnate, were full of the hope and fear and pain and joy that we know as the human condition. They were not remote unrecognizable beings. So the idea of the continuity of a core selfhood became more concrete.

Death, birth and loneliness

It was reassuring also, that few seemed to be reporting an experience reminiscent of the terrors of the Bardo. (A subject who did seem to find himself in the Bardo, was Wambach's case of the soldier who had just died in a war, quoted in Chapter Nine). The terrors of the Bardo or lower Purgatory are likely to be in the past for many; in fact for all those who have access to the mental levels, unless their centre of experience and expression is still that of markedly negative emotion. This realization calms some of the typical Western fears-my own original fears, about the after-death experience. Yet, since Wambach wasn't researching the interlife period itself, there was still a large gap in the picture of the state between death and birth. Most of Wambach's subjects were reporting that teachers and members of their group helped them choose the next life's conditions and challenges. Did this mean we were not usually alone after death? D.K. has said in response to this, and the fear of having to part from beloved people at death-theirs or ours, that it is birth not death, which is the real experience of loneliness:

> *At birth, the soul finds itself in new surroundings and immersed in a body which is at first totally incompetent to take care of itself or to establish intelligent contact with surrounding conditions for a long period of time. The man comes into incarnation with no recollection as to the identity or the significance to him of the group of souls in bodies with which he finds himself in relationship ...After death this is not so, for the man finds on the other side of the veil those whom he knows and who have been connected with him in physical plane life, and he is never alone as human beings understand loneliness (my emphasis); he is also conscious of those still in physical bodies; he can see them, he can tune in on their emotions, and also upon their thinking, for the physical brain, being nonexistent, no longer acts as a deterrent. If people knew more, birth would be the experience which they would dread, and not death, for birth establishes the soul in the true prison, and physical death is only the first step towards liberation.'* (Bailey 1953, pp. 392-3, extracted in Bailey 1985, pp. 53-4)

While this was somewhat reassuring about the loneliness which might have seemed to continue after death as before, this statement of D.K.'s was only a comparison after all, possibly of a bad situation (death) with a worse (birth). There was no comparison made with the time later in physical life when, as D.K. continues, *'this loneliness only gradually disappears as he makes his own personality contacts, discovers those who are congenial to him and eventually gathers around him those whom he calls his friends.'*

Still the nature of the after-death state continued to be mysterious.

The culminating period was the 'moment short or long' of soul contact. Then there followed the preparation for a new body and new life. When life was difficult and painful, which was often enough, as it is for many or most of us, the prospect of this return to probable suffering and unhappiness in another life on earth was unattractive to say the least. How many of us, though, would look at the life we have lived till now, a life lived in paradise by comparison with the conditions and extremity of suffering in so much of the world-and pronounce it, overall, *not* worth the effort and pain?

(Certainly some of us would, as a result of unbearable daily suffering of body or psyche-a minority I hope.) Suffering or oblivion-which would most of us choose if these were the alternatives? Suffering *is* the way of all flesh-until we are roused to consciousness by it. As the Buddha taught us, we must raise our consciousness from the vale of illusion to the mountaintop of light of the Universal Mind, or as the Christ taught us, into the inclusive love and universality of the Divine Life. By this means we cease to identify with the suffering body-personality of the small self.

Western research on reincarnation and the interlife period

Carl Jung pondered the West's faulty understanding of the nature of the pre-birth existence, in his 1927 *Psychological Commentary* to the *Tibetan Book of the Dead*. He noted that the Western mind with its *'existing biological ideas'* had been pushed to the limits even in the discovery of intrauterine consciousness. This was because we believed that consciousness only began at birth. (The idea that babies in the womb can hear and feel and therefore are *conscious in utero*, is more generally accepted now). Jung is suggesting the West would not tolerate or cope with, the investigation of consciousness and therefore life, before conception. He speaks of psychoanalysts claiming to have probed intrauterine memories:

> *Here Western reason reaches its limit, unfortunately. I say 'unfortunately', because one rather wishes that Freudian psychoanalysis could have happily pursued these so-called intra-uterine experiences still further back; had it succeeded in this bold undertaking, it would surely have come out beyond the Sidpa Bardo (of Rebirth) and penetrated from behind into the lower reaches of the Chonyid Bardo* [The emphasis is mine. Jung is saying that psychoanalysis would discover the later or rebirth bardo first, and the earlier, the Chonyid or afterdeath bardo next as a result of approaching from the intrauterine experience.] *It is true that with the equipment of our existing biological ideas such a venture would not have been crowned with success; it would have needed a wholly different kind of philosophical preparation from that based on current scientific assumptions (Jung 1927, p. xliii).*

This 'wholly different kind of philosophical preparation' has been happening in the meantime, and is of course, the endeavour of this book, *Death, Our Last Illusion*. Psychoanalysts have in fact, succeeded in Jung's bold undertaking of pushing back further than intrauterine experiences. Stanislav Grof (introduced in Chapter Six) began his work in LSD and pre-birth psychotherapy just two decades after Jung wrote this Commentary for the 1927 first edition of the Tibetan Book of the Dead. We have indeed penetrated into the space and life prior to birth, as this chapter explains. So did the West begin to confront the possibility of one soul, many lives? Have we been able to challenge our 'existing biological ideas' and 'current scientific assumptions' to take account of these discoveries? As Jung noted in 1927, it is still the case that within mainstream Western thought, there continues to be outright rejection of the idea of reincarnation and all supporting evidence. Despite that, increasing numbers of people in the West either believe in reincarnation, or consider it a possibility; around four out of ten in the West, or is it higher by now? There is a great deal more openness of mind now, to what were once dismissed as the ideas of the deranged or the superstitious and uneducated.

It is fascinating to recall the attitude in Australia, in the fifties and sixties, to discarnate existence and to reincarnation. Back then they were, quite simply, ideas that no sane adult should be caught entertaining.

The Search for Bridey Murphy (Bernstein 1956), introduced in the previous chapter, was one of the books the precocious group at my Anglican (Episcopalian in the US) secondary girls' college passed around under the desk, covered in brown paper. We knew that the Hindus and Buddhists believed in reincarnation, but it was a weird superstition to us, given our scientific education, and perhaps more important especially at that age, our religious instruction-that this our only life would end in Heaven with Christ if we believed in Him and followed His example. The American housewife Ruth Simmons had, when under hypnosis, become the Irish Bridey Murphy; not a dual personality, but a former one. When the geography, situation and aspects of this nineteenth century Irish life were investigated, there was a remarkable degree of corroboration. So, Ruth Simmons had lived before! This was impossible according to the Western construction of the cosmos, which was of course, considered the only tenable one. Even if we accepted the Bridey Murphy story, we still saw other lives as something that only happened to her and a few other lucky individuals. She was some freak of nature, outside the bounds of God's kingdom.

Clinical findings challenge the 'one life only' basis of Western psychology

Psychologists and psychiatrists generally had a similar attitude, that reincarnation was merely the stuff of archaic myth. They were, however, increasingly using hypnosis, and some- those who searched beyond birth for the origin of problems- found their views uncomfortably challenged by their clinical findings.

In her book *You Have Been Here Before* (1978), Edith Fiore discusses her use of hypnosis to heal her clients' presenting problems by regressing clients to their earlier years, to the birth experience, and eventually even to experiences in the womb.

Dr Fiore reports that until two years before writing the book, she was utterly uninterested in the idea of reincarnation. Then a young man came for treatment of crippling sexual inhibitions:

> *When I asked him...under hypnosis, to go back to the origin of his problems, he said "Two or three lifetimes ago, I was a Catholic priest". We traced through this lifetime... and found the source of his sexual difficulties. I was aware that the patient believed in reincarnation. Therefore, I felt that his vivid description of his past life, coloured by a great deal of emotionality, was a fantasy. However, the next time I saw him, he told me he was not only free of his sexual problems, but felt better about himself in general. I began to take note of this new therapeutic tool.*

Fiore didn't suddenly believe in reincarnation, and therefore begin to practise past-lives therapy; she discovered a 'therapeutic tool', one that might prove useful in helping patients, and decided to try it out.

From reincarnation to discovery of the interlife-Fiore, Wambach, Whitton and Newton

Shortly after, Fiore treated a social director of a cruise ship for two apparently contradictory fears:

> *The first was the dangerously strong impulse she would experience to jump overboard, and the other, paradoxically, was an irrational fear of getting lost at sea. Under hypnosis she found herself as a small Norwegian boy, Sven, on his father's boat, being urged to jump as the boat crashed onto rocks. He disobeyed his father and drowned. During the same session she found herself in two other lifetimes, one as a fisherman, the other as a sailor, both lost at sea, both eventually drowning. ...Again, I felt that she was 'reliving' fantasied existences...Six weeks later, back from a trip across the Pacific, she was exuberant when she told me she no longer had either of the two problems.*

This patient also believed in reincarnation. So Fiore still wasn't convinced. Another patient, whose fear of snakes had no origin in the present lifetime, prompted Fiore to test the reincarnation hypothesis:

> *I asked her if she had had an encounter with snakes before she was born. She saw herself as a fifteen-year-old Aztec girl in front of a pyramid, watching*

priests dancing with poisonous snakes in their mouths. She trembled with
emotion and reported the bizarre rites in vivid detail...[Afterwards she]
stated vehemently, "I don't believe all that stuff!"' (Fiore 1978, pp. 15-16).

Fiore's instructions to her client are very carefully chosen. The therapist does not suggest that there is necessarily anything 'before you
were born', unlike Wambach, who actively suggests other lifetimes.
The client may, if thinking rationally (supposedly not the case under
hypnosis), conclude that Fiore is referring to the time in the womb,
in this phrase *'before you were born'*. Or give Dr Fiore the expected answer *"There wasn't anything before I was born"*. Despite this, the client
in these examples and no doubt, her other cases, goes immediately,
not to intrauterine experiences, but to those in other lives. Fiore
discovered that it didn't matter what either she or the patient believed about reincarnation; when (and only when) the true origin of
the problem was 'located' and 'experienced', the problem would disappear. So, whenever the origin of symptoms was not found in the
present life, Fiore began routinely regressing patients back further
than this life, with great success.

Dr Helen Wambach's 1979 study, *Life before Life*, which has
been considered in Chapter Nine, presented us with some solid
evidence of reincarnation, and was one of the important studies to
begin to change attitudes. However, I suspect not too many of us
found it possible to rearrange our worldview to take account of this
evidence, especially its *interlife period* implications, despite that she
had taken her subjects back to the moment before their birth into
their present lives, to answer questions about the choices they made
about time period, parents, sex, and life's tasks in the coming lifetime. Many of us had no trouble accepting as a working hypothesis,
the existence of the soul and reincarnation. Yet we may still have experienced vast unease about the process as we then understood it.

The West discovers the Bardo

It seemed then that the entity who was there after death and before
birth, was the soul...**outside of incarnation rather than between
incarnations**. There was no knowledge of between lives, only incarnation or eternity and an entity with a consciousness entirely separate from one's own. What 'I' did between lives, or the state 'I' inhabited, was a non-question, as there was no 'I' between lives, only a
separate 'I' for each incarnation, an idea owing something to my
then (poor) understanding of Buddhism. Two books which had a
profound effect on the attitude of many Westerners, and brought

about this critical change in my own understanding and attitude to the inter-life period, were Whitton's *Life between Life* (1986) and Newton's *Journey of Souls* (1994). Between the publications of these two studies came another influential study, which took a quite different approach, but also ended up exploring the interlife period and reinforcing the findings of Whitton, Newton and later Andy Tomlinson and others. This was Brian Weiss' *Many Lives, Many Masters* (1988).

These highly qualified and experienced North American psychological researchers, the Canadian psychiatrist Dr Joel Whitton in 1974, Dr Michael Newton, a Californian hypnotherapist, and Dr Brian Weiss, at the time Chief of Psychiatry at 'a large university-affiliated hospital in Miami' (1988, p. 10), came upon the Bardo or interlife in the course of their investigations. Recognition of the Bardo in clinical psychology and psychiatry was new. Yet they were far from being the only ones who made before-birth discoveries through Western research rather than Eastern mystical practices. There is a fact that is very much to the credit of the objectivity of researchers into past lives, from the late nineteenth century onward. They almost universally rejected the idea of reincarnation. Dr Sir Alexander Cannon, mentioned in Chapter Nine, was convinced his patients were talking rubbish when they found themselves in past lives under hypnosis. Yet despite their original dismissal of reincarnation, these researchers stumbled upon what they were eventually forced to recognize as fact: the connection between a client's present life and one or more past lives. It is this recognition that deserves credit.

This connection alone was nearly impossible to accept for most, given their immersion in the Western materialist mindset, that matter is all there is. So, far from drawing conclusions based on Eastern mysticism, about the period of time between those lives, clinicians seem not to have ever 'gone there'; that is, they didn't even speculate about the period between lives. This is the only explanation for the fact that it was not until the interlife actively revealed itself through their research, that the idea of a post-death consciousness was more to them than just an Eastern superstition. This is notably true of Dr Whitton and Dr Newton, whose discoveries of the interlife came about in similar fashion, and somewhat differently from the interlife discoveries of Dr Edith Fiore (1978). The latter discovered the interlife period as a result of working with patients whose problems were located, not in the events of a previous life, which meant investigating a past incarnation, but in the experience of a previous death. This meant the client took the therapist into the period just before, during and, importantly, just after a previous death; and thus into the state between lives.

Fiore discusses the implications of her findings about consciousness after death and before the next birth:

All that I shall show you corroborates the findings of Raymond A. Moody...[His subjects'] descriptions of their experiences before resuscitation are virtually identical to those of my patients under hypnosis-except that many of my patients recall events in the interim between lifetimes whereas Moody's do not. And for obvious reasons. His patients never made the transition complete. His patients chose not to die or were forced to return.... **One of the outstanding features in accounts of the death experience is that consciousness continues without a break...[my emphasis]**....(Fiore 1978, pp. 228-9).*

Occasionally patients weep after their death as they look down and see relatives grieving. The sadness is always for others, not for the person they were- no matter how traumatic their death. It is as though the release from the agony, and the newly experienced joy and ecstasy overcome the past suffering. For many, death is a rather gentle slipping into a different, -- better, state. Almost all people experiencing dying under hypnosis use the word 'floating' to describe the immediate bodily sensations after death....(Fiore 1978, pp. 228-9).

Fiore goes on to summarise her patients' experiences of tunnels and lights and waiting family and friends, but only discusses the time immediately after death; that is, in Purgatory or the astral or emotional realm: 'A description of the interim between lifetimes, taken from my patients' fascinating accounts, will have to wait for a future publication. It is a book in itself!' (Fiore 1978, p. 235).

Dr Joel Whitton became chief psychiatrist of the Toronto school system, among other distinctions. His discoveries, as reported in the book written with Joe Fisher, *Life between Life* (1986), are similar to, and complementary to, Michael Newton's in *Journey of Souls* (1994).

Joe Fisher, Whitton's writer, introduces Whitton's interest in reincarnation. He had been a skilled party-trick hypnotist since adolescence, then, in his early twenties, began to refine his technique to investigate reincarnation, discovering as other hypnotherapists do, that anyone capable of regressing in deep trance to infancy, was equally capable of travelling into an earlier life (Whitton & Fisher 1986, pp. 3-4).

Psychological researchers Whitton and Newton discover the Interlife

Dr Whitton stumbled upon the realm between lives in a manner similar to, and earlier than, Newton. He was already a practicing psychiatrist when the Bridey Murphy phenomenon, and other similar accounts of individuals having lived before, made past-lives therapy a sudden trend in the West, especially in North America. Concerned that there were as yet no serious scientific studies to establish the credentials of past-lives therapy, Dr Whitton proposed an experiment into the validity and use of hypnotic regression techniques for the recovery of past lives data, to the Toronto Society for Psychical Research, in 1973, and began to search for a suitable subject. He settled on Paula Considine, a woman in early middle age, who was stable in temperament and had no particular belief pro or anti reincarnation. She was 'a typical North American housewife':

Many sessions and several past lives later, Dr Whitton made a mistake in the precise and literal instructions needed to direct the mind of the hypnotized subject, just as Dr Newton would do in his turn. He was attempting to get Paula to go from her life as Martha Paine to that as Margaret Campbell. 'Go to the life before you were Martha' was his instruction. Following an enraptured silence, she struggled to express her experience, shocking Dr Whitton by announcing that she was in the sky.

> *"I can see a farmhouse and a barn...It's early...early morning. The sun...is low and... making long shadows across the burnt fields...stubbly fields.'* [The confused Dr Whitton asked what she was doing up there. The reply from his subject was that she was 'waiting to be born' and watching her mother protectively as she struggled with the farmhouse pump and her unwieldy pregnant body. 'What is your name?' Whitton then asked, trying to orient himself by locating the lifetime in question.]

> *'I...have...no...name.'...Could it be that Paula's unconscious mind was somehow tapping into the fabled bardo of the ancient Tibetans?* (Whitton and Fisher 1984, pp. 20-21)[1].

Whitton 'thoroughly confounded', returned Paula hastily to the present, and had to put aside any questions this experience raised until he'd finished the study and the report on reincarnation explored under hypnosis.

---

1. Life between Life, © 1984 by Joel Whitton and Joe Fisher, published by Harper-Collins Publishers Ltd. This and other extracts used by permission of the publisher.

Then the following year, 1975, Raymond Moody's book *Life after Life*, his collection of NDE of people who claimed to have died and returned to life, was published, causing a sensation. Dr Whitton then decided to begin his researches into the place to which the NDErs reported journeying. Perhaps it was the same bardo-type place as Tibetan mystics knew, and Paula Considine had reported. It is to this book of Dr Whitton's as well as Dr Michael Newton's *Journey of Souls* that I owe the clarification of my understanding about the *nature of the life after death and before birth*.

In his preface to Whitton's book, author Joe Fisher summarizes the findings:

> 'The message from deep trance is that life after death is synonymous with life before birth and that most of us have taken up residence in this other world many, many times as disembodied entities ... Dr Whitton's subjects, whose religious backgrounds are as varied as their initial prejudices for or against reincarnation, have testified consistently that rebirth is fundamental to the evolutionary process in which we are enveloped. At death, they say, the soul leaves the body to enter a timeless, spaceless state. There our most recent life is evaluated and the next incarnation is planned according to our karmic requirements' (Whitton & Fisher 1986, p. 24).

This summary is entirely consistent with Hindu and Buddhist teachings, with D.K.'s elaboration of the scheme of life, and with the evidence from NDE, at least as far as it goes.

Whitton's own preface deals with the doubts and scepticism inevitably aroused by any claim to have knowledge of the other side of death. Dealing with the difficult issue of proof, he writes: '*There are important hidden assumptions in the theory of reincarnation as well as complex psychological issues in a memory of a past life. We do not articulate these issues in this book, but believe we have addressed them and have included only those cases wherein the hypothesis of past lives is the only valid one* [my emphasis]' (Whitton and Fisher 1986, p. 12).

Whitton also addresses the issue of criticism from some of his colleagues and others:

> *The aposiopesis of the classical psychoanalysts will proclaim, as with Richard Bucke, infantile omnipotence in the belief in the possibility of the impossible, or the longing for the lost-father object in the quest for mystical experience...The uninformed will simply, ad populum, cry fantasy*' (Whitton and Fisher 1986, p. xiii).

My crude translation goes thus: The classical Freudian psychoanalysts will offer a half-explanation that these reports (from a land and a life after death and before birth) are nothing more than the products of the unconscious. These if analyzed, they would say, would reveal themselves to be the Id, or Child, believing in the impossible (as in I can jump from the roof and fly if I wear this cape; if I close my eyes and wish I can die and still be alive), or the attempt to rediscover the lost father-object through a mystical encounter with the father of all fathers, God. This response of Whitton's critics is category or quadrant denial, in Wilber's terms.

Some of my readers will have no need of this translation; but my guess is that most would have to reach for the dictionary as I did, to discover the meaning of 'aposiopesis' –incomplete thought, possibly 'half-baked idea' in Whitton's use. What then is the point of my quoting a part of such a highly specialized and technical defence at all? The reason is that it makes it very obvious that Joel Whitton has considered, and been able to reject on good grounds, the possibility that these reports from his subjects are no more than fantastic or a-rational products of his subjects' unconscious. And that it also makes abundantly clear that Dr Whitton is, in his capabilities and approach to the subject of life after death and before birth, the opposite of gullible and ready to fantasize; his intellect is clearly of a very high order, and he is likely to prove rigorous in his investigations. These investigations and their outcome are discussed more fully below, once the later and more startlingly controversial work of Dr Michael Newton has been examined.

Dr Michael Newton discovers the place of souls

The next moment in this series of revelations came with Michael Newton's studies in *Journey of Souls: Case Studies of Life between Lives.*

Newton's work was begun in the decade prior to 1994 and the book's publication. Dr Newton, working as a hypnotherapist in private practice, was using standard regression techniques to take his clients back to childhood for the origins of their presenting problems. This extended to include past lives therapy to meet a need. Then quite by accident, he took a client into the between-lives state and began the work that led to this book. Its information has been drawn from hundreds of accounts of the life after the last death of his clients, (the experience of the interlife period). Newton has chosen 29 typical accounts to illustrate the nature of the journey and the places of the soul. My discovery of this book was the cause of great excitement. It has provided answers to my urgent questions about the nature of consciousness and the self between lives, and about the relationship of NDE to the real thing (given the assertions by its critics, that little or nothing could be judged from NDE, because the subjects did not die, and it is the experience of death which matters). Here were *first-hand reports of the soul in the disembodied state*, and the nature of life and consciousness beyond the Six Realms (Hell, Animal, Hungry Ghost...the lower astral states).

In prefacing remarks, Dr Newton observes the similarity of the Near-death experience and the early stages of his regression sessions, and notes his discovery that *it is possible to access the state after permanent death*, not just NDE, once in a deep trance state (Newton 1994, p. 9).

Could this study be a hoax?

Midway through the early drafts of the book, I wrote in great excitement: 'What revelations awaited me in Newton's book! It reads like science fiction; few will believe it, I think. Yet it fits well with the rest of the theoretical structure gained from my reading, especially of Alice Bailey. I can't see why the author would have invented all this. To write a piece of fiction posing as fact, which becomes a bestseller, and makes a lot of money? The book's About the Author statement cites a long list of qualifications and accomplishments, which would surely have the universities, psychological associations and institutes of which he is supposedly a member, wanting to discredit him via legal means if nothing else, if it were a fiction. And if Newton really is the expert of the citation, then he has risked his reputation and career on this book; both could well have been ruined by the outrageous statements about life on earth and elsewhere, which his clients have given him.

This still leaves two alternatives if the book is a fiction or a hoax. The first is that his clients were deliberately leading him astray by their clever but absurd inventions, which he was gullible enough to believe, and worse still, publish! This would have required several hundred unrelated people from all over the U.S. and over a space of years, to be involved in an elaborate conspiracy, given that their evidence about the post-mortem world is repetitious and consistent, even, it seems, on the most improbable details.

The remaining alternative is that Dr Newton's clients are themselves deluded; that their imaginations are running riot. This possibility is struck out by the way in which hundreds of clients report the same otherwise unknown and 'unbelievable' things. Newton himself responds to a similar charge, in saying that even if subjects could fantasise deliberately or work up a free-association scenario about their afterlife, *'these responses would soon become inconsistent with my other case reports'.* Perhaps they are seeing what they have been culturally programmed to expect in the afterlife? The trouble is, they are not... Newton continues, observing that his clients' prior spiritual ideas and beliefs ran the gamut of possibilities from deeply religious to atheist. Yet their beliefs were often flatly contradicted by their experiences in the post-death world. *"The astounding thing I found ... was that once subjects were regressed back into their soul state they all displayed a remarkable consistency in responding to questions about the spirit world"* (Newton 1994, pp. 4-5)[2].

It could be argued that they all know of the literature on NDE, and have merely regurgitated some version of that. This argument is that mounted by Dr Susan Blackmore, when she says that NDErs are merely reporting what they expect to find after death, on the basis of prior information (from the media, friends' accounts, and visits to hospitals). This argument is invalidated by Newton's findings: The similarity and consistency of the reports of Newton's subjects on the interlife period don't stop where the NDE stops at all. They continue right through the cycle of experience to the point of rebirth. Dr Blackmore is relying heavily, in her attempted denial of the reality of NDE, on the argument that the phenomena of the dying brain cause visual effects like the tunnel and the light, and produce hallucinations responsible for the rest of the descriptions such as the Life Review and the meeting with loved ones who have already died.

The problem with this argument now, is that Dr Newton's clients are not seeing lights and tunnels because of malfunctioning of the dying brain (patients have in any case been shown to be brain-dead, as noted in Chapter Three), or because of hallucinations produced by drugs, prescribed or otherwise, which Blackmore says partially replicate the dying brain effect. So, if they are not dying and not hallucinating, they can't be said to be suffering from delusion thus caused.

That brings us to just one last possibility-that Newton has doctored the data he received in client sessions to make it appear more similar and consistent. There is a possibility of this. But the problem previously mentioned remains-that is, that the story he would be striving to make appear more consistent and solid, is a story none but a gullible new-age faerie child is likely to believe regardless of its presentation, if not for its origin and genesis. It is just

---

2. *Journey of Souls* by Michael Newton, Ph. D. © 1994 Llewellyn Worldwide, Ltd. 2143 Wooddale Drive, Woodbury, MN 551252989. This and other extracts used by permission and with best wishes from the publisher. All rights reserved.

too far-fetched. This takes us back to the argument that he was risking career and reputation in telling this story at all: why would he risk making things worse? Why not doctor it the other way-to be less alarmingly outrageous? So- I was inclined to believe him, at least about the general outline and much of the detail, even on initial reading.

There are reasons however, not to take as gospel every detail that Newton's subjects report about the interlife. The first is that these are indeed, humans like ourselves, who, despite having access to states presently inaccessible to most of us on earth, are still limited in their understanding of those states and the whole scheme, by the degree of their development. The second is that even the most articulate struggle to communicate their discoveries within the limits of language. The third is the considerable limitation on bringing back, clearly bringing through, everything encountered in the beyond-brain states when once again limited to brain-consciousness.

Newton takes us beyond the NDE

Subjects talk about their experiences in the same way as travellers into the Near-death experience do, with the same elements- until their passage through the 'gateway' into the spiritual world, which is where those who return to their bodies are turned back. These clients of Dr Newton did not re-enter their bodies after a short NDE. They are instead, recalling their journey after physical death, in one of Dr Newton's sessions. They describe their return - 'homecoming' to a beloved place and soulmates and teachers; an assimilation of experience and of the lessons to be drawn from the latest life, then, for some souls at least, 'R&R', rest and recreation, before the process of selecting a new life and body and preparation for rebirth.

Souls- who and what are they? Beyond the astral death

The discovery of Newton's studies, (and later, of Whitton's), and eventual acceptance of most of their conclusions, has made the critical difference to my fear of death. They have been in fact, the missing pieces of the puzzle. My excited first reading of this book made me think for the first time, that souls were a recognisable part of ourselves; knowable, reachable! The consideration of these studies and their conclusions may not have the same effect upon others approaching the problem from a different life experience, background or discipline. However I'm hoping that my explanation as to why it provided the missing pieces which made the picture emerge in rich colour and a certain amount of detail for the first time, may be equally clarifying and reassuring for my readers.

There are enough accounts around of life in the astral plane, such as Cardinal Benson's, quoted earlier, to reassure us about that stage at least. But after the death of the emotional or astral body? We knew nothing. If the place beyond that wasn't quite the everlasting bliss of our various religious teachings -- which I found unappealing, what was it? The Tibetan's teachings give an outline only, and souls still seem too remote, too pure and inhumanly perfect, to be accessible to anyone but a saint, a Master of the Wisdom or a Buddha. And Mahayana Buddhism, in struggling to point to even the relative 'bliss which is nothingness', is not much help to the uninitiated.

The Tibetan assures us: *For those who know themselves to be souls there is no death.* Well, that fixes everything then, except for all of us who still haven't the foggiest idea whether we can even claim to be the proud possessors of such an elusive divinity as a soul! (Or claim to be in the safe possession of that august Being). Many key concepts seemed only to reinforce the idea that the soul had little or nothing to do with ordinary humans still struggling with life in the physical world.

Life after death came across as something cold and remote and inhuman, an experience of disjointed or wraithlike or semi-conscious existence for anyone not evolved to the point of capacity for a degree of universal consciousness. *Was it pretty much a blank until we contemplated the return to earth,* and were ready to begin the process of consultation and choice tracked by Helen Wambach? If that were the case, our experience as souls would be almost entirely of incarnation and its hardships. This was a dismal and depressing prospect. Surely this was a mistaken reading, I kept thinking, but I couldn't, still, put flesh on the bones of the abstractions given by D.K., and by Tibetan Buddhism, to get much feel for the life and experience of the discarnate soul.

It was Newton's book particularly, which filled in the picture so it finally made sense, by giving a remarkably solid, continuous and lively account not just of the astral experience, but also of the life and world of the soul post-incarnation. That alone would not have made the impression it did. It was the compatibility of the accounts of Newton's subjects, and Whitton's, with D.K.'s explanation of it from a spiritual-scientific point of view, and its ability to be reconciled, too, with Sogyal Rinpoche's and Buddhist teachings generally, with the findings of Helen Wambach, Stanislav Grof, Fiore, Weiss, Tomlinson and others, and with accounts of, and research into, the

Near-death Experience, that bore great weight, and produced some assurance.

However, the Near-death Experience and all the Reports Back to Earth from individuals like Cardinal Benson, were still not reliable enough guides. This is due to the illusory nature of the astral plane, and the improbability that most of these reports came from anywhere higher. That meant we still needed reports back from those who had gone beyond the astral level...who had undertaken the whole journey, from shedding the physical and astral and mental bodies, to rejoining their souls. *"Journey of Souls"* does in fact contain these reports, as does Whitton's *"Life between Life"*, the first report of experiments and studies into the intervening life, published eight years earlier. The critical aspect of *"Journey of Souls"* was that the entire interlife experience was explored in its consecutive stages, and in sufficient detail that it became possible to be sure that it was indeed the journey of the soul, not just of the astral aspect of the discarnate self, which was being reported by Newton's subjects. They weren't just wandering around in the fogs and miasmas of the Bardo or the lower astral plane, and happening on the same delusional fiction as each other.

I had remembered from readings of Helen Wambach that we are usually reluctant to return to Earth. Wambach had concluded *'Sixty-eight percent of my subjects felt reluctant, anxious, or resigned to the prospect of living another lifetime. Only 26 percent ...looked forward to the coming lifetime...So death was experienced as pleasant by 90 percent of these subjects, but being born -- living another lifetime -- was unhappy and frightening. What a strange reversal of what I had expected!'* (Wambach 1979, p. 63).

I still couldn't, it seems, mentally process that to make a difference to my fear of death. This fear is now gone, after reading Newton especially. It became clear that subjects' reluctance to return to earth wasn't just due to earthly life being the greater of two evils, but to their unwillingness to part from the beauty, companionship, love and joy in which they were immersed as souls. Many, perhaps the majority of Newton's subjects are reporting as discarnate human souls, *'functioning in or limited by, the mental body'* as D.K. puts it about Devachan-that is, from devachanic consciousness. None of these reports is likely to come from a subject's *immortal* soul, which would require an exceptional degree of soul-personality coordination -- in fact, identity. This identity must indicate a consciousness at or beyond Wilber's Fulcrum-8, Turquoise, that of the Witness or Watcher; by definition a consciousness in no need of Dr Newton's help.

The chapter headings of Newton's book give a quick overview of his discoveries about the soul's journey. They are: Death and departure, Gateway to the spirit world, Homecoming, The Displaced soul, Orientation, Transition, Placement, Our guides, The Beginner soul, The Intermediate soul, The Advanced soul, Life selection, Choosing a new body, Preparation for embarkation, and Rebirth.

In the first stage (labelled **Death and departure**), as already noted, Newton's subjects find themselves, just like those who undergo a Near-death Experience, hovering above their moribund bodies, and passing straight through solid objects. They try to talk to distressed survivors and medical staff and discover that in this new state, they can't be heard by those still in bodies. Both groups feel pulled away from the deathbed or place; both report peace and anticipation, not grief or fear. Both report brightness around them: Some subjects see *'brilliant whiteness totally surrounding them at the moment of death, while others observe the brightness is farther away from an area of darker space through which they are being pulled.'* This, he says, is the well-known tunnel effect (Newton 1994, p. 9).

A detail is given by one client, which corresponds with D.K.'s teaching about the way in which we leave the body at death, from one or other of the apertures at the crown, the heart, or the solar plexus, depending on level of advancement. This case also bears out D.K.'s assurance that death is quick and painless once it arrives, regardless of the level of pain leading up to it.

Sally has been shot on the American frontier by a Native American arrow, and tells Dr Newton that she is indeed in pain; the point has torn her throat: (pp. 10-11).

> S: *'I'm dying (subject begins to whisper while holding his hands at the throat). I'm choking ... blood pouring down ...Will (husband) is holding me ... the pain ... terrible ... I'm getting out now ... it's over, anyway.*
>
> *Note:... After calming techniques, I raise this subject from the subconscious to the superconscious level for the transition to spiritual memories.*
>
> *'Dr N: Will you please describe to me the exact sensation you feel at the time of death?*
>
> S: *Like ...a force ...of some kind ... pushing me up out of my body.*
>
> Dr N: *Pushing you? Out where?*
>
> S: *I'm ejected out the top of my head.*

When asked what this 'I' is, moving out of the top of Sally's head, Dr Newton is told of a transparent white, radiant energy referred to by the subject as 'my soul'. The sensation is like: *'peeling a banana. I just lose my body in one swoosh!*

Dr N: Is the feeling unpleasant?

S: Oh no! It's wonderful to feel so free with no more pain, but... I didn't expect to die ...'

This subject, a man in the current life, came to Dr Newton to cure a lifetime of throat discomfort.

Gateway to the Spirit World

Newton's examples of client reports give an excellent idea of the passage through the stage after exiting the body, and clearly show the identity of NDE and the real thing; the experience of dying without any return or reprieve. It is marvellous that, instead of the recall after the event, dependent on memory of the NDE, what we get under hypnosis is the direct communication of the experience itself.

This subject, Case 3, (pp. 18-19) has just passed through the tunnel:

S: It's so...still...it is such a quiet place to be in...I am in the place of spirits. [It is interesting that there is immediate recognition of this. The impression of this place is that it is one where the physical has given place to the mental. How wonderful! No oppressive noise!]

S: I feel the power of thought all around me...thoughts of love...companionship ...empathy......as if others are...waiting for me.

... I feel secure...I'm aware of thoughts reaching out to me... of caring ... nurturing. It is strange, but there is also the understanding around me of just who I am and why I am here now [My emphasis].

This is a corroboration of D.K.'s advice quoted earlier, that once on the other side of physical death, the veils of seeming drop away and *'men know'* that they are immortal souls passing through mortal lives. The next client quoted, Case 4, describes in detail the *appearance* of the world in which he finds himself, as he moves away from the tunnel's exit.

'I see layers...levels of light...they appear to me to be translucent ... indented...

For me it is mostly sweeping, non-material energy which is broken into layers by light and dark color variations. I think something is...pulling me into my proper level of travel and trying to relax me, too...' (Newton 1994, p. 20-21).

Orientation. According to Newton's subjects, once our reception committee of close family and friends has greeted us, we move to a place of healing, where the accumulated negativity of the finished life is cleansed by light and sound. The next 'stop' assists the soul to reorient to this spiritual environment, sometimes accompanied by an examination by the subject's guide. Newton notes the 'remarkable' similarity of his clients' descriptions of the nature of the next two stages, despite the different names they use. (p. 53).

Transition. Newton's clients say their next stop is a place he calls the staging area. The reports of his subjects change from the earlier descriptions of '*layering and foggy stratification*':

> The experience becomes one of travelling through '*a mighty galactic cloud into a more unified celestial sphere... [S]ubjects...are dazzled by an eternal world spread out before them and believe that somewhere within lies the nucleus of creation...I hear nothing about the inky blackness we associate with deep space*' (Newton 1994, pp. 71-2).

This description of a transitional staging area is, as far as I can discover, unique to Newton. (Sogyal Rinpoche refers to a 'transit lounge', as noted in Chapter Six-but is it the same place?) Does this uniqueness invalidate everything he has said? If he or his clients were fantasising or fabricating on the basis even, of everything that has now been written on the subject, a discrepancy like this one could not appear, since no one else had 'invented' it-and still hasn't, to my knowledge. If Newton's study were a hoax, he would not wish to add an invention unique to his fiction, as this would tend to show up the hoax. This gives his research added authenticity.

Newton includes the debriefing session with what he calls the **Council of Elders**, as part of the Transition phase and chapter. Whitton gives it a separate chapter "The Board of Judgement", and goes into greater detail. Newton provides a typical report:

> "*After I meet with my friends, my guide takes me to another place to meet with my panel of Elders. She is at my side as an interpreter for what I don't understand and to provide support for my explanations of my conduct in the last life...There are always the same six Elders in front of me...Their faces are kindly, and they evaluate my perceptions of the life I have just lived and how I could have done better with my talents and what I did that was beneficial. I am freely allowed to express my frustrations and desires...*" (Newton 1994, pp. 85-6).

Homecoming

Souls come home, not to a location, but to their group and their position within the world of souls-their relationship to all other souls. Newton usually means by 'soul', not the divine or spiritual soul, but the human soul-the discarnate consciousness with whatever admixture of astral and mental aspects, and infusion of (divine) soul-consciousness, that individual has developed:

> *One subject remarked " As I come near my place, there is a monotone of many voices sounding the letter A, like Aaaaa, for my recognition, and I can see them all vibrating fast as warm, bright energy, and I know these are the disembodied ones right now."*

Souls within the group who are still incarnate are only able to radiate *'a dim light with low pulsating energy patterns and don't seem to communicate much with anyone.* They are still able to *'greet the returning soul in a quiet fashion within the group setting'* (Newton 1994, p. 85).

There is a quite telling corroboration of another aspect of these reports: Andy Tomlinson's (2007) subjects told him that they must decide how much soul energy they take with them into incarnation, and that the balance helps to sustain the group on the soul level in their work.

The group life of souls vs. traditional ideas and developmental psychology

Newton remarks on the difference between expectations of soul life, and the reality:

> *'...After awakening, it is no wonder that (my clients) express surprise with the knowledge that everyone has a designated place in the spirit world...I was (also) unprepared to hear about the existence of organized soul support groups. I had pictured souls just floating around aimlessly by themselves after leaving Earth.'* (Newton 1994, p. 87)

Newton describes these groups as they emerge through his clients' reports. Souls rejoin their primary support group, a close 'family' of three to twenty-five souls all at a similar level of knowledge and spiritual development, referred to as the 'primary cluster' by Newton. There, in places they describe as like earthly libraries and places of learning, they study, learn, reflect and come to greater knowledge and wisdom about all aspects of their development especially relating to their just-finished life. They are under the immediate tuition of more advanced souls who are supervised in their turn by those more advanced again, and who might have the charge of two or more secondary cluster groups, with at least a thousand souls, and composed of many primary groups. Meantime the whole vast group of human souls is watched, guided, helped and administered by 'master souls'. Each soul belongs first and foremost to their primary cluster.

> When there is contact between different groups, it is *'governed by the lessons to be learned during an incarnation. This may be due to a past-life connection, or the particular identity trait of the souls involved'*. These connections will only be peripheral ones in the lives concerned. *'An example would be a high school classmate who was once a close friend but who you now see only at class reunions.*

> *Members of the same cluster group are closely united for all eternity. These tightly-knit clusters are often composed of like-minded souls with common objectives which they continually work out with each other. Usually they choose lives together as relatives and close friends during their incarnations on Earth* (Newton 1994, p. 88).

This grouping of souls, with its characteristic of powerful group bonding; the feeling of deep love between the group members, the strong identification of souls with their group, and the group cohesion and group purpose, was a totally unexpected finding, as Newton says. His original view of solitary souls, whether 'aimlessly drifting' or going to an individual reckoning and reward in a place of single souls, not groups of souls, is the usual picture of life in the world beyond physical death, both in the popular imagination and in most of the world's great scriptures and religious teachings. It is in fact, what we could expect to be 'discovered' about that world if the subjects of any study were dreaming, fantasizing or tapping into the collective psyche on the subject of life after death. There simply isn't any obvious justification for making up or imagining the group life of souls. This group life is in direct contradiction with what we as a culture, expect to be the case after death.

Yet it is exactly what The Tibetan also teaches-that souls are an intimate part of a group, and are strongly group oriented, and rather uninterested in the solitary personality life. Not only do souls exist in groups, so that the very nature of the soul is a group nature, but during incarnation, he points out constantly, we are steadily learning to relate to larger and larger groups, and broaden the area of our compassion and concern, our activity and our responsibility to larger groups, as our consciousness expands ever further beyond the narrow confines of the little personal self. Eventually we advance to the stage of being ready for a higher form of group life and activity – the work of some form of active service in the world, in a group of students, or disciples, under the direction and tuition of a Master or a senior disciple. This stage is likely to be under-represented (though it is present) in Newton's sample; his conclusions, above, apply to a more general stage of Western humanity.

Newton's discovery of the group life of souls is also the nature of the soul life as it would appear *if we attempted to predict it on the basis of Western developmental psychology*-the consciousness expanding to include ever larger groups, family to ethnic group to nation to world, and beyond.

D.K. wrote to one of his own disciples-that is, students:

> *'All the work that I seek to do with you and my other disciples has been with the objective of intensifying their group relation, to deepen their group love and to bind them together as a group. For this is group work which the Hierarchy and those associated with it do, and my group is not one wherein personal training is given in order to bring about personal growth. Let me emphasize this again, my brother. I am not training you so you can grow. I am training a group of disciples so that they may function as a unit, and as a welded totality. That subjective inner unity has been neglected by you whilst you wandered down a byway of high grade personality and emotional beauty but which in reality belonged to the world of illusion* (Bailey 1944, p. 239).'

The stress placed by D.K. in his instructions to his disciples, in Discipleship in the New Age, Volumes I and II, is upon the vital importance of the development of the group relationship and the group skills and aptitudes, of group love and group strength, and finally upon the group's work in service to humanity, to offer its unique contribution to the whole. It is not upon the individual in the group, although in the middle stages of evolution especially, the emphasis is necessarily upon personal development of love, will and wisdom within individuals, as is reflected in subjects' reports of examination before the Council of Elders. True group identity and work is a step or two beyond just belonging to a group and being conscious of it. It is a reason that we are taught in groups upon soul levels, as D.K. explains below, and as Newton also discovered.

Teachers, groups and the spiritual classroom: Newton and D.K.

Newton summarizes his findings about guides as follows:

> *The system fosters enlightenment and ultimately the perfection of souls. It is important to understand that while we may suffer the consequences of bad choices in our educational tasks, we are always protected, supported and directed within the system by* **master souls** *(emphasis mine)... **The whole idea of a hierarchy of souls** (emphasis mine) has been part of both Eastern and Western cultures for many centuries* (Newton 1994, pp. 104-5).

Though there is a tradition in most world religions, of guardians or Buddha-like preceptors and discarnate teachers, I was not alone in dismissing them as fantasy until quite recently. It was the description of her discovery of, and growing relationship with, her own guide by Dr Elizabeth Kubler-Ross (1997) that made me stop and think again. It was even later that I connected these "guides" with The Tibetan's description of a hierarchy of teachers who oversee our spiritual growth and development, and report back regularly to the senior members of that hierarchy, the Masters of esoteric tradition, who are themselves under their senior, the one known in the West as the Christ, *The Master of all the Masters and the teacher alike of angels and of Men'*, and the Buddha, who is senior even to the Christ.

Newton discovered that every one of his clients taken into the interlife had a guide. He reports:

'The recognition of these spiritual teachers brings people into the company of a warm, loving creative power. Through our guides, we become more aware of the continuity of life and our identity as a soul...The awareness level of the soul determines to some extent the degree of advancement of the guide assigned to them. In fact, the maturity of a particular guide also has a bearing on whether these teachers have only one student or many under their direction. Guides at the senior level and above usually work with an entire group of souls in the spirit world and on Earth' (Newton 1994, p. 107).

The Tibetan's advice on the teaching received by every soul in the system (Bailey 1922b, pp. 64-9) is amazing, involving as it does both those out of incarnation and those of us in bodies on earth.

'Advanced egos and the spiritually inclined, who are not yet on the Probationary Path, attend instructions from disciples, and on occasions large classes are conducted for their benefit by initiates. Their work is more rudimentary, though occult from a worldly standpoint, and they learn under supervision to be invisible helpers ... The very advanced, and those on the Probationary Path and nearing initiation, work more frequently in what might be termed departmental work, forming a group of assistants to the Members of the Hierarchy (Bailey 1922b, p. 65).

This is amazing stuff! Is D.K. saying that classes are held, and souls treated as students? If that is the case, are they organized, formal classes? Are these classes graded, as this suggests they might be? What then, would be the qualifications for entry to any grade? And what would be taught in these classes? Do they bear any relation to courses of instruction, grades and classes on earth?

Whilst the man is on the Probationary Path (and termed a probationer) he is taught principally to know himself, to ascertain his weaknesses and to correct them. He is taught to work as an invisible helper at first and for several lives he is generally kept at this work. Later, as he makes progress, he may be moved to more selected work. He is taught the rudiments of the Divine

> *Wisdom and is entered into the final grades in the Hall of Learning. He is known to a Master, and is in the care (for definite teaching) of one of the disciples of that master, or if of rare promise, of an initiate.*

There are three levels of tuition and learning, for the three broad levels of soul maturity-the Hall of Ignorance, the Hall of Learning, and the Hall of Wisdom, the last being the soul's university:

> *Disciples are taught in groups in the Master's Ashram, or classroom, at night, if in incarnation. Apart from these regular gatherings, in order to receive direct teaching from the Master, a disciple (for some specific reason) may be called to the Master's study for a private interview. This occurs when a Master wishes to see a disciple for commendation, warning, or to decide if initiation is desirable. The major part of a disciple's tuition is left in the hands of some initiate or more advanced disciple,* [called a guide in Newton and elsewhere] *who watches over his younger brother, and is responsible to the Master for his progress, handing in regular reports. Karma is largely the arbiter of this relation.*

> *Initiates receive instruction directly from the Masters or from some of the great devas or angels. These teachings are usually imparted at night in small classes, or individually (should the occasion warrant) in the Master's private study. The above applies to initiates in incarnation or on the inner planes* [i.e. out of incarnation]. *If on causal levels* [i.e. they are advanced enough to be functioning consciously as souls on the causal level] *they receive instruction at any time deemed advisable, direct from the Master to the Ego* [the soul] *on causal levels.*

Jung's personal instruction from 'Philemon' indicates that he was at least a disciple, though more likely an initiate. However, this and the other similar cases I've cited form yet another category-where the Master (or a very senior disciple?) makes an appearance on the physical plane to give personal instruction. D.K.'s own work with Alice Bailey began like this. (He materialised before her and asked her to help with his work. She refused, and continued to refuse for some time; she considered the paranormal had a bad reputation and she didn't want to be involved, as she relates in her *Unfinished Autobiography* of 1951. The Tibetan asked her to please just give it a trial; Alice's talents and attributes were needed by the Masters working to evolve the consciousness of humanity. The work began, and of course Alice was won over by the quality and content of these communications; by the inescapable fact that these were indeed high and authentic teachings, of a kind that could not be known and communicated by anyone in normal incarnation.)

Has Newton discovered anything that would give support and substance to both accounts? Is there any mention, among his clients' reports, of such a thing as spiritual learning? And if so, is there any suggestion that it might be remotely 'official'–structured and formalized, as distinct from the natural learning which takes place with experience? He refers to guides as teachers: Do they function as teachers in any more formal sense?

In his first book (1994, p. 85) Newton reports on the learning of the soul. He notes that average souls, at a basic level of spiritual work, describe their spiritual groups as separated into classrooms, or even separate schoolhouses: *The analogy of spiritual schools directed by teacher-guides is used so often by people under hypnosis that it has become a habit for me to use the same terminology.'*

Later in his writing, Newton appears to have gone a step further, no longer seeing 'classroom' and 'teacher' as mere analogies. It becomes clear to the reader that the experience of *'spiritual schools directed by teacher-guides'* is identical to that on earth except that the concrete physical setting is lacking.

> 'Some of my subjects object to my characterizing the spirit world as a place governed by societal structure and organizational management ...On the other hand, I listen to these same subjects describe a planned and ordered process of self-development influenced by peers and teachers. If the spirit world does resemble one great schoolhouse with a multitude of classrooms under the direction of teacher-souls who monitor our progress-then it has structure (Newton 1994, p. 104).

Newton had accumulated more data by the time of writing his second book, 'Destiny of Souls', and is able to add to the picture about classes, teachers and grading. He had already discovered that souls don't all progress at the same rate. Some in the group progress faster although this may not be equal across all curriculum areas. Souls at intermediate level who demonstrate special talents such as healing and teaching, *'are permitted to participate in specialty groups for more advanced work while still remaining with their cluster group'* (1994, p. 106).

Newton describes levels of learning and advancement: *'six levels of incarnating souls'* ascending from Level One. Souls who have reached Level III are formed into independent studies work groups. *'Usually, their old guides continue to monitor them through one master teacher. Thus, a new pod of entities graduating into full Level III could be brought together from many clusters within one or more secondary groups'.* Nearing level IV, souls are given greater independence from the group learning. *'Although group size diminishes as souls advance, the intimate contact between original peer group members is never lost'* (Newton 1994, p. 106).

The extent of corroboration in these sources about the Interlife, and spiritual advancement through the teaching and training given by more advanced individuals, is truly remarkable. There is no sign that Michael Newton had any knowledge of the teaching of the Tibetan, D.K., through the Alice Bailey books. It was his clients, though, who had to had to have worked their way through these esoteric texts, and then succeeded in regurgitating selective, and altered, details, under hypnosis. And not just a couple of his clients, but all of them. It is impossible. I can't see how it could be attributable to any cause other than the reality that is being described. The mechanism of creation of the Hierarchy or Communion of Saints or the (human aspect of the) Great Chain of Being, is visible in these sources. It is further explored in Chapters Twelve and Thirteen.

It is just as striking that we as spiritual students whether in incarnation or in the Interlife, are grouped by our spiritual masters and teachers, according to a more elaborated, but otherwise utterly recognisable, Western developmental psychology!

The next chapter, Eleven, examines in detail Dr Joel Whitton's discoveries on the Interlife, in order to compare them to Dr Newton's, and to discover if the corroboration of evidence from these two sources is more than superficial.

Chapter 11
The Soul's World

Whitton and Newton compared

Summary Points

- NDE research agrees with Interlife studies; independent researchers' Interlife studies also agree
- Whitton's post-death stages similar to Newton's and those found in NDE
- The Bardo identity
- **The Judgement, Life review and planning for a future life**
- Whitton's and Newton's subjects report a panel of Elders or a Judgement Board and life review
- **Planning the next life; choosing parents, setting and goals**
- Case studies of karma; cause and effect in incarnation: Newton, Whitton and Tomlinson
- **Comparison: Newton's and Whitton's accounts of the true nature of the soul's realm**
- Karmic debts and soul choices

- Soul learning through personality experiences; choosing more difficult lives
- Homosexuality: soul, personality or genes?
- The nature of the soul
- **The laws of spiritual and physical evolution; soul control will end suffering**
- The stages and major events of the after-death experience
- Souls returning under the Law of Karmic Liability or the Law of Necessity
- **Soul vs. Personality; Logotherapy's definition**

The Soul's World

There is a critical test for these case studies of the Bardo or Interlife period: Do they support or contradict- or bear no relation to, the findings of Moody, Sabom, and Near-death Experience researchers? If they do not, then the foundations of my argument are a degree shakier than otherwise. If they do, the sceptic's position would be that Whitton's and Newton's subjects knew of the work of Moody and others and were regurgitating aspects of the NDE. I've answered the sceptics regarding Newton's work in the last chapter. What about that of Whitton? Although his work was not published until 1986, Dr Joel Whitton's clinical discovery of the Bardo took place in 1974, and Moody's *Life after Life* was not published until 1975.

Validity testing NDE and Interlife studies

Whitton's findings on the interlife, as Fiore's, reported in the last chapter, supported the findings of the NDE pioneers. Yet the earlier studies had been investigating only the Near-death Experience, not the Interlife, which was then almost unknown to Western researchers. Dr Michael Newton's later studies were also completely consistent with NDE investigations. The sceptics' position fails to account for the seamless continuity of the known and the unknown: the accounts of those who had apparently travelled into the Bardo during NDE, and the accounts of the Interlife period given by Whitton's and Newton's subjects, alive and lying on the clinical couch.

This chapter may be the most controversial and testing of the entire book, and not only for those whose view of life, the universe and everything has materialist bounds. Christians and Buddhists, even the new agers who haven't just accepted a dogma, but have chosen a spiritual tradition after exploration -- a relatively new development in history, may find it hard-as hard as I did originally, to take these super-cloud lands seriously. Part of the problem is that our vague and therefore unchallengeable, ideas of life and consciousness beyond death, are being given confronting form and detail in Newton's and Whitton's work. And it was possible to read the last chapter, about Newton's discoveries, and dismiss it as the findings of just one maverick investigator.

However, if Whitton's findings corroborate Newton's (as they do), what remains but cautious acceptance? And when still further evidence accumulates, from newer studies, such as those of Brian Weiss (U.S. 1988) and Andy Tomlinson (U.K. 2007), what defence remains for materialism? All these studies evidence the same 'absurd' elements of the interlife experience: One example is the Board of Judgement or Council of Advisors which, though given different names, is to be found in all of them.

In *Exploring the Eternal Soul; Insights from the Life between Lives*, the most important new study, Tomlinson selects eleven of the interlife reports of 160 clients, mostly British, Dutch, German and Scandinavian. He acknowledges the work of the pioneers, Whitton, Newton, Fiore, Cannon and Modi particularly. Through the text, Tomlinson compares his findings with those of these pioneers, and gives a diagram of comparison between the elements and nature of the interlife as discovered by each. Tomlinson's work fully corroborates and extends these earlier findings. Once the comparison has been made between Whitton's and Newton's work, it will be useful to look at this further evidence.

We have seen in the last chapter, how Whitton stumbled upon the Bardo and began his research. Joe Fisher, Whitton's co-author, outlines the conduct of a session exploring the interlife. The subject, under Dr Whitton's hypnotic direction, will return to the moment of the past death, then *'gradually begin to relate events very similar to the* [Near-death] *accounts collected by Dr Raymond Moody, Dr Kenneth Ring, Dr Michael Sabom* [and others]... (Whitton & Fisher 1986, p. 52).

NDE research agrees with Interlife studies; independent researchers' Interlife studies also agree

Beyond this physical death, which is being relived via hypnosis, Whitton has identified stages similar both to Newton's and those reported in the Near-death Experience (Whitton & Fisher, 1986, pp. 32-9). The first, *Brilliant beginnings*, is about the stage of entry into the Light. The section titled *I think, therefore I am*, is about the nature of our being now we no longer perceive or relate through the five senses.

The domain of the discarnate is summarized using the words of Rudolph Steiner "After death, all our thoughts and mental representations appear as a mighty panorama before the soul".

In the section titled **The Bardo identity**, Whitton equates meta-consciousness and the soul:

To enter metaconsciousness is to be one with the timeless oversoul which is the invisible cornerstone of the powers of the individual...(p. 62) When Jesus Christ said 'Lo, the Kingdom of God is within you', he was probably referring to the oversoul...' (P. 63)

Whitton also explains in this section, that many oversouls know each other from past lives.

The next section, *The Board of Judgment,* explains the reality behind the idea of the post-death Judgment or testing of the soul according to the value of every thought, word and deed during the lifetime now finished. Although Whitton does not catalogue the stages of return in the same way as Newton or D.K. because of a different approach, it is clearly the same experience which is being described, ending in the same 'place' (where degree of evolution permits); the metaconscious state of the spiritual soul or oversoul, in Whitton's term.

The Judgement, Life review and planning for a future life

The post-death Judgement is a feature in all our spiritual and philosophical traditions, onward from the ancient Egyptian 'weighing of the soul', according to Whitton and Fisher (1986, p. 65). Yet despite the fact that The Judgement has been regarded in modern times, as a medieval myth, Dr Whitton's subjects reported that they found themselves before this very Judgement board.

> *The members of this... tribunal are highly advanced spiritually... Knowing intuitively everything ...about the person who stands before them, their role is to assist that individual in evaluating the life that has just passed... If there is a private hell... it is the moment when the soul presents itself for review... While incarnate, one's negative actions can be rationalized and repressed...*

Another old myth turns out to have some kind of reality: In the interlife review, all emotional suffering we have inflicted on others *'is felt as keenly as if it were inflicted on oneself*.

Both Whitton's and Newton's subjects reported that some time after their entry into the higher worlds, they were called before a panel of Elders or a Judgement Board. Newton summarizes his findings in his second book *Destiny of Souls*:

> *' A step or two above our guides, these ascended masters are the most advanced identifiable entities my still-incarnating clients see in the spirit world. They give them different names such as the Old Ones, the Sacred*

Masters, the Venerables, and pragmatic titles like the Examiners or the Committee. (Newton 2002, p. 201)[1].

Both researchers agree that the purpose of this is not the ancient idea of the passing of judgement and condemnation of our souls when we have sinned, but the objective evaluation of the effort, actions and achievements of the just-past life especially in the light of the goals set before it began. Whitton's work, however, gives more detail about 'The Board of Judgement' and the life review process which is wonderfully clarifying.

The Life in Review. Whitton's subjects reported, like Newton's, that they underwent a flashback life review, with the Elders presiding, to assist them in assessing their motivations, their actions and the outcome in that life, and as part of the process of identifying the tasks to be undertaken in future lives. One subject says:

'It's like climbing inside a movie of your life. Every moment from every year of your life is played back in complete sensory detail...' And yet it is instantaneous.

This means that the soul cannot avoid realising

'when happiness was thrown away or when thoughtlessness caused pain in another or when life-threatening danger was just around the corner...This [self-analysis] is the soul's moment of truth, and, as it proceeds, the judges tend to remain in the background' (p. 65).

Surprisingly, regardless of our traditions' picture of stern taskmasters, the Elders do not act as judges, but rather as

'loving teachers whose aim is to encourage their student to learn and benefit from past mistakes' (Whitton & Fisher 1986, p. 65).

Important events are discussed-what happened there and why; did you succeed in your aims? How could you have handled it better? What are the next lessons on the agenda? It becomes obvious that our teachers don't measure our success by some standard of perfection we will not reach for many lives to come, but according to the standard which is relevant to our present stage of development, and to the specific goals established with their counsel and assistance, before taking incarnation in that life.

Shedding 'skins'. Having said that, the standard set before us to reach eventually, is perfection, says Whitton. According to one subject, there are many ascending planes encountered in working

---

1. *Destiny of Souls* by Michael Newton Ph. D. © 2000 Llewellyn Worldwide, 2143 Wooddale Drive, Woodbury MN 55125-2989. All extracts used with permission and with best wishes from the publisher. All rights reserved.

towards greater spiritual unity. This ascent, she indicated, takes place both after an incarnation and over the course of evolution; an understanding in agreement with Tibetan Buddhism and the perennial philosophy:

> *"There are many higher planes and to get back to God, to reach the plane where His spirit resides, you have to drop your garment each time until your spirit is truly free...[We] are allowed glimpses of the higher planes-each one is lighter and brighter than the one before'* " (Whitton & Fisher 1986, p 75).

This is corroboration by ordinary humans who have experienced it, of the 'onion-peeling' process of shedding of bodies described in Tibetan Buddhism, in D.K.'s teaching through Alice Bailey's books, and in other sources quoted in Chapters Six and Seven. The process of psychological development from the midpoint of greatest separation, individualization and autonomy to the point of cosmic, unitary consciousness can also be described this way: In order to get back to God or Self 'you have to drop your garment each time until your spirit is truly free'.

Planning the next life. The most significant finding of Dr Whitton's research is that it is usual to plan our next life while discarnate. The judgement panel, *'mindful of the soul's karmic debts and its need for specific lessons, give wide-ranging counsel* (p. 41). Whitton's subjects discovered that they chose their parents, the setting and goals of the coming life, and the souls who would play significant parts in that life, according to the lessons to be learnt and karmic needs. Whitton's writer Fisher then quotes the Tibetan Book of the Dead: *'Examine where you are going to be born and choose the continent.'*

In the extraordinary Rolf De Heer film *Ten Canoes*, we are taken into the pristine beauty of the Dreamtime proximity, by its descendents. It is a life of survival work, rigid roles and extremely limited horizons, but lived in the paradise closer to the beginning of the journey than we have been privileged to see. It is a thing of awe that we can for a moment, look into this vanished paradise, at a certain cultural order and beauty that existed before colonial invasion with all its horrific consequences for the original Australian people. David Gulpilil is one of the great actors of the age. He is also a living link to this world: He and his clan group, who made the film with him, live an adapted version of the traditional way. We have little idea about Aboriginal spirituality. Most Westerners and perhaps some urban Aboriginal viewers will think indulgently that these are merely primitive myths on display. And be grateful we are no longer confined in such a limited world, as I am. But here too, just as in every spiritual tradition worldwide, including in the five great faiths, the core truths shine out through the cultural accretions surrounding them. One of these is the expectation that the kinsman or woman who has just died, will be reborn into the group -- as a son's or daughter's child. This is pretty much what would have happened, either due to the 'rushing back into incarnation' of the less-evolved, discussed in Chapters Eight and Nine, or under the direction of the soul and the 'Old Ones'; in Aboriginal terms, the Wise Ancestors who oversee incarnation.

Coming back to earth. Whitton's research backs up the teachings already explored; that the less evolved will have an overwhelming desire to be back in a body, and won't linger in the between life state:

> *Nor will those who see an early opportunity arising on the earthbound plane to make karmic compensation for actions in earlier lives. Extended stays may arise from the desire to expend great effort in preparation for the next earthly existence or may stem from an apathetic attitude which often results in disembodied slumber ...*(p. 69).

Newton's description of the 'step one, step two' of the process of planning a new life, selecting a new environment and body, parents and associates, is far more detailed, while Whitton is concentrating on the different causal or karmic aspects of the process, such as the link between karma and genetic inheritance, and the relationship between the interlife plan and the earthly experience. He evidences the detailed blueprint of the less-evolved versus the sometimes mere general outline of more evolved souls, the case of repeated failures to meet set challenges, and the case of revision of plans even as the incarnation proceeds. Can we tell, while in the midst of this planned life, how well we are doing? Those of us who are succeeding, or have even completed the set plan and are now improvising, *'have an inner sense that life is unfolding as it should. Those who have strayed from their blueprint feel, instead, that everything is out of control...* (Whitton & Fisher 1986, p. 76).

Whitton goes on to discuss a different situation, where there is general scripting, but no detail, which happened with one client who had been lured into bushland and raped, though no rape had actually been planned. She said of her discoveries: *'My plan was that I would pick a tragic event which would cause me to change my entire soul complexion during my thirties'* (p. 77).

Curiously, there was an aspect and stage of the entire futuristic romance (as it first seemed to me to be) that especially read like science fiction. This was Newton's description of the place of life selection, where souls look at possible futures on what seemed like big computer screens. Yet I was amazed to discover a brief reference to this in Whitton also, giving the notion greater credibility. One subject visualized *'a sort of clockwork instrument into which you could insert certain parts in order for specific consequences to follow*. He had to work with this machinery, making *'alterations to the interlife plan in order that they might transpire in my forthcoming life on Earth'* (Whitton & Fisher, p. 72).

This subject's statement predates the arrival of computers into our homes, so he has used an older analogy and symbol –'clockwork instrument' rather than 'computer' as used by Newton's (later) subjects, to 'translate' the experience into terms earthlings can understand. But whatever the reality behind this experience or this perceived 'instrument', the event will only be processed by the human mind via assimilation to something familiar-clock or computer.

Andy Tomlinson's subject, Liam Thompson, uses still another symbol, when he says of the scene of his next-life preview 'It really is a cinema, with seats in rows and a big screen. Except I think I'm in control of what's on the screen and I can see what I want' (2007, p. 101). I have chosen Liam to use as the exemplar of Tomlinson's work, since he committed suicide -- not once but repeatedly, yet, in line with my earlier comment on suicide, suffered no terrible retribution. I comment further about this later in the chapter.

Newton gives more of the fleshing-out of the process that takes us from body-personality to soul: from the moment of exiting our used body to the return to the soul world and to one's own group, that I especially needed to make sense of the nature of the soul and the soul's world. The stages of return are clearer. The interaction between souls is also clearly illustrated there.

Tomlinson has built on this work by questioning his subjects similarly, and probing sometimes further, into the same areas as Newton, so we get the same fleshing-out of the process. This produces *corroboration, not replication*, giving us further understanding, and some new insights. For example, Tomlinson prompts his subjects to discover more about predetermination versus free will. Do we have to accept the life the Council of Elders advises for us? '*As Liam Thompson reported, 'We're not forced to do anything. A soul can remain in the spirit realms rather than incarnate, and continue the learning from there'.* However as Jack Hammond commented about the reluctance to accept a life plan, *'we become restless and our spirit guide encourages it [the new plan] by showing us the benefits'* (2007, p. 129).

The shuttle of rebirth: our journey so far. Joe Fisher, Whitton's writer, includes a brilliant chapter, carefully researched, on the idea of reincarnation through the ages:

> 'Rebirth has always been espoused by the wisest of spiritual and philosophical sages- from Plato to Jesus Christ' (p. 87). All traditions teach, says Fisher, that 'repeated incarnations are as essential for spiritual evolution as the succession of years is to physical development' (p.88).

The authors ponder Saint Augustine's rejection of reincarnation, and comment that he may not have known, along with modern Christians, that Jesus Christ testifies to reincarnation in both the Bible and the Gnostic gospel Pistis Sophia , where Jesus says that *'souls are poured from one into another of different bodies of the world'* (p. 91).

The Cosmic Classroom. There are wonderful insights here, into the true nature of the workings of karma. The idea that 'an eye for an eye' is its essential nature, has changed over the millennia from the advice of verse 28 of The Instruction of Ptahhotep (Egyptian, 2,600 B.C.E.): 'Your deed turns into judgment of you'.

> Fisher explains 'The Old and New Testaments were equally uncompromising and displayed an even keener taste for vengeance. Revelation 13:10 says, "He that leadeth into captivity shall go into captivity; he that killeth with the sword must be killed with the sword". [St Paul meant in another lifetime, surely-since it was obvious that this balancing did not happen to most people in the lifetime in which the act was committed. And not in Purgatory, Hell or Heaven, where it isn't possible to be killed again by sword or other means. However, this harsh interpretation evolved, says Fisher]:

> *The Christian Gnostics and the Hebrew Cabbalists came to understand karma as a law of compensation. Anyone who killed another would not necessarily be condemned to die in similar circumstances but would be expected to make amends for the act in some way, perhaps by returning in a future life to care for the dying and the maimed* (p. 70).

Case studies of karma: Cause and effect in incarnation

The second part of Whitton's book is devoted to 'Karmic Case Studies'. These reveal the relationship between karmic requirements, soul choices, life circumstances, and our incarnate handling of, and responses to, those circumstances.

In life after life, whether male or female, Ben Garonzi had reacted to violence by killing the perpetrators, and was thus caught in a vicious karmic circle. In the life under review, he had been brutalized by a father he came to hate:

> 'One evening, when his father had become insensate from alcohol, Ben went to a kitchen drawer and pulled out a carving knife with every intention of slitting the man's throat. Then, listening to the promptings of an inner voice, he changed his mind and replaced the knife...This decision to desist became a major turning point in Ben's life' (p. 71).

Another client, a high school teacher, struggled to reconcile the spiritual and erotic aspects of his nature:

> The very vivid woman's face which appeared 'told me that the erotic element provided the yeast for developing conscience, altruism and benevolent concern. Eroticism, being a rudimentary force that provokes interaction, forces people to become intimately involved and can therefore initiate and assist in spiritual development' (p. 73).

Newton and Whitton are in agreement regarding the nature of the law of Cause and Effect, its workings in our lives and the process of learning and evolving. Newton's second book 'Destiny of Souls' covers more of this process.

Newton, Whitton and Tomlinson compared

Is there any corroboration of the results of these two pioneers, in more recent studies, particularly Tomlinson's *Exploring the Eternal Soul*? Tomlinson notes the elements and nature of the interlife in his study, and in the findings of these pioneers. He includes a diagram of comparison. The diagram is based on that of Ian Lawton, and comes from his *The Book of the Soul (2006)*. These close colleagues worked together after Lawton wrote this first book, and ended up separating their material into two books, Lawton's being *The Wisdom of the Soul (2007)*.

The diagram is titled *Comparison with Other Interlife Pioneers*, (Tomlinson 2007, p. 166-7) and organizes the work of Tomlinson, Newton, Ramster, Whitton, Cannon (Dolores not Alexander), Modi and Fiore into a list of major findings, and notes with a bullet point in the researcher's column, if that particular element is present in their findings. Since I have isolated some of the same, and some different, common elements, it would be useful to summarise the diagram here. The elements of the interlife period covered in this *Comparison* diagram are: Transition via a tunnel or light (found in reports of all seven researchers); Met by friends, family or spirit guides (found in eight reports); Varied perception of surroundings (4); Initial rest and energy restoring (4); Healing shower of energy

(4-but never the same four in these last three headings); Delayering as part of energy healing (1-Tomlinson's new discovery); Rehabilitation for traumatized souls (3); Soul group members at similar level (6); Review with elders (6); Replay/role-play via life-books and films (6); Ongoing classroom learning (6); Non-judgemental nature of reviews (7); Next life planning (7); Choice to reject the life plan offered (7); Multiple life plans offered (3); Training in specialisation (4); Relayering as part of reincarnation (1).

Tomlinson has discovered the clinical evidence for what he names 'delayering'. This is the shedding of 'skins' known to the perennial wisdom; described by the Tibetan, D.K., in Chapters Seven and Eight, and called 'dropping your garment' by Whitton's client, quoted above. As we have seen, there is in Buddhism, a strong tradition of teaching about the process of moving upwards through steadily refining substance and consciousness. Even in Christianity there are indications of it in the process of ascent from Purgatory to Heaven. If death and birth are in fact, the reverse of each other in terms of movement between the universal and individual, the unified spiritual and the separated concrete, Tomlinson would have to report on that reverse process. Significantly, Tomlinson's subjects do indeed discuss their 'relayering'; the process in reverse as they descend into incarnation.

What are the similarities between Newton's and Whitton's accounts of the afterlife?

1. **The nature of the experience.** Clients of Dr Newton and Dr Whitton, like NDEr's, travel into a place like the old myths, our ancient faiths, and the wisdom of the sages -- a place located in a profoundly moral universe. It is a place that Buddha, Jesus, Plato, Mohammed, and the Hebrew Patriarchs from Abraham onward, would recognise. Newton and Whitton agree that the psyche is set free from the body and material plane, to return by stages 'whence it came', and to reintegrate with a greater whole. The metaphysics by which this happens is continuous with our materialistic conceptions, but extends far beyond them, and reverses our materialistic idea of the physical plane as the cause of all other manifestations of life. How much agreement is there between these two researchers, about the nature and significance of the experiences beyond death, and about the events and aspects of what all their clients apparently experience as a journey, not just a set of unrelated incidents like a dream-jumble?

2. The significance of the experience. This journey, the place and the experience are profoundly meaningful; the discarnate individual is integrated into a scheme far greater than anything guessed at in earthly life, and into an all-embracing purpose, to which all subjects of both Newton and Whitton testify. The life review, the reflections after, the new life's design and the reasons for choosing any particular design over any other all have significance for and within this larger, deeply moral scheme. Subjects report they have come to understand that the present life has in fact been chosen and designed by themselves, with assistance from teachers and counsellors.

3. The reality of the place. Whitton's and Newton's subjects clearly agree with Dr Fenwick's summary in Chapter Three on the NDE, of his patients' experience of this place as one where we are surrounded by universal love.

'So powerful, so ineffable is the experience that first-time visitors are rendered speechless' reports Dr Whitton, *'their faces contorting with emotions of awe and bewilderment'.* He quotes one subject describing the experience:

> *Unworldly ecstasy. Bright, bright light. I didn't have a body as on Earth. Instead, I had a shadow body.... There is no ground and no sky... [W]hen we want to communicate, we can do so without having to listen, without having to speak* (p.25).

This subject may have been in a higher body- perhaps the mental body, but had no reference point for that. When NDErs arrive on the astral plane (as all but the most evolved do, as we have seen in previous chapters), they typically see wonderful cities of light or beautiful pastoral scenes or magnificent gardens. A formless world such as is being described here, is necessarily more abstract than the astral world, further from physical reality, and closer to the Ultimate. The proof of its existence there, and at all, is that we can't imagine it, even when told what it's like, and certainly not dream it up as the quintessential after-death world.

After listening to their subjects, Dr Newton and Dr Whitton are in agreement that this place has a reality that is, unimaginably again for us earthlings, more real than our anchor and reference-point for reality-our waking consciousness on earth. According to Whitton *'the life between life is not a fairy-tale world. Those who have tasted its richness know that they have visited the ultimate reality'* (p. 25).

Newton (2002, pp.135-6) relates a client's experience of creating oranges in the spirit world, perfect in every way, and yet the client says *"'without a body...well...to me they have the flavour of imitations.'"* He goes on to philosophize about this, to harmonize clients' perceptions of the spirit world as the greater reality, with the lack of sensual reality of these mere thought constructs of earthly objects.

> *'Despite this client's comments, I have had subjects tell me that they see the spirit world as reality and Earth as an illusion created to teach us...[T]he reality of an interdimensional spirit world with its lack of absolutes allows the soul a magnitude of experience far beyond the physical.'*

This reflection also suggests that Newton would agree with Whitton, that this world of spirit has no similarity with and cannot be conflated with or mistaken for, imaginary worlds.

Whitton's writer Fisher says of it, that this blissful state 'can be defined as the perception of a reality beyond **any known state of existence** [Emphasis mine]. It is distinct from dream states, out-of-body experiences, the reliving of past lives and all other altered states of consciousness' (Whitton & Fisher 1986, p. 25). (There is one exception; this 'blissful state' is one of the altered states known to mystics, sages and those who have achieved a measure of self-transcendence).

4. Unearthly bliss. There is also agreement that it is likely to be the most glorious experience; joy or even bliss beyond anything we know on earth. Whitton describes the state of metaconsciousness as *'to surrender one's sense of identity only to become, paradoxically, more intensely self-aware than ever...to feel at one with the universe...'* (p. 25). Newton describes it more modestly in this passage, to take account of the shock or bewilderment of those less-evolved, or those who have been thrust suddenly into this new sphere: *'Regardless of their state of mind right after death, my subjects are full of exclamations about rediscovered marvels of the spirit world. Usually, this feeling is combined with euphoria that all their worldly cares have been left behind, especially physical pain'* (1994, p. 25).

5. Familiarity. There is agreement as to the familiarity of this place. Those who recall leaving the mortal body and arriving in that place, experience it as their real home. Whitton's subjects knew it as: *'our natural home from which we venture forth on arduous journeys of physical embodiment'* (p. 11).

In the chapter 'Homecoming', Newton (1994, p. 30) reports his subjects also experienced it as a return home. One subject reports quite typically: *"It's so warm and comforting. I'm relieved to be away from Earth. I just want to stay here always. There's no tension, or worries, only a sense of well-being."* This subject says her next major impression is one of *familiarity.* Newton comments: *'The most common type of reaction I hear is a relieved sigh followed by something on the order of, "Oh, wonderful, I'm home in this beautiful place again"'* (p. 19).

6. No spatio-temporal properties. There is agreement that this is a place which *transcends earthly categories and boundaries of time and space*, and where there are no discrete objects, no physical 'things'. *'At death the soul leaves the body to enter a timeless, spaceless state...'* (Newton 1994, p. 3). *'Only through symbols can travelers in the bardo hope to understand and describe this world devoid of time and space'* (Whitton & Fisher, p. 25).

Each one of Newton's illustrative cases also demonstrates this. He says: 'Quite a few people who come out of trance tell me that there is so much about the spirit world they were unable to describe in earthly terms. Each person translates abstract spiritual conditions of their experience into symbols of interpretation which make sense to them.' Newton 1994, p. 97).

7. **Rebirth is part of the scheme**

There is agreement that rebirth is a necessary part of the scheme. This doesn't so much seem to merely follow from the fact that subjects are experiencing That Place from the view of their present incarnation, and are therefore coming upon it as the place they have gone after death released them from a previous incarnation (so they are now aware of at least two such incarnations and must begin to conclude that rebirth is normal). They seem primarily to know it as an incontrovertible truth; something as obvious as our possession of a sense of selfhood, or the knowledge that the memories we carry from early life are in fact our own experience.

This is a knowledge to which Newton and Whitton both testify, giving added conviction to D.K.'s statement: 'On the inner side, men know that the Law of Rebirth governs the experience-process of physical plane living, and they realize then that, prior to the elimination of the kamic, kama-manasic or manasic bodies, they are only passing through an interlude between incarnations...' (Bailey 1953, reference edition 1970, p. 495).

Joe Fisher comments (p. 3), 'Dr Whitton's subjects, whose religious backgrounds are as varied as their initial prejudices for or against reincarnation, have testified consistently that rebirth is fundamental to the evolutionary process in which we are enveloped.'

This is implicit in Newton's report of his findings, rather than explicit in any statement. However, he remarks, '... when souls are in the spirit world preparing for a new life, they laugh about being in rehearsal for their next big stage play on earth. They know all roles are temporary' (2002, p.12).

8. **The universe is a morally ordered place**

There is agreement, not only about the nature, but also about the structure and workings of this moral universe in which we find ourselves. Newton's researches, which resulted in *Journey of Souls*, took his personal answer about the nature of the universe from that of 'original cynicism' and atheism to the polar opposite position. In the book he concludes '*...order and purpose in the universe emanate from a higher consciousness*' (p. 273).

Both researchers discover the existence of a universal moral law, and report similarly on the way this law works out.

9. The law of spiritual cause and effect is a reality

Both researchers conclude that that we are who we are and where we are on earth because of the way in which this karmic law -- the law of cause and effect, operates given the choices we make in life.

Whitton quotes one client saying *"There are people I didn't treat too well in my last life, and I have to go back to the Earth plane again and work off the debt. This time, if they hurt me in return, I'm going to forgive them because all I really want to do is to go back home [to spirit]"'* (p. 41).

In the following case of Steve the Texan, Newton demonstrates the ordered and inevitable operation of the law of karma, and the way the law of karmic compensation works. Debt is incurred automatically with every act of harm to others, and must be repaid (as the opposite kind of karma is also earned with every act of love and kindness, and is also repaid in kind). The necessity of repayment of karmic debts is also shown in this case. Newton replays with Steve, the moment of making the decisions about his next life. It is very clear how reluctant Sumus, the higher self of Steve, is to be in close relationship in this coming life, with certain other souls with whom he has 'unfinished business'.' As Newton gets him to focus on his connection to them, Sumus/Steve 'grabs' Newton's hand in his anxiety:

> S: *It's...Eone...she wants to be ...my mother again.*
>
> Dr N: *Is this the soul of the woman who is Haroum's and Steve's mother?*
>
> S: *Yes, she is...oh...I don't want to...*
>
> Dr N: *What's going on?*
>
> S: *Eone is telling me it's time for us to ...settle things...to be in a disordered life as mother and son again.*
>
> Dr N: *But Sumus, didn't you know this at the place of life selection when you viewed Steve's mother taking her baby to the church?* [She was about to abandon him on its doorstep.]
>
> S: *I saw the people...the possibility...it was still an abstract consideration...it wasn't actually me yet. I guess I need more convincing because Eone is here for a reason...*

Dr N: Why did you and Eone wait 4000 earth years before discussing a balancing out of your treatment of her in Arabia? [Sumus as Haroum, a north African tribal chieftain, ordered his mother executed. When famine struck, and her appeals to Haroum had failed, she had broken into stores under his control, to feed his starving people.]

S: Earth years mean nothing; it could have been yesterday. I just wasn't ready to offset the harm I did her as Haroum.

Dr N: If your soul joins with the body of Steve in Texas, will Eone consider this karmic payment for your debt?

S: My life as Steve is not supposed to be punishment. [Here the subject focuses on one aspect of the question and misses answering its intended import.]

Dr N: I'm glad you see that. So what is the lesson to be learned?

S: To...feel what desertion is like in a family relationship...deliberate severing...

Dr N: The severing of the mother and son bond by deliberate action?

S: Yes...to appreciate what it is like to be cast off (Newton 1994, pp. 237-8).

Karmic debts and soul choices

We learn over a series of lives, to make better choices, more in harmony with the law. The soul itself learns through the personality's experiences. It is the personality (the incarnate aspect of the soul, plus the mechanism of incarnation, the body and the bodymind which they create) who makes the choices earlier on, wanting only to play in the playground of life. Later on the soul, reluctantly at first, accepts the advice of wise teachers and decides to undertake more difficult lives to learn the needed lessons.

Whitton says *'the judges' recommendations are made according to what the soul needs, not what it wants'.* He gives two examples of his clients' responses to this (pp. 41-2). The first client, who doesn't want to take on the challenges recommended because of not feeling strong enough, but sees the need, says '*I know we have to be given obstacles in order ...to become stronger, more aware, more evolved, more responsible [my emphasis].'*

The second example from Whitton is instructive about the way karma and physical obstacles interact. It doesn't seem to be the case that our souls make defective bodies where we need those lessons, but that a physical inheritance with suitable defects is chosen. This subject reports:

I chose my mother knowing there was a high incidence of Alzheimer's disease in her family...But my karmic links with my mother were much more important than any genetic deficiency. [That is, deficiency didn't sufficiently counterbalance the links to her mother, for this subject to be justified in rejecting this opportunity.] *...The judges told me that I should undergo the experience of being raised without a father in this life and I was aware that my parents would soon be divorced. I also knew that my choice of parents would put me in the ideal geographical location for meeting the man I was destined to marry.*

So when we grumble about our lot in life, are we always grumbling about something ultimately self-chosen? In the larger scheme, the answer from both Whitton and Newton is yes, our lot is either self-chosen or self-deserved and submitted to consciously on soul levels...*'We are thoroughly responsible for who we are and the circumstances in which we find ourselves. We are the ones who do the choosing'* says Whitton (P. 53).

Newton comments 'Although souls are not yet omniscient...they have no doubts about karmic lessons and the part they played in past life events' (2002, p. 192).

Suicide and retribution

This is being written firstly for a beloved sister whose incurable condition causes daily suffering not sufficiently relieved by morphine, and whose ability to live any kind of meaningful life is steadily contracting as a result of pain and disability. Those who suffer thus are likely to contemplate euthanasia, but end up rejecting it from fear that it is the moral equivalent of suicide, and will carry the retributive consequences about which our traditions warn. I've already mentioned Andy Tomlinson's subject Liam Thompson in connection with suicide, initially in Chapter Eight. I commented there, that intuitively I felt there was no terrible retribution for suicide; we ourselves would choose to made amends and balance the account in following lives. Tomlinson comments that Liam's is an interesting case *'because a number of the pioneers agree that (suicide) seems to be the one act that is looked on unfavourably in the light realms'* (p. 61). Liam chose to end his previous life via suicide, because as a young man in Ireland, the girl he loved had chosen to stay and care for her sick mother, rather than running away with him to a new life.

'After his death he describes entering a "black vortex, spinning away"' (2007, p. 23). The next experience though, is positive-one of healing in an energy shower, and a clearing out of *'all the negative energy from my previous life',* including those around and built up by, his suicide.

When Tomlinson instructs him *'Just describe what you're experiencing and feeling',* Liam replies *'Pure joy and love. It's like I'm an empty cup after the negative energy leaves and I'm being filled up with new energy...'* *(2007, p. 29).* Some suicides will travel into a dark lower Bardo space created by their own negativity for a time. It depends very much on the reasons for suicide-as well as the overall degree of evolvement of the soul involved.

But what about that 'unfavourable reaction' Thompson has mentioned in the light realms to suicide-how bad is it? When Liam meets his guide for a review, he is standing with arms crossed, shaking his head. *'Tell me what happens in this review'* instructs Tomlinson. *'He's asking me why I always take the easy way out. I have a problem facing up to problems* (p. 61). When asked what his guide has to say about the suicide, Liam reports that he's done the same thing in the last couple of lives, so his guide *'doesn't want to repeat himself*! (p. 62). He does however, project information about those lives to help Liam to understand his patterns, while also projecting love. Much of the subsequent discussion and interlife planning with his guide was deliberately blocked from Liam's recall because as he said, he was facing a similar situation in his current life, and had to work it through himself. Tomlinson comments: *'Suicide is apparently one of the worst situations we can face in the light realms unless it relates to serious illness. However this account is hardly a serious judgement from on high'* (p.63).

Newton's findings support this view. After his client tells him there is no punishment for suicide, just dealing with 'the same thing ... again in a different life,' Newton notes that intolerable physical pain is different:

> This [disappointment of teachers and friends] is the usual spiritual attitude towards suicide, but I want to add that those who escape from chronic physical pain or almost total incapacity on Earth by killing themselves feel no remorse as souls. Their guides and friends also have a more accepting view towards this motivation for suicide (Newton 1994, p. 58).

Homosexuality: soul, personality or genes?

Any circumstance in our lives can still have one of several causes. It can be chosen and initiated by the personality regardless of or despite what the soul may wish. It may be an event to which the soul has reluctantly agreed when the teachers suggested it. The soul may, however, have freely chosen it. Or the causes may be initiated by another personality or soul, or by a group, or even by humanity as a whole-as in the plight of farmers all over Australia and other parts of the world, with the desertification of land, as global warming sets in. Then there are still larger causes-planetary, systemic or cosmic in origin.

Whitton has a story that illustrates more than one of these:

> *A man who had once used and abused young boys in ancient Greece was re-vulsed at having to return as a persecuted homosexual. "Oh, fuck! Oh no, not this. Anything but this!" he screamed in trance. "There's no way I could go in-to that body", he said later. "But I had made my choice-unwillingly-on the advice of the judgment board and I just had to go through with it. I felt pushed.* (p. 48).

This subject's abusive treatment of others in Greece was chosen by his personality not his soul; the karmic compensation was something dreaded by him but advised by his teachers; yet he ac-knowledges the compensatory life as something ultimately chosen by his soul. Finally, the abuse suffered by those young boys in an-cient Greece is an example of circumstances in our lives caused by someone else's personality choices. Curiously enough, though this deeply moral universe is a place which clashes rather violently with our science and its views of the nature of reality, it is the one with which we are most comfortable and which we find most supportive of our sense that life has meaning: It is the most motivating of us to pursue higher values and live a true and better life.

It is worth noting that this cause of homosexuality is far from be-ing the only one. That highly evolved human being we call William Shakespeare, was a married man, as was the actor under whose name he published his plays and poetry. The sonnets, and the dedication of them to W.H., have aroused speculation and debate as to his pos-sible homosexuality. According to Douglas Baker, John Richardson, 'Shakespeare', did indeed fall in love with a beautiful youth, whose name and biography are given in Baker's book *Shakespeare: The True Authorship* (1994). Baker's knowledge comes, he says, from the akashic records and from his teacher, the English Master, the real Shakespeare, who was later Robert Browning. John Richardson, who paid William Shakespeare to be the front man for his plays (it had to do with control of copyright) became this young man, W. H's, philosophical and literary tutor, his mentor and it would seem from the poetry, his lover, in a perfect replay of the traditions of classical Greece, where this age-bestriding genius and initiate had been the great dramatic playwright Aeschylus. In that society, male homosexuality was a virtue, not a vice, as is evident in the quote from Plato's Timaeus in chapter Sixteen. It was a cultural choice, not the biological given it tends to be in the present society. With the exception of the children who know from very early on, that they are homosexual, girls and boys usually grow up expecting to be heterosexual, but may suddenly find, often to their dismay and even distress, that they are simply not. The bodies in which they find themselves around mid-adolescence (or earlier) have their own in-built sexual responses which may quite tragically, run foul of every cultural rule and expectation, causing self-hatred, denial, family breakdown, and even suicide. This is just beginning to change.

On the inner level however, it will often be the case that the soul has chosen, or accepted, a homosexual life, and not necessarily for the reasons that are evident in Whitton's case. It may not be a case of repetition of ancient patterns or even repayment of debts. There may be lessons that can best be learnt through the experience of ho-mosexuality in the present society. There is one other reason for choosing to incarnate in a homosexual body. The sensibility of the homosexual man or woman is definitely different from that of their heterosexual peers; the gift they offer the world particularly when this is highly developed, is considerable. Is it really that different? Would there have been no other John Richardson/Shakespeare, Rudolph Nureyev, Cole Porter, Virginia Woolf, Iris Murdoch...? It's a hard case to argue, I'll admit, but not without merit. Certainly women are very clear about the attributes of many homosexual men they find attractive.

Newton's discussion of the case of Steve/Sumas illustrates this view of karma as the universal moral law which cannot be evaded. The idea of karma underlies the substance of the case studies through the entire book. Newton doesn't theorise about it or dis-cuss its history; his task as the researcher is to record the idea only as it arises through his subjects' experiences. Karma arises instead, as *the foundation of the entire process of evolution through rebirth* as he re-ports on it through the history of his cases.

This summary is entirely consonant with Hindu and Buddhist teachings, with D.K.'s elaboration of the scheme of life, and with the evidence from all available sources about life after death.

The existence of the soul

There is agreement about *the nature of the entity whose home place this is*. Both psychologists refer to this entity as 'the soul', identify-ing it as the relatively enduring entity, distinct from the body-per-sonality and separating from it in stages through death, spoken of in the sacred texts of the world. Whitton also calls it the 'higher self'. *Past-life therapy identifies the higher self that transcends lifetimes and exerts a telling influence on the way we think and behave. Dr Whitton's study of the between-life state...has further enhanced our knowledge of this higher self* (p. 6).

Earlier, Fisher prepares us for the revelations of the book; the case histories that reveal what actually happens after death. He then turns to the inevitable question; how is it possible to make contact with the soul through hypnosis? He answers it through explaining that the structure of the mind and consciousness, (accessible through hypnosis), reaches to the Self. This is in complete agreement with every teacher of the perennial philosophy, and as seen in earlier chapters:

> *The third, the innermost core (of the mind) is what we are now calling the superconscious mind. This level exposes the highest center of Self where we are an expression of a higher power. The superconscious houses our real identity, augmented by the subconscious which contains the memories of the many alter-egos assumed by us in our former human bodies. The superconscious may not be a level at all, but the soul itself* (pp. 2-3).

The nature of the soul

There is agreement about *the characteristics of this soul or higher self*, which is also consonant with religious teachings about it. The soul has a degree and kind of awareness impossible to humans. Dr Whitton discovered that *' human awareness in the interlife reaches a far higher pitch than that experienced during regression either to an earlier phase of this life or to a previous life...'* (pp. 6-7).

This is certainly the experience of every other researcher, including Grof and Fiore. The soul has knowledge far beyond that of the incarnated aspect, though as we have seen in the cases cited above, it is far from complete and perfect. The soul has a degree of moral rectitude, which in the earlier phases of the cycle of incarnations, is foreign to the personality. The quintessence of the nature of the soul is love. The soul evolves by learning through the experience of incarnation -- practicing, testing, growing faculties and qualities through persistence and application, making plans and fulfilling them or wandering far from them and failing to achieve objectives set for that lifetime, making mistakes and rectifying them. One of Dr Whitton's clients -- a social worker, describes the movement between normal awareness and soul awareness, as she experiences it when in the interlife state. She gives a clear description of the nature of this soul consciousness. She then contrasts this consciousness

with that of the personality and world to which she returns at the
end of the session with Dr Whitton:

> *I'm flooded with the most euphoric feelings I have ever known. These feel-*
> *ings are accompanied by total awareness and understanding of who I truly*
> *am, my reason for being, and my place in the universe. Everything makes*
> *sense; everything is perfectly just. It's wonderful to know that love is really in*
> *control. Coming back to normal consciousness, you have to leave behind that*
> *all-encompassing love, that knowledge, that reassurance.* (p. 31).

This subject says instead of fearing death, especially when life is
hard, she regards it with longing for a return to that *'marvelous state of
being'*.

The laws of spiritual and physical evolution

There is agreement that the universe is a place of steady progression
from unconsciousness through grades of limited consciousness to
something like universal awareness, and that this takes place
through trial and error and through learning, via the taking of form -
- more and more complex body-personalities, which require, and eli-
cit, more consciousness. In the following extract, Newton (1994, p.
100) discovers that there are distinct levels of soul advancement indicated by the colours of each soul! His subject has just spoken of
two of her teachers, Karla and Valairs, and their auras:

> *DR N: Why is Karla's energy radiating yellow and Valairs blue?*
>
> *S: That's easy. Valairs precedes all of us in knowledge and he gives off a*
> *darker intensity of light.*
>
> *Dr N: Does the shade of blue, compared to yellow or plain white, make a dif-*
> *ference between souls?*
>
> *S: I'm trying to tell you. Blue is deeper than yellow and yellow is more intense*
> *than white,* [and the colour that a soul radiates is] *depending on how far*
> *along you are.*

Newton later gives a classification, in table format, of these colours
and their indicated levels of soul development. There are six levels
or learning stages, with their associated Kinetic colour range, and
their student, guide or teacher status, from Beginner through to
Highly Advanced, given on page 103 of *Journey of Souls*. In *Destiny of
Souls*, this scheme is extended by one stage, and the colours filled in
more precisely and with their variations, in the section titled Colour
spectrum of spiritual auras (p. 171). The colours run from white
through off-white (reddish shades) to yellow, dark yellow (gold),
light blue, the dark bluish-purple (surrounded by radiant light) of

the Master, to the deep violet surrounding still more advanced entities.

Whitton gives a remarkably detailed and insightful list of the earlier stages of soul growth via the psychology of each stage, which provides a useful comparison to Newton's spectrum and all previous classifications, including that of developmental psychology especially as systematized by Wilber (2007). Of course, Wilber's first books were already in print before Whitton's. Wilber's The Spectrum of Consciousness, written when this genius was just 23, was published in 1977. Whitton or Fisher could have read Wilber. The language, and the contents would seem to deny this, however; the stages are merely similar, rather than matching one-to-one.

1. **Materialism:** *'The search for physical well-being, a state dominated by sensual craving...There is no recognition of an afterlife or a supreme power'* (Wilber's Fulcrum-3, pre-operational, egocentric Red is suggested here. However the next stage, superstition, sounds more like a transitional, mauve stage between Wilber's Red and his Blue, which is post-magical, mythic thinking and consciousness).

2. **Superstition:** An awareness of a higher power dawns. *'Practically nothing is known about this omniscient power: there is solely the appreciation that something is out there which cannot be controlled except, perhaps, by amulets and rituals...'*

3. **Fundamentalism:** This stage is characterized by *'superstitious... thinking about God...There is belief that prayer, adherence to ritual, and the practice of certain attitudes and behaviour will guarantee the supreme reward-a place in heaven or the afterlife. A leader is usually required to intercede with the all-powerful God, who must be appeased...*(This fits neatly with Wilber's Fulcrum-4, concrete operational, conventional Blue).

4. **Philosophy:** *Early awakening to the awareness of self-responsibility...This stage is marked by respect for life, tolerance of the beliefs of others, and an understanding of the deeper teachings of the orthodox religions.* (This description seems to parallel that of the post-conventional, formal operational mind of Cook-Greuter's Achiever, and Wilber's Fulcrum-5 Orange Modernist, with her or his Enlightenment values-Liberty, Equality, Fraternity.)

5. **Persecution:** This stage is marked by tension and anguish *'which springs from the intense desire to understand the hidden meaning of life... The search for answers frequently takes the form of extensive reading, study and membership in various mystical and metaphysical groups. The title of this stage is taken from Christ's Sermon on the Mount and the phrase "Blessed are the persecuted" (Matthew 5:10)* This is a quite different, but apt, description of the post-formal, postmodern pluralist who can find no

ground to stand on; Cook-Greuter's Individualist, her Stage Five, and Wilber's Fulcrum-6, Green, emergence of the Existential self.

The paths leading from these neophyte stages *'may lead up the Eastern side* [of the evolutionary mountain] *through meditation... or they may climb the Western face through mysticism and intellectual metaphysics.* (This point opens up and leads from Loevinger's Autonomous stage, Cook-Greuter's Strategist stage, and Wilber's Yellow, Integral Fulcrum-7 stage.)

So long as the desire remains to be, to do, or to possess, karmic consequence will continue. (Whitton and Fisher, pp. 77-8).

Every one of these aspects of soul life and its implications for our understanding of reality is amplified and much more fully explained in the teachings of the Tibetan. D.K. has summarized it (Bailey 1942, reference edition 1970, p. 5):

'(*A)s the third aspect* [the body-personality awareness] *is consciously developed, man arrives at a knowledge of matter, of substance and of outer creative activity. Then he passes on to a realization of the underlying qualities which the form is intended to reveal, and **identifies himself with the ego, the soul or solar angel** [my emphasis]. This he comes to know as his true self, the real spiritual man. Later, he arrives at the realization of the purpose which is working out through the qualities, as they express themselves through the form...It is apparent as we study, how this entire sequential process of realization pivots around form manifestation, and has relation to the quality and purpose of the divine Mind...It deals therefore with the outer personality expression of that great all-encompassing Life, **which we call God, for lack of a better term'** [my emphasis].*

The Tibetan elaborates this scheme with its purpose of developing ever-higher and more inclusive levels of consciousness, and therefore with its hierarchy of being (Bailey 1942, reference edition 1970, p. 5):

(*T)he objective of the evolutionary purpose ... is to enable man to manifest as a soul in time and space and to tune in on the soul purpose and the plan of the Creator, as it is known and expressed by the seven Spirits before the Throne, the seven planetary Logoi... (A)ll that the highest of the Sons of God can grasp is a partial realization of the purpose and plan of the Solar Logos... The reason is that each of these planetary Logoi is, (in His place and term of office) conditioned and limited by his own peculiar point in evolution....* [This is in the higher perspective, the reason for our suffering. To put it another way, matter still rules us, not spirit. When the soul in us and in all life has more control, suffering will disappear. The Tibetan continues]:

The average human being '*is a sum total of separative tendencies, of un-controlled forces and of disunited energies, which slowly and gradually be-come coordinated, fused, and blended in the separative personality*'.

The soul-controlled human being ' *is the sum total of those energies and forces which are unified, blended and controlled by that 'tendency to har-mony' which is the effect of* [the soul quality of] *love and the outstanding quality of divinity*'.

The individual ruled by the still-higher spiritual or monadic con-sciousness '*is the synthetic expression of the purpose of God, symbolised through revealed, divine quality (in the soul) and manifested through the form.*'

The stages and major events of the after-death experience

Do the researchers agree on the stages and elements?

Both researchers may have anticipated that their results would flatly contradict, or more likely just bear no relationship to, those of Dr Raymond Moody and later researchers in the field of the Near-death Experience. This would have cast grave doubt on the authen-ticity of both areas of research. Instead their subjects reported the same experiences- Looking at their vacated corpses and attempting to communicate with those still in bodies; the Light, the bliss, the sense of total freedom, the vastly expanded awareness; the Being of Light, the meeting with others who knew them; the life-review. It is important to note that their results *supported the hypothesis of life after death* in that those experiences replicated the near death experience as far as it went, then simply went beyond that point, as is to be ex-pected if there is life after death.

It is equally important that the two researchers are in complete agreement regarding the major events in the *post-death* experience. This is not to say that there is replication of every aspect and detail. There are differences in the two researchers' approaches and per-spectives; in the questions they ask subjects, in their methodology and their areas of focus, which cause highlighting or downplaying of different stages and events. It is significant that despite these differ-ences, their subjects report the same major events.

The detail of the process that is given here is unique to Newton's study, -- or was until Tomlinson's study, though all the major points also appear in Whitton's book.

Liberation, the bardo and rebirth: Tibetan Buddhism & the perennial philosophy, vs. modern sources

How does this compare though, with the description of the rebirth process of Tibetan Buddhist teachings in The Tibetan Book of the Dead? There we are told that those who recognize Rigpa, the dawning of the Light, have no need to reincarnate; they achieve liberation. And that a degree of liberation can be accomplished at any one of several stages in the after-death process.

It's only those who fail to recognize the Light, - who don't understand that everything in the material realm is illusory, who must undergo reincarnation- and then it will be a matter of 'choosing wisely' the place and parents, or of being pulled back into incarnation, and to the place where the parents-to-be are making love, without choice. At first sight this conflicts with everything discovered through the research of Westerners, which would seem to suggest that nearly all souls within the system are still incarnating, regardless of their mental and spiritual development. All Newton's subjects have reincarnated, obviously, and therefore would seem *not* to be among those who have seized the opportunity presented at death to liberate themselves from reincarnation. They have had no specific training recently, at the essential practices for liberation at death, as practiced by Tibetan Buddhists, so it looks as though they must have experienced the dark bardo, and were candidates for being thrust helplessly back, or drawn inexorably down, into the present life. Yet most of them report a degree of latitude and choice about the process, which differs markedly from the experience as described in the Tibetan Book of Living and Dying.

Is one or the other just plain wrong? No: the original Tibetan advice to the dead in the Bardo Thodol is addressed most urgently to those who will, without its assistance, wander helplessly in the darker regions before finding themselves back in a body on earth. There is not yet enough soul; they do not as discarnate psyches, 'ascend to heaven', but remain in lower astral spheres until being pulled into incarnation by their own desires, or 'pushed' from soul levels. Most others will also reincarnate, but not in this driven or forced way. It is only necessary to return to the Ageless Wisdom in the teachings of the Tibetan to reconcile the two accounts.

Souls returning under two Laws; the Law of Karmic Liability and the Law of Necessity

Some of Newton's and Whitton's and Wambach's clients seem to have spent little or no time in the astral part of the Bardo, unlike those described as reincarnating in the texts of the Bardo Thodol, and the Tibetan Book of Living and Dying. This last group, who have been thrust helplessly back, or drawn down by their desire to be back in a body, is the group D.K. quotes the Old Commentary describing as 'the prisoners of the planet...held in durance hard by low desire'. They are compelled to ride the train of reincarnation, and presently know of no way, and have no desire, to get off.

Those who have managed to find the carriage door and climb off the train have seen a different reality. Satisfaction of desires in the material world is no longer their goal. They are not totally immersed in that as the only existence. They have indeed discovered something higher and of greater value, even, than success and happiness on earth, however they might have measured that. So if I am claiming that these research subjects reincarnated despite achieving a measure of freedom from the illusion, and finding their way off the circular line, how is this possible? Does Tibetan Buddhism have it wrong?

Those who are not compelled to ride the train of incarnation, who get off at an earlier station in the loop, but who are shown in Whitton and Newton and Wambach as reincarnating despite that, do so in a different way, and under a different law, the Law of Karmic Necessity. Those to whom the Bardo Thodol is most urgently addressed, are the bulk of the human population, who reincarnate under the Law of Karmic Liability. What is the difference between these two laws?

> *The majority of souls in the human family come into incarnation in obedience to the urge or the desire to experience, and the magnetic pull of the physical plane is the final determining factor... (Generalising), human beings can be grouped into four classes:*
>
> 1. *A few who are under the influence of their souls, or who are rapidly becoming susceptible to this influence.*
>
> 2. *Personalities, of whom there are many today.*

3. *A vast number of people who are awakening to mental consciousness [but who are not yet the emotionally and mentally integrated 'personalities' of group two].*

4. *The great mass of humanity, who are the unawakened human beings and the bulk of the population of the world.* [It is this majority who incarnate under the urge to experience and the Law of Karmic Liability].

In every phase of human history, the quality of the civilization is the only thing that can in any way be conditioned by the Great White Lodge. The Members of the Lodge are only permitted to work with the emerging qualitative aspects of the divine nature. This is, in its turn, slowly conditioning the form life, and in this way the form aspect is steadily altered and adapted, as it progresses towards increasing perfection. This conditioning process is carried forward through the souls who are returning to incarnation, for just in so far as they are awakened or ... awakening, is it possible for the Hierarchy to prevail upon them ...[my emphases]. These awakening souls are the ones who can at times be influenced to retard ...[or hasten, as D.K. next explains] their entry into physical plane life in order to effect a conditioning of the processes of civilization... It will be apparent, therefore, that the needed changes in our civilization can be brought about rapidly or slowly, according to the number of those who are living as souls in training (Bailey 1942, reference edition 1970, pp. 259-60).

There are two greater groupings given here by D.K.: the Unawakened and the Awakened, corresponding to the two groups in Tibetan Buddhism. The Unawakened have no choice about returning; they are pulled into incarnation by the physical plane, as D.K. says. They are the ones who rush blindly into a new birth, or are dragged back in, as Tibetan teachings point out, or feel that someone else, a higher authority, did the planning. They have as yet no soul contact. So they incarnate under the Law of Karmic Liability, automatically. They are unable to get off the train, even if they wished to do so. This only becomes possible as they begin to awaken.

Those who are awakened or awakening have by definition begun to see the (lesser) light, and will enter into it at some stage after exiting their physical bodies, for a shorter or longer time. They will return under a different prompting, for a different reason, and under a different law, the Law of Karmic Necessity. The soul itself is now becoming more and more involved in incarnation, and is consequently, often decidedly reluctant. It is now possible though inadvisable, to refuse to reincarnate: this is one basis of the Tibetan Buddhist teachings that, having entered into Mind, the **entrapment** *within incarnation is at an end*. Many of those incarnating under this law return as conditioning souls, who do at soul level make a choice, however reluctantly, to return to the suffering Earth, to aid and lift the Prisoners of the Planet. It will be obvious why it is this group upon which 'it is possible for the Hierarchy to prevail', to advise on their return to incarnation and to a particular set of circumstances and challenges which will aid in 'conditioning civilization'.

So, dear reader, where are *you* in this process, you may well be asking? You may already have been able to place yourself in one of the stages of developmental psychology (despite the brevity of my descriptions). If you are reading this book, and especially if you have persisted with it to this point, it is impossible that you could be in D.K.'s Group 4. It is almost certain that you are 'up there' among the members of Group Two or One, and quite probable that you are in Group One. The reasons are simple: anyone capable of reading this book has a mind developed to a high degree, comparative to the bulk of humanity, and a conscious interest in spiritual matters different from the blind faith of the Group 4 individual. These two facts alone guarantee some degree, limited as it may be yet, of soul contact[2].

The primacy of Mind

Does Mind have the same place in the cosmic scheme according to Whitton and Newton?

Both researchers report their subjects returning to a place where thought is dominant, and is the organizing energy. This implies that they must be in the place of Mind. *'I think, therefore I am'* is one of the subtitles in Whitton (p. 32).

The subject chosen by Newton to describe the immediate experience of arrival in the between-life place, said, as already quoted *'I feel the power of thought all around me'* (p. 18). There is frequent

---

2. It would require at least a highly intelligent and mentally capable formal-operational Fulcrum-5 Orange, (there are plenty around), to read this text. A reader at this stage may baulk at the paradoxical nature of the worldview presented, and the denial of the ultimate reality or primacy of the material world. A Fulcrum-6, Green reader might enjoy the intellectual challenge, while disagreeing, even violently, with what I'm claiming is a post-existentialist view of the world. This text is both pluralist, which is valid and good, and hierarchical, which to a Green, is not! The contents may be a better fit with the Fulcrum-7 Integral Yellow worldview, with its capacity to integrate all perspectives, and weight them. And with the levels above that, beyond Wilber's Ego-Witness divide. Their increasing personal experience of the trans-mental, spiritual realities of these higher stages of consciousness will give the text greater validity to these readers.

reference in both studies, to thought as the mode of communication in the spirit world.

Does it, however, follow that both have concluded that evolution is about developing our higher, mental faculties and beyond, and operating more and more from the mental or higher levels here on earth? Whitton's levels of development, already quoted, from Materialism and Superstition through Fundamentalism, Philosophy and Persecution as the 'neophyte' stages of evolution, do imply a steady growth of consciousness, mental functioning, and constructing and confronting the world and experience through thought and ideas, and moving out of the evolutionary stage dominated by emotions and superstitions, knee-jerk reactions and platitudes.

It was while interviewing a beginner soul under hypnosis that Newton stumbled across an exciting discovery, referred to above, that the level of advancement of our souls is indicated by the colour of their auras. He began to ask about soul colours as a matter of course. Another client than the one who first introduced him to this idea, had just told Newton that her energy was sky-blue; it occurred to him to ask about the colour of Kumara, her highly advanced guide. He was told that it was violet. (Newton 1994, p. 153)

> *Dr N: How does light and colour identify the quality of a soul's spiritual attainment?*
>
> *S; The intensity of mental power increases with the darker phases of light.*

Newton concluded that both as souls pure and simple, and incarnate in bodies, we emit and receive light energy:

> *As souls, the density, color, and form of light we radiate is proportional to the power of our knowledge and perception as represented by increasing concentrations of light matter as we develop...From my cases, I have learned the more advanced souls project masses of faster moving energy particles which are reported to be blue in colour, with the highest concentrations being purple...With each incarnation, we grow in understanding'* (p. 102). The colour of our aura changes accordingly, from white to deep violet.

It is clear that both Whitton and Newton conclude that advancement is about the getting of wisdom, and this also implies the increasing use of the mind. So progress from one stage to another requires the development of knowledge, perception and understanding, which are powers and attainments of the mind. So there is complete agreement with Buddhism and the Tibetan's presentation of the Ageless Wisdom, about the importance of Mind in the overall scheme, and its primacy over Matter. Progress is away from the physical level, and occupation and immersion in the material universe, towards the level where Mind predominates.

Is Mind the final stage, or level of Being? No, except in Buddhism's all-encompassing use of the word, though the same levels of being and of evolvement are seen in Buddhism also, just differently defined. Mind is the focus and tool of a consciousness centered (for a long period of our development) in the Soul. It is awareness through Mind of ourselves as *souls*, working through and growing through, bodies and personalities, (and not, as we mostly see ourselves, those bodies and personalities themselves), which liberates us from the world of phenomena and permits us to live in the world of the Real. As the ancient Sanskrit Prayer goes:

> *'Lead us from darkness to Light, From the unreal to the Real,*
>
> *From death to Immortality.'*

Soul vs. Personality; Logotherapy's definition

But what is the Real, as distinct from the Unreal? And what is of the Soul, what is of the Personality? In his classic book, *Man's Search for Meaning*, the renowned psychiatrist Viktor Frankl, founder of Logotherapy, defines the difference with amazing clarity from a medical and therefore entirely earthly perspective. He developed Logotherapy partly as a response to his experiences in a German concentration camp during the Second World War. This 'Third Viennese School of Psychotherapy', sees that the *'striving to find a meaning in one's life is the primary motivational force in man. That is why I speak of a will to meaning in contrast to the pleasure principle (or, as we could also term it, the will to pleasure) on which Freudian psychoanalysis is centered, as well as in contrast to the will to power on which Adlerian psychology, using the term 'striving for superiority' is focused* (Frankl 1984, pp 123-5).

The neuroses treated by Freudian and Adlerian therapy are 'psychogenic neuroses': these have their origin in the drives and instincts which define the personality. Noogenic neuroses have a different cause:

'Noogenic [from the mind] neuroses ...emerge... from existential problems. Among such problems, the frustration of the will to meaning plays a large role...The appropriate and adequate therapy is logotherapy; a therapy, that is, which dares to enter the specifically human dimension.' [Frankl cites the case of a 'high-ranking American diplomat' who came to him after Freudian analysis. He had been told that his inability to comply with American foreign policy was due to projected hatred for his father. Frankl discovered he was not actually a patient; the cure was a more meaningful vocation.] *It is clear that he also needed to*

understand that his frustration was not negative, but positive – that it was not something to refer to infantile projections [as had been done in his Freudian analysis], *but to work with as creative of meaning.*

The drive to pleasure and the drive to power and superiority arise in the personality. The urge to meaning and the search for meaning have their origin in the soul or in what is termed 'mind' in the English translation of Frankl's book. None of us suffers from existential anguish until we reach the point of evolution where existential problems even exist -where we have a sufficiently developed mind to comprehend them.

The next chapter considers the nature of God or the Ultimate, and whether it is possible for little humans such as we are, to have any relationship with that level of consciousness. If that is the case, what is the nature of that relationship according to Christianity and Buddhism-and is there any recent evidence for its existence?

Chapter 12
The God Argument

Christians Vs. Buddhists, Homo Erectus and Evolution

Summary Points

- The nature of Ultimate Consciousness or Deity, and our relationship to That
- Newton's subjects' experience of a divine Being.
- From the traditional cosmos via materialism to Death-of-God Christianity: Is there an alternative?
- Science, Richard Dawkins and *The God Delusion*
- Bishop Spong and Christianity without God the Father
- Evolution: Teilhard de Chardin, the Ageless Wisdom, Darwin and Forbidden Archeology
- The Ageless Wisdom's evolving cosmos found in Hinduism and Buddhism
- The Divine Milieu and evolution
- Forbidden archeology-ignored evidence for the presence of humans *alongside* our ape 'ancestor'

- Java Man: Missing Link or colossal mistake?
- A caring God, or materialism's vast indifferent Emptiness?
- God in Buddhism: A personal God vs. no God at all?
- Did the Buddha believe in God? The Dalai Lama on Buddhism's No-God
- The Ultimate in Buddhism and Christianity; no contradiction
- 'There cannot be a God; there is too much suffering'
- Soul control and the limits to suffering

The God Argument

This chapter ponders the Big Questions about the Ultimate. What would be the nature of Supreme Mind or Deity, and is there any evidence for such a Being? Is our relationship to the rest of the manifest world a Darwinian one, or is it that of Teilhard de Chardin's *Divine Milieu*, the evolution of consciousness?

Christianity and Buddhism appear to be at opposite ends of the faith continuum on the nature of this ultimate reality. Is one of the two faiths right? This chapter deals with the nature of Ultimate Consciousness or Deity, and with the nature of our possible relationship to Deity. There is an alternative to mediaeval Christianity and modern Death-of-God Christianity in the perennial philosophy, but can it explain evolution as it appears in nature? Can this alternative also explain the structure of our relationship with God or Supreme Being?

What is the Nature of the Absolute?

Michael Newton's further investigations into the life between lives, recounted in his second book, *Destiny of Souls*, uncovered a great deal more of his subjects' reports of teachers and guides, about the Council of Elders, and about the nature of God, or the Absolute. So what *was* their experience of That Nature? Does it bear any relation to that known in Christianity or Buddhism?

Under the heading *'The Chain of Divine Influence'* Newton writes about his clients' experience of a divine Being, and ponders if this is God. It was a surprise to me that the recounted experience isn't just a reiteration of previously held beliefs. Subjects do not prejudge the experience, or categorize it, preferring simply to call this Being 'The Presence':

> *To many of my clients, the Presence [experienced during interviews with the Council of Elders] seems not to be a 'who' but that which 'Is'. For others, the Presence is an entity who functions as an equalizer, harmonizing the greater awareness of Elders to the lesser awareness of the souls who come before them...*

A client is then quoted explaining more about the effect of the Presence.

> *'When I sat on a panel (of the Elders) it was like being inside the soul in front of you. What you feel is much more than empathy towards someone who has just come back from a life. You are really in their shoes. The Presence gives you the power to feel everything the soul feels at the moment. The prism of light from the Presence touches every council member in this way.'*

Newton continues:

> *Does the same Presence move from council to council, is there more than one entity, or is "It" simply God, which is everywhere?... Other than fleeting moments with a more powerful and loving Presence, the Council of Elders is the highest authority people directly encounter in their spiritual visions. As a result of what they see in a trance state, my subjects do have the sense of a vertical tier effect of soul attainment in the spirit world* (Newton, 2002, p 249).

From the traditional cosmos via materialism to Death-of-God Christianity: Is there an alternative?

This Presence, and the tier effect or chain of lives from less to more evolved, may all seem highly unlikely even to those reared in the Christian tradition of the Communion of Saints. But it will seem less likely than science fiction, to Westerners for whom reality is our rational and scientific Western construction of the world. It has taken us a century or two to adjust to the idea that we ourselves, humanity, are neither the center of the universe nor the pinnacle of all creation.

However, now we have arrived here, any alternative to the rationalist and materialist view of life seems an illusion. The furnishings of our God-house have been wittily catalogued, and demolished as fantasy, by Richard Dawkins in his *The God Delusion (2006)*. But having hauled down his false idol, God, should we instead, bow down to the Supreme that Dawkins raises up in God's place, the supposedly victorious, glorious Science?

At the Name of Dawkins, should God tremble and quake? Well, when one has enemies like Richard Dawkins and Phillip Adams (2008), who needs friends? An intelligent and vital skepticism, or downright atheism, is infinitely to be preferred to the opposite; fanaticism or slavish, uncritical devotion. Dawkins quotes Bertrand Russell, responding to the question *'What will you answer God, when He asks why you didn't believe in Him?'* *'Not enough evidence, God, not enough evidence'*, was Russell's reply. It's impossible to be rational, and not credit that position.

Dawkins' success, though, requires his argument (well-presented, but not watertight; naively reductionist, it could be argued), that the physical is the beginning and end of everything. As you've seen, I disagree with that Material Universe idea, and have amassed some evidence to back my position. However, a mass of evidence for survival of physical death doesn't, I have to admit, logically guarantee us a God. But can God be discovered through empirical research, or through philosophical reasoning? Or only through higher modes of mind such as the contemplative?

This form of discovery (direct experience through contemplation or meditation) is the basis of the perennial philosophy, Buddhism, Christianity, and our other spiritual schemes. Ken Wilber's cogently argued cosmological map, divided into four quadrants, Subjective, Intersubjective, Objective and Interobjective, each with a type of knowledge and truth, and means of validating which cannot be reduced to any one of the others, makes this clear. (See Diagram 1, in Appendix). Validation is never automatic; it always involves the community of experts undertaking the experiment and examining the evidence gained from that exercise.

The Western idea of Deity has evolved from the mediaeval idea of the Supreme King on his throne in Heaven. The Death-of-God Christianity of recent decades is far more sophisticated, but is it more reasonable or more satisfying?

Traditional Christianity's great chain of being led from the meanest creatures on earth, to humanity in its graded ranks from serfs to kings. It then passed via the ranks of angels, to the feet of God. Humanity was at the apex of God's Creation, and the reason for the existence of the rest of the universe. Earth was created as the dwelling-place of humans, and its plants and animals were for our use and enjoyment. The countless millions of other stellar bodies in the universe had no real place in this scheme, and certainly no explanation as to their existence or purpose. Even the Copernican and Newtonian revolutions failed to totally dislodge this view. It was Darwin's theories which caused a radical remodelling of the homocentric, anthropomorphic God and universe. The Darwinian chain was the product of a natural, non-divine process: The higher species including humans evolved over long ages from the lower, in a progressively elaborating sequence. This 'chain' had absolutely no spiritual content whatever, and of course, no Deity inherent in it, despite Darwin's statements about the logical need for God. He wrote on April 2, 1873 in a letter to a Dutch student, that the chief argument for the existence of God was *'the impossibility of conceiving that this grand and wondrous universe, with our conscious selves, arose by chance'* (Darwin 1995, p. 57). Perhaps he wasn't a good enough Darwinian?

This revolution in worldview, bolstered by the discoveries in astronomy, the Einsteinian revolution and quantum physics especially, was instrumental in producing the Death-of-God Christianity of which the American bishop, John Selby Spong, is a famous proponent.

Bishop Spong and Christianity without God the Father

John Spong, touring Australia in 2003 promoting his book, *A New Christianity for a New World,* was interviewed for *The Age* by Barney Zwartz:

> *"In the past"* Spong says, *"God was depicted as a supernatural being who lived above the sky and periodically invaded the world to do a miracle. Then along came Copernicus and Kepler and Galileo, and suddenly the sky was empty, it was just infinite space.* [This only removed God to a sphere above and beyond material existence, as the Newtonian Watchmaker who made the mechanism and left it to run on its own.] *So the idea of God sitting above the clouds keeping record books on every individual seems less than believable".*
>
> *Before Charles Darwin wrote, he says, we thought of ourselves as a little bit lower than the angels (Psalm 8). After Darwin wrote, we thought of ourselves as a little bit higher than the apes.*
>
> *"We could go on and talk about Freud, Einstein and Hawking,"* Spong says. *"The intellectual revolution of the past 400 years has totally reshaped the way we think of the world, and Christianity has to think in terms of that world...My book is an attempt to spell out a way to be Christian without checking your brains at the door of the church* [that is, putting your brains along with your coat and bag into the checking-room or holding-area]. *You can embrace the fact that you are a citizen of the 21st century."'*

In Spong's youth in fundamentalist South Carolina, there were the *'cardinal precepts'* seen as God's will and judgement. These were black segregation, women as inferior, and homosexuals and Jews as evil. *'Traditional theology says God is creator, all-powerful, all-knowing and everywhere...To Spong, this is pre-modern mumbo-jumbo. No-one can say what God is, but he is not a being. The book calls 'it' a presence that can be experienced but never defined'* (Zwartz 2003, A3, p. 4).

Spong's new Christianity has ricocheted off the Bible Belt version, tearing it to pieces, not without cause. Yet he remains uncritical of our newer scientific orthodoxy, whose cardinal precepts have come to frame our worldview, which we take to be 'the truth'. This view, though, is as vulnerable to revision in the light of better science, as those Spong criticises. (Curiously, Dawkins, in a not dissimilar rationalization, enshrines Science in the place of the toppled statue of the God of Ages, as noted above. He seems oblivious to the threat that today's science will become tomorrow's myth or partial truth; and to the very imperfect reputation of science as a strictly rational pursuit).

We continue to make the mistake of believing that we now, at last, possess The Only Truth. Spong hasn't quite swung to the opposite extreme as so many reared in the 20th century Church have done, and become atheist, but he sees his new Christianity as more evolved than it actually is. Deity as a great Being, or Deity as not a Being of any kind; is either more plausible given our present knowledge of the universe? Kitty Ferguson, quoted in earlier chapters especially Five, concluded that science might never be able to answer the question even of God's existence (1994, p. 282).[1]

It is admirable that Spong has had the courage to undertake such radical surgery – to his own attitudes as well as to the Church's. Yet do we really have to choose between Creationism or some versions of the Intelligent Design idea, where every creature is created uniquely and for all time by Jehovah; and Evolutionism, where blind chance and the battle for survival are the only creators of serendipititious new combinations to evolve life? Is there an alternative, which provides us with a synthesis of these two opposites of one dialectical movement of the Western mind?

There is a spirituality, and a theism, which are encompassing, which are not based either on blind faith, reaction, or the science of a particular period. This theism is inclusive not divisive: It doesn't throw the baby out with the bathwater of modern scholarship; the bathwater of the washout of the Bible as the eternally true and undiluted Word of God, for example. (Rachael Kohn notes the dismay of the Catholic Church when the translation from the Latin of the

---

1. 'One of the questions science hasn't answered and may never be able to answer-let none of us assume otherwise-is whether there us a God. We have not been able to say that it requires double-think or other intellectual dishonesty to have great faith in science as we know it at the end of the twentieth century and also to believe in God – even a personal and intervening God' (Ferguson 1994, p 282).

Bible became widely accessible, and critical scholarship unpicked it.)[2] This spirituality and theism I am proposing to elaborate, reconciles the two versions of the Great Chain of Being, rather than discarding either the mediaeval or the Darwinian version, and restricting the debate to one or the other as the only valid answer.

Evolution: Teilhard de Chardin, the Ageless Wisdom, Darwin and Forbidden Archeology

The Ageless Wisdom places humans, and their life and death, in a scheme that encompasses and relates everyone and everything in the universe, including Christianity, Judaism, Islam, Hinduism, Buddhism and every other approach to God and the puzzle of human existence, along with all scientific endeavours. The older religions of the East still present the large part of this vision. It is a constantly evolving cosmos, and every element and aspect of it is evolving too, including humans.

What is this evolution? Is it Darwinian-the adaptation of species to the available habitats, and their development of physical characteristics that give them the edge over competitors in the struggle for survival? (There is an important side argument here, of Ken Wilber (1982) especially, that natural selection cannot possibly account for physical evolution, because the physical characteristics such as wings or eyes, that confer an advantage over animals without them, have to develop *before* they can be selected. And that these mutations would take forever to occur if left to random mutations of the genes, which could or must produce half a leg or half a wing on the way to full development-a mutation which would ensure, not competitive survival, but extinction. Richard Dawkins (2006) argues in support of Darwin, that the Anti-natural selectionists ignore the

---

2. This dismay began when Lutheran scholar Wellhausen (1844-1918) established that the Bible was a collection of accounts written in different periods, casting doubt on it as the 'dictated' Word of God.

Fuelled by the philosophical and political rationalism of the Enlightenment, Protestants would... produce sceptical interpretations of its miraculous narratives that would positively shatter the central tenets of Christianity. In study after study, scholars would deny or disprove some of the fundamentals of the faith. The following were among their conclusions: the Gospel texts were ambiguous on whether Jesus believed himself to be the Messiah; they were inconsistent on whether he was born of a virgin; they were not at all clear as to the meaning of the Hebrew expressions 'the son of God' and 'son of man'; and the plain meaning of certain passages was contradictory to the notion that Jesus himself was God (Kohn 2003, p27). The Gospels were the work of inspired but fallible humans, who recorded their understanding of extraordinary events long after their occurrence, not the One Truth.

sophistication of recent developments in our understanding of natural selection, genetics and mutation.)

Curiously, this cosmic evolution encompasses the Darwinian kind, which is the evolution of matter and life forms-however that takes place, to be fitter vehicles, better adapted for the expression and learning of the inhabitants. It is evolution in its spiritual aspect and true nature: it moves towards a greater perfection in wisdom, love and compassion, greater omnipotence and omniscience, greater responsibility towards all lesser beings, and greater usefulness towards the Whole. So, is there any evidence that humanity is evolving in this more inclusive sense, not just physically?

The Divine Milieu and evolution

The great French Jesuit priest, Pierre Teilhard de Chardin, gagged by the Vatican for his revolutionary views, certainly saw it that way. He wrote in *The Divine Milieu* (1968) of the 'Omega Point', the moment in history when the *consciousness of humanity will reach critical mass*, and we will take the evolutionary leap into a new, interconnected and ethical way of being.[3] In his classic 'Mysticism: A Study and an Anthology', F.C. Happold writes that the evolution of ideas and of scientific instruments has radically changed our perception, resulting in a new image of the universe:

> *The new image does not ...annihilate God, or the possibility that there are spheres of existence other than the material and levels of consciousness and perception different from those of most human beings...It compels us to consider afresh our ideas of the nature of the universe, of man, and of God, to search for new and more adequate images.*

> *With the appearance of the human line a new form of biological existence emerges; there is, in effect, a new creation. This new creation is characterized by the emergence of the power of reflection. Father Pierre Teilhard de Chardin, in his Phenomenon of Man, coins the vivid word hominisation to describe this leap in the evolution of life... (W)hat line may evolution be expected to follow? May it not be the growth of an ever higher form of consciousness, spreading out ever wider and wider, until it embraces more and more of mankind...an expanding interiorization and spiritualization of man, which will result in an ability to see aspects of the universe as yet only faintly glimpsed? ...(M)ay we not see in mystics the forerunners of a type of*

---

3. Is it possible that the Omega Point could occur in time to save us and the planet -- given that presently, less than 2 percent of us have reached Integrated consciousness? But what is critical mass? It may be 10 percent of us at and beyond this, Wilber's Yellow stage, given the effect this would have on the other 90 percent.

consciousness which will become more and more common as mankind ascends higher and higher up the ladder of evolution? It is not an irrational hypothesis (Happold 1963, p. 397).

It would seem self-evident, even just from the historical record of the past ten centuries, that we are evolving. We grope our way toward freedom, justice, equality and a decent life for all in the human family, the principles and the goals first announced in the eighteenth century Enlightenment movement. After the Second World War, in 1948, these values were declared to be the rights of all humans, not merely the French or white Americans. Since then, this Universal Declaration of Human Rights has become the platform of global citizenship of individuals and states, and these values have become generally accepted, even though their implementation and practice are spreading too slowly. Yet despite this obvious evolution of humanity, the ideas of Teilhard de Chardin were seen as heretical by Rome --and revolutionary; likely to cause revolt.

The Ageless Wisdom is at the other end of the spectrum from traditional Christianity, at least in its view of the nature of the universe. It has recently been updated for a humanity now much more advanced and teachable, by the Tibetan Master D.K., who works under the World Teacher, the great individual known to us variously as the Christ, the Messiah, the Imam Mahdi, the Maitreya, and the Lord Krishna (Bailey 1955, reference edition 1979, p. 314).

The Ageless Wisdom's evolving cosmos in Hinduism and Buddhism

The constant flux of evolution taught by the Ageless Wisdom, occurs both within the physical level of its order, and beyond, in its mental and spiritual levels. Everything from atoms and unicellular plants, rocks and primitive creatures to mammals, the great apes, humans upward and onward to the Great Intelligences informing planets and star systems, is related and connected in one evolving cosmic scheme or web of life and its inevitable great chain of Being. This scheme, much more inclusive than traditional Christianity, is scientific in its construction and its evolvement, yet it remains bound together by that apparent airiest of fantasies, divine Love.

It is a scheme in which the individual units evolve through taking embodiment in different times and places, in different parts of the scheme, in different types of bodies. These bodies are themselves being steadily evolved: matter, the lowest level of energy vibration, is being worked by spirit, or the higher levels of energy vibration, *through the consciousness within* those bodies. The individual units of consciousness move upward via steadily more complex incarnations and life situations. There is a perfectly scientific principle, the universal law of cause and effect, or karma as it is known in the East, in Hinduism and Buddhism especially, which in combination with reincarnation, *operates to bring about the evolution of every unit of life*. Evolution produces greater awareness, greater contact with the life around, greater capacities, and greater ability to be interested in all beyond the little centre of self, and to care for and be responsible for, an ever widening circle of that life. This is exactly Einstein's vision of our task and goal in life; Western developmental psychology has discovered this kind of evolution is taking place in humanity as a matter of course.

Forbidden Archeology

Teilhard de Chardin's rather similar 'spiritual evolutionist' stance was not restricted to humans, nor was it merely a (radical) Jesuit priest's theology. Teilhard was a skilled paleontologist connected with some of the most famous digs of his time-all of them fuel for the controversy of a recent study, *Forbidden Archeology* (Cremo and Thompson, 1993). The book contains startling revelations about the development of Darwin's theory especially as it applies to the *Descent of Man* from an ape ancestor of the present great apes, and from the trees to the ground, upright stance and moving on two legs not four. The original study, *Forbidden Archeology*, has been condensed to become *The Hidden History of the Human Race* (Cremo and Thompson 1999). It traces the attempt to find or create the Missing Link that would prove the descent of humans from apes, and where this attempt went disastrously wrong. Authors Cremo and Thompson then examine the entire paleontological record, and discover that no Missing Link has yet been found, despite two centuries of archeology and paleoanthropology-the study of early humans via fossils. Though there hasn't been skullduggery on quite the Piltdown Man level, (the clever forgery that had us fooled for years) the response of the scientific community to evidence which disputes human descent from apes, has often been refusal to publish the research, and silencing and dismissal of the researchers, even to the point of forcing reburial of the finds. But we have gone on assuming that the case is proven, in ignorance of the original debacle about evidence. *So what actually happened?*

Java Man: Missing Link or colossal mistake?

German scientist Ernst Haeckel had already proposed and researched a hypothesis like Darwin's Descent of Man theory. So certain was Haeckel that the Missing Link would be discovered, that he
commissioned a large painting of the creature whose bones, when
found, would prove this new idea of the evolution of Homo sapiens
right. (It is no longer easy to imagine or understand how shocking
this was to Western civilisation! We had until then, believed
ourselves uniquely created by God or force unknown, and not
merely superior to, but a separate creation from mere animals).
Haeckel called the creature *Pithecanthropus*; that is, ape-man. Where
would such evidence be found, pondered Eugene Dubois, an admirer of Darwin and Haeckel? Dubois applied for the post of army
surgeon in Dutch-colonised Sumatra. He resigned his lucrative lec-
tureship in anatomy, sailed to the East Indies and started digging for
the evidence. It duly arrived, at Trinil in Java in 1891-2: a skullcap
and a femur or thighbone, which were eventually taken to be from
the same creature even though they lay some forty-five feet apart.
Two molars were also found separately. Dubois' original classification of these fossils, was as those of an extinct giant chimpanzee.
The skull was more primitive than any known to be Homo sapiens,
yet the femur was that of a creature of upright, bipedal or two-
legged, habit.

Correspondence with the expert Haeckel seems to have changed
Dubois' mind: *'Obviously, both men had a substantial emotional and intellectual stake in finding an ape-man specimen. Haeckel, on hearing from
Dubois of his discovery, telegraphed this message: "From the inventor of
Pithecanthropus to his happy discoverer!"'* Dubois was now under significant pressure to construe his finds according to Haeckel's
desideratum.

Controversy ensued in the scientific community on Dubois' return to Europe with the specimens of *Pithecanthropus erectus*. When
world experts met at the Berlin Society for Anthropology, Ethno-
logy, and Prehistory to decide the evolutionary status of the specimens, the president of the Society, Dr Virchow, refused to chair the
meeting:

> *In the controversy-ridden discussion that followed, Swiss anatomist Kollman
> said the creature was an ape. Virchow himself said the femur was fully hu-
> man, and further stated: "The skull has a deep suture between the low vault
> and the upper edge of the orbits (eye sockets). Such a suture is found only in*

apes, not in man. Thus the skull must belong to an ape... a giant gibbon, in fact. The thigh-bone has not the slightest connection with the skull" (Cremo and Thompson, 1999, p. 159)[4].

Other experts gave similar opinions; the Selenka expedition to Trinil in 1907-8 to resolve the question found both animal and human remains, but no missing link. The authors spend a whole chapter reviewing the research and expert opinions up to the present:

In summary, modern researchers say the Trinil femurs are not like those of Homo erectus but are instead like those of modern Homo sapiens. The Java thighbones have traditionally been taken as evidence of an ape-man existing around 800, 000 years ago in the Middle Pleistocene. Now it appears we can accept them as evidence for anatomically modern humans existing 800,000 years ago (Cremo & Thompson 1999, p. 162).

But it was too late-the damage had been done. It may be, the authors conclude, that fossils will be found to fill in the gaps between the great apes and humans. However, given the evidence to date, there is nothing to suggest that any further fossils found, will necessarily support Darwinian evolutionary theory:

What if, for example, fossils of anatomically modern humans turned up in strata older than those in which [fossils of] Dryopithecus (the supposed Pliocene ancestor of modern apes and humans) were found?

In fact, such evidence has already been found, but it has since been suppressed or conveniently forgotten. Much of it came to light in the decades immediately after Darwin published The Origin of Species, before which there had been no notable finds except Neanderthal man. In the first years of Darwinism, there was no clearly established story of human descent to be defended, and professional scientists made and reported many discoveries that now would never make it into the pages of any journal more academically respectable than the National Enquirer [a US Yellow Rag chiefly interested in controversy and scandal].

Java man was found in Middle Pleistocene deposits generally given an age of 800,000 years. The discovery became a benchmark. Henceforth, scientists would not expect to find fossils or artifacts of anatomically modern humans in deposits of equal or greater age. If they did, they (or someone wiser) concluded that this was impossible and found some way to discredit the find as a mistake, an illusion, or a hoax (Cremo and Thompson 1999, p. 7).

There are not just two, or ten, such 'mistaken' archeological finds. Page after page, chapter after chapter, of *The Hidden History of the*

---

4. Extracts from Michael Cremo and Richard Thompson 1999, The Hidden History of the Human Race, Bkhaktivedanta Publishing Los Angeles, are taken with permission of Michael Cremo.

Human Race catalogues these finds. To call this a major scandal impacting negatively on the credibility of the way we do science, scarcely overstates the case. Homo erectus -- Java man, has remained the proof of the Missing Link, still found in school texts and coffee-table books on human evolution. The entire archeological record has been distorted to fit this error of judgement on the part of careless enthusiasts -- Haeckel especially (he had already been found guilty by an academic court of the University of Jena, of falsification of the facts of embryology to fit his view of the Darwinian thesis). As for Eugene Dubois, in old age he told his scientific community that he had been wrong; this skullcap was only that of a large gibbon. But the record was set; no one would now listen to a 'cantankerous' old man. This is not a case of Wilber's quadrant denial; the distortion of the record created what Cremo and Thompson refer to as a *knowledge filter*, which distorts all subsequent findings. Such filters operate in every area of science.

Hobbits and other anomalies

There was the recent discovery of Homo floresiensis, dubbed 'Hobbits', which excited not just the archeological community, but the general community too. Aren't they a Missing Link, readers may ask? These fossils, found with animal bones and artifacts on the Indonesian island of Flores, are of hominids around three feet tall, and with a skull just one-third the size of modern humans, in strata dated to 13,000 years ago. But humans are known to have already been present in the Archipelago!

The facts only add to the problem. The tiny cranial capacity of these 'hobbits' puts them down near the bottom, ape end of the line, whereas their advanced toolmaking ability puts them in the fully human part of the line heading up towards Homo sapiens sapiens. This dilemma has proven really useful in making a start on unpicking the mistaken fabric of evolutionary record produced by 'Java man'. The anomalies were at first attributed to a deformity of the single female skeleton of the first find-a group of U.S. scientists set out to establish that she had suffered from dwarfism or microcephaly. This was eventually ruled out. When other fossils were found of the same tiny stature, in deposits dated to as early as 94,000 years, there was no alternative but to accept that we humans had lived alongside these little people also of the genus Homo, for nearly a hundred thousand years. They have been designated Homo floresiensis. And scientists had to admit that the smooth ascent of the Darwinian line of human evolution was beginning to look a bit jagged, even fictional.

Cremo and Thompson are not asserting that there have never been animals halfway between apes and humans in evolutionary terms. (Perhaps they were produced by mating between apes and primitive humans.) They are stating, with simplicity and clarity, that there is absolutely no evidence (yet found) that modern humans *evolved from apes*, and a mass of ignored evidence for the presence of humans *alongside* the ancient ape Dryopithecus, the supposed ancestor of both modern apes and humans.

Recent finds are challenging textbook 'facts' about human evolution, as reports in the National Geographic News show. Formal bone tools 70,000 years old, from the Blombos cave in South Africa, show humans making sophisticated tools twice as long ago as we had believed possible. A *homo* skull from Dmanisi, Georgia, 1.2 million years old, is so tiny that evolution of large brains cannot, as previously thought, have been the advance that allowed humans to move out of Africa.

Several generations of the Leakey family have pioneered in archeology, thrilling the world with their finds in Africa. A Leakey team dig in Kenya in search of contemporaries of the famous 'Lucy', Australophithecus afarensis, turned up the skull of Kenyanthropus platyops (flat-face), 3.5 million years old. The fact that these utterly different hominids, one with a tall, flat face and small molars, the other (Lucy) with a protruding face and large teeth, lived side by side, produces confusion in the lines of the human family tree, which was supposed to be a linear evolution of one species from the one before. Similarly, at Dmanisi, several hominid species were found who must have lived alongside each other. Scientists now propose that there were multiple species, only one of which survived to become modern humans. The story of human evolution is experiencing ongoing revision of most of the previously accepted 'facts'. I actually don't mind being physically descended from an ape, if it turns out that way! In an incident in 2008 that threatened international cricket, Australian cricketer Andrew Symonds was apparently called a monkey by Indian opponent Harbhajan Singh. He saw it as a racial insult, as it was probably intended-yet rationally, how could it be, when according to accepted science, we are all descended from 'monkeys'?

So am I a Creationist or Intelligent Designer, or an Evolutionist? I am bits of all, and none-perhaps an idealistic monist, spiritual evolutionist would be a good description. I think we may look back on our current understanding of human evolution with a certain self-critical amusement, even disbelief. Though impossible to imagine at this moment, may it yet come to seem strange that we ever imagined we were descended from apes, rather than that humans had a separate line of evolution, beginning in however primitive an ancestor? The only reasonable alternative is to admit into the record all the genuine finds of the genus Homo, however early they appear to be, and then to search for and find, the common ancestor if it exists, back before that time. At any rate, we must cease distorting the facts to fit the (Darwinian) theory.

A caring God, or materialism's vast indifferent Emptiness?

Science has shown us a universe so vast in both time and space, and a humanity so shrunken in stature, that we therefore see the cosmos as profoundly indifferent to the lives of mere humans, - of each little individual among the billions of us crowded onto the planet. Surely it could not be such an ethical place, where every apparently trivial action is noted, and counts in the overall scheme, so that the moral debts of each of us must all be paid, as in both Hinduism and Buddhism? The idea provokes profound skepticism in many Westerners. Religion and a caring God may strike the rational side of us as a fairy-tale, charming in its quaint antiquity of notions about the importance of humans, but in the end as irrelevant as the bygone culture which produced it. The Christian teaching of a Son of God who died for us on the Cross to save little individual humans, all 6 billion of us, from our sins, may seem to us moderns almost quainter and more fabulous, and in the same vein.

We, who have inherited the Christian worldview, find that after the scientific revolution, we have become mere animals, *'a little higher than the apes'* as Spong says, tossed out to cling to the fringes of a vast, dehumanised universe. Some of us clutch at traditional ideas -- of a God scarcely big enough to create and run a solar system, yet a God who is at least comfortingly human and accessible. Meantime, many of us wonder how any God could possibly even be aware of such insignificant creatures on a speck of a planet.

God in Buddhism: The East's conception of the Ultimate attracts Westerners

The inadequacy of the tribal god of traditional Christianity (and our skep-ticism about other aspects of our faith) creates different responses.[5] Some of us become outright atheists. Some find an expanded Christianity, which retains both God and Christ; some adopt the secular Christianity solution and reject a divine Christ, along with God as other than an amorphous Energy. Variations on this theme abound; they include the ideas of two Australians. In John Carroll's meditation upon the 'dark saying' that he finds is the gospel of Mark, he brings a fresh mind and heart, and a fresh translation, to the central text of Western civilization, from which its cohering mythos has been derived. This is the original gospel, the one from which Matthew, Luke and John were written. Carroll finds neither claim to, nor evidence of the Church's idea of divinity. Instead, he finds 'The Existential Jesus' (2007), the philosopher of Being who makes God redundant.

Melbourne institution Francis McNab, theologian and psychotherapist, the dynamic and influential Minister of St Michael's Uniting Church in the city's heart, preaches that Christ's resurrection from death has no factual, only mythic reality. He is promoting the New Faith, a version of Christianity similar to Spong's; saying in ABC 1's Stateline programme (5 October 2008) that the *old faith has no interest or grip for many people'*. Interviewer Cheryl Hall paraphrased McNab as asserting that Abraham is probably a concoction, Moses a mass murderer and Jesus though very important, not 'necessarily' the Son of God. Hall introduced McNab to listeners as an outspoken rebel, and possibly *'the best ad man'* of the Christian Church, after he erected billboards attacking the negativity of the Ten Commandments. (There was an outcry, and they had to come down). McNab goes one step further than the Catholic Church-he doesn't just dismiss Hell as a myth, but Heaven as well, leaving only Earth and its inhabitants, in contradiction of Chapter Eight of this book!

McNab's position seems to be at the opposite end of the rope from that of traditional Christianity and the more conservative members of McNab's own church, the Uniting Church of Australia (who 'deconstructed' those billboards). Then there is the position of a third Australian, David Tacey, whose views are something of a synthesis of both – a synthesis achieved by the incorporation of surprising new elements.

---

5. Rachael Kohn writes of the response of priests and ministers to this dilemma, that once in office they find themselves having to suppress the critical Biblical scholarship they learned in theological college: This is necessary because it is at odds with the requirement on them to *'preach the creedal truths of Christianity'*, which are questioned by this scholarship (Kohn 2003, p. 35). All quotes from The New Believers by Rachael Kohn are reprinted by permission of HarperCollins Australia.

In *ReEnchantment: The New Australian Spirituality* (2000), Tacey proposes that Australians who are open to the experience, colonial descendants and recent arrivals alike, are being spiritualised through putting down psychic roots into the land; by the sacred rocks and earth, just as the original Australians have been and are. In the present this land-based spirituality naturally includes responsibility for the environment and respect for the unique indigenous relationship to the land, and custodianship of it. (The original Australians are born from and out of the land, and belong to that sacred being in just the way that the rocks and trees and animals belong. This is in profound opposition to the European attitude: the land is an inert commodity, one we parcel up in legal transactions, buy, sell and fence off into lots we consider *we own*.)

These battles over the interpretation of Christianity have been enough to send many of us into the arms of religions with a more vast conception of the Ultimate-a significant group. So at the opposite end of the scale of responses is this Western fascination with Eastern religions, Buddhism in particular, which teach that there is no personal God, only Infinite Mind. Although this has proven immensely attractive to Westerners seeking an alternative to traditional Christianity or Judaism, we struggle with the ideas of karma, reincarnation, and the apparently empty, inhuman Fullness of this Mind, and of Nirvana, the ultimate state of consciousness. How can a vaster universe be somehow still aware of little human lives, and sympathetic to, or accommodating of them? It is a contradiction insoluble to modern science. At the same time, the apparently more reasonable idea of God as something like an impersonal (and to us it seems, unconscious) Energy leaves many of us feeling ultimately isolated, alienated and alone.

Rachael Kohn explores these dilemmas, and the solutions we've created, in The New Believers (2003):

> *Today's new believers are re-imagining God to embrace the self-help movement, the Westernisation of Buddhism and the moral agenda of environmentalism. Undeterred by the sharply secular dissection of the Bible, they have unearthed fresh ways of experiencing its wisdom'*, summarizes the back jacket[6].

The new believers are remodelling the mainstream religions, and creating new creeds, to take account of critiques made by the educated, rational and skeptical modern mind. There are such numbers of Jewish Buddhists that a term has been coined to identify them:

---

6. All quotes from Rachael Kohn's The New Believers (2003) are used with permission of HarperCollins Australia.

'Jubus'. The existence of the term is evidence of the extent to which this remodelling, including cross-fertilisation, is a recognized phenomenon.

There is a fascinating comment and prophecy from D.K. about Buddhism and its Vedanta antecedents, and their Westernisation, made prior to 1942:

> The East has had this teaching for ages and has produced numerous commentaries upon it-the work of the finest analytical minds that the world has ever seen -- but it has made no mass use of the knowledge, and the people of the Orient do not profit by it as a whole. It will be different in the West, and is already modifying and influencing human thought on a large scale; it is permeating the structure of our civilisation, and will eventually salvage it (Bailey 1942, reference edition 1971, p. 511).

A pivot of the dilemma of the modern mind is the question of the nature of the Divine. Neither extreme – the personal God versus no God at all, seems to make enough sense, and any kind of a *via media* or compromise position looks logically impossible. We are attracted to, and find reason in, the Eastern conception of the Absolute as unknowable and unapproachably non-human because so vastly greater than the little specks of humanity upon the tiny blue planet. At the same time, we long for the comfort of a God who is indeed a Divine Father, who knows and guides and loves us, the Christian conception of the Ultimate.

Westerners including the writer have found it difficult to grasp the nature of the Ultimate according to Buddhism. Here is a seriously brilliant mind attempting to understand it. It is that of the U.S. NASA scientist Frank Tipler, who has just quoted Ghandi (a Hindu) who *'ridiculed the idea that Nirvana is extinction'*. Tipler then quotes an eminent Buddhist monk and professor of Buddhism at various American universities, the Rev. Dr Walpola Rahula, who is answering the question: What is Nirvana? He says that the debate which has produced 'volumes' has merely confused the issue:

> [H]uman language is too poor to express the real nature of the Absolute Truth or Ultimate Reality which is Nirvana. ... Nirvana is beyond all terms of duality and relativity. It is therefore beyond our conceptions of good and evil, right and wrong, existence and non-existence. Even the word 'happiness', which is used to describe Nirvana, has an entirely different sense here. Sariputta once said, "O friend, Nirvana is happiness!" Then Udayi asked: "But friend Sariputta, what happiness can it be if there is no sensation?" Sariputta's reply was highly philosophical and beyond ordinary comprehension: 'That there is no sensation itself is happiness'".

Tipler goes on to give us his summary of the nature of Nirvana:

.... Sariputta's reply was perfectly within ordinary comprehension: he meant that Nirvana is total extinction, but he didn't want to say it. By playing word games, he hoped to convince both Udayi and himself that total death is not really total death' (Tipler 1995, p. 277). [7]

Tipler's is the very type and paradigm of the scientific Western mind struggling with the subtleties of Buddhism. Tipler also quotes from Anne Gage's *The One Work, a Journey towards the Self*, a conversation Anne has with a Buddhist monk, which begins with her question "How can one say what has value in this present world?' to which the monk replies:

'Only one thing has value: Enlightenment.

'Does Enlightenment mean Nirvana?'

'Yes.'

'But doesn't that mean annihilation and the death of the soul?

'Not of the soul, but of ignorance and separation.' [D.K. refers to this as the ultimate sin, the great sin of separateness, which is that of the personality immersed in the material world, pursuing its own ignorant and thus selfish little goals and holding itself apart from all others and thus the One Self or God.]

'But I have read that the Buddha did not believe in any permanent entity or essence like the Real Self: that Nirvana is an experience of Bliss followed by utter dissolution; that he denied the existence of both God and the soul.'

'This is the interpretation given to Buddhism by men who have understood neither the teaching nor themselves' [my emphasis].

'Why did he say that everything was unreal?'

'Can you say of what passes through you, of fleeting emotions and thoughts, of the circumstances that come to you, this is I; this is permanent; this is Real?'

'No, I suppose not.'

'Do you know what is permanent and real?'

'No, unless God is, but I don't know that God exists. Did the Buddha believe in God?' [I would want to answer that the Buddha knew, and in the nature of that ultimate knowledge, Buddha himself was not separate from the object of his knowledge, and therefore could not speak of God, the concept of Whom is separate in our thinking from All that Is. The monk's reply was wonderfully simple and perfectly adapted to his inquirer's need.]

---

7. All extracts from The Physics of Immortality: Modern Cosmology, God and the Resurrection of the Dead, © Frank Tipler 1995, published by Macmillan, London, are used with the author's general permission.

'He didn't speak of God, which is different. If a man realizes God and is among other men who do not, it is useless to speak about Him for they would not understand. Man must discover God and his true Self or Ego by following the Path of Enlightenment'" (Tipler 1998, p. 83).

This is full of the clarity of grace and the simplicity of deep wisdom, so that the distinction between the monk and the Buddha himself, or the Bodhisattva, disappears for a moment. So surely, given his reference to God, the Buddhist monk with whom Anne Gage is conversing is a Western convert -- perhaps a Californian? This is not the case; he is a monk of Bangkok. It is interesting to note also, that the term he uses for the Self is Ego -- the term used by the Tibetan, D.K.

Yet both the Eastern idea of the Impersonal Ultimate and that of God as our Heavenly Father have truth in them. Beyond our entrapment within that net of conceptions about the material universe as all there is, lies a vast new understanding. *The truth may not be either-or, but both, and...*

Superphysical Materialism? Or just two sides of the coin?

The Dalai Lama spoke to Dr Peter Michel, about the creation of consciousness being impossible from non-consciousness: *'Consciousness has no beginning. A consciousness can only emerge from something that is an unchanging source-that is from another consciousness [emphasis mine]-not from something lifeless. Therefore, we say that it is without beginning'* (Dalai Lama 1997, p. 24).

It appears that the Buddhist Ultimate can be conceptualized as supreme Consciousness, though without the focus of Personhood. If the Absolute is Mind, or Energy, 'It' must be superhuman and superconscious.

Deity must be conscious in a way and to a degree we cannot imagine, infinitely beyond our own level of consciousness. Those of us who insist that Deity is only energy and no more, forget that we mean that 'just energy' *has no consciousness*, and cannot possibly also be Deity, or be cognizant of anything, certainly not of the entire universe. Mere preconscious energy cannot create anything by itself, let alone such a cosmos as the one we inhabit. (Richard Dawkins' argument in *The God Delusion (2006)* is that consciousness created itself from preconscious matter- via known and unknown mechanisms of evolution. This is a necessary argument if you insist on the position of materialistic reductionism, that there is nothing but physical matter in the universe).

Such a Consciousness as this overriding one surely is superhuman in the final degree, not subhuman or otherwise unrelated to humanity, and unable to be met in relationship by the humanity He has created. So the love which binds the universe together and holds the stars in their courses as well as giving our own miniscule and brief lives goal and meaning, must be the outstanding quality of this Divine Consciousness, and the nature of the relationship we have with Him. Such Consciousness, I would argue, must be able to be related to and reached, in contemplation or through invocation or prayer and must be infinitely capable of response. (The nature of that response is in question, especially given our own inadequacies to make connection, and our desire for an intervening father figure). This response would only be impossible if the Ultimate were an "It" and not a "Thou". So we come back to something that is not so very different from the highest Christian conception of God, however unrelated to the God made in the Image of Humanity from which common-and-garden Christianity has often suffered.

It is, in the end, merely a clash of words and definitions. These profound philosophical probings into the nature of Ultimate Reality are utterly necessary, yet doomed to inconclusion. Dualism can never perceive or conceive Unity. The profoundly limited can never conceive the Unlimited. Both Christianity and Buddhism (to confine the debate to those two for the moment) understand something of the truth, and have expounded and placed their emphasis on different vital aspects of it.

Buddhism's great contribution is the insight that the Ultimate is far greater than the gods humanity has erected in the place of worship in the past, as in Egypt, Greece or Rome, for example. The Ultimate is not merely a deified human, not just the Galilean writ large, not just Jesus' big dad, as many Christian groups, such as the Mormons with their idea of God as in a body like us, seem to conceive Him. A God so small could never have created even the physical universe with its billions upon billions of galaxies, let alone the rest of Reality-the superphysical levels of being!

On the other hand, to say that there is no God means there is no Creator, and we seem to be back to a universe confined to the physical level, and evolving haphazardly and unplanned, out of primordial nothingness. This is a universe in which humanity is merely an accident of material collision-the profoundly materialistic view of nineteenth and twentieth century science. This is certainly not the view of Buddhism in any of its branches, nor the intention of even the most radical Death-of-God Christians. And, as I have argued, the signs by the early twenty-first century point in the opposite direction, to a universe which didn't just happen, but was deliberately created, by the design of an unimaginably great Intelligence, who is both the One in whom we live and move and have our being, and the Self of all of us.

God and no-God, intimate and impersonal; there is no contradiction

The Tibetan, D.K., comments upon this great debate:

> 'We have spoken here of God in terms of Person, and we have used therefore the pronouns, He and His. Must it therefore be inferred that we are dealing with a stupendous Personality which we call God, and do we therefore belong to that school of thought which we call the anthropomorphic? The Buddhist teaching recognizes no God or Person. Is it therefore, wrong from our point of view and approach, or is it right? Only an understanding of man as a divine expression in time and space can reveal this mystery.
>
> Both schools of thought are right and in no way contradict each other. In their synthesis and in their blending can the truth as it really is, begin -- aye, dimly, -- to appear. There is a God transcendent Who 'having pervaded the whole universe with a fragment of Himself can still say: "I remain." There is a God Immanent Whose life is the source of the activity, intelligence, growth and attractiveness of every form in all the kingdoms in nature. There is likewise in every human being a transcendent soul which, when the life cycle on earth has come and gone and when the period of manifestation is over, becomes again the unmanifest and the formless, and which can also say "I remain"'(Bailey 1942, reference edition 1971, pp. 229-30).

The contribution of Christianity is the understanding that this vast, immeasurable Ultimate, this Creator, is still accessible to us, and still relates to us with boundless Love, regardless of the immense gulf of consciousness and understanding which separates us. He can still be related to, and desired as the Divine Beloved, by us in our turn. He remains the Father of us all, and His Nature is indeed reflected in the tiny scrap of the cosmos inhabited by us as it is in every other part, including its reflection in the relationship of parents and their children on earth. Happily for my argument, this idea or apprehension *has* to be as old as contemplation of the Divine. It appears in Teilhard de Chardin's *Mysticism*, where he says: *'The Centre of this spiritualised Matter (spiritual Whole) has to be supremely conscious and personal. The Ocean collecting all the spiritual streams of the universe is, not only something, but somebody. It has, Itself, a face and a heart'* (Teilhard de Chardin, Mysticism, p. 398.

To know the Creator, you need only look at His creation. 'As above, so below' remains eternally true. This relationship is mediated for us through the Great Beings who stand on the evolutionary ladder between us and the Godhead, -the Buddha and the Christ especially in these traditions, and thus make it easier and more accessibly human for us.

Every one of Humanity's attempts to conceptualize and recognize the Ultimate, presents humanity as a whole with some indispensable jewel of the entire truth, including of course, Islam, Judaism, Hinduism and Christianity. In the end, no substantial disagreement will be found between their core teachings.

The Tibetan further comments:

> *Thus in human thought, preserved for us by the great Teacher of the East, the Buddha, we have the concept of the transcendent Deity, divorced from the triplicities, the dualities, and the multiplicity of manifestation. There is but life, formless, freed from the individuality, unknown. In the teaching of the West, preserved for us and formulated for us by the Christ, the concept of God Immanent is preserved, - God in us and in all forms. In the synthesis of the Eastern and Western teachings, and in the merging of these two great schools of thought, something of the superlative Whole can be sensed - sensed merely - not known* (Bailey 1942, p. 231).

The view of the Ultimate of all the differing faiths will be found to come together like the most magnificent and beautiful stained-glass mosaic, to filter the Light which streams from the Godhead so a limited humanity may look at it and see its shapes and colours. Saints and sages, mystics, contemplatives and meditators of every tradition have borne witness to this; to the nature of the Divine; and the essential Love of the One in Whom we live and move and have our being. They do not need to speak of it as a matter of rationality, of deductive logic, as I have done here. They struggle to find words for the ineffable, for that which is beyond words and even thought, to present us with a morsel, a small taste, of their direct experience of the nature of the Divine.

It is an experience of the loss of self and the merging with the Self; of moving from the periphery, where one merely exists, to the fiery heart of Reality, into the eternal beauty and immortal love of the One who is All that Is, where one knows oneself to be identical with That One, and with humanity and all life, in the glorious cosmic dance which is the expression of Deity and the Life of the One Self. This truth about the nature of the Ultimate, has come to us from the contemplatives of every tradition, from Indians Shankara and Patanjali to the Tibetan Milarepa, from Rumi the Sufi poet and mystic, to the Essenes and the Cabbalists, from St Augustine, Julian of Norwich, and St Teresa of Avila, to Baha'u'llah, the Iraqi saint from whose wisdom the exemplary and pioneering Baha'i teachings of the oneness of all faiths and divine revelations sprang, and down to the present, to Yogananda and Simone Weil and the teachers of what might be called the American Dreaming–to mention some representatives only. This is also the experience that awaits every one of us in the natural course of evolution; the evolution of the self-concept from personality to soul to spirit and beyond, increasingly as we cross the border, or dismantle the conceptual boundary between ego and Witness consciousness. Teilhard de Chardin writes in *Christ in Matter*:

> *I live in the heart of a single element, the centre and detail of All, personal love and cosmic power. In attaining it and merging myself in it, I have the whole universe in front of me, with its noble endeavours, its entrancing search for knowledge, with its myriads of souls to be perfected and healed...We could say that God, eternal being in himself, for us is in process of formation all around us. And God, too, is the Heart of Everything* (Quoted in Happold 1963, p. 397).

The Dalai Lama is internationally respected as a spiritual leader. This is due to our capacity to recognise his luminous spiritual presence with its deep humanity, and because he actively promotes this understanding of the Ultimate or God, the one humanity, and the many paths we take to Enlightenment and Divinity, even while teaching Tibetan Buddhism to a world which needs its perspective. In an interview (shown on ABC TV in February, 2002) the Dalai Lama commented: 'Westerners like the people of Great Britain and the United States, should stick to Christianity.' Buddhism at its best is an aware and tolerant faith capable of the maturity to recognize other faiths and their validity, and therefore has a superior world-view- one which in the 21st century, and post-September 11 2001, is desperately needed just for our survival as humanity, and that of the planet.

Sadly, Christianity in its extremist and fundamentalist sects particularly, along with Islam and Judaism in their fundamentalist manifestations, is a good deal less tolerant and mature. There has been some progress along with some backsliding in Roman Catholicism since the great Pope John XXIII, followed by Paul VI, opened up interfaith dialogue in Vatican 11, teaching Christians that the God who was worshipped by Islam or Buddhism or any other faith, was the same God as claimed by Christians. (It follows that those of faiths other than Christianity were no longer *heathen*.) The Papal declaration *Nostra Aetate*, on the Relation of the Church to Non-Christian Religions, which was proclaimed by His Holiness Pope

Paul VI on 28 October 1965, deals with this subject, as noted in Chapter Two. Rachael Kohn in her book *The New Believers* refers to Hans Kung the theologian, also censured by the Roman Church in 1979 for his criticisms of the papacy, seeing the Church since that time, *'turn its back on the liberal and democratic ethos of the Second Vatican Council, (1962-65)'*. Kohn speculates that this, and the inspiration of the First Colloquium on Religion held by UNESCO in Paris in 1989, may have prompted Kung to formulate *'an ethical agenda which could be applied to all existing religions'*, which Kung titled *Global Responsibility: In Search of a New World Ethic* (Kohn 1997, pp. 184-5).

All this makes the vision of Baha'u'llah, the founder of the Bah'ai faith, seem more astounding, more visionary, in its ideal of human spiritual unity, than ever: *'One of the most important of Baha'u'llah's teachings is the concept of progressive revelation. The great religions are not separate and unrelated phenomena, but stages in the gradual unfoldment of a single Divine purpose, the preparation of humankind for the tasks of the long promised age of its collective maturity'* (The Baha'i Faith, c. 2005).

The intolerant and divisive creeds are those who see humans of any other persuasion as Heathen or Infidel, to be destroyed via Crusade or Jihad, or other forms of elimination such as the genocide of Muslims by Christians and non-Muslims in Kosovo, Israel's treatment of non-Jews within its borders, Turkey's persecution of Armenians around the turn of the twentieth century, the attitude of Al Quaeda or Jemaah Islamiah that the only good Westerner is a dead one, or the wars of religion between Hindus and Muslims in India. 'They' are considered an abomination to God or some other institution such as the Fatherland or the Holy Land or the race or culture of the state, and not worthy to survive. Most creeds have been guilty of this kind of amazing arrogance and its devastating consequences.

In the end, it may well be the case that every possible position or statement, and its equal and opposite negation about the nature of the Ultimate, are equally true. This includes "There is a God", and "There is no God"; "There is a Soul", and "There is no Soul". So what does this mean and imply for the loneliness of the long-distance Western enquirer into alternative Eastern ways? Does The Ultimate have any aspect or quality recognizable to humans, and therefore providing comfort for us about what lies beyond the death of the physical body?

Given that God or the Supreme Consciousness exists, the cosmos is not accidental, but is evolving according to His[8] Plan. Humanity is a part of that Plan.

It is impossible that we could be purely accidental, unless the entire majestic universe with its intricate order and vast design can be considered just an accident. The chances of such an entity with its zillions of interrelated events coming about by chance is, as we have seen in the calculations of Fred Hoyle and Chandra Wickramasinge, and the conclusions of others on the basis of these calculations, not even less than megazillions to one. It is zero. So if the universe isn't accidental, it is the result of a plan. It follows from this that The Supreme Consciousness has a plan for us, as for every aspect of the creation, and that we, too, have a part in this plan. And that the part we play is neither unimportant nor insignificant. If we had no real part to play, we would be the one discordant element in a minutely ordered scheme. (Even if we could for a moment, imagine that contradiction, a creation such as our universe, yet no creator, the intimate interlinking of all lives in what Teilhard de Chardin called the co-becoming of the universe, all of us evolving together and by mutual interaction, makes us co-creators. We must therefore choose very carefully, what we do with our lives and with all other lives on the planet. It won't be just our children and grandchildren who suffer if we destroy the environment-it will be ourselves returned.)

It makes logical and philosophical sense that regardless of our indescribable insignificance and inferiority, and the Absolute's infinitely vaster Being, we as His creations and creatures, must share something of His nature, which must be pure consciousness and pure love. This is despite the fact that our own share of both consciousness and love is a scrap, until we evolve further. As His creatures, we must by definition be fully comprehended by Him and suffused with Him, and therefore be like Him in some small degree. The Creation that issues from the Godhead, the Parabrahm, the Ain Soph, is of that same Nature, made of that same 'stuff', since there is no other 'stuff' in the entire universe. We are indeed in and

---

8. It may continue to cause concern or irritation to some readers, despite the argument thus far, that I refer to 'God'. This is still the most easily recognized naming of the concept in question, and I would argue, will do as well as any alternative term. I understand the allergy we can suffer to the word 'God' because of its historic usage and connotations. Similarly, when I write of 'He' and 'His', it is not because He is a (very large and vast) human, but because no more appropriate words exist. Several writers have preferred 'It' for the Ultimate because of the difficulties with 'He'. I like that even less – it causes us to think, however involuntarily, of the Ultimate or God, as less than human.

of Him, as He is in and of us. The Tibetan quotes from a very ancient text to explain this:

> *The basic sacrifice which the planetary Logos made was when He decided to incarnate or enter into the form of this planet* [as we all incarnate and take physical form]. *This was from pure choice, motivated by His 'fixed determination' to function as the Saviour of the planet, in the same sense as the world Saviours come forth for the salvaging of humanity. The initiate, on his tiny scale, must learn to function also as a saviour, and thus express the Law of Sacrifice through the medium of the developed, pure, reasoning will, and not simply from that of impulsive love and activity...*
>
> *This sacrifice was imperative in the fullest sense, owing to the ability of the planetary Logos to identify Himself in full consciousness with the soul in all forms of life, latent within the planetary substance ... Because of this identification, He could not refuse the invocative appeal of the 'seeds of life, striving within the substance of the form, and seeking added life and light', as the Old Commentary puts it. This striving and reaching forth evoked His response and the going out of His divinity ...to meet the deeply hidden divinity within these seeds...'*

Just as other, lower, little lives form our bodies and are transformed and altered by our transformations, or even just growth, in consciousness and consequent life-changes, so also we, who as Humanity, form part of the body of manifestation of the planetary Logos, are transformed by His changes in consciousness, and lifted towards greater life and light and love, even as we help to create both light and love:

> *Under this Law of Sacrifice, Sanat Kumara (to express the idea in occult terms) 'must turn His back upon the Central Spiritual Sun, and with the light of His Countenance irradiate the path of the prisoners of the planet'. He sentences Himself to stay for as long as may be needed, 'acting as the Sun and light of the planet until the Day be with us and the night of Pralaya descends upon His finished task.'* The quotation is again from the Old Commentary (Bailey 1955, reference edition 1979, pp. 286-7).

It seems rational to turn our backs on the hubris and egocentricity of God-in-man's-image. It seems very modern and 'scientific' to see the Divine as just an infinite Energy to which humans can have only a limited relationship, but *it actually doesn't make sense.* We need to constantly remind ourselves that our perception of reality is blinkered by our science, which will inevitably move past its present fixation on the physical level as the beginning and end of the universe. Science will evolve past the idea that a mindless physical process of some kind is the only *possible* source of creation. Many top astrophysicists and scientists generally have moved on from this worldview, leaving average humanity still stuck in the view filtered down from their ranks earlier last century.

What then, does the Ageless Wisdom, through the Tibetan Master, have to say on this crucial subject?

> *It is not, however, a profitless task for the disciples and aspirants to catch the dim outline of that structure, that purpose and that destiny which will result from the consummation and fruition of the Plan on earth. It need evoke no sense of futility or of endless striving or of an almost permanent struggle. Given the fact of the finiteness of man and of his life, given the tremendous periphery of the cosmos and the minute nature of our planet, given the vastness of the universe and the realization that it is but one of countless (literally countless) greater and smaller universes, yet there is present in men and upon our planet a factor and a quality which can enable all these facts to be seen and realized as parts in a whole, and which permits man (escaping, as he can, from his human self-consciousness) to expand his sense of awareness and identity so that the form aspects of life offer no barrier to his all-embracing spirit* (Bailey 1942, reference edition 1971, p. 219).

'There cannot be a God; there is too much suffering'

Some of the finest minds -- and hearts, on the planet would still argue that there cannot possibly be a God. Sir David Attenborough is an outstanding example. He is responsible more than anyone else for making us aware of the awesome beauty and variety, intelligence and interdependence of all the rest of the life on the Blue Planet, thus bringing us to some sense of the need for wise custodianship of the planet. In one of Australian Andrew Denton's most revealing interviews, Attenborough said he couldn't believe in a God who permitted a worm to live in the eye of an innocent African child and cause blindness. *'Was there nowhere else for that worm to live?"* he questioned, angrily. Again and again, this is the response to the question; do you believe in a Creator? *'No, I cannot believe in a God who would permit so much terrible suffering, such cruelty.'* One of the final tragedies –and triumphs of the evil behind the Nazi power lust, was the loss of faith of so many good people as a result of the uncovering of the atrocities in Hitler's concentration camps: *'There cannot be a God if such things took place and were not stopped.'* The response is the same to tragedies and atrocities of every description.

Then there are those of us for whom there is no such thing as an accident, or human cussedness, or the blind forces of matter. Everything in life happens for a reason, and this reason is the Divine Will. Whether I lose my car keys or get swept away by a tsunami, it is God's intention for me personally, goes this unexamined thinking. The flip side of this coin is our rage and despair at a God who would cause, or even permit, these monstrous cruelties-concentration camps, child soldiers, refugee camps with their starving women keening over dead babies; tsunamis, hurricanes, bushfires. We expect intervention as a matter of course, and believe that evil and suffering should not exist, and if they do, that proves there is no God. If that is the case, then we have misunderstood the nature of God and cosmos. Any large intervention would have drastic consequences for all of us, and for a myriad of other lives, on this planet and elsewhere in the cosmos. At worst it would stop evolution, and perhaps life itself, on the planet. Interventions do however, take place constantly-when they don't bend the rules, or nature, too badly.

'*A mobilizing of the Forces of Light is going on upon the inner side of life*' D.K. wrote to his group of disciples or students in a series of letters at the height of World War Two. '*These Forces stand ready, but the word for action must come from the Christ, and He will give that word when the people give it to Him. We are the conditioners of our own destiny. Neither the Christ nor the Hierarchy may, at this stage in human evolution, take any step vitally affecting human evolution unless released into this activity by humanity itself* (Bailey 1957, reference edition 1972, p. 352).

Any intervention or assistance must happen '*without any infringement of the free will of the individual, group or nation. The occult law of spiritual freedom had to be recognized and respected. No such respect or safeguarding hinders the activities of the forces of evil*' (Bailey 1957, p. 340).

The problem of suffering lies in the prevailing power of matter and therefore, of what we experience quite rightly, as evil. Evil and suffering have their source in the relative intractability of matter despite its divine origin, at this point in our evolution. Evil is only unredeemed matter; it is matter not yet infused with spirit. Evil, advises D.K., is '*simply the dominance of matter and the negation of the spiritual values*'. The context is the examination of the intense evil inflicted on the world by the Nazi regime and the Axis powers (Bailey 1957, p. 340). In our lack of understanding of the scheme in which we are involved, we think of God as the ultimate benevolent dictator whom we must petition for mercies such as the easing of suffering. But it is *in and through us* and our development, that matter is 'redeemed'-that is, transformed by consciousness. We ourselves are '*the sons of God come in to the daughters of men*'-spirit or consciousness incarnating in matter, and thus not passive creatures, but *co-creators* of our realm of the universe.

The new science of epigenetics is discovering that consciousness, once believed to play no part at all in transmission of characteristics via DNA, is actually altering our DNA in the course of a lifetime or less, through the choices we make as individuals.

This raises the vital question: by what mechanism *are* we, as little individual human beings, connected to the Absolute? There needs to be a scheme of relationship that makes obvious sense. The next chapter deals with this question.

Chapter 13

The Great Chain of Being, Hierarchy and Teachers of the Race

Summary Points

- The visual Out-of-Body experience of one blind woman, and her NDE meeting with 'Jesus'
- 'What the light conveyed was love'
- **The tradition of beings who mediate the Absolute to humans**
- The hierarchy in Buddhism
- **What is this Hierarchy?**
- The work of the Hierarchy for earth and humanity; our place in a vast scheme
- Supreme Consciousness is Love; how could it be otherwise?
- **The student's relationship to her or his Master, the World Teacher and Deity**
- Newton's cases: God is never seen, just 'known'
- **Krishna, The Messiah, Christ, The Imam Mahdi, The Buddha ...who are they?**

- What is the ultimate identity of each separate person?
- **Christ for Christians only?**
- 'The Christ has no religious barriers in His consciousness'
- **Women in Islam, the veil, the West and 'Jihad Sheilas'**
- **Religious war to destroy humanity?**
- Dynamic Creation and the Chain; God to Humanity via all servers of humanity
- The group of world servers and the 'radiant Rainbow Bridge'

The Great Chain of Being, Hierarchy and Teachers of the Race

What are we to make of the Being of Light encountered by those reporting a Near-death Experience; a being who seems to stand in a mediatory role between the Godhead and us? This is the one apparently referred to in our religious traditions-variously, as the Christ, the Imam Mahdi, Krishna, the Messiah, the Bodhisattva and the Maitreya Buddha. Is there any objective reality to this Person or to the role of World Teacher seemingly played by the one known under these different names?

The visual Out-of-Body experience of one blind woman, and her NDE meeting with 'Jesus'

On February 23, 1973, Vicki Umipeg, 28, was severely injured in a road accident. She had been born at 22 weeks, and suffered such optic nerve damage as a result of over-oxygenation of her humidicrib, *'along with about 55,000 other babies in the U.S. at that time'* as to leave her totally blind. I've chosen her story from Ring and Cooper's *Mindsight: Near-death and Out-of-body Experiences in the Blind* (1999, pp. 24-5), as Ring's research makes it impossible to dismiss NDE and OOB as dreams or fantasies. Vicki is also quite typical in responding to this, the place in which she finds herself during her Near-death Experience, as the realm of completion, of perfection, of total love, of instant and complete intuitive knowledge, and of Divine Being and God.

Vicki recalled the frightening sounds and sensations leading to the crash. Then suddenly she had her sight, and could see the crumpled VW bus (or Kombi van) from an Out-of-Body perspective. On arrival at emergency in (Harborview) hospital, she found herself up on the ceiling watching a male doctor and a woman doctor or nurse, working on her body:

> *She could overhear their conversation too, which had to do with their fear that because of possible damage to her eardrum, she could become deaf as well as blind. She recalls seeing her body, tall and thin, and thinking 'Well, that's kind of weird. What am I doing up here? ...Well, this must be me (the body on the metal table). Am I dead?'*

Vicki then travelled up through ceilings and above the roof, where she had a panoramic view, and was exhilarated at the freedom of her ascension. She heard 'sublimely beautiful' music. After being sucked into the tunnel, she describes rolling out onto grass, and discovering that everyone around her was *'made of light. And I was made of light.*

What the light conveyed was love. There was love everywhere. It was like love came from the grass, love came from the birds, love came from the trees.'

Debby and Diane her blind schoolmates, no longer children, welcomed her, *'bright and beautiful, healthy and vitally alive '.* This was despite that they had been profoundly retarded, and died as children aged eleven and six. There was also a couple who had been her caretakers, Mr. and Mrs. Zilk, and finally her grandmother, who hung back initially (she had abused Vicki). Love and welcome were the only feelings present in all of this:

> *"I had a feeling like I knew everything...and like everything made sense. I just knew that this was where...this place was where I would find the answers to all the questions about life, and about the planets, and about God, and about everything..."*

> *And then she is indeed flooded with information of a religious nature as well as scientific and mathematical knowledge. She comes to understand languages she doesn't know. All this overwhelms and astonishes her:*

> *"I don't know beans about maths and science...I all of a sudden understood intuitively almost things about calculus, and about the way planets were made. And I don't know anything about that...I felt there was nothing I didn't know." As these revelations are unfolding, Vicki notices ...a figure whose radiance is far greater than the illumination of any of the persons she has so far encountered.*

She has met him in her previous NDE (1963), and identifies him as Jesus. As discussed in earlier chapters, NDE subjects reared in Islam would be likely to see The Being of Light as Mohammed, or the Imam Mahdi, while a Hindu NDEr would probably identify 'him' as Krishna, and a Buddhist as the Maitreya Buddha or their yidam, their tutelary deity; bearer and personification of the divine archetype.

Vicki conveys the joy of being in the presence of her beloved Jesus again, and the love she experiences from him. She wants to stay with him in this place of completion and perfection, but he communicates to her that it isn't time yet; she must return to her earthly life for now. Vicki is extremely disappointed, and protests that she wants to stay with him. He tells her she will return to him, but for now, she must go back to physical life to 'learn and teach more about loving and forgiving'. And in order to have the children she so desperately wants. She consents to return: This Teacher shows her *'a complete panoramic review of her life, and as she watches, ...gently comments to help her understand the significance of her actions and their repercussions.'*

Vicki's experience of the one whom she calls Jesus, is quite typical. It illustrates the way in which, in the after-death state, there may be a vast expansion of contact and comprehension of life. Yet in the midst of this disappearance of separateness and limited consciousness, there is an Individual, the Being of Light who mediates ultimate consciousness: He seems to have complete knowledge and understanding of the individual before him, in both their past life and their future.

The tradition of beings who mediate the Absolute to humans

The hierarchy in Buddhism

It would seem at first glance, that there is no equivalent of this individual, nor of the tradition of beings who connect and step down the Absolute to mere humans, in other religions especially Buddhism. Once again, the truth is subtler and more complex than this understanding of Westerners, which is likely to deny or deconstruct hierarchy, in Buddhism and elsewhere. (This denial is most marked in Wilber's F6 Poststructuralists, the Greens who insist that there is no greater or lesser, no higher or lower; we are all equal.) In a central section of The Tibetan Book of Living and Dying, Sogyal Rinpoche (1992, p. 134-5) discusses the vital importance of our relationship with the Inner Teacher, the enduring aspect of ourselves, (the soul or spirit; the higher self in the West), and with the Master of our spiritual tradition. The Rinpoche says that the Master is the spokesperson of one's own inner Teacher, and *'bearer, channel and transmitter of all the blessings of all the enlightened beings.'*

'He or she is nothing less than the human face of the Absolute'. I suspect we tend to forget that in Buddhism, ordinary humans are not expected to be capable of relating to the Unknowable by themselves. There is a long and powerful tradition of beings who mediate the Absolute to mere humans; teachers, guides and Masters who have gone before and thrown light upon the way. They can be our teachers 'in the flesh', as St Francis and St Benedict were to their disciples, as the Dalai Lama is presently, or capable of revealing themselves at need and at will to their disciples, as is the case with the teachers of so many other exceptional humans, including Jung and Kubler-Ross. But who are these teachers, guides and Masters? If they are 'the human face of the Absolute', this suggests a certain relationship between the two, which throws light on the nature of the Absolute. But what could that possibly be?

What is this Hierarchy?

Contact between the Ultimate or God and His little creatures would have to take place via a hierarchy of being. This hierarchy must and does exist because of *evolution,* which is a necessary part of the scheme. All beings evolve; they evolve in parallel with the scheme and structure of the cosmos itself, from simple and primitive to more and more complex (on the physical level of our planet, from unicellular creatures through cold-blooded animals to the lower mammals and finally humans). If there is no real death, then continuing life and evolution of all units in the cosmic scheme is inevitable. Even if understood just on the Darwinian level, evolution is an obvious and necessary aspect and law.

Those units of life and consciousness at the upper levels of the evolution in any particular part of the cosmos are those closest to Deity (and working at being closer) and most able to interpret Deity to those on lower levels, and to assist them, as each higher level is able to do for those below. Given that Deity is not remote and inaccessible, but is part of us as we are a part of that Great Being, and intends that we should know Him- (that is, be conscious of Him as He is of us), and evolve to ever greater likeness and identity with Him, this chain of communication between the more evolved and the less is vitally necessary. Human need alone calls forth teachers from a compassionate Deity; if that Supreme Consciousness is Love, how could it be otherwise? Given that we are linked to that Absolute by the Chain of Being, or hierarchy of lives, -the communion of saints in Christianity, this hierarchy also provides the structure of the inner government of the planet, again necessarily so.

The work of the Hierarchy for earth and humanity; our place in a vast scheme

The Tibetan Master has clarified this:

> *Who are the Masters? ... Even those who do not admit the existence of the Masters seek some ideal... They...visualize some great philanthropist, some superlative scientist, some notable artist or musician... The human being, - simply because he is himself fragmentary and incomplete - has always this urge within himself to seek other and greater than himself. It is this that drives him back to the centre of his being, and it is this that forces him to take the path of return to the All-Self. Ever, throughout the aeons, does the Prodigal Son arise and go to his Father, and always latent within him is the memory of the Father's home and the glory there to be found. But the human mind is so constituted that the search for light and for the ideal is necessarily long and difficult. "Now we see through a glass darkly, but then face to face";*

now we catch glimpses through the occasional windows we pass in our ascension of the ladder, of other and greater Beings than ourselves; They hold out to us helping hands, and call to us in clarion tones to struggle bravely on if we hope to stand where They are now standing....

The great Initiate, who voiced the words I quote, (St Paul) added still other words of radiant truth: "Then shall we know even as we are known." The future holds for each and all who duly strive, who unselfishly serve and occultly meditate, the promise of knowing Those who already have full knowledge of the struggler... (As) he laboriously reiterates from day to day the arduous task of concentration and of mind control, there stand on the inner side Those Who know him, and Who watch with eager sympathy the progress that he makes (Bailey 1950, ref. ed. 1985, p. 257-8).

How reassuring is this tremendous fact; of the disciple's relationship to her or his Master, and through that Master, to the World Teacher and on to Deity. Add to that the fact of being known and understood utterly, through and through, until we finally reach the point where we also have a conscious relationship to Deity, and 'know as we are known'. Even as we appreciate that the struggling, aspiring seeker's first Master is her or his own soul.

As the poet Robert Browning has so beautifully expressed it in the dramatic lyric 'Saul':

It shall be

A face like my face that receives thee,

A Man like to me

Thou shalt love and be loved by, forever;

A Hand like this hand

Shall throw open the gates of new life to thee!

See the Christ stand!

In *Initiation, Human and Solar*, D.K. tells us about the nature of the Hierarchy's four main lines of work:

a) To develop self-consciousness in all beings.

b) To develop consciousness in the three lower kingdoms [mineral, vegetable and animal].

All these kingdoms [mineral, vegetable, animal and human] embody some type of consciousness, and it is the work of the Hierarchy to develop these types to perfection through the adjustment of Karma, through the agency of force, and through the providing of right conditions.

c) To transmit the will of the Planetary Logos [the Consciousness of our planet, our planetary Lord.]

They [Hierarchy] *act as the transmitter to men and devas or angels, of the will of the Planetary Logos, and through Him of the Solar Logos.*

d) To set an example to humanity.

...This hierarchy is composed of Those Who have triumphed over matter, and Who have achieved the goal by the very self-same steps that individuals tread today. These spiritual personalities, these adepts and Masters, have wrestled and fought for victory and mastery upon the physical plane, and struggled with the miasmas, the fogs, the dangers, the troubles, the sorrows and pains of everyday living... Their apprehension of the freedom that comes through the sacrifice of the form by the medium of the purificatory fires, suffices to give them a firm hand, an ability to persist even though the form may seem to have undergone a sufficiency of suffering, and a love that triumphs over setbacks, for it is founded upon patience and experience. These Elder Brothers of humanity are characterized by a love which endures, and which acts ever for the good of the group, by a knowledge which has been gained through a millennia of lives, in which They have worked Their way from the bottom of life and evolution well nigh to the top...' (Bailey 1922b, reference edition 1972, pp. 20-25).

This is truly heartening! Yet is this concept of a Hierarchy of teachers something confined to esoteric philosophy? Have researchers like Dr Michael Newton found any evidence of its existence? Some version of the encompassing idea, that of the Great Chain of Being or Ladder of Life, has been a governing paradigm in societies and cultures as diverse and widely separated as Imperial China and Elizabethan England, where this metaphor *'served to express the unimaginable plenitude of God's creation, its unfaltering order, and its ultimate unity. The chain stretched from the foot of God's throne to the meanest of inanimate objects. Every speck of creation was a link in the chain...'* writes EMW Tillyard, in *The Elizabethan World Picture* (1963). We have a greatly truncated and modified version of the Great Chain of Being still, in the Darwinian version of evolution which underlies the current worldview of science.

The Hierarchy in D.K.'s teachings and in Newton, in Christianity and in Buddhism – is it the same?

Newton provides us with a chart of levels of soul advancement, six in all, and gives their corresponding colours:

I have never found a person who is a living grade VI, or master guide, as a subject. I suspect we don't have a whole lot of these advanced souls on Earth at any one time. Most level VI's are much too involved with planning and directing from the spirit world to incarnate any longer...

Once in a while during a session with a more advanced soul, I hear references to an even higher level of soul than Level VI. These entities, to whom even the masters report, are in the darkest purple range of energy. These superior beings must be getting close to the creator. I am told these shadowy figures are elusive, but highly venerated beings in the spirit world.

The average client doesn't know if spiritual guides should be placed in a less than divine category, or considered lesser gods because of their advancement...In my opinion, guides are no more or less divine than we are, which is why they are seen as personal beings. In all my cases God is never seen. People in hypnosis say they feel the presence of a supreme power directing the spirit world, but they are uncomfortable using the word "God" to describe a creator. Perhaps the philosopher Spinoza said it best with these words: 'God is not He who is, but That which is.'

Every soul has a spiritual higher power linked to its existence. All souls are part of the same divine essence generated from one oversoul. This intelligent energy is universal in scope and so we all share in divine status. If our soul reflects a small portion of the oversoul we call God, then **our guides provide the mirror by which we are able to see ourselves connected to this creator** *(my emphasis)* (Newton 1994, p. 122).

This recalls the explanation of the teacher's position and role in Buddhism, by Sogyal Rinpoche, quoted at the head of this chapter. *'He or she is ... the human face of the Absolute'.*

Given the disparity of their sources, it might be expected that these accounts of God, Hierarchy, and Masters, – Newton's and D.K.'s, would bear little relation to each other at best, or flatly contradict each other at worst. Yet there seems to be no point of disagreement; just a different 'angle' from each writer, and different facts. These amplify what appears to be the central truth about the nature of the cosmos: that there is a God or Ultimate who, infinitely greater than we are in consciousness and in every quality we admire, must be aware of us, and love us more completely and absolutely even, than those teachers and leaders whose capacity to love has placed them above us in the Great Chain of Being. Deity's love, care and concern for us is thus delegated and stepped down to beings ever nearer to our own level of life and consciousness, in a chain of authority and responsibility which has created Earth's own Hierarchy of Masters, through whom the chain descends, eventually including each one of us.

This Hierarchy is present and recognized in Christianity, in the Disciples of Christ and in the Apostles who were sent out to teach and to establish the Christian community, or church in each local community. It also exists in the priesthood which extends back in an unbroken line to Peter, of whom Christ said "Upon this rock shall I build my Church'. Every true disciple is said by D.K. to be a part of the true apostolic succession; each is *'A priest unto the Lord'*. The spiritual succession also exists in Buddhism; each aspirant should find a living master who is *'of the lineage'*, in order to be linked in to its spiritual power and authority, and to be initiated properly into the spiritual mysteries and the means of escape from endless cycles of reincarnation. The hierarchy of spiritual masters and teachers culminates in the Buddha.

Tibetan Buddhism, in the person of the Dalai Lama, recognizes the Christ (as does Sogyal Rinpoche as already mentioned in Chapter Five). The late Pope, His Holiness John Paul II met with the Dalai Lama in Rome, in a mutual recognition of each faith of the other. Responses of the different faiths to the terrorist attacks of 9/11 especially, were surprising; they were not merely inter-denominational, but interreligious. But beyond these, which could be just gestures of goodwill, is there any evidence of a tradition linking the different entities claimed as supreme founders and teachers by the great religions, and suggesting they might even inhabit the same world, and be something other than the skeptic's idea of the God-botherer?

The Tibetan, D.K., reminds us of the fundamental truths behind all revealed religions, truths revealed by their great avatars or prophets: 'They are essential to the spiritual growth and the progressive realizations of divinity by man.' Everything else is simply expansion upon these truths, and is due to humanity's necessary and desirable intellectual and spiritual development. *'It is the unalterable truths which must be discovered and recognized as the new world religion takes form on Earth [my emphasis] and conditions human thought and consciousness in the coming New Age'* (Bailey 1957, ref. ed. 1972, p. 288).

The connection between religion, the evolution of planetary life, the intellectual and spiritual growth of humanity, and the 'wielding of the divine laws' is revealed in D.K.'s explanation of the hierarchical organization and stepping down of the creative power:

I have been... seeking to impress upon you the eternal fact that the entire universe has been created and its evolution processed through the power of thought, which is only another word for controlled meditation... [T]he laws of this meditative work are the result of certain mental determinations, which embody the will of the planetary Logos and are imposed upon all lesser groups of lives by Those Whose task it is to wield the divine laws and enforce them. Freedom of the will is here to be noted in relation to the Time concept but not in relation to the final and inevitable divine results at the end of the immense world period... The basic purpose of Sanat Kumara [the planetary Logos or Divinity] *is revealed from cycle to cycle by His Agents in*

Shamballa, and is by Them impressed upon the minds of the senior Members of the Hierarchy...

The major thoughtform of the spiritual Hierarchy, created by joint ashramic meditation, is called by us the Plan... Each ashram... undertakes meditation upon the general Plan and thus each initiate and disciple finds his place and sphere of activity and service-from the very highest initiate to the least important disciple...

The need of (the) unthinking masses must be met by disciples of less spiritual development, and probably their greatest appeal is through the application of economic help...They... adapt the Plan to the widely differing masses and thus the hierarchical Plan can reach from the Masters of the Hierarchy, through the Ashrams to the New Group of World Servers, and [on] *to the whole human family* (Bailey 1955, ref. ed. 1979, 233-4).

The world Ashram is the Buddhist Sangha; the Christian Communion of Saints is a rough equivalent. See Diagram 3 in the Appendix for the position of this place of world teaching and training.

Krishna, The Messiah, Christ, The Imam Mahdi, The Buddha ...who are they?

The Buddha is The Christ's Great Elder Brother, Whose time of service to humanity begins to draw to its close. He will move on to higher duties in the infinite order of the cosmos:

There is an increasing emphasis being given in the West by esotericists to the Full Moon of May, which is the Festival of the Buddha and the time when He makes His annual contact with humanity. This emphasis...has not been brought about in order to impose recognition of the Buddha upon the Occident. There have been two main reasons why, since 1900, this effort has been made. One was the desire on the part of the Hierarchy to bring to the attention of the public the fact of the two Avatars, the Buddha and the Christ, both upon the Second Ray of Love-Wisdom, Who were the first of our humanity to come forth as human-divine Avatars and to embody in Themselves certain cosmic Principles and give them form (Bailey 1957, ref. ed. 1972, p. 347).

The Wesak Festival has been held down the centuries in the well-known valley in the Himalayas (if the faithful would only believe it) in order:

(1) To substantiate the fact of the Christ's physical presence among us ever since his so-called departure.

(2) To prove (on the physical plane) the factual solidarity of the Eastern and Western approaches o God. Both the Christ and the Buddha are present... (Bailey 1948, ref. ed. 1984, p. 45).

So the task of the Buddha and the Christ has been to bring these great Principles, of Wisdom and Love, to earth by incarnating them and thus manifesting them on earth in their own being, life and work. When those of us who form the congregation in the Christian churches, say the Creed in its various forms, we affirm that Christ was *'the only Son of God'*. This is both a great, eternal Truth (about the Nature of the Divine Trinity and the 'mathematics' of manifestation of the Divine) and at the same time, inaccurate in the way we tend to understand it, that the man, Jesus of Nazareth, was the *only* individual to the end of time who stood or will stand on the planet as God Incarnate. The ultimate identity of each of us is the Buddhanature, the Christ-nature:

> *When you are ultimately truthful with yourself, you will eventually realize and confess that "I am Buddha" I am Spirit. Anything short of that is a lie, the lie of the...separate-self sense, the contraction in the face of infinity. The deepest recesses of your consciousness directly intersect Spirit itself, in the supreme identity. "Not I, but Christ liveth in me" [the words of St Paul] -- which is to say, the ultimate I is Christ (Wilber 2007, p. 198).*

Thus we are all Sons of God: sons and daughters on the physical plane where there is a sexual differentiation, 'sons' for lack of a more inclusive term, beyond the physical plane. As Newton says in the quote above, 'we all share in divine status'. Christ was the first of our *true* earth humanity to achieve this spiritual eminence; the Buddha achieved this point in an earlier cycle. We are all due to achieve the same high point of spiritual attainment eventually, just as the Christ and the Buddha have done:

> *The Buddha embodied the Principle of Light, and because of this illumination, humanity was enabled to recognize Christ, Who embodied the still greater Principle of Love ... The one demonstrated the height of the attainment of the third divine aspect (Active Intelligence); the other that of the second aspect (Love), and these two together present one perfect Whole [my emphasis].*

> *The second reason* [for the emphasis upon the relationship between the Buddha and the Christ] *was to initiate...the theme of the new world religion.* ...[Through the work of the Buddha and the Christ] *the Divine Plan ...is expressing itself at present in the keen recognition by men everywhere of the need to establish right human relations, culminating in the objectives for which the United Nations are fighting. These have been voiced for humanity by two great world disciples* [Franklin D. Roosevelt and Winston Churchill-disciples despite their very real personality flaws and policy and planning mistakes], *in terms of The Four Freedoms and The Atlantic Pact...Enough light has been permitted to penetrate by the efforts of the Buddha, to lead to a world-wide recognition of the desirability of*

these formulas; and there is enough love already in the world, released by the Christ, to make possible the working out of the formulas (Bailey 1957, pp. 346-9).

Does God belong to the Catholics, the Shi'a Muslims, neither or both? Christ for Christians only?

What has happened to the vision presented to us by these Supreme Teachers, and by the Prophet Mohammed, and the great Indian and Chinese teachers along with others? Why are we fighting so hard amongst ourselves in what Karen Armstrong, titling her wonderful book about the clash of religions and cultures and the rise of Christian, Islamic and Jewish fundamentalism, has called *The Battle for God*? Why do we not see that the World Teacher is known to us by different names, but that He is the same great Being? Why do we believe God belongs only to our particular religious group?

If the God worshipped by Christians is the God of Love, then surely He must have sent a great spiritual teacher, His representative, to every group on earth. If the great teacher claimed by Christians, the Christ, is real, then His love is not just for Christians, but equally for His other flocks, which He reminded us, 'ye know not of'. A Christian is one who is a follower of Christ. But what of those who call Him by a different name? Why would we imagine that every one of His other congregations has read documents produced by some of His followers decades or more after His departure, (i.e. the Gospels) and would therefore be likely to use the same nomenclature?

There is some further evidence in support of this contention that the World Teacher is known by other names to other faith communities. The title of the World Teacher in the Hindu faith, Krishna, has the same ideational and linguistic root as the word Christ, to the point of being the same word when the spelling is equalized. Krish or Krs, with spelling rearranged to our more typical useage, becomes Chrish or Christ, which in its turn is Crist or Krish or Krs, both or all of them meaning Apex or Summit or Pinnacle. A sizeable proportion of the world's people live in India, and the majority of them are of the Hindu faith. Before we arrogantly presume to be the entire and only group of The Faithful, we should consider whether the World Teacher would refuse to recognize these others based on such a quibble as the slight difference in spelling of the Romanization then Anglicization of the Sanskrit word.

The Christ has been for two thousand years:

> *'the supreme Head of the Church Invisible, the spiritual Hierarchy,* **com-**
> **posed of disciples of all faiths** *[my emphasis].*

> *He recognizes and loves those who are not Christian but who retain their al-*
> *legiance to their Founders-the Buddha, Mohammed, and others. He cares not*
> *what the faith is, if the objective is love of God and of humanity. If men look*
> *for the Christ Who left His disciples centuries ago they will fail to recognize*
> *the Christ Who is in process of returning. The Christ has no religious barri-*
> *ers in His consciousness. It matters not to Him of what faith a man may call*
> *himself* (Bailey 1957, ref. ed. 1972, p. 612).

If this sounds as though it might be *preferable* to be a Christian, it
should be remembered that the Tibetan himself, who among his
many duties, earlier presided over a Buddhist lamasery, is not a
'Christian'. Christians already understand, as they always have, that
the Messiah of the Judaic faith is the Christ. It is the reverse of this
which is problematic: Although the underlying concept – of Messiah
and Christ, is the same, the Jews contend that Jesus of Nazareth was
not He, not the Messiah or the Christ. It is worth remembering that
the first Christians were Jews, and saw themselves, not as a separate
faith at all, but as standing at the head of, and within the long and
venerable tradition of Judaism. The continued inclusion of the Old
Testament in the Christian Bible is evidence of this fact. Early
Christians were the New Believers of Judaism, while those who
didn't recognize the Christ were the Old Believers.

In Islam, Jesus (Isa) is not the Only Son of God as in Christianity, but one of God's messengers, along with Abraham and Moses.
Jesus will return to earth at the end-time and kill the Antichrist, says
the Koran. Mohammed is first among the messengers, of course. So,
in Islam, Jesus of Nazareth was not the only messenger of God, or
elect son of God, sent to humanity.

Peter's answer to Jesus' question: *'But whom say ye that I am?'* has
long provided some sort of scriptural authority for the idea of Christ
as the only Son of God. Peter replies *'Thou art the Christ, the Son of the*
Living God' (Matt: xvi, 13-16). Dion Fortune comments on the distortion of the original teachings in the present-day religions:

> *In the mouth of Peter, and the thought of Jesus, these words have not the sig-*
> *nification the Church at a later date wished to give them: "Thou art the elect*
> *of Israel announced by the prophets". In the Hindoo, the Egyptian, and the*
> *Greek initiations, the term 'Son of God' signified "a consciousness identified*
> *with divine truth, a will capable of manifesting it." According to the proph-*
> *ets, this Messiah must be the greatest of these manifestations. He would be*
> *the Son of Man, i.e. the Elect of earthly humanity, the Son of God, i.e. the*
> *Envoy of heavenly Humanity, and as such, having in himself the Father or*
> *Spirit, who, by Humanity, reigns over the universe (Fortune n.d., p. 36).*

This is illumined by recalling the true meaning of the ancient Biblical phrase; the *Sons of God come in to the (sons and) daughters of Men*; that is, the creations of the spirit incarnating in the progeny of earthly, material origin.

Much of the conflict between faiths is due to the priests and theologians of every faith attempting to place a monopoly on the way to grace. The truth, the vision, is also as D.K. says, obscured by the *dogmas of every religion* built up over time and in response particularly to the culture and the worldview, and the perceived needs of those in power in church or mosque or synagogue or temple, and in the state. Examples of this distressing, but fairly inevitable development or corruption of the original vision and message abound in every religion. One is the anathematization of the idea of reincarnation in Biblical scholarship and the writings of the Church Fathers, 'arranged' by the Emperor Justinian, via an altogether too compliant priesthood, in the 6th Century C.E for political as much as theological reasons.

'*Pope Vigilius had been summoned by the Emperor, but he opposed the council and took refuge in a church in Constantinople*', notes I.M. Oderburg, in Reincarnation as taught by the Early Christians (1973). It was Justinian who closed the last of the great classical Greek academies in 529; the Platonic academy in Athens. Plato (c. 427-347 BCE) was by no means the first to teach the doctrine of reincarnation: it was generally accepted, though not universal, in the ancient and classical worlds.

Women in Islam, the veil, the West and 'Jihad Sheilas'

Another example of corruption of the original message is the 'burying' of the equality of men and women clearly present in original Islam, and the insistence, in parts of Islam, on outdated and extreme versions of Shariah, the religious Law, the breaking of which is met with death or harsh punishment. In Afghanistan, the Taliban showed the world just what a fundamentalist Islamic theocracy would look like. It is a bitter understatement to say that under their regime, women were not treated with the equality accorded them by the Prophet. We should remember that they were savagely beaten for 'crimes' such as showing too much face or ankle, and executed for getting educated or continuing to work out of home, even when male breadwinners were absent or dead, and they and the children were starving.

This brutal reduction of women to the status of enslaved chattels is nowhere sanctioned by the teachings of the Prophet Mohammed. It is distressing, yet instructive of *the true origins of this supposed divine command*, to hear from the women of Afghanistan via RAWA (Revolutionary association of Women of Afghanistan) that the status of women has scarcely improved despite the end of the theocracy. Rapes and murders still continue, young girls are still being killed because they dare to go to school to get an education; women all over the country still prefer imprisonment within their burkhas to the dangers of dispensing with them and drawing attention to the fact of their existence and their sexuality.

Groups of Islamic women in many countries are studying the sacred texts, and, with the knowledge gained, challenging male domination and authority in home and mosque and community. These women are able to demonstrate in many instances that such domination does not derive from the sacred writings ('Jihad Sheilas', *Compass*, ABC 1, February 2008). Compass is ABC1 TV's religious affairs programme,

Despite the restrictions of Islam upon them, the last thing the women of Islam want or need, is to be 'liberated' into the Great American Way, with (among many other abuses of dignity, privacy and sanity) its pressure on girls and women to look and act like Madonna or Paris Hilton. Many Muslim women are wearing the veil and long dress or coat because they themselves have chosen it for the dignity and freedom it offers, unknown to Western women who face a lifelong battle to keep face and body youthful, beautiful and above all, sexy. It is an important assertion of identity when used in this way, and not as a result of cultural pressure or fear of persecution:

> *Western observers were particularly dismayed by the spectacle of women returning to the veil, which they had seen as a symbol of Islamic backwardness and patriarchy...But it was not experienced in this way by those Muslim women who voluntarily assumed Islamic dress for practical reasons and also as a way of casting off an alien Western identity. Donning a veil, a scarf and a long dress could be a symbol of that "return to the self" which Islamists were attempting with such difficulty in the postcolonial period...The veiled woman has, over the years, become a symbol of Islamic self-assertion and a rejection of Western cultural hegemony... Where Western men and women...cling to this life by making their bodies impervious to the process of time and ageing, the veiled Islamic body tacitly declares that it is under divine orders and oriented not towards this world but to transcendence...'* (Armstrong © 2000, p. 295).

By contrast, there are the 'headscarf police'; the Islamic peer groups who nag and bully schoolgirls and women generally, into wearing the hijab; something more a matter of personal choice here in Australia until after 9/11. And there are the 'Jihad Sheilas', the title of the documentary aired on ABC1, in February 2008, which caused a storm. These are Anglo-Australian women, born and bred in parochial country towns, and drawn to Islam and to Muslim men by their exotic strangeness; their utter opposition to everything these girls (as they then were) had ever known. Conversion, and Muslim marriages, (five to date in the case of one of the women) have taken these Australian born-and-bred women into a fundamentalism deeply censorious of, and possibly actively hostile to, Australian culture and institutions; hence 'Jihad Sheilas'. *Their* wearing of Islamic dress- some in the burkha (I'd rather be hot and uncomfortable now than break God's commandment and end up in Hell, said one) feels to Australians, like an affront, an assault even on the Aussie way of life. Should it?

When Western colonialism bled the Middle Eastern lands dry of every resource, and failed them everywhere from Egypt to Iran (leaving them more deeply impoverished and alienated from the small but wealthy Westernised elite, and feeling like strangers in their own land), when Russian Communism also failed in Egypt and Afghanistan, when Westernisation by their own governments also failed, what was there to do but turn to their own traditions for confirmation of self and culture, and a viable cultural alternative to Americanisation? The West has failed the Middle East, and fails it again if we don't understand why Islam regards democracy, George Bush style, with suspicion as yet another imperialistic imposition, and why America, Israel, and the West are so unpopular. Karen Armstrong's wonderful book, already a classic in its field, makes all this abundantly clear, in the process of examining the histories of Christian, Jewish and Muslim fundamentalism.

Religious war to destroy humanity?

Poverty has been blamed for Muslim youths in their thousands taking up the call to Jihad against the West and Israel. Poverty is neither necessary nor sufficient to explain Islamist terrorism, but it certainly helps. Imprisonment within what have become ghetto states in Palestine, combined with impoverishment and hopelessness, might be sufficient to turn many Western youths into bitter enemies of their oppressors. Joining the Cause is an alternative to the despair and hopelessness about the future, which has prompted so many youths, boys especially, to suicide. Under different circumstances they may, as a minority of Muslim youths sadly do, find fulfillment in offering those lives to Allah as human bombs in jihad against the Infidel West.

There is a chilling warning delivered by the Tibetan, that if we fail to reach a loving understanding which eliminates mutual antagonisms, *'humanity is headed towards a religious war which will make the past war* [World War Two] *appear like child's play; antagonisms and hatreds will embroil entire populations and the politicians of all the nations will take full advantage of the situation to precipitate a war which may well prove the end of humanity. There are no hatreds so great or so deep as those fostered by religion'* (Bailey 1957, ref. ed. 1972, p. 545-6).

This was written in 1948, when the 'past war' was only just over, and could not have been imagined by anyone on earth as 'child's play' by comparison with a war to come. And who apart from D.K. and his superiors would then have seen a worldwide war of religion as anything but the nonsense of medieval crusaders?

The two commentators, Armstrong and Kohn, have different views as to the origin of Islamist terrorism. Kohn points to the continued oppression of their populations by Middle Eastern governments, and to the intense hatred in Islam for America, Britain and everything Jewish fuelled by what amounts to paranoid propaganda. The Protocols of the Elders of Zion, *'the nineteenth-century Tsarist Russian forgery written to incite pogroms against the Jews'*, was published as the record of a Jewish cabal plotting to take over the world. It is widely disseminated and believed in the Muslim world, says Kohn (2003, p. 186). The previously Christian myth that Jewish clerics shed Christian blood to make the special cakes of the feast of Purim is also widely seen as truth not fiction in the Middle East, where it has become Arab blood which is used. Was its original dissemination as mischievous as the use later made of the four cartoons depicting the Prophet Mohammed published in a right-wing Danish newspaper in 2006? These cartoons, inoffensive except that they dared to picture Mohammed, which is forbidden, received malicious additions before being published and disseminated in Islam. It was a deliberate attempt to incite rage and hatred of the West, and led to rioting crowds committing arson and homicide.

Kohn also points to the complete lack of a discipline of self-criticism in Islam. Karen Armstrong gives a much more sympathetic assessment, and she also teases out the tragic history which has made this almost inevitable. Or has it? Her history implicates the West heavily in the practice of veiling the women of Islam, and in the lack of educated and critical opinion in many Islamic societies to counterbalance paranoia and fanaticism, and to promote the lively exchange of differing views, which is at the heart of a free and democratic society.

Dynamic Creation and the Chain; God to Humanity via all servers of humanity, (the New Group of World Servers)

Jung states a radical truth about the incarnation of the One Self:

> *Although the divine incarnation is a cosmic and absolute event, it only manifests empirically in those relatively few individuals capable of enough consciousness to make ethical decisions, i.e. to decide for the Good. Therefore God can be called good only as much as He is able to manifest His goodness in individuals. His moral quality depends upon individuals. That is why He incarnates. Individualisation and individual existence are indispensable for the transformation of God the Creator* (Moacanin 1986, p. 90).

Those generous and courageous humans attempting to do something practical to help, with this or any other of the conflicts and problems creating crisis for humanity, mostly have no idea that they belong to a subjective worldwide group, which is part of the great Chain of Being. But how does it work? How does the connection from God to humanity actually take place? It is not just a structure, but an active, dynamic entity, through which evolution itself proceeds, via the divine energies and activity being steadily stepped down, as is explained here. The connection between the Plan in Shamballa, and its implementation by humanity takes place via the emerging group D.K. has termed the *New Group of World Servers*.

This group was gathered 'out of the many groups', beginning in the earlier 20th century. It is the link in the Great Chain of Being, which connects the Hierarchy to humanity:

> *Its members are all in physical bodies but must work entirely subjectively, thus utilizing the inner sensitive apparatus and the intuition. It is to be composed of men and women of all nations and ages, but each one must be spiritually oriented, all must be conscious servers, all must be mentally polarized and alert, and all must be inclusive...*

> *It is a group that has no exoteric organization of any kind ... It is a band of obedient workers and servers of the WORD, obedient to their own souls and to group need. All true servers everywhere therefore belong to this group, whether their line of service is cultural, political, scientific, religious, philosophical, psychological or financial. They constitute part of the inner group of workers for humanity,... whether they know it or not (my emphasis)...*

> *This group gives the word 'spiritual' a wide significance; they believe it to mean an inclusive endeavour towards human betterment, uplift and understanding, they give it the connotation of tolerance, international synthetic communion, religious inclusiveness, and all trends of thought which concern the esoteric development of the human being* (Bailey 1934, ref.ed.1979, pp. 413-5).

The members of this group, according to the Tibetan, adhere to every creed and to none. They may recognize some Supreme Being or God, or not, they may think of themselves as spiritually oriented or not, they may know themselves consciously to be members of the group called by the Hierarchy, the New Group of World Servers, or they may, as is usually the case at present, never have heard of the NGWS, nor of the Hierarchy.

This was at the time of its announcement, and is now still, a revolutionary idea! Many awaiting the return of the Christ would be surprised to discover that the Fishers of Men as Christ called them, the group gathered round the World Teacher to do His work will not be of their particular creed and theirs only. They will be shocked to discover that some of the Elect will have no religious faith whatever, and may even call themselves agnostics or atheists. It may come as a further surprise (as the entire notion did to me originally) that essentially, the members of this group elect themselves:

> *They are being gathered out of every nation, but are gathered and chosen, not by the watching Hierarchy or by any Master, but by the power of their response to the spiritual opportunity, tide and note... through the very selflessness of their service... Their characteristics are synthesis, inclusiveness, intellectuality and fine mental development...They have no barriers set up around themselves, but are governed by a wide tolerance, and a sane mentality and sense of proportion* (Bailey 1934, ref.ed.1979, p. 400).

Emergence of the New Group of World Servers

Thirty years ago, when I first heard of the New Group of World Servers and the Hierarchy, it all seemed impossibly theoretical and far-fetched. In the meantime, it has become sufficiently factual to be a part of my lived experience. I can look back now and trace the emergence of this group over the decades since the 'sixties and the appearance of mass civil rights protest movements against the Vietnam war, the segregation of black Americans and Australians, nuclear weapons and militaristic solutions. These popular movements threw a searing light on the oppression of the powerless by the powerful in government or big business, and the materialistic agenda of conservative governments, which were destroying the environment and communities and futures everywhere. These modern movements are far less driven from the top by a leader, as in the past; they are a great groundswell of protest such as broke out all over the world quite spontaneously, with very little organisation, in March 2003, when U.S. President George Bush and U.K. Prime Minister Tony Blair, backed by others notably Australia's P.M. John

Howard, decided to invade Iraq because Saddam Hussein had weapons of mass destruction, which it turned out, he didn't any longer. (Saddam concealed this as long as possible from the enemies of the Iraqi dictator and his state-Iran especially; it should be no shame to have believed, as an ordinary citizen, that there were WMD hidden in Iraq).

These movements are no longer simply revolts by the oppressed against the oppressors; they are as often action by those who seek to redress the wrongs done to other, powerless groups in the society, and who seek justice, peace, freedom and rights for all of humanity. All over the planet, we gather in groups to work together on achieving some aspect of this vision, thinking globally, acting locally. It may be work for refugees or third-world farmers, indigenous people or street kids or those orphaned by war or AIDS, endangered animals or work to raise the political consciousness of a state or a nation. It should be work to rescue our living environment, and the other life in the planet, from imminent destruction.

Whatever the work, what a joy it is to recognize one's own tribe, and to become aware of being a part of that tribe with a unique contribution to make, yet sharing the journey and the work with mates! Perhaps the easiest way to identify the nature of the Group is through a concrete experience of it – my own, necessarily. At a recent conference on reconciliation, multiculturalism, immigration and human rights, I became more aware of the breadth of the vision and inclusiveness of the agenda of this worldwide group, of its achievements and the spread of its membership and influence that had happened in the half-century since it was little more than an idea. All this, and the almost startling recognition of my membership of this group and the effect of being 'us', not just 'me' was a cause of excitement as well as the joy I've mentioned.

This conference was organised by the founder of Common Ground, my publisher, Bill Cope, with partner, Mary Kalantzis. CG creates conferences and knowledge communities that are worldwide-in their addressing of major issues for humanity, their venues, and their participation; education conferences in Beijing, for example.

Other examples of world service groups are Oxfam and Avaaz, operating supranationally, rallying activities and funds against world poverty, war, injustice and environmental destruction.

Other, co-operating groups work consciously with a spirituality that includes all our traditions-and goes beyond, urging us to become agents of human and planetary evolution. These include Andrew Cohen's EnlightenNext, Claire Zammit's Feminine Power

/Evolutionary Women, and Craig Hamilton's Integral Enlightenment, along with the Lucis Trust's World Goodwill meditation and service organisation.

The group of world servers and the 'radiant Rainbow Bridge'

It strikes me that these are indeed 'intimations of immortality'. At these moments, we seem to be tugged by recollections of the love and joy that are the natural atmosphere of soul life. These are above all, soul qualities, soul capacities and feelings. This group experience is an experience of the world of the soul and of its essential nature. It is not possible to be a member of such a group, and experience that love and joy in being together and sharing, unless you already have some degree of 'soul infusion'. The Tibetan uses this phrase in the following extract, which discusses the way in which the soul world is being increasingly connected to the place of embodied human living by this work we are doing as a worldwide group. It is said to be part of the preparation for that impossible, millennial, mythical Second Coming, which becomes a great deal more rational once we understand that we are not the only ones around, and we cease to think of the universe as an accidental creation of matter, and the material level as the only 'real' one, from which all others are derived:

> *All soul-infused personalities are creating the human antahkarana* [bridge between personality and higher self]... *In the beautiful Eastern symbology, 'The Bridge of Sighs' which links the animal world with the human world, and leads all men into the vale of tears, of woe, of discipline and of loneliness, is rapidly being replaced by the radiant Rainbow Bridge (antahkarana), constructed by the sons of men who seek pure light. They pass across the bridge into the Light serene which there awaits them, and bring the radiant light down to the world of men, revealing the new kingdom of the soul; souls disappear, and only the soul is seen'.*

> *Then follows that stupendous event for which all soul-infused persons prepare: the externalization of the Hierarchy and the reappearance of the Master of that Hierarchy, with the Personnel of which it is composed; this group of liberated and functioning souls will appear on earth as part of the manifested phenomena of the outer plane...*

> *The Masters (in this long interim) have not come forth to contact humanity on any large or group scale; many of Their senior disciples have, however, emerged at varying intervals and when needed; The World Teacher has also come forth to sound the key or note for each new civilisation. Men have had, therefore, to find their way alone to the Hierarchy; in silence that Hierarchy has waited, until the number of 'enlightened souls' was so great that their invocative appeal... could not be denied. (T)he balance of equilibrium, attained*

between the Kingdom of God on Earth and the Kingdom of God in Heaven (to use Christian phraseology) became such that the "Gates of Return" could be opened and free intercourse established between the fourth and the fifth kingdoms in nature. The gates (and I am still speaking in symbols) are already opening and soon will stand wide open to admit the passing of the "Son of Man, the perfected Son of God" back to the place-our Earth-where He earlier demonstrated perfect love and service (Bailey 1955, ref. ed. 1979, p. 408-9).

The Christian Church has taught that the Second Coming will be, not the ushering in of the New Age, but the end of all ages, culminating in the Resurrection of all the bodies out of all the graves (to me that is grotesque as well as ridiculous; no wonder modern minds rebel!) in concert with the Last Judgment of God on the one life of each corpse and everyone living on earth, before we are assigned to Heaven or consigned to Hell for all eternity. D.K. sets the record straight : *'(T)he circumstances of His return are only symbolically related in the world Scriptures'*. The Tibetan uses the plural 'Scriptures' here; he is not just referring to the Bible. Recognition of this symbolic not literal, statement about the return of the World Teacher *'may produce a vital change in the preconceived ideas of humanity'* (Bailey 1957, ref. ed. 1972, p. 611). Another world scripture, the Hindu Bhagavad Gita says of the return:

Whenever there is a withering of the law and an uprising of lawlessness on all sides, then I manifest Myself. / For the salvation of the righteous and the destruction of such as do evil, for the firm establishing of the Law, I come to birth age after age.' Book IV, Sutra 7, 8.

The ordinary Christian can be expected to reject these ideas about the Christ presented by the perennial philosophy, says D.K; while the intelligent will increasingly refuse *'the impossible Deity and the feeble Christ'*, known to historical Christianity. The intelligent public will accept the reality, a present and living Christ:

Who is known to those who follow Him, Who is a strong and able executive, and not a sweet and sentimental sufferer, Who has never left us but has worked for two thousand years through the medium of His disciples, the inspired men and women of all faiths [and of none, as earlier stated]; *Who has no use for fanaticism or hysterical devotion, but Who loves all men persistently, intelligently and optimistically, Who sees divinity in them all, and Who comprehends the techniques of the evolutionary development of the human consciousness...*

They [the New Group of World Servers, his disciples] *will prepare and work for conditions in the world in which Christ can move freely among men, in bodily Presence; He need not then remain in His present retreat in Central Asia.*

In case this still sounds as though the Second Coming might be an event recognized only by a few mystics, here is the Tibetan next writing in very concrete terms about it:

> *His reappearance and His consequent work cannot be confined to one small locality or domain unheard of by the great majority, as was the case when He was here before. The radio, the press and the dissemination of news will make His coming different to that of any previous Messenger; the swift modes of transportation will make Him available to countless millions, and by boat, rail and plane they can reach Him: through television, His face can be made familiar to all, and verily "every eye shall see Him." Even if there is no general recognition of His spiritual status and His message, there must necessarily be an universal interest...This creates an unique condition in which to work, and one which no salvaging, energizing Son of God has ever before had to face'* (Bailey 1948, ref. ed. 1984, p. 16).

What would happen if we heard, for the first time, the message of the World Teacher through all our religious traditions down the ages? Would it 'sink in' and make a difference if we heard it directly from Him, and could have no doubt about its origin? If we all began to live with a new recognition that we are after all, people of the One Life, the One God?

The next and final chapter casts light on the idea of soulmates, from Plato to the present, and on dealing with the grief of separation in death, through understanding that no real separation takes place. When it becomes clear that death does not exist except for the physical body, it must radically change our thinking about separation from those we love, and consequently our whole outlook on life.

Chapter 14
Soulmates

Just a Myth?

Summary Points

- Dream encounters with the Higher Self
- The idea of soulmates in Plato
- **Marriage in the Heavens or marriage made in Heaven?**
- Soul love and group love
- The experience of soulmates in Newton and Whitton -- close relationships of several kinds
- **Are soulmate relationships always harmonious?**
- Spiritual recognition class in Newton
- Love at first sight?
- **The soul bond; foundation of our main earthly relationships**
- More than one primary soulmate? Whitton's discoveries
- **Death of a partner is not the end of the relationship**
- Dealing with grief
- Conscious shifting to the astral plane in sleep; Richelieu's experience
- 'The peace that passeth understanding', when separate loves and group love become the One Love

- Funerals and the elimination of death from the consciousness of humanity

Prelude

At Antares Bay, in the cottage. I wake from a dream of an unknown man, the perfect Lover, full of an unearthly joy. It's such a long time-years, usually, between sightings of Eros-Agape, the mating principle of spirit as well as flesh.

The place of the dream is gilded by midsummer light, and so warm! I return to a chilled, ice-rimed world-the lake, the sky, all the terrain between, one frosted layer of shadow blue which must crack through to the substance. The golden cypress, dawn-lit, is the one solid nameable object; where yesterday were trees, little holiday places, the jetty and its boats, the scene is erased, substance and shadow are so mingled and confused.

I wake quite alone, yet without any sense of need, in the silence of this place which is almost mine. I feel warm all through, exultant, wanting to laugh or sing about it, lying still curled round the feeling of this man's extravagant, uncounted loved for me, his delight in me. Marco had walked round the rock shelving on the little beach under the cliff. He found us there on that zenith summer day, our feet in the heaven-reflecting water, both naked, and this young, young man with his soft ashen curls and milky skin, cuddling me from behind. I can't say that he was a beautiful youth-he was, but that would make him an object of my gaze, and he was somehow invincible Subject.

I wonder at the feeling of him, it was so acute-the hardness of pectoral muscle, the softness of genitals, and the encompassing, protective spirit of his love. The presence with which he graced the day itself was so careless and debonair, so light of heart and spirit, that his name might have been Bliss.

How hard it seems to tell ourselves the truth; that the way has been long and difficult, arduous effort and pain and a cramped, partial existence at best, in the search for completion. Even to see it in those terms -- as a way between places, is the experience of arrival; its sudden awareness that this was a journey after all, and here the point at its end that had always been the destination. Until then, there is nothing; stasis, tedium, immobility are words spoken from the journey's end, and there is no journey, no word: There is only present horror-the eternal unchangeable fact of the way things are.

So much of the diary is loaded with, saturated with, this pain and distress. But it is a record of what might well be regarded in the future as life in the Dark Age...at a time when love, the necessary essence, was so rare that we were all obsessed with it, crazy for it like junkies desperate for a fix. Though how could we crave what we had never known – a love which may

be nowhere available? So the diary, I see now, is a traveller's log...of a jour-
ney in search of a state known at the beginning, only in dreams...'

Or in the taste of the Eternal. The One Love, savoured in meditation; elusive, not to be pursued, lasting only as long as the supreme
effort of attention which permits access to it. Or descending as an
inexplicable Grace, the answer to a tortured soul's cry from the
abyss; a sweet, soaking rain onto long barren earth.

The completion we crave in union with the One

Journey's end, I knew, twenty-five years ago when I wrote this diary
entry into an abandoned novel, was the embrace of the Perfect
Lover. This was the one mystics yearn towards, the Christ – all the
spiritual and the erotic elements gathered, then dissolved utterly into completion; into union with the One Love. I knew that this was
what I hungered for, longed for: the consummation of all striving
and effort, the end and justification of all suffering.

I am including another dream-encounter with the Higher Self.
Although these are my dreams, they are not particularly personal; we
are not suddenly switching into biographical mode. The hope is that
the lyrical writing of this first one especially, and the content, will
strike a chord with my readers, and arouse recognition of similar encounters. The dreams also help to illustrate and elucidate the connection between the personality and the archetypal Self, the kris,
the apex or Christ.

I awoke this morning still wrapped in the embrace of another of these
rare dream lovers. He was Jacqui's son, Stephen Chris, a decade or so young-
er, another Jungian Young Man of the Spirit, though older than Edward of
Antares Bay. [My friend Jacqui did indeed have a son Chris, who was
at the time, a shortish, chubby, sandy-haired boy. The dream does
not refer to this child, but uses his name only, and his relationship
with his mother and younger brother Nicky.]

He was immensely, somehow eternally, tall and omnipresent in himself,
though in his manifestation merely a very tall, well-built young man, won-
derfully but not gorgeously handsome, with ash-blond hair again, but
straight this time, worn quite long, and blue-grey eyes. Yet his physical char-
acteristics were never particularly obvious or even very clear – it was his
presence that was so dominant. He was remarkably strong, matter-of-fact
and practical, unlike the sensuous young man of Antares Bay, who was there
because he just was, as an echo of the I Am of Divinity, and to simply,
lazily, laughingly but truly, love me, and make me understand how

beautiful I am - as is every one of us, if only we could see it; to celebrate our eternal youth and beauty and the fact of this incredible love.

Chris was striding across the sports oval towards the gate at Greenhills School, out of context there, but come to pick up his younger brother, Nicky. I had no expectation that he would even notice me, though I realized that I'd loved him since always. In a movement of instant recognition, he came through the groups of parents and the kids pouring out of the school doors, straight towards me, as if there was no-one else present. He took my hands and smoothed my hair back from my cheek, and we moved together into a kiss, a searching, profound communion. It was a moment of repletion of love, not of the cravings of passion; we supped together from the chalice of Love. Then he disappeared, back to the task of looking after the children, including one injured and another disabled, in his resolute and practical way – but not as if it were his domain or role, but because he had the strength and took responsibility, despite having Manly things to do. He sorted out a fight between an older boy and Nicky, then he carried the injured older boy into the pickup truck to join Nicky and a disabled boy and me. Jacqui began driving to the hospital. I thought he had forgotten all about me, permanently, since there seemed no room for such a passion in his life or indeed, his person. His arm lay oblivious, along the top of the bench seat behind me. Jacqui took a sharp corner and we all slid towards her. Chris's arm came automatically out and around me, protectively, but still unconscious, I thought. But as we straightened out, he turned to me, bent towards me and kissed me, all of himself in the gift and the taking, and we sucked at each other like bees at honeysuckle nectar.

The following day I note that the one element which keeps appearing is his hair – its length and cut and fair sheen, and the way it floats, detachedly, into my inner sight. It is like a young knight's or page's, yet it keeps disturbing me with its femininity. There is something else here I haven't understood. There is nothing feminine, in the ordinary sense, about him. He is not actually a male human being. Nor is he a female human being. He is simply a Man.

As I reflect on what I already knew at the time of the diary entry, and the knowledge still to come, it became clear that there were bits missing – Chris and Christ were not perfectly identified yet: I turned from earthly loves to the heavenly one, seeing one as profane, the other as sacred. Yet weren't both Chris and Edward, as Jung has taught us about beautiful young men in dreams, just representations of my own Spirit?

How is it that we can 'crave what we have never known' as I wrote in the Antares passage? Perhaps we had known this kind of undying love after all... Could it be that the lovely myths of soulmates and heavenly marriages were the permanent substance of truth underlying our craving? I kept coming across strands and permutations of this idea in books and conversations and oral teachings-the idea that for each one of us there was someone, somewhere in the world, who was the one and only mate for us. There was a perfectly matching man for me, perfect because we were essentially one unit before time began. Or there was a twin soul who was also my true love, the one for whom I would yearn, and wait, and search until he was found. Or there was my ideal mate and partner who was the missing male part of me, as I was the missing female part of him.

The idea of soulmates in Plato

This idea has been strengthened in Western consciousness through a version of it in one of Plato's philosophical dialogues. The playwright Aristophanes sets it forth as his idea of love in Plato's *Symposium*, which harks back to the banquet held by Socrates in Athens in 416 B.C. He regales the diners with a myth that attempts to explain why we long for each other: the gods split each of us from our other half as punishment.

Aristophanes says:

> 'And when one of them meets with his other half, the actual half of himself,
> whether he be a lover of youth or a lover of another sort, the pair are lost in
> an amazement of love and friendship and intimacy, and one will not be out
> of the other's sight, as I may say, even for a moment: these are the people who
> pass their whole lives together; yet they could not explain what they desire of
> one another. For the intense yearning which each has towards the other does
> not appear to be the desire of lover's intercourse, but of something else which
> the soul of either evidently desires and cannot tell, and of which she has only
> a dark and doubtful presentiment' (Plato 1942, p.181).

I dallied with these charming and comforting ideas, while on the rational level I regretfully came to the conclusion that there was no such thing. There couldn't be a male-female partnering on the soul level, because there was no masculinity or femininity, no sexual difference, beyond the physical level. Yet didn't it come to the same thing -- Jungian Other or Soulmate, I pondered? No, at least for the very long, aeonial present. The idea of true marriage as with the soul -- my own soul and therefore more of the same, was boring to me; I was filled with excitement only at the prospect of 'marriage' with a separate soul. Though in the end, there is no difference -- all loves are resolved in the One Love.

Soul love and group love

There was a teacher who insisted to a group of us who were in our teens and twenties, and going through the ecstasies and agonies of the search and the finding and losing -- *'All earthly loves between the sexes pale into insignificance beside the* **true** *love. Just wait till you have a taste of it in meditation! Once you meet your Divine Self, all the heartaches and cravings for 'him' or 'her' just disappear. Your whole perspective on love and sex and marriage changes dramatically.'* This was an American touring Australia in the seventies with her own interpretation of the Tibetan's teachings; the Reverend Alma Brown.

Later I came across The Tibetan's words regarding the post-death experience on the astral level:

> *'May I again remind you that there is now no physical brain to respond to impacts generated by the inner man, and also that sex, as it is physically understood, is nonexistent. Spiritualists would do well to remember this and so grasp the foolishness as well as the impossibility of those spiritual marriages, which certain schools of thought in the movement teach and practice. The man, in his astral body, is now free from the strictly animal impulses which, upon the physical plane, are both normal and right, but which now have no meaning to him in his kamic (ie astral or emotional) body'* (Bailey 1985, p. 40).

Of course this is even more the case beyond the astral level, when the desire body has been shed, and we are functioning in the mental body, or have shed that also, and are merged into the soul. And once these 'strictly animal' impulses are gone, the focus turns in a truer, purer way to the soul relationship between us.

I knew from D.K.'s writings through Alice Bailey that on the soul level, it is the group that matters, not the individual. The Mantram of the Soul was something I'd been saying for years: *I am one with my group brothers, and all that I have is theirs. May the love which is in my soul pour forth to them. May the strength which is in me lift and aid them. May the thoughts which my soul creates, reach and encourage them.* The group I mentioned above, which I'd instigated, (or did it take place by spontaneous combustion?) gave me a profound experience of belonging to 'us' not just 'me'. The moments when we were bonded into a single entity by genuine love of each other, were sublime; they remain among the high points of my life and the lives of those who were part of the Group. These moments were sparked and underpinned by deliberately constructed ceremony with meditation at its heart.

The significance of this has only slowly become evident to me, and that is partly through Newton's work, again. Soul love and group love were then an unreachable ideal, a concept without wings, which often found itself in the same nest as other spiritual ideals such as universal love, compassion and charity to all including those who have harmed me–or on a global level, harmed groups of innocent people. (I'm thinking here of Hitler, Pol Pot, Saddam, Mugabe and the rest). Absolute harmlessness in thought and word and deed, and the complete forgetting of self in the service of others are hard ideals.

So, although the group was paramount in importance, and although I knew we returned again and again with that group to play many roles, have many experiences and learn many lessons, I saw souls as so detached from ourselves here on earth that love between a man and a woman had no basis or echo in the world of souls.

There are no soul marriages because the soul knows no sex. That must mean, I thought, that all sexual loves and partnerships are temporary; limited to the span of a single lifetime. The love between a woman and a man became just another delusion of the physical and temporary self, another aspect of the Great Illusion, untrue in the larger scheme, and unworthy of any real attention. I had to cease thinking of people as men or women, and see them instead as souls manifesting just for now, in bodies of one sex or another. While this was true in the larger perspective, I think now that the pendulum had swung too far in the opposite direction, taking with it much of the joy and savour of earthly relationships.

The experience of soulmates in Newton and Whitton -- close relationships of several kinds

The corrective view didn't arrive until I read Newton's *Journey of Souls*, and even then, I needed to encounter Newton writing on the subject of soulmates in *Destiny of Souls* to fully comprehend it. Important additional understanding came from Joel Whitton's research into the roles and relationships of souls through several lifetimes, in *Life Between Life*.

I hope the following selection from *Journey of Souls* (1994) gives you as much of a thrill, and as much comfort, as it did me. All quotes from that book in the following section are taken from Chapter Fourteen, *'Preparation for Embarkation'*, (pp. 249-62). Life is like a stage play in which we always have the lead role, says Newton. Our soulmates are our supporting cast, as we ourselves are the cast of the

stage play of any other soulmate playing the lead in their own production. But how will we be able to recognise them on earth?

Newton's subjects tell him that that an essential aspect of preparation for the new incarnation, is something they refer to as Recognition class. But whom do we need to recognise? 'Soul\mates' is
the answer. These are not just our 'nearest and dearest', husbands,
wives or partners. These close relationships come in several categories, Newton explains:

> First, there is the kind of relationship involving love which is so deep that
> both partners genuinely don't see how each could live without the other. This
> is a mental and physical attraction which is so strong neither partner doubts
> that they were meant for each other.

> Second, there are relationships based upon companionship, friendship and
> mutual respect.

> There is a third category, of more passing acquaintance, but all of
> these are 'designated companions to help you and themselves accomplish mu-
> tual goals...In terms of friends and lovers, identity recognition of kindred
> spirits comes from our highest consciousness. It is a wonderful and mysterious
> experience, both physically and mentally.'

So, here was the revelation that main roles and relationships, especially in this context, our love and marriage partnerships, are therefore sanctioned by our higher selves (at least when we get it right
and choose according to soul plans) and not something to cause us
to feel guilt, nor something to be automatically renounced for
'higher things'.

Are soulmate relationships always harmonious?

Newton comments on the assumption that since our relationships
are 'designated', they must be harmonious:

> ...I have had clients come to me with the assumption that they are probably
> not with a soulmate because of so much turmoil and heartbreak in their mar-
> riages and relationships. They fail to realize that karmic lessons set difficult
> standards for each of us and painful experiences involving the heart are de-
> liberate tests in life. They are often of the hardest kind.

Just because things aren't perfect, doesn't mean there's no such
thing as a soulmate. Nor is it an indication that we have messed
things up and missed our soulmate.

I would now have other things to say about this. Hard tests such
as learning to live independently and survive alone (a lesson which
may involve separation by death), or karmic adjustments such as

suffering the rejection we earlier inflicted on our soulmate, (which may involve other forms of separation while both are still in physical bodies), make for turmoil and heartbreak. This doesn't mean that all deaths and divorces are 'intended', along with all unhappiness in relationships. There is also the simple, all-pervasive factor of descending into incarnation and taking on the human condition, and with it the trial and error that is an integral part of living and completely unavoidable. We will inevitably make many mistakes; we will inevitably do things less than perfectly –or we wouldn't be here on earth.

'All the world's a stage, and all the men and women merely players' (Shakespeare)

Newton uses the analogy of the scripting and performance of a theatre piece about the playing-out of our incarnate lives together: It is perfect, almost not an analogy, but just the correct description, until a certain point, where it breaks down and therefore becomes misleading. Script changes are the result of free will, he says. We immediately think of the producer, director and actors discussing and implementing changes which are intended to improve the play. However, it is not a play with all the lines studied and the ending already known to the actors who dramatize it for the benefit of the audience. The actors in this play, once incarnate, retain no memory of the intended ending: They've been set loose on the ensemble and the public with only some knowledge of the parts they are playing and an intuitive response to the major turning-points in the unfolding drama. Comedy, tragedy, farce or inspiring legend? Which will it be? They must ad-lib all the lines, and apart from major events, they must attempt to structure the play as they go. Script changes are not so much the result of free will consciously applied, implying that we know the lines but choose others; they are the result of having to improvise because we don't know the script, and thus lose touch with the intention of this play. (Then, of course, there are those who return to the physical world without a script, sometimes by choice, sometimes by chance.)

Is it closer, at this point, to a psychodrama, where the main issues to be worked on and the roles people will play are known, but where the outcome will be determined by the process? Perhaps it is like a major architectural project such as the Sydney Opera House or Melbourne's Federation Square, where all that exists is a blueprint on architect's paper, which must now be translated into concrete three-dimensional physical reality: The project's builder, the personality, must interpret the soul-architect's design and translate the mental diagram into the built environment.

Even when we make the best decisions and produce the best self we can for the present incarnation, we are still likely to experience something less than perfect harmony with our soulmates, because we are as yet our soul's partially completed project. The one constant consolation, regardless of how we handle our relationships on earth, how we deal with our karmic relations or make new karma, or how badly things turn out for the usual earthly and human reasons, is that *the true, indestructible, eternal relationship and its everlasting love are there,* waiting for our return at the end of a life, or our recognition right now.

It's all been prearranged, mate! Spiritual recognition class in Newton

Newton prompts our recognition of the truth of a vital first meeting (pages 250-51):

> *Is it coincidence, ESP, déjà vu, or synchronicity when the right time and place come together and you meet someone for the first time who will bring meaning into your life? Was there a fleeting forgotten memory-something familiar tugging at the back of your mind? I would ask the reader to sort through those memories involving a distinctive first encounter with someone important in the past... What did you feel at that moment?*

> *I hate to tamper with your fond recollections of a supposedly spontaneous past meeting, but such descriptions as chance, happenstance, or impulse aren't applicable to crucial contacts. This makes them no less romantic. In cases involving soulmates, I have heard many heartfelt accounts of close spiritual beings who journeyed across time and space to find each other as physical beings at a particular geographic spot on Earth at a certain moment.*

It is important to note that not everyone chooses to make a plan before incarnating: Some souls, some of them quite evolved, just decide to 'wing it' instead; they only begin with an overall intention as to what this life needs to achieve.

Newton then takes us to his interview with a subject who is describing Recognition Class. He asks if there will be special signs, or memory triggers, set up for this subject to recognize every member of the reincarnating group gathered for the class.

> *S: ...The signs are supposed to click in our memory right away and tell us, "Oh, good, you are here now...It is time to work on the next phase."*

We discover that his client has been given a sign that he must recognise as a seven-year-old. It's the silver pendent round the neck of a neighbour who teaches him about people and life.

Then quite thrillingly, Newton (p. 257) takes his client, and us as readers, to the moment of preparation in Recognition Class, for meeting the client's soulmate. He asks about the most important sign David must remember, which turns out to be the way his wife-to-be laughs:

S: When we meet, her laugh is going to... sound like tiny bells...chimes...I really can't describe it to you. Then, the scent of her perfume when we first dance...a familiar fragrance, her eyes...

Dr N: So, you are actually given more than one trigger sign for your soulmate?

S: Yes, I'm so dense I guess the prompters thought I needed more clues. I didn't want to make a mistake when I met the right person.

Dr N: What is supposed to trigger her recognition of you?

S: (grins) My big ears...stepping on her toes dancing...what we feel when we first hold each other (p. 255).

I love this! He's so lyrical about Melinda and so funny about himself; it's so *real*.

Newton comments on the importance of eyes, the 'windows to the soul: *No physical attribute has more impact when souls meet on Earth...*' However, all five senses may be *'used by spiritual prompters as recognition signals...'* (Newton 1994, p. 257).

This is wonderful enough, but Newton via his usual skilled and precise questioning, is about to take us to the moment of activation of these signals, to enlighten us as to *what happened* between David and Melinda when they actually met on earth for the first time.

S: ...My idea to go to the dance was sudden. I hate to dance because I'm so clumsy. I didn't know anybody in the town yet and felt stupid, but I was guided there.

Dr N: Had you and Melinda scripted the dance scene together during the spiritual prep-class?

S: Yes, we knew about it then and when I saw her at the dance, alarms went off. I did something very uncharacteristic of me...I cut in on the man she was dancing with. When I first held her, my legs were like rubber.

Dr N: And what else did you and Melinda feel at that moment?

S: As if we were in another world...there was this familiarity...it was so weird during that dance...a knowing without doubt that something important was unfolding...the guidance...the intent of our meeting...our hearts were racing...it was enchantment (Newton 1994, p. 259).

There is some discussion here about missed cues and false trails; what will happen if we miss the turnoff to our main destination. Dr Newton asks why David's former girlfriend Clair was in his life at all, if he was always meant to be with Melinda. David's answer is instructive; a life with Clair was a 'false trail', which he needed to be discriminating enough to avoid. Yet if he had taken that path, he would still have learned valuable lessons (p. 259).

Seriously, you couldn't make this stuff up! We judge the fictitious tale that attempts to reproduce reality (in order that we may take it seriously enough to engage with its world and its propositions) by standards of probability that turn out to be wide of the mark when the truth is discovered. Truth is stranger than fiction, we say, unaware till now that 'the truth'-what actually happens in the realm we experience as solid reality, is something which in many instances started out as a form of fiction - a deliberated and acted construct with all its theatrical parts workshopped by our souls beforehand and aiming to achieve a definite outcome.

Love at first sight? Michael Newton's own amazing story of being led to 'the woman in white'

But for an even more amazing tale of this stranger-than-fiction fictitious truth, nothing quite beats Newton's own experience of meeting his primary soulmate via three specific clues! I've marveled at it and pondered over it often since first reading it myself. The three clues are *not* the reason that this particular How We Met story takes the reader's prize. Newton recounts that he was so struck as a teenager by a Christmas advertisement in Look magazine that he never forgot the face or name of 'Peggy' the beautiful dark-haired woman holding a Hamilton wristwatch. It was the same brand as one he received at twenty-one:

A few years later, while attending a graduate school in Phoenix, I was washing a load of white laundry one Saturday. Suddenly, the first trigger was activated in my mind with the message "It's time to meet the woman in white". I tried to shake it off, but the face in the ad pushed all other thoughts away. I stopped, looked at my Hamilton watch and heard the command "Go now". I thought about who wears white. Acting as if I was obsessed, I went to the largest hospital in the city and asked at the desk for a nurse matching the name and the description.

I was told there was such a person who was coming off her shift. When I saw her, I was stunned by the resemblance to the picture in my mind. Our meeting was awkward and embarrassing, but later we sat in the lobby and talked non-stop for four hours as old friends who hadn't seen each other for a while-which, of course, was true. I waited till after we were married to tell my wife about the reason I came to her hospital and the clues given to me to find her. I didn't want her to think I was crazy. It was then that I learnt that on the day of our first meeting she had told her astonished friends "I've just met the man I'm going to marry" (Newton 1992, pp. 260-61).

This was, when I read it, almost incredible. And yet I knew Newton was simply recalling what actually happened-and that if Peggy's friends or the staff on the desk at the hospital were to be asked about that night, their accounts would fit Newton's own. It was a revelation. Yet it fitted with my own experience and that of friends, and explained the otherwise inexplicable about those crucial meetings with soulmates.

This is the 'Love at First Sight' phenomenon, which I along with intelligent sceptics everywhere, took to be nothing more than a sorcerer's potion of lust and sentimentality, mixed by the atavistic drive to perpetuate the species, the sort of thing studied by television documentary guru Robert Winston. Yet it is widely reported, and not just by the randy and sentimental. The first meeting of Jennifer Byrne and Andrew Denton is a case in point. These two are leading lights in the Australian media, Jennifer latterly as newsreader and reporter for the ABC, now First Tuesday Book Club host; Andrew initially as a comic for the same organisation. He has since become one of the most feared and respected interviewers of the world's famous, newsworthy and notorious, who was compared to Michael Parkinson, arguably the world's best-known interviewer. (Denton, like Parkinson has now retired from interviewing). Jennifer and Andrew talk with what seems to be a degree of embarrassment about their Meeting; they are both too bright and too intellectually and otherwise aware to be candidates for the lust-and-sentimentality at first sight phenomenon. *'Our eyes met across a crowded room-quite literally'*, Andrew confesses in an Australian Women's Weekly interview (August 2003), in which their then secret marriage is revealed.

The soul bond as the foundation of our main earthly relationships

How immensely comforting all this proved to be! It meant that our souls were and my soul was more knowable; that my soul was more involved; that *we have profound earthly connections which seem to us to be accidental and a matter of purely personal choice, yet which in truth emanate from the soul bond.* I really did have a soul connection with those who were central in my life. It wasn't even just a connection from past lives together triggered only when back on earth in physical form. It also meant the replacement of one determining order with another very much higher. It meant that our lives are not governed solely by random events, entropy or market forces, Murphy's Law, or the law of the mating jungle, though these will have their place while ever unregenerate matter is in the ascendancy in earthly life.

There is another consideration of interest in this story. Newton doesn't merely do what most of us do; go somewhere different – or even somewhere familiar, and have a Sydney Olympics fireworks display explode inside him, on encountering The One. I imagine that this is what happened when Crown Prince Frederik of Denmark travelled to the opposite side of the world, and Mary Donaldson flew from Tasmania to Sydney in September 2000. Neither would have been aware of any intention other than to see the Sydney Olympics. I expect both would say what amazing luck it was that Mary happened to be in the bar of the Slip Inn when Frederik chose it as his watering-hole for the night, and that if it weren't for the Olympics, they would never have met. Yet if they are soul mates, and their meeting was important for a dynasty and a nation, perhaps contingency plans were laid in case something went wrong on that day, and they failed to meet.

It's time to return to the point about the extra significance of Newton's programme for meeting his wife. He is told Go Now, and must work with the clues he has to pinpoint the place in an entire city where his 'primary soulmate' is to be found at her place of work. The process is more specific, requiring a more aware and intelligent response. Above all it is more conscious than it is for most of us. I think the likely reason was that the details of the encounter were intended by Newton's soul, and his soul group including Peggy, to be related in the book it was intended he would later write. The encounter had to be clearly memorable for Newton, clearly inexplicable by the usual invoking of chance and luck, and so unusual and thought-provoking to Newton's readers that it might be something of a trigger to soul consciousness in us too. None of this would have worked with anyone less evolved and therefore soul-connected than Newton.

SOULMATES

More than one primary soulmate? Whitton's discoveries

Dr Joel Whitton's research in Life between Lives (1986) changes the picture of soulmates in an important way. He details one case study for the purposes of exploring and illustrating the nature of soul connections and the way they work out on earth in our sexual relationships and marital partnerships. This case suggests we may have more than one 'primary soulmate'.

Gary Pennington was a happily married man, still in love with his wife after 16 years, when he found himself being irresistibly drawn to a woman whose gaze met his across a crowded room at a cocktail party. There was instant affinity, to the point where he told Dr Whitton *'It was like being welcomed home'* (p. 166). They became lovers, until Gary's wife Elizabeth, desperate at the increasing estrangement from her husband, took an overdose. She survived, and Gary abruptly broke off the relationship with the other woman, Caroline. Her response was to move in with an attentive admirer, then despair in her turn and hang herself. She was discovered in time and lived, but the guilt, the concern over his uncharacteristic behaviour and worry as to its roots sent Gary in search of answers.

Dr Whitton looked in the obvious places first, in the present life, but, finding nothing there, directed the search for Caroline into earlier times. This case, which is unusually instructive about these soul mate connections, is explored in detail in Life between Lives (pp. 165 ff).

Gary saw himself as Peter Hargreaves, an English R.A.F. intelligence officer standing beside an aircraft before his takeoff from a base near Salerno, Italy, in 1944. He was about to undertake an ill-advised reconnaissance sortie to spy on German counterattack preparations. German fighter aircraft intercepted the plane, and he was injured and forced to crash-land.

Hargreaves was captured and taken north to a German interrogation centre, where his shattered leg was left untended and became gangrenous. He was beaten and then tortured to extract information. Heroically, he revealed nothing useful to the Germans, and he died of their cruelty.

Gary was incredulous at some of the details revealed under hypnosis, especially the name Monte Cassino. He didn't understand what a casino was doing in a war zone. Lacking knowledge of the war's Italian campaign, he did not know that the Monte Cassino monastery, bombed by the Allies, gave its name to the associated battle.

There was no sign of Caroline. Yet at the following session with Dr Whitton, she appeared, in connection with this wartime experience in Italy. Caroline had been Elena Bocchi, his main contact with the Italian resistance movement; they had fallen in love.

Elena's father has recently been killed in combat, and Hargreaves steps in to provide as best he can for the destitute Bocchi family. He promises to marry her as soon as the war is over (p. 173).

After Peter's death, Elena sank into profound depression, and finally threw herself off a cliff. Peter Hargreaves, earthbound by anger at the Nazi infiltration of the partisans which was responsible for his death, and deep concern for Elena, attempted to materialize to stop her.

The connection with Caroline/Elena went further back – to a Russian life when Gary was Sevastjan Umnov, envoy of the Empress Elizabeth Petrovna to the French court of Louis XV during the mid eighteenth century, when much of his work was as a secret agent. In this life, Caroline is Lisenka, the younger sister of Sevastjan, who was living with him in an incestuous relationship. She is jealous and fearful that her brother is having affairs with other women in the French court or Paris. She responds to one rumour by marrying an admirer.

Only a few weeks later, she hangs herself in despair at having denied herself all hope of continuing the relationship she treasures most. Sevastjan is heartbroken when the news reaches him in France, and he never again returns to Russia (p. 176).

That accounts for Caroline and her tendency to suicide as a way out. But what about Elizabeth? It was discovered that Gary had been Jeremy Everett, a nineteenth-century mathematics lecturer at Oxford University, and leading a double life. He had a wife and two young sons in the countryside nearby, and a mistress and two infant daughters in Oxford. He fully intended to provide for both families, but died of pneumonia in his thirties, leaving the Oxford family in poverty, for which his mistress blamed him. His Oxford wife is unknown today, but Elizabeth 'has exchanged roles – a hallmark of the phenomenon of group reincarnation' (p. 177). Several lives as secret lovers when Elizabeth had lost Gary had made her afraid of losing him again.

'Random universe' despair is without foundation

Once I had read both Whitton and Newton, this new knowledge of the deliberate and careful design of our lives (which is still liable to derailing by the personality) replaced any notion of contingency-of the accidental and gratuitous nature of our lives, at least in their large perspective. The despair which resulted from the random universe idea was unnecessary. It added greatly to the sense of security and peace, regardless of the violence, horror and destructiveness of so much happening in the world, and the desperate uncertainty of every aspect of our ongoing lives-that the negative, evil and destructive influences and outcomes would not prevail except in the short term: Good must triumph ultimately. The reason is clear. Regardless of how humans mess things up and destroy rather than create, the observers, monitors and arbiters of the whole scene and process are incorruptibly good, the products of Divine Love.

There is another vital implication, which is of course borne out by everything Newton and Whitton had discovered. Almost all of the earthly creators of evil, heartbreak and tragedy return to a soul, a soul-group and a group of wise counsellors and teachers intent on turning this situation around and creating only good instead in the future.

But what about when we have found our soul mate, and lost her or him again, to death? Can this knowledge assist us to pick up and go on with life, rather than falling into any lengthy and destructive grief and despair-and falling apart?

Death of a partner is not the end of the relationship

Although I knew (by the final research for this book) that there was *no death*, and although I knew too, that the place to which we 'travelled' when the physical body died, was the same place as we know from our sleeping hours, I still didn't grasp the implications of this. Although I had written, some three years before, that the only thing preventing us from seeing and communicating with those we loved after their deaths, was that we ourselves were unable to 'pierce the veil' between the worlds, it remained mere knowledge, unreconciled with living. I knew that there was no need to mourn because those others were actually very close, but I felt it provided a limited comfort and reassurance for those in grief. My friend Silvana's loss was an experience of this: her beloved son Daniel had died at just eighteen from cancer. As fellow students of the Ageless Wisdom, we both knew he was still living, in fact more so than ever; however his mother had understood that she should not attempt in the intensity of her grief, to call him back to her, as that would delay his right and inevitable progress into the Light and union with his soul. *This is true*; so how could it also be true that in our sojourn on higher levels in the hours of sleep, we can meet and communicate with, those separated from us by physical death?

There is a simple, beautiful little book by C.W. Leadbeater, *To Those Who Mourn* (1999), which talks of this separation and the nature of the communication between living and dead, so-called. He says that the beloved person we think of as dead and gone is, in reality, still with us:

> *When you stand side by side, you in the physical body and (your beloved) in the 'spiritual' vehicle, you are unconscious of his presence because you cannot see him; but when you leave your physical body in sleep you stand side by side with him in full and perfect consciousness, and your union with him is in every way as full as it used to be. So during sleep you are happy with him whom you love; it is only during waking hours that you feel the separation.*

There is a reason for our grief: most of us have not yet developed the continued consciousness which all spiritual practices assist, and which Tibetan Buddhism and the esoteric philosophies including Theosophy, are especially designed to create. Although we can, in sleep, bring the physical consciousness into the more refined post-physical/astral body, the reverse is difficult for us:

> *[M]any of us find it impossible to bring through into waking life the memory of what the soul does when it is away from the body in sleep. If this memory were perfect, for us there would indeed be no death. Some men have already attained this continued consciousness, and all may attain it by degrees, for it is part of the natural unfolding of the powers of the soul. ...[F]ragments of memory come through, but there is a tendency to stamp them as only dreams and therefore valueless...*

Leadbeater reassures us of the ongoing connection: '*[If] you have some piece of news you wish to give to a departed friend, you have only to formulate it clearly in your mind before falling asleep, with the resolution that you will tell him of it, and you are quite certain to do so as soon as you meet him.*' He goes on to say that is it still possible to consult or ask for advice, though the recollection of it next morning will be hazy; however there will remain: '*a strong impression as to his wish or his decision; and you may usually take it that such an impression is correct*'.

Leadbeater continues, following this reassurance with a warning: '*At the same time, you should consult him as little as possible, for, as we shall see later, it is distinctly undesirable that the dead should be troubled in their higher world with affairs that belong to the department of life from which they have been freed'* (Leadbeater 1999, pp. 26-31).

Dealing with Grief

Not long after the death of Daniel, my friend's son, I opened at a reading from the Tibetan about grief. The result of sharing this reading with his mother Silvana, was that we both accepted (rather than completely understood) that it is the difference between the kinds of 'calling' of the departed person. It is the type of contact we are attempting to make, what it is we are asking, or demanding, of this loved individual who is no longer clothed in the familiar flesh, and what is the *nature of our bond* with them, that determines the kind of contact we make and its suitability.

D.K. wrote to a grief-stricken disciple, in August 1936...

*Brother of mine: All severing of links produces severe reactions. Yet if you could but realise it, the severing of outer physical plane links is the least severe and the most impermanent of all such events. **Death itself is a part of the great illusion and only exists because of the veils that we have gathered around ourselves.** You, as a worker in the field of glamour (which is the new field in which humanity has consciously to work), have been deeply honoured and trusted. Death comes to all, but not for you should there be the usual glamours and distresses. I would say to you my brother, look not back at the past. In that direction lies glamour and distress. It is the usual direction and the line of least resistance for the majority. But such is not the way for you. Look not either to revelation or the imparted illusory comfort of those who hover on the dividing line between the seen and the unseen.*

D.K. is referring to mediums and clairvoyants here. Their comfort is 'illusory', not because what they tell us is necessarily untrue. Although they are capable of revealing to us, the earthbound ones without astral vision, what we cannot, in waking consciousness, pierce the dividing veil and see for ourselves, they are still harvesting in astral fields, where all is, as on earth, passing and illusory. (It is important to remember that advice given in Discipleship in the New Age Vol. 1 to this disciple, one presumably more advanced than most of us, is personal, and may apply differently to anyone else.)

Reach up to the heights of the soul and, having sought and found that pinnacle of peace and that altitude of joy whereon your soul immovably stands, then look into the world of living men–a threefold world in which all men, incarnate and discarnate are found. Find there that which your soul can and will recognise. The glamours of one's own distress, the maya of the past distort one's point of view. Only the soul stands clear from illusion, and only the soul sees things as they are. Mount, therefore, to the soul...(Bailey 1944, ref. ed. 1976, p. 463).

If we seek in our grief to contact the true person, the deathless individual, with whom we have a relationship that transcends time and space and the illusory world created by human desire, the astral, then we cannot expect to find that one in the lower worlds. They will be found where soul meets and communes with soul, on causal levels, in the relatively enduring place of souls, 'where all men, incarnate and discarnate', are to be found.

D.K. indicates in the next paragraph that he does not expect the grieving woman or man he addresses in his letter of July 1936, quoted in part above, to throw off all sorrow immediately as a result of understanding that there is no death and no separation in the true sense. He continues... *'I foresaw the agony of your coming months and sought to have you know that I was standing by* [as our teachers and soul group stand by all of us in incarnation at such times especially]. *This I am still doing. I remind you of this for the strengthening of your faith, the deepening of your assurance, and your integration in this group work'* (Bailey 1944, pp. 463-4).

So, it is the nature of the bond and the kind of contact we are attempting to make, which makes it harmful or otherwise to the one who has gone through the veil of death. A heartbroken mother who was expending all her emotional energy on trying to bring her daughter or son back to her in the physical world, would be impeding that soul's progress (and her own) by the 'weight' of her grief, and the dragging effect of the demand for her child's return to her. The released child would have spent much time trying to get the mother's attention by any means to let her know her child was still among the living. The chief mistake the mother would be making would be the failure to recognize that this soul has gone on to further and greater life. Her child is separated from her only so long as she is trapped in her thinking, upon illusory levels, and believes that the death of the body and removal of the personality mean the end of that relationship, or even the end of the existence of this soul who was her child.

Holding onto consciousness in the realms of sleep

Consciousness is everything. *It defines the difference between those who believe death to be the end, and those who know there is no death.* The Tibetan asks disciples to practice an exercise at bedtime because it ends this entrapment within material consciousness, and hastens availability for service after death. The exercise is merely to undergo the normal nightly sleeping process, yet with one single, simple difference which would change everything about the way we perceive reality. It is to remain conscious through the whole process-of leaving one's sleeping body and moving out onto the astral level. That was, is, the key. It is the key to the entire labyrinth that is the mystery of life and death. (He cautions elsewhere, in Esoteric Psychology 11, that we usually need the refreshment of ordinary, unconscious sleep). The exercise is contained in a letter to a disciple, R.A.J., written August 1946:

> *Your objective is to preserve consciousness as you withdraw it from the brain and pass out onto the subtler levels of awareness. You are not discarding the physical vehicle permanently ... The aim is for a few hours and whilst clothed in the astral and mental vehicles, to be consciously aware elsewhere. With determination you become a focused, interested point of consciousness, intent on emerging from the casing of the physical body. That point you hold...fixedly waiting for the moment when your negative attitude to the physical plane and your positive attitude to the inner planes will bring a moment of release, perhaps a flash of light, the perception of an aperture of escape, or the recognition of your surroundings, plus the elimination of all surprise or the expectation of any phenomena.*

> *You are (as you practice this exercise of withdrawal) only going through an ordinary everyday process. If facility in doing this exercise is achieved, the hour of death will find you automatically and easily-because the physical body is making no resistance but remains quiescent and negative-able to make the Great Transition without concern or fear of the unknown. This is an exercise I would like to see all the group* [of disciples in training to seed the New Group of World Servers] *undertake... I have chosen these words with care and would like you to study them with equal care* (Bailey 1955, ref. ed. 1979, p. 489).

A book I've already mentioned, the Buddhist Rob Nairn's *Sleeping, Dreaming, Dying* (2004), is enlightening on these subjects. It gives two methods for attaining full and unbroken consciousness in both realms, an attainment important in Mahayana Buddhism for the same reasons as D.K. gives. When it becomes possible to remain conscious through the transition, in sleep, to the astral world, the illusion of death as the end, and of the material world as the sum total of existence, must finally evaporate.

It was a great aid to understanding, to read the experience of preparation for astral travelling, and the process of leaving the sleeping body, as described in *A Soul's Journey* (Richelieu 1996, pp. 39-43). As seen in previous chapters, the author's teacher, 'Acharya', was sent by his own Master, who is *'one of the adepts or perfected men who help to govern this planet'*, to help Richelieu through overwhelming grief at his brother's death. Acharya asks his Master for permission and assistance to take the grieving Henry, as Richelieu calls himself in the book, onto the astral level to meet the 'dead' brother Charles. He instructs Henry as to what he must do: don't eat meat or drink alcohol; take this tablet so you are asleep by 10 p.m; once in bed, imagine a huge ceiling mirror, and work out what you would see in it, so when you see your body lying on the bed you don't panic and jolt back into it.

Conscious moving to the astral plane in sleep; Richelieu's experience

> *'Although you get out of your body every night, you do not remember anything about this because you are not conscious of getting out; now I am trying to arrange that there will be no break of consciousness at all between your falling asleep and realizing your detachment from your physical body'*, he tells his student.

Richelieu took the tablet at nine forty-five:

> *It was just when I heard the first silvery chime starting to herald in the four quarters preceding the striking of 10 o'clock, that I seemed to feel something quite unusual going on in my body. Something inside it seemed as if it were loose and I felt what I can only describe as a sliding movement ... [Then] before the clock had started to record its ten strokes, I found myself suspended in space and looking at my body lying on the bed, exactly as I was told I would do...*

There were two familiar people waiting for him. One was his guru, the other was the dearly-loved brother whose existence he believed to be ended in the fighter plane crash over wartime London, who alerted Henry to his presence with *'a merry laugh behind me... There was Charles looking exactly the same as when I had seen him last. Obviously he was enjoying my surprise and my incredulous expression, and his face was wreathed in smiles with all the jolly old wrinkles that I knew so well showing as in the days that were gone.'* Charles' handclasp was as firm as ever, and Acharya comments that he is indeed real, and that each brother is solid seeming to the other because both are in astral bodies. *'I found it difficult to appreciate that although the astral body looks like the physical so far as features are concerned, yet it is not in any way physical and has no flesh, bones or tissues.'*

The curious thing is that though Charles in his astral body has an objective reality, (that is, he can be seen by anyone on the astral level in their vicinity); aspects of his appearance do not. Henry comments in surprise on Charles being still in his RAF uniform. Acharya has to explain that Henry saw his brother dressed that way because that was what he was wearing last time they met, and the plastic astral matter had simply responded to Henry's thought. He would always see Charles dressed as he, Henry, imagined, and not according to Charles' own thought of his mode of dressing.

The after-death planes are familiar to us through sleep

So-it was as simple as that. In sleep we are not confined to the physical body and its very limited contact with Reality; it is not the case that we are condemned for the entire time between birth and death to endure this limited and claustrophobic outpost of the great cosmos. We are immured in the body just during our waking hours (which we have mistaken for the whole experience of life on earth). Why aren't we aware of this release in sleep? It is merely because our brain physiology and chemistry are not yet evolved enough and therefore sensitive enough, to register the impressions coming from the astral level.

Richelieu's book demonstrated the fact and the reality of our passage onto the astral level during sleep. It was presented as a normal everyday or rather, night, occurrence, which was usually undertaken by us unconsciously. The force of the idea that we don't exit at death to a strange and unknown realm, but to a realm which is in fact well known to us, as it is where we spend about a third of our lives, came home at last. The missing piece of the puzzle was supplied by this book, and reflections on it.

The Way of Release from imprisonment by desire

There are other passages about dealing with loss and grief, which exhort us to realize the dominance of the soul, and change our perspective accordingly. The great paradox revealed in all contemplative spiritual traditions and though modern developmental psychology, is teased out in this passage below. In order to gain the All, we must surrender it. There is only one way; *to lose the self and find the Self and enter into Peace*, as the ancient mantram goes. This is the paradox of gaining the whole, and 'attachment' and inclusion within it, by the opposite-by detachment, not grasping:

> *What is it that we are endeavouring to do? We are treading the **Way of Release**, and on that way all drops from our hands; everything is taken*

*away, and detachment from the world of phenomenal life and of individuality is inevitably forced upon us. We are treading the **Way of Loneliness**, and must learn eventually that we are neither ego nor non-ego. Complete detachment and discrimination must finally lead us to a condition of such complete aloneness that the horror of the great blackness will settle down upon us. But when that pall of blackness is lifted and the light again pours in, the disciple sees that all that was grasped and treasured, and then lost and removed, has been restored, but with this difference-that it no longer holds the life imprisoned by desire. We are treading the Way that leads to the Mountain Top of Isolation, and will find it full of terror. Upon that mountain we must fight the final battle with the Dweller on the Threshold [the personality-the 'sleazy politician' as Sogyal Rinpoche calls it], only to find that that too is an illusion. That high point of isolation and the battle itself are only illusions and figments of unreality; they are the last stronghold of the ancient glamour, and of the great heresy of separateness.*

*Then we, the Beatific Ones, will eventually find ourselves merged with all that is, in love and understanding...We are treading the Way of Purification and step by step all that we cherish is removed-lust for form life, **desire for love** [my emphasis], and the great glamour of hatred. These disappear and we stand purified and empty. The distress of emptiness is the immediate result; it grips us and we feel that the price of holiness is too high. But, standing on the Way, suddenly the whole being is flooded with light and love, and the emptiness is seen as constituting that through which light and love may flow to a needy world* (Bailey 1942, ref. ed. 1971, pp. 34-5).

This is the point beyond the personality-soul threshold, at the soul-spirit threshold. It is a point for which we have data mainly in what Wilber terms 'the performing of the experiment' of the 'community of the adequate', those qualified by meditation, study and the spiritual disciplines, to judge the results and inform the rest of us, in what is now called the perennial philosophy (Wilber 2000, p. 157 ff.)

'The Peace that Passeth Understanding', when separate loves and group love become the One Love

So the love of the soul-group, even, is not quite the point. It comforts us, doing Time in the prison of Earth, to know that there are real humans like ourselves who love us till death and beyond, and that they are soulmates even if not quite in the way we'd imagined or hoped–that is, one and one only, designated for oneself alone, for all eternity.

It is comforting too, to know that when the labour and suffering is done on earth, the place to which we return (most of us) is anyone's and everyone's idea of Heaven. Yet *the ultimate achievement and realization* is the point where we are supremely indifferent to (the need for) individual loves; when we are indifferent to whether we are in heaven or on earth, functioning in a body or out of it. It doesn't matter in the end, whether my dream-mates Chris and Edward were separate soul-mates or as Jung, along with all the masters of the perennial philosophy, has taught us, not separate spirits at all, but a manifestation of the archetype of spirit-my own and everyone's, that is, (the one) Divine Self. What in the end, is the difference? There is one, but barely-and without any practical outcome. To know oneself as utterly precious and deeply, deeply loved-as we all are-by the Divine One, the Soul of all the souls, the Cosmic Christ, the One Self, the One in Whom we live and move and have our being, is everything. Does it matter whether it is mediated through the one embodiment or another?

We become indifferent because we understand past all argument, that there is no difference and no separation; Heaven is Here and Now; all our earthly loves partake of and reflect the One Love. To seek the Eternal, to turn to the love of God is not to turn from worldly loves at all, but to incorporate them, and at the same time, to love the One in and through them, to love God as that individual, while still loving the person. Although I'm not just sermonizing, though this is quite profoundly understood, and is an intuition which has been many years in developing, it is still only fitfully implemented in my lived expression. But I do understand finally! Through the process of writing this book, I know of each separate love that *'This, too, shall pass'*, when it is revealed to be just an aspect of the One Indivisible and Immortal Love. However far off, there *will come* the moment for each of us when Lover and Beloved, self and Self, I and God, I and World are known to be One.

Funerals and the elimination of death from the consciousness of humanity

This elimination of the great fear of death, and of the entire material concept of life, which entraps and enthralls us within a very narrow range of the total reality, can be experienced now through meditation and spiritual exercises, by anyone with sufficient time and persistence. It will be at its end for humanity as a whole once we develop awareness on the next higher plane to the physical plane-the astral or emotional plane. This will happen in the future-and has begun to happen for some of the more advanced members of the race.

What are the implications of this discovery? The moment that consciousness on the astral plane is established, is the moment that death loses its reality. Then, so much of the rest of the Great Illusion in which humanity is immersed, will simply evaporate! Death will be seen as just a transitional process.

Death used to plunge the lives of the survivors into a prolonged funerary gloom. It was obligatory to wear black, for years in some cultures and times like Georgian and Victorian England, and to live in a hushed and sombre pall. This would have been hard indeed on the one who had just made the transition, who was trying to make family and friends aware that all was well; she or he was more alive than ever. The darkness and negativity of this attitude is quite poisonous, and not just to the supposedly deceased. *We need to be able to mourn, because the loss is real.* The severing of links produces severe reactions, as D.K. wrote, above.

Happily though, our approach to death and funerals has steadily been shifting away from this 'death is the end of everything' funeral of the heart. Increasingly, we choose to celebrate a life more than mourn a death at the funeral service, expressing our gratitude for the love and delight this beloved person gave us. We take stock of their achievements, making *a public summation of their life.* Hopefully this is not the first time these acknowledgements of love and gratitude for the real gift that this life was to us, have been made. We forget that those who grace us with their presence usually have no idea how admirable we find them!

The next step we need to take as a society is to extend this positive attitude to a celebration not just of their past, but of their present and future, and ours with them. Most funerals display an extraordinary confusion about survival of physical death: this beloved person, present just a few days ago, is suddenly being spoken about as not merely absent, but non-existent now. It's not just their past deeds, but their present attributes such as courage and generosity, which are described in the past tense. These are qualities of the psyche which, hard-won as they have been, are not subject to any dissolution process, but are now the soul's permanent possession.

We are told that their immortality consists in our memories of them, even when the words of the ceremony may assure us of '*the resurrection of the dead*' to everlasting life. In contrast, eulogists often directly address the departed as though they were present and listening. (They often are.) It's clear we believe they still exist.

I expect this public summation has great importance to the psyche, as the newly discarnate self begins on the stocktaking 'before God and oneself' that will now take place. However, I only know of one account of its effect; Frances Banks' response to her funeral, in *Testimony of Light*:

> *In an inexplicable way, and due no doubt to my intense desire, I was able to be present with you all in mind and consciousness, whilst still lying here [after her 'death', in the convalescence hospital on the astral level] in this silvery light...*

> *I 'saw' you all...I was grateful to those who had journeyed to Maidstone to be present at these last rites. I gloried in the beautiful flowers. I wanted to weep at Richard's mystical interpretation of the change which had separated me (though only seemingly) from you all.... I felt lifted up in mind and soul because I was being missed, because there was so much affection and because Richard was wisely making this a hopeful farewell, without the heavy burden of emphasized sorrow and mourning which would have saddened and distressed me. Then, just as inexplicably as I had become part of these scenes, it all faded. I was lying here at peace.*

> *"So this is death!" I recall saying to one of the Sisters..."Life separated by density-that is all!"*

> *Elation filled me. I knew now that I could 'tune in' and even 'see' the earthplane, if desire was strong enough to loosen the barrier between our world and my new one...This, I realised, was my first lesson* (Greaves 1969, p. 31).

In Chapter One, when I was explaining to readers what to expect from the book, I wrote:

> *I am in absolutely no doubt now about the reality of our continuance as our quintessential selves, more alive and complete than ever, and the reality of great joy at the least, and communion and love as a natural state of being, beyond the physical life.* At the least I hope I have shown you that there is some solid evidence, along with some rational argument, for this attitude. The best outcome would be that the book has changed your mind about death. Perhaps it has even shifted some of my readers from *material universe* thinking, to receiving these intimations of immortality; the love and joy which await us in the further stages of life–all of them. For most of us, once we are out of a non-functioning body, death is an adventure, and a joyous experience.

The exploration of the Near-death Experience by specialists has discounted NDE as just a physical phenomenon. It is the most likely proposition that there is continuance the other side of death. And once the AWARE study headed by Sam Parnia, comes to its expected positive conclusion, proposition must become fact. *There is no death.* There seems little room anyway, in the no-longer material universe, whether of quantum physics or developmental psychology, for the possibility that death is the end. While the research must go on, death-as-the-end no longer looks a credible enough future upon which to base a life. There's no point whatever in building an entire culture and civilization around its premise. Just as all spiritual traditions have always taught us, death as annihilation is merely our last illusion.

Appendix

Ken Wilber's Four Quadrants of Existence and Knowledge

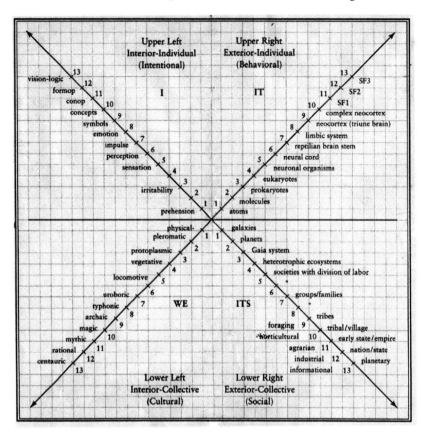

[Notes
Upper Left/I: Knowledge via introspection and reporting of individuals
Eg: introspective psychologies such as Jung, Freud
Upper Right/ IT: Knowledge via collection of external data
Eg: physical sciences, empirical psychologies such as Watson, Skinner
Lower Left: WE: Knowledge via introspection and reporting of cultural groups
Eg: culture studies
Lower Right/ITS: Knowledge via external observation of groups
Eg: social sciences]

Diagram Source: Wilber, 2007, frontispiece

The basic levels or spheres of consciousness

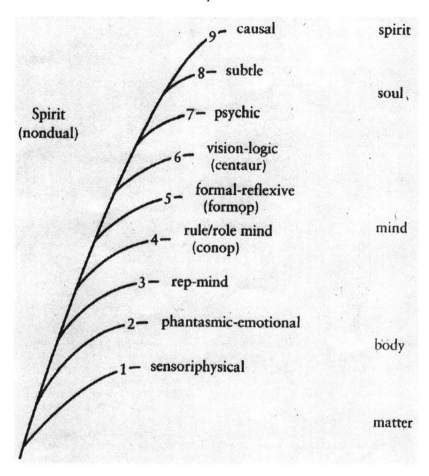

9— causal   spirit

8— subtle

         soul

7— psychic

Spirit
(nondual)

6— vision-logic
(centaur)

5— formal-reflexive
(formop)

4— rule/role mind   mind
(conop)

3— rep-mind

2— phantasmic-emotional

        body

1— sensoriphysical

       matter

Source: Wilber, 2007, p. 208.

The Seven Planes of our Solar System/The Constitution of Man

Spiritual Development and the Seven Planes

- The **Lighted Way** [see 1, on diagram opposite] leads to *Nirvana*, through the bridge in consciousness which links the lower and higher minds, via the incarnate soul, or Ego. *This 'lighted way' is the illumined bridge [or Antakharana]...built through meditation...and through a conscious incorporation into the group in service and for purposes of assimilation into the whole [the One Life, Divine Self, God]* (Bailey 1942, p. 72).

On the diagram, this is the link between three principles; the mental unit or body, the egoic or causal body, (the 'body' created by the soul in order to incarnate,) and the higher mind; the *'mental permanent atom'* or indestructible seed or droplet, in Buddhism. When this link has been made, the *'"initiate" can escape from the limitations of form life and enter into that state of consciousness called Nirvana by the Buddhist'* (Bailey 1942, p. 50). This produces the liberation of the soul from incarnation.

Nirvana is, *'in Hinduism, Buddhism, and Jainism, the attainment of enlightenment and freeing of the spiritual self from attachment to worldly things, ending the cycle of birth and rebirth'*, according to Encarta® World English Dictionary © 1999 Microsoft Corporation.

- The **Way of the Higher Evolution** [see 2] opens from *Nirvana*, at the end of the reincarnation cycle (Bailey 1942, p. 214). This end-point is the 'unitary' or 'unitive' consciousness of the highest stages of Developmental psychology; Wilber's Fulcrum-9 causal consciousness, of which he says that the Self or *'Witness is itself the causal unmanifest'* (Wilber 2007, p. 337). Yet Nirvana is only the ultimate state and final end, to incarnate humans. It is a mistake to think of it as the point where we blend with all that is, and therefore cease to exist except as an indistinguishable part of an amorphous Divine consciousness. It is just the beginning of our true usefulness, not just to humanity and all life on our tiny scrap of a planet, but to the greater whole of the cosmos, in the *'seven paths which open up before the adept of the fifth initiation'*. These paths are both planetary and systemic (solar system) in their service (Bailey 1942, p. 30).

Nirvana, an achieved stage of consciousness, is stable access to *the experience of* the *spiritual realm*, of Buddhi, intuitional or highest Mind in this context as Buddhism tells us. However, it is initially achieved when the four highest levels of the *mental plane* are linked in consciousness.

- The **planetary Ashram** [see 3] is located on the higher subplanes of the mental plane. In Buddhism, this is the **Sangha** [3] of the Buddha. The Sangha is *'the community of those who are attempting this realisation'*-of the Way pointed out, the truth realised, by the Buddha (Wilber 2007, p. 197).

- On the *third subplane* of the mental plane [see 4], *'are found the causal bodies of the individual men and women. These bodies, which are the expression of the Ego,* [i.e. the human, incarnating soul, the body or vehicle of the spiritual soul or Buddhi] *or the individualised self-consciousness, are gathered together into groups according to the ray or quality of the particular Ego involved'* (Bailey 1985, p. 136). These groups of souls are gathered into many subgroups, according to need. It includes the small group of close souls or soul mates, with whom we incarnate for aeons. The original seven groups constitute the first of the major *form* differentiations on the descent into incarnation (Bailey 1942, p. 110).

- **Devachan** or **Dewachen**, on the *fourth subplane* of the mental plane [see 5], is the 'place' where we as discarnate souls enjoy Heaven. *'It is of a higher order than the ordinary heaven and the bliss enjoyed is more mental than we ordinarily understand by the word, yet nevertheless it is still within the lower world of form and will be transcended when non-attachment is known'* (Bailey 1985, p. 136).

- **Purgatory** [see 6] is the state passed through during the purging of the emotional or astral body or aspect of the psyche. This means that purgatory is (coterminous with) the astral plane.

- Buddhism's **Six Realms of Samsara** [see 7], are realms of entrapment in the Bardo via our predominant emotions and vices of pride, jealousy, desire, ignorance, greed and anger. These six realms are states of (the lowest levels of) the astral plane.

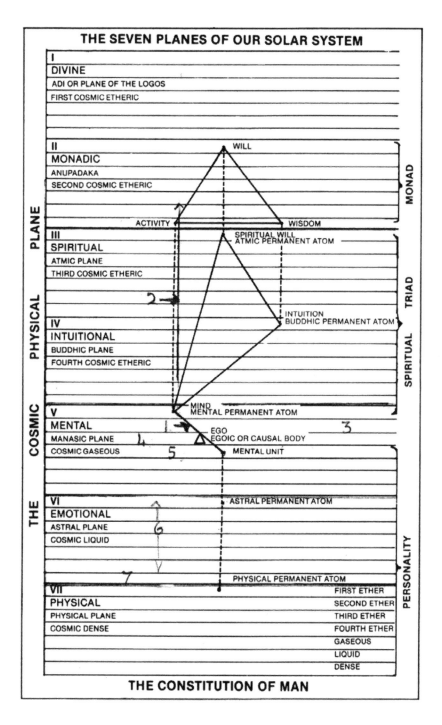

Source: Bailey 1985, p. 134.

Developmental psychology's stages of personal growth from egocentricity to self-transcendence in Maslow, Loevinger and Kohlberg. Integrated via Wilber's scheme.

LADDER Basic Level	CLIMBER	VIEW Maslow (self-needs)	Loevinger (self-sense)	Kohlberg (moral sense)
sensoriphysical	F-1	(physiological)	autistic symbiotic	(premoral) — 0. magic wish
phantasmic-emotional	F-2	safety	beginning impulsive impulsive	I. preconventional — 1. punishment/obedience
rep-mind	F-3	safety	self-protective	2. naive hedonism
rule/role mind	F-4	belongingness	conformist conscientious-conformist	3. approval of others
formal-reflexive	F-5	self-esteem	conscientious individualistic	II. conventional — 4. law and order
vision-logic	F-6	self-actualization	autonomous integrated	III. postconventional — 5. individual rights
psychic	F-7	self-transcendence		6. individual principles of conscience
subtle	F-8	self-transcendence		Kohlberg has suggested a higher, seventh stage:
causal	F-9	self-transcendence		7. universal-spiritual

Source: Wilber 2007, p. 218.

Bibliography and List of References

Adams, Phillip 2005, 'Late Night Live', ABC National Radio, 12 May 2005, 10.30 p.m.

Adams, Phillip 2008, *Adams vs. God; the Rematch*, Melbourne University Press, Carlton.

Alder, Vera Stanley 1968, *The Finding of the Third Eye*, Rider, London.

Armstrong, Karen 2000, *The Battle for God*, London, HarperCollins.

Ashton, John F. 2001, *The God Factor: Fifty scientists and academics explain why they believe in God*, HarperCollins Australia, n.p.

Assagioli, Roberto, 1965, *Psychosynthesis*, Turnstone, London.

Atwater, P.M.H. 1988, *Coming Back to Life; the Aftereffects of the Near-Death Experience*, Collins Dove, Blackburn, Victoria.

The Baha'i Faith c. 2005, Bahai International Community Office of Public Information, New York.

Bailey, Alice A. 1922a, *The Consciousness of the Atom*, New York, Lucis. Written by Alice Bailey alone. Reference edition 9th, 1974. *All extracts from the Alice Bailey books are reprinted with the permission of Lucis Trust,* See http://www.lucistrust.org

Bailey, Alice A. 1922b, *Initiation, Human and Solar*, Lucis, New York. (Reference edition, 1972).

Bailey, Alice A, 1925, *A Treatise on Cosmic Fire*, Lucis, New York. (Reference edition, 1979).

Bailey, Alice A. 1934, *A Treatise on White Magic, or, The Way of the Disciple.* Lucis, New York. (Reference edition 1979).

Bailey, Alice A. 1936, *A Treatise on the Seven Rays, Volume 1, Esoteric Psychology I*, Lucis, New York. (Reference edition 1970)

Bailey, Alice A. 1937, *From Bethlehem to Calvary*, Lucis, New York. Written by Alice Bailey alone.

Bailey, Alice A. 1942, *A Treatise on the Seven Rays; Volume 11, Esoteric Psychology II*, Lucis, New York. (Reference edition 1971).

Bailey, Alice A. 1944, *Discipleship in the New Age, vol. 1,* Lucis, New York. Reference edition 1976.

Bailey, Alice A. 1948, *The Reappearance of the Christ,* Lucis, New York. (Reference edition 1984.)

Bailey, Alice A. 1950, *Letters on Occult Meditation*, Lucis, New York. (Reference edition 1985).

Bailey, Alice A. 1951, *The Unfinished Autobiography*, Lucis, New York.

Bailey, Alice A. 1953, *A Treatise on the Seven Rays; Volume 1V, Esoteric Healing*, Lucis, New York. Reference edition, 1975.

Bailey, Alice A. 1955, *Discipleship in the New Age*, vol. 2, Lucis, New York. Reference edition 1979.

Bailey, Alice A. 1957, *Externalisation of the Hierarchy,* Lucis, New York. (Reference edition 1972).

Bailey, Alice A. 1960, *A Treatise on the Seven Rays*, vol. 5, *The Rays and the Initiations*, Lucis, New York. Reference edition 1976.

Bailey, Alice A. 1985, *Death, the Great Adventure*, Compiled by Two Students From the Writings of Alice A Bailey and the Tibetan, Djwal Khul. Lucis, New York.

Baker, Douglas, c.1974, *The Techniques of Astral Projection*, Little Elephant, Essendon, Herts.

Baker, Douglas, 1975, *The Jewel in the Lotus*, vol. 1 of *The Seven Pillars of the Ancient Wisdom: the synthesis of Yoga, Science and Psychology*, Little Elephant, Essendon, Herts.

Baker, Douglas 1979, *Beyond the Intellect,* Little Elephant, Essendon, Herts.

Baker, Douglas 1994, *Shakespeare, the Real Authorship*, Little Elephant, Essendon, Hertfordshire.

Barlow, Maude 2007, *Blue Covenant: The Global Water Crisis and the Coming Battle for the Right to Water,* Black Inc., Melbourne.

Bernstein, Morey, 1956, *The Search for Bridey Murphy*, Doubleday, New York. 2nd ed., 1965.

Besant, Annie 1893, *Death-and After*, Theosophical Publishing House, Adyar, Madras.

Besant, Annie 1959, *A Study in Consciousness; a Contribution to the Science of Psychology*, Theosophical Publishing House, Adyar, Madras.

Blackmore, Susan 1993, *Dying to Live: Science and the Near-Death Experience*, HarperCollins, London.

Blavatsky, Helena 1888a, *The Secret Doctrine: The Synthesis of Science, Religion and Philosophy,* vol. 1, *Cosmogenesis*, The Theosophical Society, London.

Blavatsky, Helena 1888b, *The Secret Doctrine: The Synthesis of Science, Religion and Philosophy,* vol. 11, *Anthropogenesis,* The Theosophical Society, London.

Bloom, Harold 1996, *Omens of Millennium*, Fourth Estate, London.

Bone, Pamela 2007, *Bad Hair Days*, Melbourne University Press, Carlton, Vic.

Borgia, Anthony 1954, *Life in the World Unseen, as told to Anthony Borgia*, Psychic Press, London.

Buber, Martin 1970, *I and Thou,* Charles Scribner's Sons, London.

Buddhist Texts: Through the Ages, 1954, Newly Translated from the Original Pali, Sanskrit, Chinese, Tibetan, Japanese and Aprabhramsa, edited by Edward Conze in collaboration with I.B. Horner, D. Snellgrove, and A. Waley, Bruno Cassirer, Oxford.

Butler, Tom and Butler, Lisa 2003, *There is No Death and There Are No Dead, Evidence of Survival and Spirit Communication through the Voices and Images from Those on the Other Side*, AA-EVP Publishing, Reno, Nevada.

Carroll, John 2007, *The Existential Jesus,* Scribe, Carlton North, Melbourne.

Challoner, H.K. 1976, *The Wheel of Rebirth, An Autobiography of Many Lifetimes*, Quest, Wheaton, Illinois.

Chogyal Namkhai Norbu 2000, *The Crystal and the Way of Light; Sutra, Tantra and Dzogchen*; compiled and edited by John Shane. Snow Lion Publications, Ithaca, N.Y.

Chogyam Trungpa 2000, *The Tibetan Book of the Dead*, Shambhala, Boston.

Coleman, Nicholas G. 1999, *The Worlds of Religion*, McGraw-Hill, Sydney.

Cook-Greuter, Suzanne 2007, *Stages 5, 6 and 7, Individualist, Strategist and Magician,* in Integral Naked Premier vol 5, issue 4,

April 2007, (videorecording), Integral Institute, Boulder, Colorado. (www.integralnaked.org).

Cremo, Michael & Thompson, Richard 1999, *The Hidden History of the Human Race*, Bhaktivedanta Publishing, Los Angeles.

Dalai Lama XIV 1997, *The Buddha Nature: Death and Eternal Soul in Buddhism*, Bluestar Communications, Woodside, California.

Darwin, Francis 1995, The Life of Charles Darwin, Studio Editions, London. First published in 1902 by John Murray, London.

Dawkins, Richard 2006, *The God Delusion*, Bantam Press, London.

Doore, Gary ed. 1990, *What Survives? Contemporary Explorations of Life after*

Death, edited by Gary Doore, Tarcher, L.A.

Evans-Wentz, W. Y. ed. 1927, *The Tibetan Book of the Dead, or, The After-Death Experiences on the Bardo Plane,* according to Lama Kazi Dawa-Samdup's English Rendering. Oxford, Oxford University Press, 1927. Reference edition one, 1960. Reference edition two, with a new foreword and afterword by Donald S. Lopez, Jr. Oxford University Press, 2000.

Ferguson, Kitty 1994, *The Fire in the Equations; Science, Religion and the Search for God,* Bantam, London.

Fiore, Edith 1978, *You Have Been Here Before: A Psychologist looks at Past Lives,* Coward, McCann & Geoghegan, New York.

Fortune, Dion n.d. *The Esoteric Orders and their Work*, Rider, London.

Frankl, Viktor 1984, *Man's Search for Meaning*, Pocket Books, Simon & Schuster, New York.

Fremantle, Francesca & Chogyam Trungpa 1975, *The Tibetan Book of the Dead*, Shambhala, Berkeley.

French, Christopher C. 2001, 'Dying to Know the Truth: Visions of a Dying Brain, or False Memories?' *Lancet*, vol. 358; pp. 2010-11, 15 Dec. (http://www.thelancet.com).

Goswami, Amit 2001, *Physics of the Soul: the Quantum Book of Living, Dying, Reincarnation and Immortality*, Hampton Roads Publishing, Charlottesville, VA.

Greaves, Helen 1969, *Testimony of Light*, Churches' Fellowship for Psychical and Spiritual Studies, Saffron Walden, England.

Grof, Stanislav 1985, *Beyond the Brain: Birth, Death and Transcendence in Psychotherapy,* State University of New York, Albany.

Haisch, Bernard 2000, 'Brilliant Disguise: Light, Matter and the Zero Point Field', in *Science and Spirit*.

Hall, Cheryl 2008, 'Controversial clergyman advertises his new faith on billboards', Stateline, ABC 1, 5 October 2008.

Happold, F.C. 1963, *Mysticism: A Study and an Anthology*, Penguin, Harmondsworth, Middlesex.

Harris, Bill c. 2008, *Oneness isn't Metaphysical*, Centrepointe, Beaverton, Oregon. See also the Centrepointe/Holosync website at
http://www.centrepointe.com

Harris, Thomas A. 1970, *I'm OK – You're OK*, Pan, London.

Hawking, Stephen 1988, *A Brief History of Time*, Bantam, London.

Humphries, Christmas 1928, *A Dictionary of Buddhism*, Curzon. London.

Huxley, Aldous 2004, *The Doors of Perception*, & *Heaven and Hell*, Vintage, London. Published in the U.S. by HarperCollins, New York.

James, Clive 1981, *Unreliable Memoirs*, Picador, London.

Jihad Sheilas [videorecording] c. 2008, produced by Renata Gombac, Mary Ann Jolley and Lisa Millar, TapeSeries, Hindmarsh, South Australia.

Jones, Tony 2000, Interview with Dr Peter Fenwick, 'Lateline' (videorecording), ABC Channel 2, 10.30 p.m. 30 Oct. (http://www.abc.net.au/lateline)

Jung, C.G. 1938, *Psychology and Religion*, Yale University Press, New Haven.

Jung, C.G.1963, *Memories, Dreams, Reflections*, Collins and Routledge & Kegan Paul, London.

Keene, Michael 1993a, *Believers in One God: Judaism, Christianity, Islam*. Cambridge University Press, Cambridge,

Keene, Michael 1993b, *Seekers after Truth: Hinduism, Buddhism, Sikhism*, Cambridge, Cambridge University Press.

Kohn, Rachael 2003, *The New Believers: Re-imagining God*, HarperCollins, Sydney.

Kubler-Ross, Elisabeth 1970, *On Death and Dying*, Macmillan, New York.

Kubler-Ross, Elisabeth 1981, *Living with Death and Dying: How to Communicate with the Terminally Ill*, (Touchstone edition 1997), Simon and Schuster, New York.

Kubler-Ross, Elisabeth 1997, *The Wheel of Life; a Memoir of Living and Dying*, Scribner, New York.

Leadbeater, Charles 1999, *To Those who Mourn*, The Theosophical Publishing House, Adyar, Madras.

Leadbeater, Charles 2004, *The Life after Death*, The Theosophical
 Publishing House, Adyar, Chennai, formerly Madras (First
 Edition 1913).
Levine, Stephen 1990, 'What Survives?' In *What Survives? Contem-
 porary Explorations of Life after Death*, edited by Gary
 Doore, Tarcher, Los Angeles.
MacGregor, Geddes 1978, *Reincarnation in Christianity*, Quest Books,
 Wheaton, Illinois.
Marcel, Gabriel 1965, *Being and Having*, Collins Fontana, London.
Merzel, Dennis Genpo 2005, *Big Mind, Big Heart; Finding your Way*,
 Big Mind Publishing, Salt Lake City. See Genpo's website
 at
 http://www.genpo.com. (Accessed 12/5/08.)
Moacanin, Radmila 1986, *Jung's Psychology and Tibetan Buddhism:
 Western and Eastern Paths to the Heart*, Wisdom Publica-
 tions, London.
Moody, Raymond 1975, *Life after Life: the Investigation of a Phenomen-
 on, Survival of Bodily Death*, Mockingbird, Covington.
Morse, Melvin & Perry, Paul 1991, *Closer to the Light: Learning from
 the Near-Death Experiences of Children*. Ballantine Books,
 New York.
Nairn, Rob 2004, *Living, Dreaming, Dying; Practical Wisdom from the
 Tibetan Book of the Dead*, Shambhala, Boston.
Newton, Michael 1994, *Journey of Souls; Case Studies of Life between
 Lives*, Llewellyn, St Paul, Minnesota.
Newton, Michael 2002, *Destiny of Souls; New Case Studies of Life
 between Lives*. Llewellyn, St Paul, Minnesota.
Oderburg, I.M. 1973, 'Reincarnation as Taught by Early Christians',
 Sunrise, May 1973, Theosophical University Press,
 Wheaton, Illinois.
Parnia, S. Waller, D. Yeates, R. & Fenwick P. 2001, 'A Qualitative
 and Quantitative Study of the Incidence, Features and Ae-
 tiology of Near Death Experiences in Cardiac Arrest Sur-
 vivors', *Resuscitation*, vol. 48, Issue 2, 2001, 149-156.
Parnia, S & Fenwick P. 2002, 'Near Death Experiences in Cardiac
 Arrest: Visions of a Dying Brain or Visions of a New
 Science of Consciousness?' *Resuscitation* 52, Issue 1, January
 2002, 5-11.
Parnia, Sam 2005, 2008, *What happens when We Die; A Ground-Break-
 ing Study into the Nature of Life and Death*, Hay House UK,
 London.

Parnia, Sam 2008, 'Beyond the Mind-Body Problem: New Paradigms in the Science of Consciousness', *Morning Keynote Address, U.N. DESA Mind-Body Symposium*, New York, 11 September 2008.

Peat, F. David 1997, *Infinite Potential: The Life and Times of David Bohm*. Addison-Wesley, Reading, Mass.

Plato 1942, *Five Great Dialogues*, trans. B. Jowett, Walter J. Black, New York.

Polkinghorne, John 1992, 'The Mind of God?' *Symposium: Hawking's 'History of Time' Reconsidered. The Cambridge Review,* March 1992: 1.

Ram Dass 1990, Thoughts at the Moment of Death, in *What Survives? Contemporary Explorations of Life after Death,* edited by Gary Doore, Jeremy P. Tarcher, Los Angeles.

Ramster, Peter 1980, *The Truth about Reincarnation*, Rigby, Sydney.

Rhodes, Leon 1998, *Tunnel to Eternity: Beyond Near-death*, Swedenborg Lending Library, Sydney.

Richelieu, Peter 1996, *A Soul's Journey*, London, HarperCollins. First edition, Graphic, Durban, 1953.

Ring, Kenneth & Cooper, Sharon 1999, *Mindsight; Near Death and Out of Body Experiences in the Blind*, William James Centre for Consciousness Studies at the Institute of Transpersonal Psychology, Palo Alto.

Rogo, D. Scott 1990,'Spontaneous Contact with the Dead: Perspectives from Grief Counseling, Sociology, and Parapsychology', in *What Survives?* ed. Gary Doore, Jeremy Tarcher, Los Angeles. © D. Scott Rogo 1989.

Ryuho, Okawa 1998, *The Laws of Eternity*, Element, Shaftesbury, Dorset.

Sabom, M. 1982, *Recollections of Death*, Harper & Row, New York.

Schure, Edouard 1912, *Pythagoras and the Delphic Mysteries*, Phillip Welby, London. First published 1906.

Sheldrake, Rupert 1990, 'Can our Memories Survive the Death of our Brains?' in *What Survives?* ed. Gary Doore. Jeremy P. Tarcher, Los Angeles.

Shermer, M. 2003, 'Demon-haunted brain, *Scientific American*, Feb 10 2003.

Sogyal 1992, *The Tibetan Book of Living and Dying*, Harper, San Francisco.

Steiner, Rudolph 1983, Esoteric Studies vol. iv, Karmic Relationships, Rudolph Steiner Press, London.

Syme, Rodney 2008, *A Good Death*, Melbourne University Publishing, Carlton, Vic.

Tacey, David J 2000, *ReEnchantment: The New Australian Spirituality*, HarperCollins, Pymble N.S.W.

Tarnas, Richard 1991, *The Passion of the Western Mind*, Ballantine, New York.

Teilhard de Chardin, Pierre 1968, *The Divine Milieu*, Harper Torchbooks, New York.

Tillyard, E.M.W. 1963, *The Elizabethan World Picture*, Penguin, Harmondsworth.

Tipler, Frank J, 1995, *The Physics of Immortality: Modern Cosmology, God and the Resurrection of the Dead*, Macmillan, London.

Tolle, Eckhart 1999, *The Power of Now; a Guide to Spiritual Enlightenment*, New World Library, Novata, California.

Tomlinson, Andy, 2007, *Exploring the Eternal Soul: Insights from the Life between Lives*, O Books, Winchester, UK.

Van Lommel, P, Wees Van R, Meyers V, Elfferich I 2001, Near - death experience in survivors of cardiac arrest: a prospective study in the Netherlands, *The Lancet* 2001; 358: pp. 2039-45.

Wambach, Helen 1979, *Life before Life*, Bantam, New York.

Weiss, Brian, 1988, *Many Lives, Many Masters: The True Story of a Prominent Psychiatrist, His Young Patient, and the Past-Life Therapy that Changed Both Their Lives,* Simon and Schuster, New York.

Whitmont, Edward C. 1969, *The Symbolic Quest: Basic Concepts of Analytical Psychology,* G.P. Putnam's Sons, New York.

Whitton, Joel & Fisher, Joe 1986, *Life between Life, Scientific Explorations into the Void Separating One Incarnation from the Next,* Grafton, London.

Wilber, Ken 1980, *The Atman Project: A Transpersonal View of Human Development,* Theosophical Publishing House, Wheaton, Illinois.

Wilber, Ken ed. 1982, *The Holographic Paradigm and Other Paradoxes; Exploring the Leading Edge of Science,* Shambhala, Boulder.

Wilber, Ken 1990, 'Death, Rebirth, and Meditation' in *What Survives? Contemporary Explorations of Life after Death*, ed. Gary Doore, Jeremy P. Tarcher, Los Angeles.

Wilber, Ken 1997, *The Eye of the Spirit: an Integral Vision for a World gone Slightly Mad*, Shambhala, Boston.

Wilber, Ken 2000, *Grace and Grit: Spirituality and Healing in the Life and Death of Treya Killam Wilber*, Shambhala, Boston.

Wilber, Ken 2001, *No Boundary; Eastern and Western Approaches to Personal Growth*, Shambhala, Boston.

Wilber, Ken c.2002, *The Deconstruction of the World Trade Center*. Available at http://wilber.shambhala.com/htm/books/boomeritis.

Wilber, Ken 2007, *A Brief History of Everything*, 2nd edition, Shambhala, Boston.

Wilson, Colin 1990, 'Glimpses of a Wider Reality' in *What Survives? Contemporary Explorations of Life after Death*, edited by Gary Doore, Jeremy P. Tarcher, Los Angeles.

Yogananda 1946, *Autobiography of a Yogi,* The Philosophical Library Inc., New York, Reprinted by Axiom Australia 2004.

Zammit, Victor 2005, *A Lawyer Presents the Case for the Afterlife*. Available at http://www.victorzammit.com/book. Accessed 23/2/05.

Zukav, Gary 1979, *The Dancing Wu-Li Masters: An Overview of the New Physics*, Fontana, London.

Zwartz, Barney 2003, 'When Being a Christian doesn't mean Believing in God', *The Age,* A3, 14 Oct. (p. 4)

Zwartz, Morag 2004, *Fractured Families: The Story of a Melbourne Church Cult*, Paresis Publishing. Melbourne.

Index

Z

Zoroastrianism 33
Zukav, Gary 16

Zwartz, Barney 296
Zwartz, Morag (author of
  Fractured Families) 173

CPSIA information can be obtained at www.ICGtesting.com
Printed in the USA
BVOW032300080112

280017BV00004B/1/P

9 781863 356275